The Non-Stop Connc

C000036630

Now published for the first tir
The Non-Stop Connolly Show were first given in a 2. ...
Liberty Hall, Dublin, at Easter 1975. In epic verse and stirring dialogue they chart the life and career of James Connolly, Ireland's greatest revolutionary, from his birth in Edinburgh through his political maturation in Ireland and America to his last moments in front of a British firing squad after the abortive Easter Rising of 1916. 'Poetic powers flash through the dialogue in every sequence' *The Times.*

Margaretta D'Arcy is Irish and has worked with improvisational and theatre techniques since the fifties. She is the Irish correspondent for the Polish theatre journal Dialog. *Her work with Arden includes* The Business of Good Government *(1960),* The Happy Haven *(1960),* Ars Longa, Vita Brevis *(1963),* Friday's Hiding *(1965),* The Royal Pardon *(1966),* Muggins is a Martyr *(1968),* The Hero Rises Up *(1968),* The Ballygombeen Bequest *(1972),* The Island of the Mighty *(1972),* Keep the People Moving *(for radio, 1972),* The Non-Stop Connolly Show *(1975),* Vandaleur's Folly *(1978) and* The Little Gray Home in the West *(1978). Her play* A Pinprick of History *was performed at the Almost Free Theatre, London in 1977.*

John Arden was born in Barnsley, Yorkshire, in 1930. While studying architecture at Cambridge and Edinburgh universities, he began to write plays, four of which have been produced at the Royal Court Theatre: The Waters of Babylon, Live Like Pigs, Serjeant Musgrave's Dance *and* The Happy Haven; *while a fifth,* The Workhouse Donkey, *was produced at the Festival Theatre, Chichester. For a year he held an Annual Fellowship in Playwriting at Bristol University, and Bristol Old Vic produced* Ironhand, *his free adaptation of Goethe's* Goetz von Berlichingen. Armstrong's Last Goodnight *was first produced at the Glasgow Citizens'. Theatre and later at the National Theatre.* Left-Handed Liberty *was specially commissioned by the Corporation of London to commemorate the 750th Anniversary of Magna Carta and was produced at the Mermaid Theatre. He is married to Margaretta D'Arcy, with whom he has collaborated on several plays. Arden's first novel,* Silence Among the Weapons *(1982), was short-listed for the Booker-McConnell Prize for Fiction.*

Front cover: woodcut of James Connolly by Harry Kernoff reproduced by courtesy of Lina Kernoff.

Margaretta D'Arcy and **John Arden**

The Non-Stop
Connolly Show

A Dramatic Cycle of Continuous Struggle
in Six Parts

A Methuen Paperback

A METHUEN MODERN PLAY

First published in five volumes in 1977 by Pluto Press Ltd
First published in this one-volume edition in 1986,
in Great Britain by Methuen London Ltd
11 New Fetter Lane, London EC4P 4EE,
and in the United States of America by Methuen Inc,
29 West 35th Street, New York, NY 10001, U.S.A.
Copyright © 1977, 1986 by Margaretta D'Arcy and John Arden

British Cataloguing in Publication Data

D'Arcy, Margaretta
  The non-stop Connolly Show: a dramatic
  cycle of continuous struggle in six parts.
  I. Title   II. Arden, John
  822'.914   PR6054.A695

  ISBN 0-413-60000-9

Printed in Great Britain by
Richard Clay (The Chaucer Press) Ltd,
Bungay, Suffolk

CAUTION
All rights whatsoever in this play are strictly reserved
and application for performance etc., should be made to
Margaretta D'Arcy and John Arden, c/o Methuen London Ltd,
11 New Fetter Lane, London EC4P 4EE.

This book is sold subject to the condition that it shall not,
by way of trade or otherwise, be lent, resold, hired out,
or otherwise circulated without the publisher's prior consent
in any form of binding or cover other than that in which
it is published and without a similar condition including
this condition being imposed on the subsequent purchaser.

AUTHORS' PREFACE

James Connolly holds a unique place in early twentieth-century European history. He was the only revolutionary leader of his time who combined in his career:

– genuine proletarian origins

– a consistent record of work amongst the international socialist movement in several countries (Britain, Ireland, America)

– continuous involvement with trade-union organisations as well as revolutionary political parties

– opposition to the national hysteria of the first world war, which engulfed so much of the international labour-leadership

– practical physical expression of that opposition, in that he was one of the chief organisers of the Dublin Rising of 1916.

Throughout his career, and closely interwoven with each of the above aspects of his life, one can trace the recurrent conflict between *revolution* and *reform* – an ideological dichotomy that still plagues all who have ever had anything to do with left-wing political affairs. In Connolly's case this prolonged debate took on so many shapes and faces that we felt it necessary to explore his experience at deliberately repetitive length – hence a cycle of plays rather than one clean-cut three-act summary. Other recurrent themes that lift their coils in and out of the story, like the serpents' bodies in an old Celtic manuscript-ornament, are:

– the perennial failure of the British Left to recognise and cope with the imperialist role of Britain in relation to Ireland

– the confusion among international socialism caused by the national independence movements in such colonial and semi-colonial countries as Ireland, Poland, Serbia, etc.

These six plays have therefore taken the form of not so much a straight biography of Connolly, as a series of digressive stage-presentations of the events of his time which influenced his political views and consequent actions. They were written to be shown as one complete connected sequence, and have been so produced, both in Dublin and in London. There were certain differences of emphasis between the two productions.

In Dublin our aim was primarily to counteract what one might term the 'Conor Cruise O'Brien historical revisionism', currently much in vogue in Irish intellectual circles, and closely associated with the policies of the Fine Gael-Labour Coalition government – in which Dr Cruise O'Brien was himself a minister. This school of thought appears to maintain:

– that the 1916 Rising was unnecessary

– that Irish Independence would have been achieved anyway through constitutional parliamentary processes

– that the Protestant-Loyalist minority in Ireland (which forms a *majority* in six of the counties of Ulster) is in effect a nation of its own, quite distinct from the rest of the Irish population

– that the present anti-imperialist struggle in the country has therefore no historical validity.

To reinforce these theoretical opinions in the Irish Republic, successive governments (both Fianna Fail and Coalition) have made use of a whole series of repressive measures – including:

– trials for political offences before a Special Court without a jury

– official censorship of radio and television broadcasts

– self-censorship of the press under threat of government interference

– imprisonment of citizens upon no stronger evidence than the unsupported word of a senior police-officer that he *believes* them to be 'subversives'

– the 1976 declaration of a State of Emergency to give extra powers to the Army 'in support of the civil authority', and to permit the police to hold persons on suspicion for seven days before bringing them before a court.

Amnesty International has investigated the state of the Irish prisons: and the new Fianna Fail government has been compelled to re-examine the situation. It also appears (5 October 1977) that the seven-day detention system is likely to be shelved, as a result of widespread public disquiet.

The London production of the plays, on the other hand, was intended to demonstrate how the unwillingness of the Labour Movement in Britain to take a firm stand in support of Irish self-determination has resulted throughout several generations in a strengthening of the Anglo-Irish reactionary elements, which in turn has meant the augmentation of violence, bloodshed and widespread public suffering – a process which shows no signs of decrease. This lack of cross-channel awareness and solidarity has been directly responsible for IRA bombings in Britain, with the consequent Prevention of Terrorism Act, the censorship and crypto-censorship of Irish themes in all departments of the British media, the deportation of large numbers of Irish people without adequate means of defence, the maltreatment of Irish political prisoners in British gaols etc. etc... The latter point is to be taken up at Strasburg – where the army and police torture-policy in Ulster has already been proven – but the political impact of such revelations upon the broad British Left has, at the time of writing, been negligible.

NOTES ON THE STAGING OF THE PLAYS

Despite the apparent complexity of *The Non-Stop Connolly Show*, its staging need not present any very difficult problems. The approach should be 'emblematic' rather than 'naturalistic'; and ideally a number of stages should be used, arranged around the audience, and connected perhaps with gangways at various levels. We have suggested a series of backcloths which can be fixed either singly or two-at-a-time to give the overall atmosphere of each section of the cycle.

The large cast can be contained by a basic company of about a dozen actors, who will each have to play many different roles, not necessarily of their own sex: but stylised, easily-changed, strongly-defined costumes, and possibly stock-masks for recurrent social types (i.e. bourgeois politicians, employers, military officers, etc.), would greatly assist this technique.

The part of Connolly does not necessarily have to be played by the same actor in all six parts. It might be difficult to find an artist capable of handling him all the way through from childhood to middle-age – but that this taxing feat of character portrayal is possible was proven in Dublin by the remarkable performance of Terry McGinity, who came into the production halfway through rehearsals and became, we are convinced, truly possessed by the dead hero's *daimon*.

The music for the songs in the Dublin and London productions was found from traditional sources—there are many Irish, British and American airs which will fit the words – and we employed an improvised accompaniment, largely percussive, to give accent to the stage movement and the delivery of some of the more rhetorical dialogue and tirade.

The backcloths are described in the text. The style we have in mind should be based on the formal emblematic tradition of trade union banners, and should be carried out in bright colours with no attempt at impressionism or naturalistic representation. The cloths should include appropriate slogans and captions.

Essentially the plays need *speed* – and close attention to *rhythm*. Each scene or episode should be understood as a self-contained combination of voice, movement, colour and music, with a precise dramatic momentum of its own, which makes its point as sharply as possible and is then withdrawn from the stage, as sharply as possible, to be replaced by the next grouping. We would emphasise finally that the play will work only if the actors are more concerned with understanding the political arguments and implications of the story than with 'creating character' in the normal theatrical sense. A few books which could be usefully referred to for this purpose, as well as the works of James Connolly:

C. Desmond Greaves, *The Life and Times of James Connolly*, Lawrence & Wishart.

T. A. Jackson, *Ireland Her Own*, Lawrence & Wishart.

George Dangerfield, *The Strange Death of Liberal England*, MacGibbon & Kee.

Ray Ginger, *Eugene V. Debs*, Collier Books.

Richard M. Watt, *The Kings Depart*, Penguin Books.

James Connolly, *Selected Writings*, ed. by Peter Beresford, Penguin.

Jack Gale, *Oppression and Revolt in Ireland*, Workers' Revolutionary Party Pocket Book No. 15.

The Non-Stop Connolly Show received its first production in Dublin, at Liberty Hall (headquarters of the Irish Transport and General Workers' Union) on Easter weekend, Saturday–Sunday, 29/30 March 1975

Cast

Connolly Terence J. McGinity

Larkin Gerry O'Leary

De Leon Barrie Houghton

Other parts were played by:

Paschal Finnan	Frank Macken
Niamh Fitzgerald	Vincent McCabe
Don Foley	Dave McKenna
Meryl Gourlay	Kevin McKenna
Des Hogan	Fionnuala Rogerson
Boris Howarth	Sandra Rudkin
Margaret Howarth	Paddy Scully
Garret Kehoe	

together with the following members of the Irish Workers' Cultural Centre:

Mildred Fleming	Sheila Moran
Maura Heffernan	Virginia O'Reilly
Paul McGrath	Eamon Walsh
Mick Moran	

Children's parts were played by:

Members of na Fianna Éireann

Finn Arden

Jacob Arden

Neuss Arden

During the subsequent tour of the production in Ireland the part of **Connolly** as a boy was played by Neuss Arden.

The direction of the production was co-ordinated by:

John Arden

Margaretta D'Arcy

Jim Sheridan

Robert Walker

who were also members of the cast.

Others involved in the general administration and preparation of the production:

Senator Michael Mullen and the General Executive Committee ITGWU, Premises Manager and Staff of Liberty Hall, Eoghan Harris, Tom Kilroy, Des Geraghty, Peter Sheridan, Paddy Gillan, Brian Flynn, Tomas Mac Giolla, Mairin de Burca, Tony Ebbes, Bill Whelan, Eric Fleming, Eamonn Travers, Eamonn Smullen, Cathal Goulding, Cathal Og Goulding, Paula, Niall Stokes, Joe Deasy, Margaret Gaj, The Union of Students in Ireland, Jim Nolan, Students Representative Council UCD, Jim Campbell, Des O'Hagan, Bronwen Casson, Norah Lever, Sean Byrne, Raymond Flynn, Felicia McCabe, Ottavio di Fidio . . . and many more.

The production was sponsored by the Irish Transport and General Workers' Union and the Official Sinn Fein Party.

The London presentation of *The Non-Stop Connolly Show* was produced by Inter-action Ltd at the Almost Free Theatre, as a series of rehearsed readings at lunch time, from 17 May–19 June 1976, under the direction of the authors, with a cast recruited in England.

Part One: Boyhood 1868–1889

James Connolly, born among the Irish in Edinburgh, can find no work, so joins the Army and is sent to Ireland. He discovers Irish nationalism and international socialism: he discovers a wife: he discovers his political destiny. He determines to go elsewhere.

List of characters:

JAMES CONNOLLY
LILLIE REYNOLDS

Connolly's MOTHER
Connolly's FATHER
McBRIDE [Connolly's Uncle]

GRABITALL
3 EMPLOYERS

FOREMAN of a printing-office
PROOF-READER
FACTORY INSPECTOR
CUSTOMER at a ceramic studio
ASSISTANT at a ceramic studio

SPEAKER of the House of Commons

3 Army OFFICERS
SERJEANT-MAJOR
3 SOLDIERS
Military Policeman

POLICE CONSTABLE

AGENT of a great estate
BAILIFF
Mrs LYNCH
3 Evicted TENANTS
MYLES FLANAGAN
Flanagan's 2 Brothers
Wild WOMAN in crowd

NATIONALIST AGITATOR
SOCIALIST AGITATOR

workmen, peasants, soldiers, rioters etc

Part Two: Apprenticeship 1889–1896

James Connolly, in Edinburgh once more, and married, gains experience in the pioneer socialist movement. He seeks political office and fails to find it: he seeks to earn a living and fails likewise. He determines to go elsewhere.

List of characters:

JAMES CONNOLLY
LILLIE CONNOLLY

Connolly's FATHER
JOHN [Connolly's Brother]

JOHN LESLIE
3 Socialist COMRADES
LEO MEILLET
Trade-union LEADER
ANNIE [a Student]

GRABITALL
3 EMPLOYERS
MAGISTRATE
POLICE CONSTABLE
BISHOP

3 HECKLERS
citizens, demonstrators, socialist comrades, etc

To the memory of Liam MacMillen of the Belfast Republican Clubs, whose vigour and enthusiasm made possible *The Non-Stop Connolly Show* in that city: and who was shot dead in the street only a few days after we had played there.

Margaretta D'Arcy and John Arden

Part One: Boyhood

SCENE 1

A view of Edinburgh, slum tenements below the Castle, which flies the Union Jack from the top turret. (Backcloth I.)

Enter MOTHER CONNOLLY (*and* GRABITALL, *at the side, lurking*).

Mother Connolly

It is the right of every man on earth
(Who for his life must bend his back and work)
To own, control, and finally enjoy
The produce of his labour at its greatest worth.
Did I say every man? Each woman, girl, and boy
Is equally entitled to such a right –
If not, why do we live? But yet we have not got it:
Through all of history it has been withheld:
Though frequently, after a fearsome fight,
Some grudging portion has been slowly granted
Only because the mighty were compelled
By greater might of those whom they oppressed –

Grabitall (*lunges forward*)

Ha ha, ha ha, such sentiments are best
Ignored and scorned, for if we were to take
Too seriously the exhalations of this well-meant verbal fog
It would give cause for every snarling under-dog
To try and seize from me the wealth I make
Through all my enterprise. By disposition of paper and of gold
And power of armed men all well-paid with regular wage, I hold
My domination over all the world –
Three-fourths – two-thirds – at any rate, a lot:
And there is nothing I will not do to stop you getting what I have
got!

Mother Connolly

Proud demon, avaunt! You can and shall be beaten!

Grabitall But at what cost of lives and love and waste of food that could
be eaten . . .
Be sensible, leave such affairs to those who understand
Manipulation of money and the government of land.
My dear, it is not worth it – let it alone.

Mother Connolly

For all his sneers and jeers, I know it can be done.
Water, like blood, *can* be squeezed out from a stone

Yet no shed blood nor water has been known
To quench the fire of freedom in the heart of man.

Grabitall Ha ha, ha ha, attempt then what you can!

Mother Connolly (*drives him away with her bag and umbrella*)

Get out, get off – !

Grabitall I go – I shall return

To confound all my enemies before they are even born . . . !

Exit GRABITALL.

SCENE 2

Enter FATHER CONNOLLY.

Father Connolly (*sings*)

In the royal town of Edinburgh
That stands so dark and tall
There's many a mouse and many a rat
Live deep in a narrow hole:
And many a boy and many a girl
Observe them as they crawl
Between the cradle and the bed
And up and down the wall.

In eighteen hundred and sixty-eight
In a dark and smoky hole
In Edinburgh town a child was born
Who was both pale and small:
His mother came from Monaghan
And his father from God knows where –
But that they both were Irish folk
Their poverty did declare.

Their patches and their poverty
And the famine that they had fled
From their youngest child's first day on earth
Lived deep inside his head.
His knees were bent and bandy
And he waddled as he walked
He was unhandy and cantankerous
And he stammered as he talked.

He talked as little as he could,
His tongue was made of wood,
He was a cautious quiet child,
He never had much good food –
But his eyes were as bright and glittering
As a bullet that flies by night –

(*Speaks*)

James Connolly, that careful child –
He was born in the dark and he looked out for the light . . .

CONNOLLY (*as a small boy*) *has entered during the song.*

Mother Connolly For all your small size, Jim, you are eleven years old, and we cannot afford to keep you at school any longer. We must go out into the town and find work for you today.

Father Connolly In two or three years I will be able to get the boy a place alongside myself on the corporation dustcart. But that work is too heavy for one so young. Besides, he can read – –

Mother Connolly And even write a wee bit – –

Father Connolly So it would be best you should take him where his accomplishments will be needed. Now don't forget this, Jim: they will tell you your duty is to your master to work as hard as you can. But you have another and a greater duty – to the men who work beside you. If you are called upon to join with them for fair dealings and proper justice, you must never creep away from them and seek your own small advantage. Or they will put on ye the name of blackleg. And no man of that name comes under this roof. That's absolute. Good-bye, boy: good luck to ye, so.

Enter UNCLE MCBRIDE.

Uncle McBride Mary, is the boy away, yet?

Mother Connolly He is not.

Uncle McBride I want a word with him.

Mother Connolly Your Uncle McBride, Jim, has something to say.

Uncle McBride Do ye know why it is I never come to this house except after dark? I thought ye did not. Well: I'll tell ye. No, Mary, no, he is of an age to earn his living, he is of an age to hear the truth.

For the past twelve years I am known as McBride:
My own name, which is your mother's name, I have had good reason to hide.
If the police should find me out
They'd put a rope around my throat.
For in the Rebellion of sixty-seven I took my gun and I fought
Against the man-eating lion of Britain. Down the gullet of that monster
I have thrust in my hand and I had hold for one instant
Upon the slippery round surface of his ravening heart!
Therefore for all my life I am an outcast man apart,
A man wanted, wandering, compelled to be concealed.
It would be no good to anyone if I did not always retain

The memory of my poor country: she lies captive in the rain,
Her white skin, her dark hair, her red petticoat all dirt with the mud
    of the bog:
But the strings of her harp can still sound out their note
And at her feet one old fierce dog
Still snarls on her behalf through the corner of his mouth . . .
I am a member, d'ye see, of a brave and secret Brotherhood:
Once in, you're never out!
Once remembered, not forgotten:
Once you catch them you yourself are caught!
You who will live and work in Scotland: you too must not forget
Above all things, Jimmy Connolly, you are an Irishman yet.
It is time for me to disappear again . . .
Good luck to ye, boy: today ye become a man.

Exeunt FATHER CONNOLLY *and* UNCLE MCBRIDE.

SCENE 3

Enter FOREMAN *of printing-office, and* PROOF-READER (*who sits down to his work*).

MOTHER CONNOLLY *leads* CONNOLLY *up to them.*

Mother Connolly Come on, son, here is a printing-office. We will see what they have for you here. Is the master on the premises, please?

Foreman He is. What's your business?

Mother Connolly I was after hoping he would find me some employment for my son.

Foreman He's gey dwarfish. What's his age?

Mother Connolly Eleven.

Foreman It's against the regulations to take them on as young as that.

Mother Connolly But he can read and he can write and – –

Foreman Aye? That's in his favour. Mr MacCrook!

Enter 1ST EMPLOYER.

1st Employer Mr Dreich?

Foreman He can read and he can write, sir.

1st Employer What's his age?

Foreman She says eleven.

1st Employer I didna hear that, Mr Dreich. If he's twelve years old or over, we'll take him on. One shilling a week.

Mother Connolly One-and-six is the regular wage.

1st Employer Aye. But I didna entirely hear precisely how old he was. Ye can take it or leave it.

Mother Connolly We can try somewhere else, Jim, but there are very few vacancies . . .

Foreman Irish, are ye no? Catholic, are ye no? Then I doubt ye'll find nae employment anywhere else in this trade . . .

> Save for the fact that Mr MacCrook
> Prints notices and hymn-sheets and now-and-then a wee book
> For the priest at the chapel at the back of the Lothian Road . . .
> By my advice, ye'll accept his offer as well and truly made.
> So leave the wee lad this minute, and let him get on with his work.

Mother Connolly

> When and how will he get paid?

Foreman On Saturday night in the public bar across the street at ten o'clock.

> He gives good value for good work, does Mr MacCrook.

Mother Connolly Be a credit to your people, Jim, and let nobody take advantage . . .

Exit MOTHER CONNOLLY.

Connolly The work was hard, the pay was poor:

> The wind blew in at the workshop door
> And scattered the papers on the floor –
> And always I must pick them up
> And always I must pack them up
> And carry the type and mix the ink
> And clean the press and scrub the sink –
> I thought that men wrote words for men to print
> For other men to read: and thereby cause men think
> Of what the world has been and what it is
> And what it yet will be.
> I was informed that this was not for me.

Foreman Put that bloody book down and get on with your work!

Connolly The wage being paid within the public bar

> Was drunk at once in many a stinking jar.
> The man who paid it never drank one dram.
> His business was as firm as the jaws of a clam.

1st Employer Drink in the realm of Scotland is a curse.

> And since we had the Irish in, the curse is three times worse.

Foreman Mr MacCrook, sir? The Factory Inspector. He's making a tour of the shop.

1st Employer Then put that wee laddie where his age will not be called in question. There: at a table –

The FOREMAN *shoves* CONNOLLY *into the Proof-Reader's seat.*

Hang something to hide his feet!

Foreman (*drapes the front of the table with a cloth*) There ye are, Irish, for today you are promoted! A bloody proof-reader, no less! (*to* PROOF-READER) Here, you, sweep the floor.

Proof-Reader (*aside*)

>Why, they've sat the wee bugger at my proper table!
>I'll put a stop to that as soon as I am able.

Enter FACTORY INSPECTOR *on his rounds.*

Factory Inspector The ventilation, Mr MacCrook, does not come up to standard. Ye should have casements the length of the building that are 'capable of being opened'. Ye have only the fixed glazing: insufficient. I must mark it down.

1st Employer Aye, aye, I'll attend to it. I understand the Chief Inspector is about to retire, by the way? I doubt there'll be competition to succeed him in his post . . . ? The Lord Provost of this city is married to the second cousin of my good wife . . . I not infrequently meet him upon occasions of social import . . .

Factory Inspector Of course there's no more needed than screw a wee pair of hinges to the upright of each frame. It says 'capable of being opened' in the book, do you see: but there's no rule that compels me to actually *put* them as it were on the jar . . . That's a very wee lad ye have working at that table. What's his age?

Foreman His age is twelve, sir.

The PROOF-READER, *with his broom, catches the table-covering and sweeps it off, revealing* CONNOLLY'S *feet, high up above the floor.*

Factory Inspector Mr MacCrook, the boy's feet are eighteen inches from the floor! Without a birth certificate I can never permit this. Birth certificate? No? So I am sorry: I have no choice.

1st Employer Mr Dreich, ye should be ashamed. Employing a bairn among grown men! Send him home to his mother.

Proof-Reader Praise to the Lord and valiant Moses

>Who made the law that fixed our noses
>Safe upon our Protestant face!
>MacCrook daur bring no bloody papist
>Nevermore to take my proper place –
>Horroo horroo horroo – !

Exeunt all save CONNOLLY.

SCENE 4

Enter MOTHER CONNOLLY.

Mother Connolly

>The Irish baker in the Lawnmarket is in need of a smart wee boy.
>Come with me, son, we will see will he accept you in his employ.

Enter 2ND EMPLOYER *and* BAKEHOUSE-ASSISTANTS. CONNOLLY *is left with
them, his mother departs.*

2nd Employer My name is O'Toole and I love to bake
        Scones and loaves and sweetly-savoured cake,
        For folk that have full pockets and can afford
        Such fare as would grace the table of a lord.
        But for the poor who in the dark Lawnmarket dwell
        I must cook many and many a chalk-filled hard-crust roll:
        And from the scores of such that I with scorn must sell
        I earn the great part of my living. Before the sun is up
        I have already filled and cleared my shop.
        But wealthier patrons come all through the day till late at night:
        Therefore my bakehouse fires must keep alight
        Hour after hour with no relief nor rest.
        A wee child to watch their burning is the best.
        He costs me no great wage, two pence per day,
        And being small, he keeps out of the way –
        The space we have to work in is very tight,
        A grown man piling fuel gets under every boot
        And spoils the good bread that the quality will eat.
        So long as the fire is ever hot and high
        It makes no difference if he shuts his eye –
        So long as when he's wanted he awakes –
        Ye idle wee bugger, the fire is down, ye'll ruin the cakes!
Connolly I wasn't asleep.
2nd Employer Then what the hell *were* ye doing? Writing, is it?
Connolly I was after copying a wee writing with a bit of a burnt stick.
2nd Employer Ye can read?
Connolly I can so.
2nd Employer What is it ye have there?
Connolly It's a ballad. Printed out. Ye had it lining a pie-dish.
2nd Employer I did? Very like the best place for it . . .

He looks at the song-sheet and hums a line of the chorus:

        Glory-oh glory-oh to the bould Fenian men . . .

Ah, sure, 'tis a fine song, it has blood in it and pride. But we use it in this
island, boy, for the wrapping up of dough . . . 'tis behind us, all o' this,
concluded and finished, didn't His Holiness the Pope himself condemn
the Fenians – and true for him, they're not respectable. You don't mention them again. Get on with your work.
Connolly (*tries to write some more*)

        C is round, and O is round, and N is straight –
        I cannot keep my eyelids open:
        I can think of nothing but their great weight . . .

> I fall asleep upon the hard stone floor
> And dream a dream that I have dreamed before . . .
> I am in prison by the fire and in the fire
> There is no way I can get out of here
> Except to let the flames run over all
> Burning the floor the window and the wall
> And I am free and all the bread is burnt to ash
> Out in the street the people rush
> And cry aloud: 'Bread, bread, where is our food?
> This child destroys our life!' they cry – the hungry crowd
> Will starve to death because I would be free.
> Every time I go to sleep that is what I hear and see.
> Oh mother, mother something is wrong with me
> I cannot stand, I think my brain runs out at my ear . . .

Enter MOTHER CONNOLLY, *to take him away.*

Mother Connolly

Come on, son, come home, you don't stay here . . .

And yet, he must work somewhere. Small though he is, we cannot afford to keep him without his wage . . .

Exeunt 2ND EMPLOYER *and* ASSISTANTS.

SCENE 5

Mother Connolly

He lay in bed one week, one month, then more –
He was not well till after the New Year,
Not fit to work till the gorse grew gold on the Pentland Hills:
I found a back-street studio where they made ceramic tiles.

Enter 3RD EMPLOYER *and* ASSISTANT. MOTHER CONNOLLY *brings* CONNOLLY *over to them.*

3rd Employer Mosaic work, marble mantlepieces, bathrooms fitted out with the extremity of decorative finesse. We employ nobody here but artists of high-class qualification, young ladies of good family are accepted as pupils. I would take on a wee lad now at the very moderate premium of one hundred pounds per annum. Does he have his School Certificate? A most interesting and sensitive physiognomy, he might well be suited to – –

Mother Connolly One hundred pounds per annum – – !

Connolly Oh mother, that's an enormous wage!

3rd Employer I said premium, not wage. I don't pay you, you pay me. I said a pupil . . . Bide a moment. We do require the occasional assistant to grind pigment and prepare glazes and generally lend a hand with what I prefer

to term the 'kitchen end' of the business. The wage would be in the nature
of eight shillings per month. If the boy desires to employ himself in his
free time on any practical experiments of his own, thereby fitting himself
eventually for a craftsman's career, the cost of materials used and workshop space taken-up would of course be defrayed from the wages at the
rate of one shilling per week. The cumulative benefit of such experience
would of course be inestimable. I'll take him on.

Mother Connolly

> Can you assure me, sir, the work will not be too severe?
> He has been very ill, and we have to take care.

Exit MOTHER CONNOLLY.

Connolly For a time indeed the work that I was given

> Was agreeable enough: if the bakehouse had been a kind of hell,
> This place in comparison was like to be heaven.
> They were gentle-spoken artistic folk with a good word and a smile
> The customers furthermore were such people as I had never seen –
> They had bathrooms in their houses, and their finger-nails were so
>   clean –

Enter CUSTOMER.

Customer Oh, Mr McHook –

3rd Employer Madam – ?

Customer The little wash-stand we are installing in my husband's dressing-
room, if the decorative feature could perhaps be reconsidered? You remember we suggested a representation of the Bride of Lammermoor –
but the heroines of Sir Walter Scott are perhaps a little bit *passé*? My
sister has suggested that the Maid of Astolat would be more in accordance with contemporary taste . . . ?

3rd Employer Certainly, madam, Tennyson has captured the hearts of us all.
Miss Pennycuik, forward, please! An illustration of the Maid of Astolat
is now preferred by Mrs Guthrie. The wash-hand-stand, look sharp, girl,
get the album. We will show you, ma'am, a number of sample composi-
tions . . .

ASSISTANT (*brings Folio and uses* CONNOLLY *as a book-stand*).

Hold the folio for the lady, Jim – hold it straight, thank you . . .

Customer Oh there is one other matter, Mr McHook, I'd be so pleased if you'd
accommodate me. Poor old Mrs Haggerty, who has been my cleaning-
woman for the past five years, she supports, you know, her young grandson – the mother, well, it's a sad story . . . the father, alas, he drinks . . .
Irish, you understand . . . be that as it may, Mr McHook, she is very
anxious the poor wee creature should make his own way in the world.
You don't happen to have a place in your establishment, Mr McHook?

3rd Employer And what age, ma'am, is the laddie?

Customer Ten or eleven years old.

3rd Employer Oh I feel sure we can fit him in . . . Jim Connolly, how old are you?

Connolly Fourteen, Mr McHook, sir.

3rd Employer Mphm . . . The Maid of Astolat . . . Miss Pennycuik, an indigo motif, I think, for the gown: and heraldic emblazonments in the corner of the design . . .

>Jim, a short word. We're going to have to let you go.
>You have grown up so much lately, for the kind of work that you do
>I cannot in conscience pay out a man's wage.
>I have really nothing for you now you have reached your present age.
>I wish I could say that your abilities in this trade were as high
>As your character is good. I daresay you can try
>To obtain an apprenticeship in some other firm by-and-by . . .
>Young Haggerty, Mrs Guthrie, should come to me next week.

Exeunt all save CONNOLLY.

SCENE 6

Connolly And once again young Connolly had his fortune once more to seek.
>Up and down the whole of Edinburgh I could find no more work.
>For my first job I was too young
>For my next I was too ill
>For my third I was too old:
>What place is there left now where my sweat may be sold?

Enter GRABITALL, *passing across the stage.*

Grabitall After all, if they don't like it here, they can always go back where they came from . . . A boy of your age ought to be ashamed to have nothing to turn your hand to. At the very least one would expect you to think of serving your Queen and Country.

Exit GRABITALL.

Connolly I began to consider my elder brother John,
>At the same age as myself the same bad luck had come down
>Upon him: he had changed his name and he had gone
>In secret for a soldier, told no-one what he had done
>Until it was too late for his mother to call him home.
>In India now he lodged, he marched, he beat the drum,
>He dealt out death and he did not complain:
>For in the Queen's black book
>His wages were marked up with regularity every week.

> To go thus for a soldier is an easy thing to do: but before I decide
> There is a question I must put to my Uncle McBride.

Enter UNCLE MCBRIDE.

> If I serve the Famine Queen for meat and for bread,
> Does it mean my Irish blood has been thereby betrayed?

Uncle McBride

> Ah sure, it is common enough, don't they do it all the time?
> I myself was a royal soldier and considered it no crime.

Connolly But for Ireland you fought, the insurrection, sixty-seven – you told me the story –

Uncle McBride

> Some of it. No more than half of it. I was compelled to hide the glory
> Of my national cause beneath the English coat of red:
> Indeed there were so many rebels in the Queen's regiments, it was said,
> That at that time, had the word been given, one-third of the British host
> Would have turned against their officers and the whole empire would have been lost!

Connolly So why was the word not given, if so many were prepared to obey?
Uncle McBride

> Because as ever by spies and informers we were thoroughly betrayed.

You see, Britain was at peace and prosperous. She needs a gaff in her gills already, before a small nation dare slash out at her: and we chose the wrong time. With what results ye can imagine –

> Oh the gallows were set up and the graves were dug deep
> And our dumb deluded country never woke from her long sleep.

Look, boy, if you feel that you have to take the shilling, go ahead now and take it. Don't enlist under your own name – that was the mistake *I* made: I'm under false colours ever since. No good. Learn all that you can of military tactics and weaponcraft and the methods of British government all over the world, for which this ravenous army in so many thousands has been mustered. Whenever you meet an Irishman that wears the same uniform, have a quiet word and an understanding, and find out what goes on. And don't defy the discipline. Be proficient. Let the buggers put trust in you.

> When the time comes to declare to them who you are
> You will know that it has come and your course will be quite clear.

Exit UNCLE MCBRIDE.

SCENE 7

Enter SERJEANT-MAJOR.

Serjeant-Major

And so up the steep street to the high castle-rock:
For the small boy the great gate is opened a wee crack:
And then at his back it is banged shut and locked.

Other RECRUITS *enter, exchanging their civilian clothing for scarlet jackets and helmets, etc. The* SERJEANT-MAJOR *drills them into line.*

He is not here alone. Many others have come
To strip off their ragged jackets and put on the uniform.
From now on you belong to neither father nor mother
Nor yet to the workhouse-master, nor yet to yourselves alone:
The very motions of your body are no longer at your own command.
Put your feet together, so: hands down by the seams of the trousers!
There: that is how you stand.
And you will move like a wooden doll that hangs and jerks from my
huge thumb.
You, the young one, small one: forward. You will beat upon this
drum.

He hangs a drum round CONNOLLY'*s shoulders. The* RECRUITS *have now become* SOLDIERS, *and are drilled up and down.* CONNOLLY *taps the drum for their movements.*

You beat your drum for every step they take
To plant the flag of England's order on the neck
Of servile superstitious men whose skins are yellow and black,
Whose ways are treacherous, they will knife you, shoot you in the
back,
Whose women are hot and easy and full of disease,
Whose temples are full of loot and the foul priests of a strange
creed –
And there are jungles and deserts and hospitals under the hot sun . . .
How many of you will come back home
With five strong fingers still upon your gun?
The Queen's control throughout the world is large
It is given into your charge!
You: to Malta.
You: to Gibraltar.
You: to Egypt.
You: to India.
MARCH!

The SOLDIERS *march round and out.* CONNOLLY, *beating the drum is left alone.*

And now, boy, for you, who set to them the tune.
It is your turn.

SCENE 8

Enter, at a distance, the SPEAKER *of the* HOUSE OF COMMONS, *in wig and robe, the mace borne before him.*

Speaker Her Majesty's faithful Commons in Parliament assembled – –
Serjeant-Major Stand absolutely still, boy: pay attention to the legislation!
Speaker – taking into consideration the grave level of agrarian crime at present manifest in the provinces of Ireland, and in particular the formation of a seditious body known as the Land League, having as its object the forcible reversion of Irish estates from the hands of their lawful owners and the illegal parcelling out of the said lands into areas of unprecedented peasant proprietorship, we have drafted, debated, and passed through this Parliament, an Act known as the *Coercion Act*, whereby all forms of resistance to the acknowledged rights and privileges of hereditary landlords are immediately forbidden. Any violation thereof shall be visited at once with the utmost rigours of the Law – every agent of state authority, including the troops, to be placed upon instant readiness for the implementation of this Act.
Serjeant-Major Did you hear that? You've got your orders: Dublin, my lad, for you!

You are now to be sent to where the whole thing first began:
To the original grumbling conquest of the very first conquering
King!

Exit SPEAKER *etc.*

You will accompany the draft to the Caledonian Station at o-eight-thirty hours, thence to entrain for Liverpool. Immediate embarkation on the night boat to Dublin. Report on arrival to the Garrison Transport Officer at Islandbridge Barracks, who will give you your orders as to how to proceed by the Great Southern and Western Railway to the city of Cork. On arrival at Cork, you will report to the Orderly Officer and take up your duties with the First Battalion of the Regiment in whatever Company you are assigned. If you can't remember it, don't worry – *I'm* coming with you. Get on with it – MOVE!

More SOLDIERS *enter, they all march rapidly round the stage,* CONNOLLY *beating his drum.*

SCENE 9

The SERJEANT-MAJOR, SOLDIERS *and* CONNOLLY *group themselves as though on the deck of a ship.*

Connolly (*sings*)

    The exile from Erin on shipboard is wavering

    The boat it rolls wide and the waves they mount high

    He comes in the shape of the ancestral enemy

    With the crown on his cap and coercion in his eye.

1st Soldier Hey – Irish – Paddy – you – you *are* Irish?

Connolly I am.

1st Soldier Hey, what kind of place is this city of Cork?

Connolly I dunno.

2nd Soldier How's it off for cunt, Paddy, in the city of Cork?

3rd Soldier Tuppence a toss in the backyard of a boozer.

1st Soldier Ye'll want to mak nae bargains in the dark over there – for a stone of potatoes they'd sell ye the hole in the arse of a pig and pretend it's their ain sister, wad they no? Hey, Irish, I said – wad they no? Hey?

2nd Soldier Leave the poor wee sod alone, Jack, he's fucken seasick.

3rd Soldier So am I . . .

Connolly (*sings*)

    What does it matter that he is but a child yet

    What does it matter that he carries no sword?

    The drum on his shoulder is the burden of his infamy

    And death is prefigured when its roar shall be heard.

SCENE 10

An idealised view of the Irish countryside, lakes, mountains, green fields, white-washed cottages, a gallows with a hanged man, a round tower, an allegorical female with a wolfhound and a harp. (Backcloth II.)

The SERJEANT-MAJOR *brings his* SOLDIERS *to attention and marches them off the boat. They fall in, as it were on the quay. Enter* 1ST OFFICER.

1st Officer Garrison Transport Officer, Islandbridge, Dublin. Serjeant-Major, where's that draft of yours from Edinburgh, they should have come in on the boat?

Serjeant-Major They have, sir. They're here, sir.

1st Officer A quick breakfast in the cookhouse, march them to Kingsbridge Station, ten-thirty train to Cork! Hurry it up, carry on!

Serjeant-Major Very good, sir. Detachment, detachment, 'SHUN! Right turn, quick –

Enter 2ND OFFICER.

2nd Officer One moment, Captain Whatnot!

Serjeant-Major As you were!

2nd Officer What the devil are you doing with these men, what are they on?

1st Officer Draft en route to Cork, sir, as per HQ Transit Order of the 23rd – –

2nd Officer No! Cancel that.

1st Officer Sir! Cancel that, Sar'nt-Major.

Serjeant-Major Sir! Detachment, left turn, stand-at-ease! I didn't say stand easy, what the hell d'ye think you're doing, that man at the back there he knows who he is – (*etc . . .*)

2nd Officer (*to* 1ST OFFICER) Have you not heard the news? The Chief Secretary of Ireland, Lord Frederick Cavendish, and the Under-Secretary, Mr Burke, were carved up last night by Fenian butchers in the middle of Phoenix Park! The pair of them – DEAD!

1st Officer Good God.

2nd Officer It's less than a week since the agitator Parnell was released from Kilmainham Gaol upon signing an agreement with Mr Gladstone assuring him absolutely of his repudiation of all terrorism!

1st Officer Good God, sir, the man is already foresworn.

2nd Officer That is nothing to the purpose, Captain Whatnot. The immediate effect will be widespread civil disturbance followed by massive coercion on the part of government – that means *us*. All troops confined to barracks pending further orders. Any regiments known to contain Irish personnel must have their weapons removed from the custody of the men and placed under secure guard in the armoury. *At* the same time heavily-armed patrols in support of the civil police are to be deployed at all strategic points. Carry on.

Exit 2ND OFFICER.

1st Officer Sar'nt-Major, relieve those men of their rifles.

Serjeant-Major Detachment, pile arms! Place your bayonets alongside the butts of the rifles. Get them bloody kitbags out of the way and keep yourselves alert!

Re-enter 2ND OFFICER.

2nd Officer Captain Whatnot, these men are required at once to patrol St Stephen's Green. What the devil are they doing divesting themselves of their weapons? Serjeant-Major, an issue of ball-cartridge to every man!

Serjeant-Major Sir! Detachment, about turn; *to* the armoury to draw ball-cartridge, by the left, quick –

Enter 3RD OFFICER.

3rd Officer Where the deuce is that damn detachment that's supposed to be going to Cork?

Serjeant-Major As you were!

3rd Officer Major Whosit, are these the men? What on earth do you think

you're doing, fooling around with them here? Kingsbridge Station, at
the double, or you're going to miss the train!

Serjeant-Major Grab them guns and get fell in! 'Tenshun, right turn, double
march, left-right, left-right, left-right, left . . .

3rd Officer (*sings*)

> Agrarian crime and the assassination of landlords
> Has increased to such a degree in the County of Cork
> That the greatest number of soldiers we can possibly send there.
> Will scarcely be sufficient for the immediate urgent work.

The OFFICERS *go out. The* SERJEANT-MAJOR *marches his men round the
stage.*

SCENE 11

*The Detachment runs into a crowd of people, angrily demonstrating with
green banners and placards reading 'No Coercion', 'Parnell for ever', etc.
An effigy of Parnell is borne heroically aloft.*

Crowd No coercion! Open the Gaols! Reprieve the fenian prisoners! Parnell
and the Land League! Court-martial the redcoat murderers! Send the
bloody sodgers home! Parnell! Parnell! Parnell!

A Wild Woman in the Crowd (*sings*)

> Sure no-one knows yet whether Parnell is a traitor
> Signing his damned agreements with ould Gladstone on the side:
> Or whether in the long run he will prove the people's hero
> Securing us Home Rule and our own true national pride!
> Whatever it may be, ourselves and the cruel army
> Are locked in sworn enmity, good against bad:
> And whatever the result, there's such fervour of emotion
> At the thought of Lord Cavendish lying dead in his matted blood!

Parnell and the Land League! Up the cause of the people! Home rule
and no evictions! A nation once again!

The CROWD *starts singing* 'A Nation Once Again'.

> A nation once again
> A nation once again
> And Ireland, long a province, be
> A nation once again . . . (etc.)

The SERJEANT-MAJOR *holds his men in hand, and they stand off, on the edge
of the crowd, unable to pass across.*

Enter, at a distance, the SPEAKER *of the* HOUSE OF COMMONS – *as before.*

Speaker It is true that Mr Parnell, as leader of the Irish Home Rule Party, has
declared himself in favour of the Land League agitation: but these
people should know that he has also denounced violence. And has in-

dicated his support to Mr Gladstone's Liberal Government in all measures necessary for the preservation of peace – provided, in due time, that Mr Gladstone and the Liberals will introduce Home Rule. Half a loaf, thinks Mr Parnell, is much better than no bread. We do not consider the name of this tribune to be as dangerous as his supporters believe.

He crosses the stage, removes the head of the Parnell effigy, and carries it away, tucked under his arm.

Carry on, Serjeant-Major: Cork is where you should be.

The CROWD *is now confused and disconcerted. Frightened by the rifles of the* SOLDIERS *(which the* SERJEANT-MAJOR *has ordered to be levelled), they disperse uneasily. The troops push their way through them, and take their places, as it were in the luggage-van of a train. The* SPEAKER *goes out.*

SCENE 12

Enter GRABITALL, *at a distance.*

Grabitall On the way to Cork the young soldiers marvel at the Irish countryside:

Such ruin, such ignoble apathy, such incompetence far and wide.

1st Soldier Not a roof without a hole in it

Not a stone wall without a crack.

2nd Soldier Boulders and rocks instead of a front garden

Heaps of shit piled up at the back.

3rd Soldier And the rags and tatters that the folk here wear –

Ye'd wonder they'd not prefer to gang about wi' their arses bare!

Connolly In every field where good corn ought to sprout

The weeds and nettles grow so thick

Ye'd need an earthquake-shock to root them out.

The only vigour and order that I can discover

Are the soldiers and the constables with their bright brass and polished leather:

They glare out over the green, where at every crossroads they stand –

It is as though their cold blue eyes had poisoned the whole land.

Serjeant-Major

Boy, I'll tell ye the one thing that's wrong with this country:

Priests, boy, idolatry, like they call it the fucken Popery.

They squat in their confessionals and they smell the young women's mouths –

They have one hand out for the money and the other hand ye can guess where else!

Connolly I hear them all laugh at his ignorant remark . . .

To contradict my officer would put me in the wrong.

>At all events my own religion is not very strong . . .
>And at all events we have reached Cork.

Another CROWD *surges forward, shouting the same slogans as in the previous scene, they also have an effigy of Parnell.*

>And here we are again with the shouts and the abuse
>And the thrown stones in the street . . .

Serjeant-Major (*gathers them together to make a dash through*)
>Come on, now, keep moving, we'll soon be at the barracks –
>Keep up them fucken feet!

The SOLDIERS *are hurried out, and the* CROWD *surges after them, enraged.*

SCENE 13

CONNOLLY *enters, beating a slow drum-beat.*

Connolly Here is what James Connolly saw and did
>While serving the Queen in Ireland in her coat of scarlet red.

GRABITALL *comes forward.*

Grabitall Here is an English lord. In Westminster I abide.
>My lands in County Cork measure fifty miles from side to side.

Enter AGENT.

>Here is my agent, with a fine house in Dublin town.
>All the rents and revenues for the great lord he passes on and writes
>them down.

Enter BAILIFF.

>Here is the agent's bailiff, poor man, he is compelled to dwell
>Upon the estate of the great lord – it may be thought he lives well
>He eats roast beef and turkey: but his life is a very hell.
>We are three Christian gentlemen, we say our prayers in the
>Protestant church:
>The sworn soldiers of the Crown will not leave us in the lurch.

Enter SERJEANT-MAJOR *and* SOLDIERS, *and line up in the background.*

>I have fallen victim to an inexplicable crisis in international trade.
>I don't pretend to understand it, but my stockbroker, who is highly
>paid
>Informs me that my shares in steel and coal and shipping have
>begun to drop.
>I must sell one of my gilded carriages and get rid of half my stable –
>A coachman and some grooms must be given, as they say, the chop:
>What a pity, he was a cheerful coachman and exceedingly able.

Until this loss to my prestige has been recouped I cannot rest
content.

My Irish tenants, I suppose, must pay me some small increase of
rent.

Sir Reginald Fitzgerald, if you would be so good, pray assess the
desired amount.

Attend to the requisite business and have it paid into my account.

Agent I will apply myself to this matter with my utmost contrivance.

However, I do fear, my lord, it won't come off without disturbance.

Grabitall *I* live in Westminster: it will hardly disturb *me*.

Besides, the Coercion Act makes it possible for me to obtain
My rightful rents without delay: and if necessary, you must distrain.
By intimidating my representatives they will not put *me* in fear.
My legal dues, in the London Parliament, have been made
abundantly clear.

Agent I have written to the Lord Lieutenant and let him know what you
desire.

He assures me of his full support: my preparations are now made
To communicate with the bailiff and give him my instruction:
Captain Blazer, if the increased rents are not immediately paid
You have my firm authority to commence proceedings for eviction.

Bailiff A British officer, retired. No coward. Sir: I am afraid.

Agent Sir, you must do your duty or you lose your situation.

The garrison has been forewarned: the troops are on parade.
You have the law, you have the army, an impregnable combination.

He hands the BAILIFF *a paper.*

Grabitall Ironical that a Tory like myself should have to wait
For the Liberals to hand me my own dinner upon a plate.

Bailiff In my hand I hold a judge's writ.

Agent Then get about your work, sir: issue it.

Grabitall I am on my way to the Prince of Wales for a game of baccarat –
I hope to meet an high-priced courtesan who has just come out of
France.

Agent I am on my way to the Viceregal Lodge in Phoenix Park:
There is a ball, my wife and I are invited, I will drink and she will
dance.

Exeunt GRABITALL *and* AGENT.

Bailiff And I am my way to the hovel of an unreliable feller named Lynch.
Before the work is set on foot his mouth must be opened an
approximate half-inch.
Terence, are ye there?
'Tis Captain Blazer before your door!

MRS LYNCH *appears at the door of a cottage.*

Mrs Lynch Indeed, sir, I'm sorry to tell ye himself is not within –

Himself has heard terrible tidings of the brutal work is to be done.

Ye will evict them four bold Flanagans from the house beyond on the hill?

The word is out them four stout blackguards have put your name down to be killed

And Myles Flanagan, the fearful creature, has got himself a new long gun.

Ye understand I have said nothing and himself is not here at all . . .

As ye rode past my house this morning, I turned my poor face to the wall.

The BAILIFF *pays her and she goes in.*

Bailiff Thank you, Mrs Lynch, that will do me very well . . .

It is not only a question to evict the brothers Flanagan –

For their murderous treason they must be locked into prison

And locked up so securely they can never get out again.

In the meantime I must evict the Widow McDuffy and Seamus O'Dowd

And John Cusack and his wife Nora who live by the river where it flows through the wood,

And three families furthermore across the bridge on the open moor.

Serjeant-Major, are ye there?

The brothers Flanagan with their long gun

Have me walking in mortal fear.

Serjeant-Major (*deploys his men and comes forward*)

I am here, sir, you may proceed

Without undue panic or rush.

I have a soldier prepared and concealed

Behind every convenient bush.

Bailiff Very well.

He goes to the first cottage on his list.

*Mrs McDuffy, you are ordered by the court this very day

To vacate your rented premises without hindrance or delay.

Mrs McDuffy, do you hear?

Or do we have to break the door?

Tenant (*inside cottage door*)

Oh God for this poor roof

So many years it did cover my head

And now in bushes and in bohereens

I must go forth and beg my bread.

Bailiff Distasteful, but it must be done.

Serjeant-Major, break it down.

The SOLDIERS *break open the cottage and the people are evicted.**

(*Business and dialogue between asterisks is repeated for* MRS O'DOWD *and* MRS CUSACK.) *As* MRS CUSACK *is flung out of her cottage,* MYLES FLANAGAN *appears at a distance with a gun, and shoots. The* BAILIFF *falls.*

Flanagan Mad Myles Flanagan has let fly with his long gun.
   He is observed and he will be caught:
   But he passes it on.

He passes the gun to his 1ST BROTHER *as he is caught by the* SOLDIERS. *The* 1ST BROTHER (*pursued*) *throws the gun to* 2ND BROTHER – *offstage –who is chased in his turn. It appears from the sounds that he has passed it to the* 3RD BROTHER – *sounds of chase and shots recede into distance.* 1ST BROTHER *has evaded capture. He watches* MYLES FLANAGAN *taken away under guard.*

1st Brother Bloody Bill Blazer is good and dead:
   The curse of God upon his head.
   The curse of God upon Terence Lynch and his spiteful hungry wife
   Who told the soldiers where to find the men who sought Bill
    Blazer's life.

MRS LYNCH *passes slowly across the stage.*

An Evicted Tenant
   From this day forth until they walk out of this land
   No word from an Irish mouth shall they receive
   No help from an Irish hand
   No food from an Irish pot
   Nor warmth from an Irish fire:
   The silence of hell shall enfold them round
   In their shame and hatred and fear.

MRS LYNCH *creeps out. The* SOLDIERS *take* FLANAGAN *and the dead body away. The* TENANTS *form a sullen crowd, and stubbornly try to sing* 'A Nation Once Again'. CONNOLLY *remains at the side of the stage.* GRABIT-ALL *re-enters carrying a rolled-up Union Jack, which he slowly unfurls as he speaks:*

Grabitall Senseless resort to violence and vindictive motiveless murder of course do far more than any reasoned argument can ever do to discredit the concept of Home Rule. What, give this herd a parliament? They are lucky to be even permitted to send their members to Westminster. If Parnell prevails on the Liberals to grant them anything more than that, then Parnell must be destroyed.
   Already this noble gentleman, both in prison and now free as the air,
   So long for the cause of the people has chewed at the liver of power,
   Has at last, though it is yet no more than a half-shaped thought,

Blunted the edge of his beak and his talons are cropped off short!
Here is the form in which shortly he will appear:

He whips the flag round, showing on the reverse side an indecent picture of Parnell and Kitty O'Shea, on a green background.

The sordid bedmate of a Protestant whore!
The man whose venal lechery let Gladstone off the hook
And blew Home Rule for ever from the page of the statute book!
Take it, you fools, and flap it, from Liverpool to New York –
Let the whole world regard the poor tool with which you thought
    you could work!

He tosses the flag contemptuously at the TENANTS, *who moan with frustrated rage and tear it to pieces. Exeunt all save* CONNOLLY.

SCENE 14

Connolly I was the boy that stood and beat the drum
Upon the green fields of County Cork where these evil deeds were
    done.
I sat lonely in the barracks the night that Myles Flanagan was
    hung:
I had no excuse for the use I had been put to
Except that I was small and young –
Being a soldier under discipline I could do nothing but hold my
    tongue.

He takes out some cheap magazines and papers.

What the tongue may not handle the eyes can take in . . .

One penny each from a little bookstall in a back street. I am the villain, and the hero, of all of these stories. *Wolfe Tone and the Glorious Deeds of the United Irishmen of 1798. Robert Emmet Condemned to Death and his Brave Speech from the Dock. The Liberator O'Connell. The Fenian Brotherhood. The Manchester Martyrs.*

He sings:

My body was small but my brain it was growing.
Each word I stored up in it ran down to my heart:
For five years and six years I served and said nothing.
Confirming my confusion distorting my thought.
I am starting to think I will soldier no longer:
To desert these cruel colours I am turning my mind.
The regiment tomorrow is ordered to Dublin –
Perhaps in that city some chance I will find . . .

SCENE 15

Enter MILITARY POLICEMAN.

Military Policeman
>It is not altogether so easy to desert from Dublin town
>With the Provost-Serjeant and his men patrolling up and down:
>And he who wears the uniform is observed where'er he goes –
>The jacket of the blood-red Queen as red as any rose.

Hey, Soldier! You. Come here.

Connolly Corporal.

Military Policeman What are you doing out o' barracks all on your tod in this part o' town? There's no boozers nor tarts round here, y'know. It's a respectable neighbourhood, this.

Connolly I was just taking a stroll, Corporal.

Military Policeman Oh yes? You got permission?

Connolly Yes Corporal. All afternoon.

Military Policeman Let's have a look at it.

He checks Connolly's pass.

All right. Carry on. But be careful.

Connolly What of?

Military Policeman This weekend being the *Golden Jubilee* of Her Majesty the Queen, the native Irish will be celebrating with seditious demonstrations. Personnel of all ranks are being warned to steer clear. We don't want no riots at the sight of the uniform. You take my advice, lad, and confine your Saturday strolling to the redlight district as is customary. Not but what it might not be put out o' bounds if there's like to be commotion. Carry on.

Exit MILITARY POLICEMAN.

Connolly (*sings*)
>So I went on up through Dublin city
>Just at the hour of half-past twelve:
>I was never a one for the public houses,
>What was I going to do with myself?

Enter NATIONALIST AGITATOR *with a green banner reading 'No Jubilee Until Home Rule!' A crowd gathers round him. He picks up the fragments of Grabitall's Parnell caricature, which are still lying about the stage.*

Nationalist Agitator Aye, they try to destroy him, not once, not twice, but over and over again! Yet dauntless he defies the eternal alien tyrant that drinks your children's blood – he knows and you know that the people of Holy Ireland, strong in their ancient faith, throw back in the teeth of the monster all inducement to apostasise, all forgery and all slander that would take from them the meritorious object of their God-given loyalty! Our uncrowned king has dedicated himself, in parliament and out of it, to the sacred cause of Home Rule and the establishment in Dublin of our own free national assembly – the English Tories tremble at him, and the English Liberals under Gladstone are wound around his thumb. Sure, Gladstone lost the last election: but he knows and you know that he will never win the next one unless Parnell and the Irish Party will give him their support. Fellow-Irishmen, our great leader controls the scales of English politics, and until we get Home Rule he will throw in his national weight upon whichever side best suits this country. Uncrowned king of Ireland? He's the uncrowned king of *Britain*: and the Jubilee of Queen Victoria is a mockery and a phantasma! A Nation Once Again –

They all join in 'A Nation Once Again', and he leads them out singing in frenzy.

Enter SOCIALIST AGITATOR, *with his red banner reading 'International Workingmen's Association, Dublin Branch'. He is followed by a few not very interested people.*

Socialist Agitator Uncrowned king, do they call him, or a beggar at the back door, knocking first at the house of the Liberal and then at the gate of the Tory – inadequate delusion, that the parliamentary parties can accord any sort of power to a representative of the oppressed! Tweedledum and Tweedledee, taking their turns on the bench of office, both equally determined to protect property and privilege and the capitalism that finances them. How can we believe that Home Rule as Gladstone sees it has anything in common with an independent Irish nation? Because what does Home Rule mean but a parliament in Dublin, composed of Irish capitalists – taking orders in every detail from the parliament in London, and unable to control policy upon anything more important than the appointment of sub-postmistresses and the pay of the police. What's a capitalist? He's a rich man with an embroidered waistcoat round his belly, who buys you and your work for the smallest wage he can afford and then sells your work in the market for the largest profit he can get! If two men's work instead of ten is sufficient for the profit, then eight will be unemployed. There are riots all over England because work is not to be had: there are riots all over Ireland because land is not to be had. Yet those over there who cannot find the work are supposed to be the national enemy of those here who can't find land: and your Parnells and your Gladstones with their talk of Home Rule are in fact doing nothing other than confirming that supposition! They are dividing you, and they are ruling you: if you won't lie down to London, then you must lie down to the power of Dublin, and either way there's troops of soldier-boys in their red jackets to see you do. But if you were all to get together, both English proletarians and Irish proletarians, and if all of you were to determine to destroy capitalism once for all – take away its enormous power and the power of its lackey parliaments – then with what could we replace it? I'll give you the word – *socialism*! Now that takes some explaining, but . . .

He is interrupted by a WILD WOMAN, *screeching as she rushes on:*

Wild Woman Come on to College Green, come on to College Green – th'patriotic procession's been disrupted be th'bloody peelers, they're after burning th'British flag from the roof of th'Bank of Ireland, and there's blood in th'gutter and th'sup'rintendant's been stretched flat!

Socialist Agitator Now wait a minute, don't be misled, it's a deliberate diversion –

But he finds himself left alone except for CONNOLLY.

So there you are, lobster: divide-and-rule. That's how it works. But you'll know about that already, I suppose. Are you English – or are you Irish?

Connolly I'm Irish, but born in Scotland.

Socialist Agitator So there you are, then: divided already, before you were even thought-of! And entirely ruled-over, yet they send you here to do the ruling. Now it seems to me, squaddy, you want to think about that.

He makes as if to go.

Connolly Aye. I am thinking. I did think of it, already . . . I did think, I'd like to change it. What's this 'socialism'?

Socialist Agitator (*turns back again as he is going out*) In place of the old society, with its classes and class antagonism, we shall have a free association, in which the free development of each is the free development of all. In proportion as the exploitation of one individual by another is put an end to, the exploitation of one nation by another will also be put an end to. Difficult words, sure: does it make any sense?

Connolly I think it does, aye . . . but how to get it? Seems to me, if it's to be got, it'd be my duty as a soldier to – to, like, put a stop to it . . . ?

Socialist Agitator Like, you think it might come under the terms of the – –

Connolly Coercion Act.

Socialist Agitator There you are then . . . But let me tell you: we disdain to conceal our views and our aims. We openly declare that our ends can be attained only by the forcible overthrow of all existing social conditions. Let the ruling classes tremble at the thought of revolution! We the proletarians have nothing to lose but our chains, and moreover we can win the whole world! Just a minute, was that a peeler's helmet at the bottom of the street? I'd best be on my way – –

Connolly No! You don't go before you've explained to me – –

Socialist Agitator Look, rather than talk to you, why don't you read the literature? Here you are, take these. By rights I should ask you to pay for them, but it's such a rare thing and so useful to get them into an army-barracks, you can have 'em for nothing.

He gives CONNOLLY *some pamphlets.*

Connolly (*glances at the titles*) Karl Marx? Frederick Engels?

Socialist Agitator Aye, they're a pair of Germans. And they are both of them socialists. When the Irish Fenian prisoners were being tortured in British gaols, Karl Marx and Frederick Engels were two of the only men in England who spoke out in their defence. And furthermore it's these two men who have made the scientific study of the laws that compose capitalism, and therefrom deduced the method, by means of *science*, to get rid of it!

Connolly To lose the chains.

Socialist Agitator I quoted Marx. Look it up. You'll find it there.

Connolly This red coat will be *my* chain. But before I get rid of it, you answer me this question. Come back: you *answer* me!

He again prevents the AGITATOR *from leaving.*

Is it practicable? Can I do it?

Socialist Agitator For Godsake, do what?

Connolly Get hold of this socialism. I mean, *make* it, set it to work. Don't ye see, you silly man, I have a need to make something!

Socialist Agitator By yourself? Of course not. Oh it will be made, it will be made soon. It'll be made by an entire class. It's up to you whether you are a part of it.

Connolly (*follows his gaze and sees a* CONSTABLE *entering*) All right, but before you go – you tell me where I can get in touch with you.

Socialist Agitator You can't, because next Tuesday I'm away to New York. Sure it's a key condition of capitalism, boy: the mobility of labour. Already, I'm not here . . .

As the CONSTABLE *approaches, he slips off.*

Constable Hey, soldier, who was that?

Connolly Oh a mad feller, believes the world is a quite different shape to what all of us have been taught.

Constable Ah . . . I thought he might ha' been – you know – seditious agitator. There's a lot of 'em about. Keep away from the city-centre. There's heads are broke and all to hell there.

Exit CONSTABLE.

SCENE 16

Enter LILLIE, *and stands waiting for a tram.*

Connolly (*sings*)
  I went on up through Dublin city

Just at the hour of half-past one:
What should I see but a fair young woman
A-waiting for the Kingstown tram?
I stepped up slow to stand beside her
I hardly dared to catch her eye
I did not think that a ruffian soldier
Would be the boy to make her smile.
Toor-i-ah the doodle-addy
Toor-i-ah the doodle-ay.

Lillie (*sings*)

As I stood still in Dublin city
A-waiting for the Kingstown tram
A shy young soldier stood beside me –
I wish I could tell him who I am:
A servant girl from up the country
With not one friend in all this town –
If I could smile at him for a moment
Perhaps he would no longer frown?

Connolly (*joins in on her refrain*)

Toor-i-ah the doodle-addy
Toor-i-ah the doodle-ay . . .

Both (*embarrassed together*) I – I beg your pardon . . .

A RIOTER, *brandishing a half-burnt Union Jack, rushes across the stage, yelling for help. The* CONSTABLE *pursues him with his truncheon, and catches him. There is a short scuffle and the* RIOTER *escapes, knocking the* CONSTABLE'*s helmet off.* CONNOLLY *picks up the helmet and returns it to the breathless* CONSTABLE, *who puts it on and glares at* CONNOLLY *and* LILLIE.

Constable There'll be no trams running today be reason of the disturbances.

He resumes his pursuit and leaves them alone. They look at one another and smile.

Lillie (*sings*)

By reason of the disturbances at last we come together:
A slavey and a ruffian on a day of sunshine weather –

Connolly (*sings*)

A ruffian and a slavey, begod I think it'll rain . . .

I still didn't know what to say to her: but she told to me her name.

Lillie Lillie . . . Lillie Reynolds . . .

Connolly (*takes a step or two backwards*) That's a Protestant name. She's a Protestant. I'm a Catholic. This ends here.

Lillie He told to me his name.

Connolly Connolly.

Lillie He's a Catholic. I'm a Protestant. Does this have to end here?

Connolly No! Divided already, before we have even thought of it – and entirely ruled over? A free association, in which the free development of each is the free development of all! I will *not* have them antagonising us!

Lillie All those words he had just learnt
In his mouth so fiercely burnt,
He held my wrist, he had no choice
But shout them out in a roaring voice –
Do I want, do I want
I should do as I have been told,
And leave him alone and turn my back
And refuse to be wild and bold?
He talked of a pair of Germans
Whose names I had never heard,
He talked of a man called Capitalist
Who wanted to eat up the world –
He never talked of me
But I knew and I could see
That waiting for the Kingstown tram
No-one but me could make him say –

Connolly At last today I know now who I am!
This uniform you see me wear is neither here nor there:
I am a man is now aware of how this world is made!

Lillie And I am a girl no more afraid
Whether good or bad from this betide –
My mind made up, I now today decide
Here is the man with whom I wish to live.
I hold his hands, I give him all I have
And never ask him what he does with it –

A tattoo of drumming heard.

Connolly (*helplessly*)
Back to the barracks – inside the great black gate – ?

SCENE 17

Enter MILITARY POLICEMAN *with a patrol, one of the* SOLDIERS *beating a drum.*

Military Policeman All personnel back to barracks at the double! Emergency order by reason of the disturbances! All personnel back to barracks at the double!

CONNOLLY *whips off his jacket and cap. He is spotted, and* LILLIE *grabs them and runs off one way, while he goes the other.*

Hey you there, that man there – I can see you, come back here!

A chase. CONNOLLY *and* LILLIE *dodge about, on and off the stage. The patrol catch her for an instant, but she drops the uniform and gets away. During the chase she and* CONNOLLY *pass one another once or twice, and exchange a few flurried sentences.*

Connolly Done with it – finished – on the run – –

Lillie You, *and* me – together – wait – at the house where I work, the gardener keeps his work-clothes in the shed – come on with me – I'll get you out of it – !

She comes in with a civilian jacket and cap, which she thrusts into his hands as he runs past. When he next appears, he is wearing them. The patrol are still after him, but the MILITARY POLICEMAN *re-enters out of breath onto an empty stage.*

Military Policeman Where the hell's that bloody drummer! Come here!

The SOLDIER *with the drum comes in.*

Will you beat the fucking thing, call the silly buggers back! There's a mob of five hundred fenians advancing down Baggot Street, they'll murder us if we run into them.

The SOLDIER *beats the drum. The rest of the patrol straggle back in.*

Come on, we're getting out of this – this town's a fucking madhouse.

A Soldier But what about the deserter, Corporal?

Military Policeman What about the fucking deserter? He had his mot with him, didn't he? He'll be picked up in the brothel, same as they always are. Come on, get out of it – run!

They run off, hurriedly, pursued by a gang of drunken RIOTERS.

LILLIE *re-enters.*

Lillie (*sings*)

> In eighteen hundred and eighty-nine
> Young Jimmy Connolly jumped the line
> He left the army far behind
> And ran away to –

CONNOLLY *re-enters.*

Connolly (*sings*)

> He'd be –
>> Slyly biding, quitely hiding, yet confiding
>> He will not be caught in Scotland!

Lillie (*embraces him*) Why ever Scotland?

Connolly My people are in Scotland – I've a brother there – he was in the army himself, he'll know the score, he'll hide me, no doubt of that. He has work there, he'll find work for me. Now I think of it, he's involved in some class of politics. Trade unions, he said. Would that be socialism?

Lillie I haven't the least idea!

Connolly Never mind that. You come too. Dundee, he said. We'll get married!

Lillie In Dundee we'll get married. It's not safe to stay *here*.

Come away, there are windows on all four sides of this square.

Connolly Sure what do the windows care!

Their glass will be shattered and their frames will be broke
Before all that this soldier has to say will have been spoke.

Ah, by means of *science*, to get rid of the enormous power and win the
whole world – Lillie, my love, love me – disdain to conceal your views –
let the ruling classes tremble: we have nothing to lose but our chains!

They walk away arm-in-arm.

Enter GRABITALL.

Grabitall So blind, so young, so foolish and so small:
They have not thought about their life at all.
What can she make, what can he make with her
But futile struggle and unending care?

Lillie (*as she and CONNOLLY walk out*)
So small, so young, so foolish and so blind:
We are no smaller than are all mankind.
Between the trees of this quiet Dublin street
A pair of giants plant their seven-league feet. . .

Exeunt.

END OF PART ONE

Part Two: Apprenticeship

A view of Edinburgh, slum tenements below the Castle, which flies the Union Jack from the top turret. (Backcloth I.)

   Enter LILLIE.

Lillie (*sings*)

>In eighteen hundred and eighty-nine
>Young Jimmy Connolly jumped the line
>He left the army far behind
>And ran away to Scotland –
>He was –
>>Slyly biding, quietly hiding, yet confiding
>>He would not be caught in Scotland.
>
>In eighteen hundred and eighty-nine
>It seemed as though the glorious time
>Of revolution was at the prime
>In England and in Scotland –
>There was –
>>Socialism, syndicalism, radicalism
>>All fermenting up in Scotland!

   Enter GRABITALL.

Grabitall (*sings*)

>The song she sings is not a lie
>Its truth is plain and sore
>The Social Democratic
>Federation has been formed!

Lillie (*sings*)

>The Scottish Socialist
>Federation also is alive:
>Trade unions without politics
>Can scarcely now survive.

Grabitall (*sings*)

>Where Whig and Tory ruled the roost
>And divided out the power
>Will a Labour Party now arise
>To threaten us in this hour?

Lillie (*sings*)

>So rousingly, so rapidly,
>So dangerously they grow – !

Grabitall (*sings*)

> What can be done to make them safe
> If away they will not go – ?

(*Speaks*)

> The answer to that
> Is not far to find out:
> Revolution aims to finish
> All good society in one minute –
> Is it not possible to arrange
> Perhaps a slower rate of change?
> An inch of change – I did not say a yard!
> If we are shoved too strong, we hit back, hard:
> No precedent must be formed that would permit
> Occasional grants of grace to be received as though by right!

Lillie (*sings*)

> That's not the kind of language
> To deter us from the fight –
> There's such a lot already got
> And even more in sight!
>
> So hoist up the slogan
> And let your banners flee –

Enter MAGISTRATE.

Magistrate (*sings*)

> There are twenty thousand marching
> In the city of Dundee . . . !

Exit LILLIE. GRABITALL *and the* MAGISTRATE *nervously take up positions at one side.*

Grabitall Now *that* ought to have been put a stop to for a start and we will!

SCENE 2

Enter a crowd with red banners reading 'Free Speech for Dundee', 'Scottish Socialist Federation', 'Social Democratic Federation'. They gather round a rostrum, on which LESLIE *and* JOHN CONNOLLY *take their place.*

John Connolly People of Dundee! This open-air meeting has been organised by the Social Democratic Federation and the Scottish Socialist Federation in order to protest against, and to resist, the recent action of the magistrates of this city, who have taken upon themselves to forbid all public assembly in Barrack Park and the High Street. As you know, the SDF and the SSF have put forward regular speakers in both of these places since the beginning of spring: and we, more than any other organisations, have proved the chief users of both the High Street and Barrack Park. We are convinced that because of the unexpected success of our Socialist meetings, this ban has been directed primarily against ourselves: but we must regard it as a general affront to the liberty of speech of every citizen in Dundee! Now, upon that reflection, I will immediately introduce our principal speaker – a man whose celebrity as a pioneer of Scottish socialism is already second to none – Comrade John Leslie!

Leslie My friends, Comrade John Connolly has very conveniently anticipated the theme of my discourse, which for a change is not socialism, but something far more historic and perhaps more fundamental. Socialism is an ideal – it is not yet a fact – it has yet to be achieved. But freedom of speech is an inherited right, which we, as Britons, have long claimed to possess peculiarly for our own. And yet, in Dundee, it is suddenly denied to us . . . Twenty thousand citizens, cheerful and not violent, will therefore proceed, in an orderly manner, first to the High Street, and then to Barrack Park: and the Social Democratic Federation and the Scottish Socialist Federation will address you in both places. The infamous new bye-law will be openly broken: and we will see who will prevent it! Comrades: to the High Street!

CONNOLLY *has entered among the crowd. He is left alone for a moment as the whole gathering, led by* LESLIE *and* JOHN CONNOLLY, *march round the theatre, singing.*

Crowd (*sings*)
    Oh dear what can the matter be?
    All Dundee's gone mad on a Saturday
    Marching around and creating catastrophe
    Talking aloud in the street!

    Oh dear who will be stopping us,
    How many cops will it need to be dropping us
    Into the gaols of a city so populous –
    They'll never be able to dae't!

The procession arrives back at the rostrum, as it were at the High Street. Then, starting with JOHN CONNOLLY, *they one by one mount the rostrum in turn, make their statement, and jump down again in a brisk and orderly manner. Each statement is greeted with applause.*

Each Speaker in turn (*gives name and address and says*) My name is **** and I am a citizen of ****. I am speaking here today because the magistrates have announced that I am not permitted to do so. Thank you very much.

The SPEAKERS *should come from all sorts of places in Scotland, with one or two from England and Ireland as well.*

Connolly (*while this is proceeding*)
>A demonstration of the application of historical science:
>Each speaker steps forward and presents his defiance.
>So small and brief a deed that has to be done –
>Yet life and death for centuries have lumbered on and on
>Before this day's work could even be begun . . .

The last to mount the rostrum is LESLIE. *A* POLICEMAN *who has been standing at the side, is now urged forward by the* MAGISTRATE. *After* LESLIE *has spoken, he takes him by the sleeve.*

Policeman I shall have to arrest you.
Leslie Yes, I expect you will.

The crowd begins to make an angry surge, but LESLIE *holds them back with a gesture.*

>We are informed by the police officer that he has to arrest us.
Policeman Now we don't want any trouble.
Leslie (*to crowd*) There is no need for anyone to make trouble. Bear in mind we're not out to defy *every* law in Dundee. Just the one. And we've done it! And moreover every weekend we will do it again. Until freedom of speech is once more restored to the people of this town.
Connolly And so he stood and swore
>What would be done. And it was done.
>And so they did restore
>The freedom as demanded to the people of the town.
>There were no more arrests: no punishment: they did not dare.

The POLICEMAN *releases* LESLIE, *and goes, after a whispered colloquy with the* MAGISTRATE *and* GRABITALL.

>The police were taken off the street almost before
>They had had time to be put on.
>The magistrates made no statement about the victory that had been won.
>Except to say –
Magistrate Er – we have every hope that the permission to hold meetings in Barrack Park and the High Street will not be abused to the detriment of public order . . .
Grabitall (*aside to* MAGISTRATE)
>We retreat because we have to. We shall step forward yet
>To recover our prestige the first chance that we get.
>To appear to be responsive to the people's declared will
>Is one way and a safe way to make sure that we keep control.

Exeunt GRABITALL *and* MAGISTRATE.

CONNOLLY *and* JOHN CONNOLLY *move about among the dispersing crowd.*

John Connolly

My brother Jim wrote to me he was coming across the water:
I wonder was he here today among all the shouts and cheers and
laughter?

Connolly My brother John wrote to me to meet him in Dundee –

I never thought he would be the one whom suddenly I would see
Cocked up on a high platform orating like a royal Persian
To no less than twenty thousand – begod but it makes me proud
One of our own should be the organiser of so huge an occasion!

They see each other:

John!

John Connolly Jim!

Is it safe to ask you questions – perhaps we don't want to be talking
too loud . . . ?

The crowd is now dispersing rapidly – LESLIE *remains behind.*

SCENE 3

Connolly It would be better to find a corner where we are not overheard . . .
John Connolly

Ye can speak in front of John Leslie – he will never repeat a word.

Connolly I'm honoured to meet you, Mr Leslie: I was here the entire
afternoon –

Begod, sir, this was a glorious victory for the people of this town!

Leslie Indeed it was, young man, but we must endeavour to be cool.

The more they appear to retreat, the more firmly they will keep
control.

Each slow step we make must be well dug-in and cemented hard
Or we find one poor foot forward will reel backwards an entire yard.
After enthusiasm is necessary pessimism.

Trust neither but balance both.

Round your young tree a ring of railings will bring straight and
upright growth.

John Connolly You're on the run. Are they after you?

Connolly I'm not sure. Ye see, the regiment was posted to Aldershot and after
that I think India. John, I couldn't go to India!

John Connolly Oh I dunno, there's worse places . . . I was in India until the
time of my discharge – if ye can keep clear of the cholera –

Connolly John: I want to get married.

John Connolly Oh, ye do . . . That makes it different.

Connolly It's hard enough for a soldier having a wife on a home posting, but
in India – –

John Connolly It's plain impossible. Ye'd get no married quarters out there
till ye make Serjeant at least – and then there's the cholera – I've seen it

run through the cantonment like a trail of blazing gunpowder, oh God, and the way it'd go for the women and kids . . . Well, so tell us the full story. Where is the unfortunate young lady? Dublin, I suppose?

Connolly At the moment she's in Perth. The first instant that it's practicable we intend to get together – –

Leslie Ah, but how practicable? Indeed for an Irish deserter Dundee is as safe as any place you could come to – we have more Irish here than in any other town in Britain: but for a marriage you will require to put up banns and all o' that – –

John Connolly You didn't enlist under your own name, I hope – ?

Connolly Oh no – I took good care.

Leslie The question is, did he propose to the young woman under his own name?

Connolly Oh I did. Sure I've told her everything.

Leslie Wise?

Connolly Why not wise?
> If into the eyes
> Of the girl that will be his wife
> A man cannot look straight
> He will hate her all his life.

The thing that's holding us up is nothing to do with my being on the run – it's – oh goddamit – such a nasty disagreeable distasteful performance! It's not right a young woman should be compelled to put up with it!

SCENE 4

Enter LILLIE *and a* BISHOP, *at another part of the stage.*

Bishop Let there be no mistake about it, Miss Reynolds – the Catholic Church does not approve of mixed marriages with Protestants. You must remember that your husband will carry with him into the next world before the very terrible judgement of God the responsibility for the souls of all of your children. He will be instructed that if they should fail to retain their most precious birthright of the irreplaceable Catholic faith, the full weight of the defection of each and every one of them will be visited on *his* soul.

Lillie Would it not be my fault rather than his?

Bishop You are already outside the Church. It is your husband who has the knowledge and the duty to bring you into it, if he can: and above all things the most bounden duty to make certain his children *stay* in it. You cannot be permitted to marry him unless you promise that you will in no way present an obstacle to this duty. Do you so promise?

Leslie Is she strict in her religion, the lassie?

Connolly Not to say strict. She has a colour of a prejudice, as why would she not? I have one myself, don't you see?

Leslie So the solution of a service in a Protestant church is not likely to arise?

John Connolly Oh no – we couldn't have that!

Connolly John. *My* wedding. Mine. My decision: no-one else's. The point is:
I am an Irishman. Look at it how you like, the Church and the people
are the one thing – all together. It may not make very good socialist sense:
but, a Protestant minister – to my mind – would be – –

    He'd be Oliver Cromwell at Drogheda gate

    With the Book in his hand and red blood upon each boot!

I could never agree to it.

Lillie A Catholic priest with the mass wafer held on high

    Is the smoke of the fires of Smithfield and the cry

    Of every Protestant in old England who walked forth in chains to
      die

    As a martyr for the truth of God and his free conscience before the
      Lord.

    How can I not think of that before I give my word?

    How can I not think of James Connolly and his own new-found
      word

    Whereby freedom and truth and good conscience all depend

    Upon bringing to an end

    The dominion over the world of the kingdom of gold

    And the pride of all kings, prelates, usurers, by whom we are bought
      and sold?

Bishop Will you promise?

Lillie I will promise.

Bishop You understand there can be no nuptial before the altar of the church;
you understand there can be no common grave for both yourself and
your husband; you understand that whatever may be the regulation
within your religion, for this marriage within the *true* religion – no
divorce: binding for ever: your children belong to us in a land full of
heresy – the flock in Scotland is protected!

Exeunt LILLIE *and* BISHOP.

Connolly My children will be the children of mankind –

    Determining their free future through the freedom of an aroused
      mind:

    They will reap where Lillie and I have sown,

    No longer asunder, but all together and made one.

Leslie For such promises as your wife will be compelled

    To make, it will in the end be left between

    Yourself and her to work out what they mean.

    By the time your children will be but half-way reared

    There will have been so many changes in this world

> That neither priest nor minister can foretell
> The whereabouts of heaven or of hell . . .

Connolly Oh I know where hell is. It is walking the streets of Scotland trying to find a job to earn enough money to – –

John Connolly Perth and Dundee are no good. You must try Edinburgh.

Connolly You think so? I have memories . . .

John Connolly So have we all. But apart altogether from the question of employment, in Edinburgh is the centre of Scottish socialism today – which I take it, is what you're looking for?

Connolly I came to Dundee because of the free speech agitation – –

Leslie It began in Edinburgh, so. I have just heard you put your thoughts about marriage into very good order – do you think you could put other thoughts – upon more general questions – into newspaper articles, or speeches at public meetings? Your brother has already proven himself a first-class branch secretary – you could be, as it were, his apprentice?

Connolly I have no doubt I could try –

> Provided only I could earn enough to be able to buy – –

Leslie The pen and the ink, and the leisure for contemplation?

John Connolly

> No better way than follow the old family tradition –
> Like the old man, like myself, find work with the corporation:
> Permanent status we can't yet get, I'm afraid,
> On a casual basis only, but you will work and you will be paid.
> For work there is for certain if earnestly you seek it:
> Not quite so certain you will be able to keep it.

Leslie Were you a scab or a blackleg, all week long

> You could heave and you could shovel for the price of a song!

John Connolly

> Ah, but we, the bould casuals, we're beginning to organise –

Leslie We need more men amongst them who will open their eyes.

> Not only free speech is the aim of our federation:
> Trade union solidarity craves particular agitation:
> Membership is yet small – we have begun, but we do not *move* –

John Connolly

> Pull your shoulder beneath the dead weight, Jim, help us out with a good shove!

Exeunt JOHN CONNOLLY *and* LESLIE.

SCENE 5

Connolly And so I did: to such effect that my wedding-day was delayed.

> Upon the first of the month there was a strike. I had displayed
> With my brother such militant spirit that I would have betrayed

    Himself and the federation and all my workmates if I had at once gone
    To Perth, to the church, to Lillie, the same week that the strike was begun.
    I wrote to her a letter.
    I said: 'When you know me better
    You will say to yourself God forbid that ever you should wed
    With a blackleg or a scab however eager to get to bed –
    Such a one within your loving hug
    Would be a dead rat baked into a loaf of new bread:
    You would need to burn the sheets and fumigate the room as for the plague – '
    I wrote to her that: and she took it: and she wrote back
    Whatever I thought best she would accept it for my sake.

Enter LILLIE.

Lillie No, not for *your* sake. For the sake of what you know to be right and what you must do: which is by no means the same thing. How did the strike turn out?

Connolly Oh we won. More or less. The pay remains as it was, rotten: but the hours were reduced.

Lillie It's a pity you couldn't have won all of it at once.

Connolly Yet the hours have been reduced. And by *us*! Who are we? To a skilled tradesman in a craft-union we have no right to organise at all. Bloody dustmen . . . we clear garbage . . . to three-fourths of this city we *are* garbage and that's it . . .

    Lillie, I will tell you, we are now garbage that can rise and fight:
    The very paving-stones have hurled themselves against the windows in dead of night
    The Lord Provost and the council in their shirt-tails all run out
    Gallop squealing the length of Princes Street at the audacity of the deed . . . !
    Forbye I am so proud of you – you so readily agreed
    To this new disturbance of your loving dream –
    So that at last I take your hand:
    The place and occasion as promised, though not the time,
    I take your hand and I take you and we walk toward the altar –

Lillie Lillie Reynolds and James Connolly tied, not with a halter
    But with their own chosen rope of two strands, together –

Connolly I work and I must earn.

Lillie We have rented a small room.
    I hope there is no doubt that children will come.

Connolly And if they do, they must be paid for –
    That is strand number one.
    Number two: so I work: as I work I must learn

> How to defeat the accumulation of gain.
> For the labour of my brain
> Accumulates a different gain:
> The urge and the power and the desire and the attainment of
>   change –
> We begin so slow but we will end so fast
> The world will think it came because it must!
> But we know now and we will not forget
> That history is made by those who fought for it.

Lillie That is the vow which hand-in-hand we take –

Connolly In sickness or in health we will not break.

SCENE 6

Connolly (*sings*)

> And at twenty-two West Port on the Grassmarket Corner
> We set up our home full of thrift and good order.
> My mother and father lived not far away:
> I would walk the foul streets to their house every day.
>
> They welcomed my dear Lillie with tender affection:
> And kindly she cared for them in their affliction.
> It was cold, it was dark and the walls ran with water –
> My mother fell ill and her life she departed.
>
> My father fell ill, upon one wet morning
> His cart-wheel drove over him when the horses were rearing.
> The generosity of the city-fathers was not far to seek –
> They made him caretaker of a public boghouse at seven-and-six per
>   week.

Enter FATHER CONNOLLY.

Father Connolly Aye, there's worse work in the world, Jim, if it wasn't for the bloody stink that's in it. And the wee childer in the street bawling 'Dan Dan the lavatory man' every time I wave my brush at them.

Connolly Then don't wave your brush.

Father Connolly Ah sure, 'tis expected . . . they would moider the life out of you if you didn't show some spirit. But truth to tell, without your mother, God rest her soul, there is but small conversation an old man can get, either on the job or off it. It'd be a terrible thing, if for want of a bit of notice, I was to be reduced all day long to shaking me broom like a lunatic! Did ye ever know a feller that would pass the time of day with a cleaner in a public lavatory? Ye did not. Sure, it's out, in, and button-up, then away up the steps with the lot of 'em before I've even had time to take note that they were there. And as for the ones that do choose to loiter, the regulations tell me I'm to report them to the polis! Begod, 'tis not a job – 'tis a bloody *function* they have given me. They said so in so many words and made it seem like it was a compliment.

JOHN CONNOLLY *has entered, and he and* LILLIE *are sorting out a pile of placards and posters.*

What's that ye have there, Lillie?

Lillie It's the posters I've been getting out for the federation's May Day meeting.

Father Connolly May Day? You mean the maypole dancing – sure I thought our friend John Knox at St Giles's Kirk above put an end to the likes of that centuries since?

Connolly He did. Oh this is different, and yet in a way it's the same. The International Socialist Movement has declared May Day throughout the world as a day of celebration for the struggles of labour. It's new: and begod in Edinburgh we are determined to make it big.

Father Connolly So you'll use it then to propagate – turn it round, Lillie, I can't read it – 'Agitation for the eight-hour-day' . . . ? Ye'll never get it.

Connolly We won't? And why not?

Father Connolly Because at the rate of the bloody wages as they are paid at the present time, a man that works eight hours will have enough at the end of the week to buy himself a loaf of bread and two inches of an oatmeal pudding: and that's about all.

John Connolly We don't expect an eight-hour day without increase of pay to go with it.

Father Connolly Ye don't? Then in my opinion, though I am but an old codger, ye have your placards writ out all wrong. Agitation for the Edinburgh employers to go stark off their heads would be a better form of statement.

Connolly Oh it would: and we might achieve it, if it was only the employers.

John Connolly The trade unions at top level are dead against it. Would you believe . . . ?

Enter a TRADE UNION LEADER, *at a distance.*

TU Leader The implication of the demand is altogether too radical, and will only serve to undermine the chances of success of innumerable local negotiations already in progress.

Voices (*severally from various parts of the hall*) Liverpool rank-and-file committee calls for an eight-hour day! Glasgow rank-and-file committee calls for an eight-hour day! Sheffield rank-and-file committee calls for an eight-hour day! Inverness rank-and-file committee calls for an eight-hour day! Greenock rank-and-file committee calls for an eight-hour day! *Etc., etc.*

Enter LESLIE.

Leslie John – Jim – it's happening – the plinth of the public monument is beginning to crack!

TU Leader Ahem . . . we are prepared, after consultation, and with all due reservation, to tentatively participate in the socialist agitation towards an eventual achievement of an eight-hour working-day.

Leslie Don't cheer too soon. They commit themselves to nothing.

Exit TU LEADER.

But the meeting, as advertised, is no longer a meeting – we can call it a mass rally – and we will hold it in the Queen's Park!

Father Connolly Begod, Mr Leslie, you have put the pepper where it stings!

Leslie No, Mr Connolly, not quite that. . . .

A continual dropping on a very rainy day
Into the thick skull and into the brain
Until in the end it comes out on the tongue.

Father Connolly I see you have a visiting speaker at the meeting . . . Some class of a foreigner?

Leslie He's a Frenchman.

Father Connolly What's he want?

Leslie To turn the whole world upside-down. Forbye, he nearly did.

Father Connolly It's not Napoleon, by any chance?

Connolly Why don't you come and hear him?

Father Connolly Begod, I think I will. Didn't I tell ye I was after starving for a wee bit of a social throng . . . ?

SCENE 7

Enter LEO MEILLET, *and takes his place on a rostrum, with* LESLIE *and the* TU LEADER. *A crowd assembles, with red banners, reading 'May Day Mass Rally', 'We want the Eight-Hour Day', etc. 'Special Speaker: Leo Meillet of the Paris Commune 1871'.*

Leo Meillet Just twenty years ago the Commune of Paris was established by the people of Paris upon the ruins of the discredited and fraudulent Second Empire of France. Our slogan was the slogan of 1789 – 'liberty, equality, fraternity' – but in the end we were destroyed . . . France had been beaten in battle by the Prussians: the French Emperor was overthrown: a republic proclaimed. The government of the new republic made peace, a shameful peace, with the Prussians. They ordered the people of Paris to give up their cannon, the cannon which for a whole year had kept the enemy out of our city. The National Guard of Paris – labourers, craftsmen, students, school-teachers, artists – was instructed to disband. We refused. We said: 'This Republic is ruled by the very men in embroidered waistcoats who have kept our useless Emperor in power for so long.' So we endured a second siege, and in the end we were destroyed. The generals of the new republic punished Paris with total ferocity. Thousands were butchered in the streets without trial. You see, we had been taken at the start by surprise, we never worked-out what it was that we were doing. Some of us were socialists, some of us were anarchists, most of us were hungry and angry and ashamed, and that was all. It was not enough. We could not agree. . . . There is no social salvation without the shedding of blood – *but* – it will be *your* blood: unless you are united: unless you are supported: unless you have proved yourselves to be wise as well as valorous!

He steps down. Great applause, except from the TU LEADER. LESLIE *comes forward on the rostrum.*

Leslie I was particularly impressed with the way Comrade Meillet has stressed the need for unity. We of the SDF, the SSF, the Independent Labour Party, put forward this demand for the eight-hour day against the opposition of the local trade union organisations. I am happy to tell you that that obstacle no longer exists. We are at one in our demand. A small demand, quite small. 'Yet sooner than give the eight-hour day,' the bosses have said to us, 'we will fight you to the death.' And they mean it. It's no bluff. We ask for bread: we get a stone. If we asked the whole world, we could not be received worse. Very well: we *do* ask it. We are socialists: we are revolutionists: and we will take nothing less!

More applause. LESLIE *gives way to the* TU LEADER.

TU Leader The trades union movement seeks only those practicable gains that can immediately be attained. Don't be carried away, brothers: keep your feet on the ground. Eight hours and that's all. It's a moderate demand. Nothing other and that's all. Now, all o' this high-fired continental clap-trap about bloodshed – there is absolutely no need – –

John Connolly (*jumps up at the side of the rostrum*) Aye – a moderate demand! The dockworkers two years ago in the Port of London made a moderate demand – for sixpence and that's all: they put themselves out on strike: but begod they never said, 'Nothing other – we will be satisfied – just give us what we beg for and you can sleep soundly in your beds' – they knew what they had set going and they didn't flinch from the consequence: they had the great heart to make a song of it – –

He sings:

> The people's flag is deepest red
> It shrouded oft our martyred dead
> And ere their limbs grew stiff and cold
> Their heart's-blood died its very fold!

Crowd (*joins in*)

> Then raise the scarlet banner high
> Within its shade we'll live and die:

> Though cowards flinch and traitors sneer
> We'll keep the red flag flying here!

The TU LEADER, *after an impassioned but inaudible protest to* LESLIE, *has stormed off the stage and out, in the midst of all the enthusiasm. The crowd breaks up, exhilarated, cheering, and waving red flags.* LESLIE *and* JOHN CONNOLLY *remain.*

SCENE 8

Leslie John, I told you not to do it!

John Connolly But they *loved* it –

Leslie Man, ye have them roused like chained dogs in a backyard when a wee bitch sticks her bottom against the bars of the gate – and as much good they'll get out of it! For against whom are they stirred up – ? Why, after all the talk of unity, against the trade union leadership!

John Connolly Aye, and not before time!

Leslie I never would have believed you would be so foolish as to be carried away by the mere beat of a bit of music and the enthusiasm of a rhyming verse! Dear goodness, man, that kind o' thing is not what politics is all about! Indeed there is poetry in it, or I'd not be in it myself: but the entire art of the business is to find where and when the poetry has a function to pursue. You were a soldier in the army – you were not allowed to run out with a flag in your hand every time you saw an enemy and challenge him to single combat?

John Connolly I've seen it done – on the north-west frontier – –

Leslie Was it a medal – or a court-martial?

John Connolly Sometimes one, sometimes the other.

Leslie Aye and this time it's the other. My lad, ye're for court-martial!

> But it won't be me that passes judgement.
> The trade union movement
> Will have their own proper verdict on what should be done with you.
> Your employers, forbye, will have some say in it too.

John Connolly (*to audience*)

> They did. Dismissed my job with the City Corporation.
> True, they made no mention of my participation
> In the struggle for the eight-hour day:
> None the less I protested it. But for all that I could say
> The notice was quite final.
> I took it to the trades council –

Enter TU LEADER *at a distance.*

TU Leader Unproven the fact that he was sacked on political grounds.
Were there witnesses? There were not.

John Connolly

>Or if there were they were liable to be put on the same spot . . .

Exit TU LEADER.

Leslie I warned you to expect the verdict that they found.
John Connolly

>There'll be nothing for me left in Edinburgh. I have to get out.
>Ye will need a new secretary – at least for a short while.

Leslie Not easy to find anyone who will do the work with such good will . . .

>CONNOLLY *has entered during the above dialogue, and they look at him.*

John Connolly The brother?
Leslie Why not?

>His head is not so hot
>As yours. His understanding
>Grows out like an oak tree day by day.

John Connolly

>Do you hear that, Jim? Take warning –
>Your bold brother's rash wind-bellows have run him clear away.

Leslie So what do you say?
Connolly If I can do it, it will be done.

>If not, you will have to seek for a better one soon.

John Connolly

>If you make but one mistake
>Your back will be broke.
>If you try too hard to make none
>The revolution will be dead and gone.
>Good-bye to you so. Send me word how you get on.

Exeunt JOHN CONNOLLY *and* LESLIE.

SCENE 9

Connolly So local Secretary I was made

>Of the Scottish Socialist Federation –
>And at once I must begin to write and to read
>The multifarious meticulous precise documentation
>Appertaining to such an office in such an organisation.
>In our weekly paper every week a brief report I must launch
>Defining and delineating the activities of my branch
>As recorded in the minutes of each meeting that has been held.

He sits down and busies himself with papers.

>If I am an oak tree my fingers are blunt twigs on the ends of knotted branches
>For the first time in my lifetime a regular pen they must wield –

> Lillie, they would be happier grappling with your soft haunches,
> Lillie, for Godsake help me, there are so many thistles in this field –
> I am not a bloody donkey, I don't know how to eat them:
> Lillie, you must come in with me and show me how to cut them!

LILLIE *enters and sits down beside him.*

Lillie What is it, what's the hardship? – Move over, let me see ...

Connolly For the federation's weekly newspaper, I thought it would be a good idea to – like, get together a wee article analysing the City of Edinburgh on a strictly class basis.

Lillie Oh, dear ...

Connolly No, it's not as fierce as it sounds. It's no more than a question of using your eyes and your common sense as you walk about the streets and ye talk to the people – then ye put the two together and there ye are, you have your article. *That's* not the problem. Lillie: it's the *words*: building them up and setting them out. I want *help*! Listen to this:

'The population of Edinburgh is composed of snobs, flunkeys, mashers, lawyers, students, middle-class pensioners and dividend-hunters forbye the working classes have imbibed the would-be respectable spirit of their betters thus they will look with aversion on the movement ...'

There's something wrong with it, Lillie.

Lillie Aye, there is, James, it doesn't make sense.

Connolly Why not?

Lillie Or if it does, it's not true.

Connolly Look, Lillie, if I'm ever to finish it, the criticism must be radical. But can it not be a wee bit *gradual* as well?

Lillie I'm sorry, James.

Connolly I mean, you've been to school for three or four more years than I ever did – –

Lillie It was only a wee church school – –

Connolly Aye, but you do seem to have remembered what you were taught. Which is a damn sight more than I did. So you teach me the way they taught you. What's wrong with that sentence?

Lillie James, it's at least two sentences – I don't know though, it may be three ...

Connolly Eh ... ?

Lillie You see, you have to break it up and separate it. After each new idea you have to put a full stop. You said you wanted to *analyse*: isn't analyse each different thing to be put in its own choice place? Ye've seen me clear the table when I've begun to start baking: I have the flour here, the butter here, the salt there, and the bowl in front of me, so. And then I know where I am. So: the population of Edinburgh, its snobs and flunkeys and all that. At the end of the list a full stop. Now, the next sentence. 'Forbye the working classes ...' Are the working classes not included in the population of Edinburgh?

Connolly Of course they are – but don't you see there's so many of the other crowd – –

Lillie That it seems they swamp us out. So we say so. In the first sentence then: 'The population of Edinburgh is *largely* composed of snobs, flunkeys, mashers – ' and that's it. It makes that clear. 'Forbye the working classes –' *Forbye* is not good grammar. It's dialect.

Connolly Now we don't have to be la-di-dah – *forbye* is what the folk here say.

Lillie Aye, if they're Scots. But this paper's read by English and Irish as well. There are Jews down Leith Walk . . . Does *forbye* mean *even though*, or would you say it meant *moreover*?

Connolly In a sense it means both.

Lillie And you intend it to mean both here?

Connolly Lord, Lillie, I'm not sure . . .

Lillie You want your readers to be sure? I mean, do you think the working classes really belong to this list of folk ye have set down, or do ye want they should be an exception? They are to be expected to take a different attitude from all the others ye have mentioned?

Connolly We'd have a right to expect it. And a right to expect that nine times out of ten we'd be bound to be disappointed.

Lillie And does *forbye* make all that clear?

Connolly It does not. But that's not because its dialect. It's a good word in its own place: but this here is the wrong place.

Lillie So we want to be more precise. Supposing we said: 'even the working classes' . . . 'even the working-class *portion* of the population' . . . and then there's no doubt how they relate to all the others. Oh dear: 'the working classes have imbibed the would-be respectable spirit of their betters' . . . ? *All* of them? You? Me? The binmen that were on strike with you?

Connolly Oh, well, no, but then – –

Lillie Of course if you believe the workers are all in their hearts middle-class and all they want is to aspire – –

Connolly Lillie, woman, no: the most absolute anti-socialist nonsense: continually put out in the popular press to confuse us – –!

Lillie So then it'd be as well, James, if we didn't put it out ourselves? All it needs is one word. '*Seemed* to have imbibed' . . . ? And then tidy up this 'thus they will look with aversion on the movement'. What movement? Socialism?

Connolly Begod, any movement that makes an effort to provide them with something new.

Lillie So say so. Here we are – –

Connolly Wait a minute. *Forbye* may be dialect, but surely *mashers* is very slang? I think we should be rid of it.

Lillie Oh no: because there's no question of it being ambiguous. A foreigner might have to ask what it meant – but if he does he won't be told 'sometimes it means *moreover* but in a sense it means *even though*'. Everyone knows exactly what is a masher. Didn't I run into one myself outside the

Lyceum Theatre? Drooping like a daffodil with a silver knob on his walking-stick. He had the nerve to call me his sweetheart and asked me into the bar for a quick one.

Connolly He did! I'll break his – –

Lillie Oh Jim, he's not here. And he didn't stay there for more than a twinkle. I told him he was an unreconstructed element of the petty bourgeoisie, and 'twas I would be the one to offer him the quick one as he rode past me in the tumbril – I was terrified he would ask me what I meant by what I said. I found it in one of your books. What does it mean?

Connolly It means *masher*.

Lillie I was right, so.

Connolly Oh you were. *Masher*. It's a grand word. Let it bide . . . Well, have we sorted it out?

Lillie I'll read it and you can see.

'. . . mashers, lawyers, students, middle-class pensioners and dividend-hunters. Even the working-class portion of the population seemed to have imbibed the would-be respectable spirit of their betters and look with aversion upon every movement running counter to conventional ideas.'

What about that?

Connolly I declare it's bloody marvellous! Now all we have to do is to hope the editor prints it. And when he does I can tell you I'll be selling the old newspaper on the corner of the street with five times the enthusiasm I've ever found for it yet! James Connolly in print! James and Lillie Connolly in print!

Lillie Your ideas.

Connolly But your words, Lillie. And without the one, I have discovered, we could never make out the other.

SCENE 10

CONNOLLY *picks up a sack of newspapers. He goes out to sell them as* LILLIE *narrates the scene.*

Lillie (*sings*)
And now the words are all put down
The arguments turned neatly round
Tied up in print both black and bold
Somehow the paper must be sold.
Sober language can't express
The fear felt for the gutter-press
By honest tradesmen who purvey
The decent newspapers every day.

Connolly (*tries to sell papers to passers-by, with little success; sings*)
> The comrades all swore they would come round and help
> They have not arrived: I must sell it myself.

Lillie (*sings*)
> No shop will stock this scurrilous rag
> So with an old moth-eaten bag
> Of papers at his back, he goes
> Upon the street in rain and snow.
> Upon the street in snow and wind
> A little corner he must find
> To hawk his wares and then slip off
> Before the law can catch him up.

Connolly (*sings*)
> My day's work should be over, my feet are so tired
> How many more hours of this are required?

He takes evasive action as a POLICEMAN *regards him suspiciously.*

Lillie (*sings*)
> Indeed he does commit no crime
> But what policeman has the time
> To argue every twist and turn?
> Far easier to run him in.
> For what? His headlines do defy
> The sacred law of property:
> Himself, so down-at-heel, must seem
> The very image of his theme.

Connolly (*sings*)
> We are not very many in the Socialist Party –
> So why the hell can't we turn up then, and help to perform our duty?

Lillie (*sings*)
> There he has been three hours and more
> Not yet got rid of half his store.
> If you would be an activist
> Wear woollen gloves upon each fist.

She sets off to rescue him.

Connolly (*sings*)
> And suddenly I look up and see
> My lovely wife with a can of tea.
> She's going to tell me to come home:
> How can I when the job is not half-done?
>
> Yet never let it be said that Jim Connolly was beaten:
> I'll unload it on to the lot of 'em at the next monthly meeting!

He thankfully sets down his bundle and drinks the tea LILLIE *has brought.*

SCENE 11

CONNOLLY *finishes his tea, pulls himself together and stands up resolutely.*

Connolly To write and sell the paper is not all –
  The people must be rallied with a call:
  A call requires a voice: a voice requires a man
  To stand like a fool in front of them, bellowing all alone.
  Somebody has to do it, every Saturday afternoon –
  It stands to reason, it's inevitable, one day it will be my turn.
  Being secretary I am lucky, I evade most of the odium:
  I *introduce* the speakers only from the corner of the podium.
  I'm not the man they are waiting for and they do not really care
  If I stand and swallow my tongue and nobody can hear –

But even so it's cruel difficult when ye have a stammer the same as I do –
it's not too bad when I'm at home or among friends – but for God's sake
what sort of a clown do I look in front of a brave red banner when I can't
even pronounce the word *socialism* properly? It only happens in
public . . .

As he talks to the audience, LILLIE *and a socialist* COMRADE *set up a red
banner behind the rostrum, reading 'Scottish Socialist Federation: this
week's guest speaker – Mr Keir Hardie: "Labour in Parliament"' '*

soshyism – ye see? *soslism* – that's even worse. *so-so-sosh* – oh Jasus. And
then there's the business of the gestures. I have a handbook, it says here:
'The arm should not be agitated except towards the end of the peroration.' Where to hell's the peroration of a short introduction . . . ? 'Comrades, we welcome this afternoon that celebrated so – so so – sho *so –
shee – al – ist* stalwart, Mr Keir Hardie, who will speak to you today
about . . .' Oh but will he? What's the time? Oh my God – Lillie! –
Lillie! –

A number of people have drifted on, waiting for the speeches.

  Oh Lillie, where the devil is the celebrated Mr Keir Hardie?
  He hasn't turned up, we've got everything ready,
  We've announced him in advance, there is nobody to take his
    place:
  The federation will be made a laughing-stock, how to God can we
    save our face?
Comrade Jim, he's not come yet.
Connolly I know damn well he's not come.
Comrade The speaker was advertised for half-past two.
Connolly I'm well aware of it: I wrote the posters.
Comrade Is there that three o'clock train he could possibly be coming on?
Connolly It doesn't run on a Saturday. As well you know.

Comrade There's more people to listen to *him* than we've ever had before.
Connolly We can't just let them go home, they'll have to listen to someone.
Lillie Jim, you're not going to – –
Connolly Who else?
Lillie But Jim, you've never spoken in public before – –
Connolly Ach, there's a first time for everything. Give me a kiss.

She gives him a nervous kiss and he jumps up on the rostrum.

Comrades: I – I have to apologise for the un- for the un-forewarned absence of comrade Keir Hardie. Comrade Keir Hardie. Who was, as you know, was to have been our speaker this – this afternoon . . . I can't think what's become of him . . .
1st Person in Crowd Is the meeting off then?
Connolly No the meeting is not off, so please don't go away: I'm as fed up as you are! I intend to ensure that an apology and an explanation will appear in comrade Hardie's newspaper for this – for this – for this breach of faith! (*aside to* COMRADE) It'd bloody well better . . . !

(*to the public*) With your permission: I will endeavour myself to speak for a few moments upon the – the equivalent subject-matter as Keir Hardie was himself, provisionally, bespoken to expound, under the terms of –
Comrade (*aside*) God, he's beginning to tangle himself.
Lillie (*aside*) I told him he shouldn't, I can't bear it, I daren't listen . . .

She covers her ears with her hands. CONNOLLY *sees her and glares appealingly at her, she takes her hands away and gives him a brave smile: but when he looks back at the public her hands go up again.*

Connolly Labour, in parliament. Like, the necess-necess – the *need* for so-socialists to work towards the formation of a – of a National Parliamentary Labour Party . . . Look, I'm no good at this – you must bear with me . . . or none of us'll get anywhere.

Some heckling now, which at first completely floors him.

2nd Person in Crowd You're dead right you'll get nowhere with your sho-sho-sho . . . !
1st Person in Crowd Will ye give us your definition please of the surplus value of wages?
3rd Person in Crowd (*right under* CONNOLLY'*s elbow*) What about Gladstone?
Connolly (*suddenly aroused by this last heckler fiercely counter-attacks*) Aye Gladstone, and *what* about him! I will tell you about Gladstone! *And* all the rest of 'em that you elect into your parliament and not one of 'em represents the working man of Great Britain who has given them what they have! Of course the working class are not entirely unrepresented: I mean *as* a class: as a force in the community – we're not serfs, as we

once were: we have trade unions if we cared to join them. But *politically*
– as things now stand – –

1st Person in Crowd Will ye give us your definition please of the surplus value
of wages?

Connolly (*briskly takes it in his stride*) I will not. I repeat: we are not serfs. But
that's all. We can never be more than that until labour as a mass-body
can control the machinery of state. When it does we shall have socialism.
But how to do it?

3rd Person in Crowd Assassinate the Queen!

Connolly What – you and Guy Fawkes! You're out of your mind.

A patrolling POLICEMAN *moves to arrest the seditious heckler.*

Wait a minute, Constable – wait a minute, you can't go arresting a man
for talking through his hat!

The POLICEMAN *moves dubiously away.*

I'll pick that point up then. You assassinate the Queen. So what happens
to parliament? You can't assassinate parliament. You can't assassinate
the civil service. You can't assassinate the army who get their orders from
both. No: you must *change* parliament: and to change parliament we
have elections. And we can only elect those candidates whom some sort
of party will back. So for labour to be elected we must have a strong
Labour Party. It must be based on the trade unions and informed with
the doctrines of socialism. To discover what those are – we have all these
papers on sale –

LILLIE *and the* COMRADES *pass round with literature.*

And next week, same time same place, myself or another speaker will
develop the argument further. I may say, by the way, that the Scottish
Socialist Federation is proposing to hold weekly classes in the very near
future for the training of public speakers. It's not such a difficult thing as
all that – to put forward a few notions in public. I mean, *I'd* never done
it before this afternoon.

The meeting breaks up in good humour, various people congratulating
CONNOLLY *on his achievement.* LILLIE *comes and hugs him.*

God, I wish I could remember what exactly I said to them! Was it no
more than a load of nonsense . . . ?

SCENE 12

During the next few speeches, CONNOLLY *is seen tramping indefatigably*
around, issuing pamphlets to people, button-holing individuals, making
impromptu addresses to groups, etc.

Comrade In Edinburgh and the Port of Leith,
       In small church-halls or on the street
       Or at the corner of the park,
       In rented rooms, dingy and dark,
       And in and out of public bars
       Where far too many foaming jars
       Are filled and swilled, but not by him,
       Backwards and forwards, up and down, goes Jim:
       Proving to all who care to listen
       That the socialist position
       Is one of science, common sense,
       Inherent in the future tense –

GRABITALL *has entered and is watching* CONNOLLY'*s busy activity.*

Grabitall Inevitable, foreordained,
       And yet it cannot be attained
       Without a struggle long and fierce . . . ?
       Is that the argument to pierce
       The thick lug-holes of the artisan?
       God, all they want in Edinburgh town
       Is a gallon of beer and a lassie to steer –
       Ye'll get never a man for your sober cause
       By preaching scientific laws!
Connolly If marxism can not entertain
       The working class will never gain:
       I quite agree – the didactic element
       Must be married with enjoyment.
       So I have determined to set up
       A women's branch of our wee group,
       Where wives and sweethearts may foregather –
Grabitall To bandy socialistic blather,
       To pass their resolutions and drink tea!
       It is a myth that love is free:
       Nothing for nothing you will get
       In or out of the SSF!

Young SOCIALIST COMRADES, *male and female, get together and discuss papers and so on.*

       A girl requires some time and money spent
       Not just a stimulating argument
       About the proletariat –
       You'll never get her into bed with that!
Lillie Whoever said that anyone would!
Connolly I quite agree: it is no good
       To meet for nothing but debate.

We should get out into the open air,
Forget class war, forget the bourgeois state,
And for an hour or two we'll share
The pleasures of the country-side –
Lillie Hire a bicycle and ride – –
Connolly Or take a rucksack up and ramble,
Across the Pentland hills to scramble –
Even those who cycle are sometimes forced to walk. . . .

*Young people in groups are seen cycling and hiking in a hearty fresh-air
manner. They sing:*

Singers Oh you'll take the high road
And I'll take the low road
And we'll beat the bosses before you –
For the day surely comes
When the revolution's drums
Will be sounding through all bonny Scotland!
Connolly Of course we don't forget to talk
About our prime and serious concern:
But best of all we all of us will learn
Through mutual comradeship and exercise
The bodily value of our human lives –
Grabitall So out they come and home they go
Healthy and happy all in a glow –
I doubt that any of them are that much wiser:
And certainly the apprentice organiser,
Poor man, is falling off his feet. . . .

CONNOLLY'*s bicycle has blown a tyre, and he has had to push it wearily
home. Everyone goes out, except* CONNOLLY *and* LILLIE.

SCENE 13

Lillie And yet he must sit down dead beat
And with each blunt-twig weary finger
Press out his tedious agenda:
Tomorrow's meeting and the one next week –

CONNOLLY *sits at his table and sweats over his papers.*

Connolly Issues crowd in, the miners are on strike:
A statement of support must be declared –
The newspaper once more must be prepared –
Lillie The SSF, the SDF, the ILP
Must all at once make clear for all to see
The precise fraternal terms of their political connection –

Enter LESLIE *and* COMRADES *who sit down around* CONNOLLY.

> Ah God he's not even had time to drink his tea –
> The agenda all spread out on the floor and across his knee –
> The agenda all spread out and the talk runs round and about
> And sometimes I hear them whisper but more often I hear them
> shout. . . .

She goes out: and reappears at intervals with tea, etc.

Connolly This is crucial and it cannot wait:
> For an election looms. We must at once debate
> Whether or not we run a candidate.
> I think we should. Oh God, but I forgot –
> Someone must be chosen on the dot
> At once to go to Zurich! The International Conference
> Of Socialists from all the world, of such importance
> Is this gathering we can not afford
> To fail to meet our brethren from abroad –
> Who can we send – and how to raise the fare?
> Never mind that now: the election must come first.

Leslie I tell you, begod, the city hall would burst
> If but one vigorous working socialist were thrust in
> Among those landlord councillors and their ledgermen!

Connolly Let's vote on that? In favour? Established, then:
> We're all agreed our candidate will run.
> The only question left is – what's his name?

1st Comrade In the mean-time:
> The delegate for Zurich could be selected?

2nd Comrade I move Jim Connolly.

Connolly No no, no no, I don't think I can go –

3rd Comrade I quite agree. We must have Jim *elected*!
> He is the best one we have got
> To get in on the bloody council and stir up the boiling pot:
> With the knife of his tongue carve out the fungus, the black rot –

Connolly Never mind that just yet.
> Let's settle the question of Zurich.

1st Comrade What about me?
> I've never been across the sea.

Leslie Ye are aware it is more than a joy-ride?
> There's a great deal of politics to be done on the side.

Connolly Ye heard what your man said about the Paris Commune?
> Changed its shape every day for faction like the phases of the
> moon:
> Till it ran into its ruin. We're sending you there with this
> mandate –

Leslie We give it you straight, there's no need for debate!

Connolly You keep the anarchists out:

> And that is your one vote.
>
> For the rest
>
> You will do what appears to you best.

2nd Comrade No, this ought to be discussed –

> We cannot just issue mandates in a wild run all hugger-mugger –

Leslie Don't be such a silly bugger:

> The policy of our federation is already clear enough:
>
> We accept or we don't: if we don't, we should piss off.

Connolly (*to* 1ST COMRADE)

> The one thing that matters is that you are the chap
>
> To put the Edinburgh branch on the socialist world-map!
>
> Bear in mind this is the first aye time we have sent anyone there.
>
> Now then: the election. We shall have to prepare
>
> Strategy and tactics with determinate care –

Leslie Bear in mind this is the first aye time we have chosen to expose

> To the cold wind of the vote the tip of our virgin nose.
>
> I don't think we can win. But make sure that if we lose
>
> We lose in such a manner
>
> That the flap of our broad red banner
>
> Will sound in the ears of the public for a hell of a long time after!

You have no objections, Jim, to being proposed as our candidate . . . ?

Connolly Hey-hey now, wait a minute – –

Leslie Ah there's nothing to it really. We put it to the people of St Giles's ward: do they want you? If the answer is *yes*, then you're in: if they say *no*, you're out. What harm can it do to you?

Connolly I see no reason to make a fool of myself.

Leslie You mean you think you haven't a chance. Let's have a look at it. St Giles's ward. Irish Catholic. Supports the Liberal as a matter of habit. Because Gladstone once promised he was going to bring in Home Rule. Which he never did. But the Roman clergy are all for him – because he repudiated the adulterous Parnell. The priests will tell the people to vote Liberal: and they will.

Connolly They don't have to. Bear in mind the Liberals are the biggest slum-landlords round here. We have only to – –

Leslie Point it out. Aye. But bear in mind also we have an overall theory for national and international affairs – we must not neglect to put forward our principles. I suggest the following order: demand public housing: support the just struggle for the independence of Ireland: and inquire why the hell the Tories and the Liberals have made an electoral pact . . .

Sensation.

Connolly They've done what!

2nd Comrade What for?

Leslie For their better security against socialism in Edinburgh. Of course, it's
only local. But to the Irish, your Conservative is – –

Connolly He is the ancestral enemy, the Unionist, the Orangeman – have the
Liberals decided to cut their own throat?

Leslie Only in the one ward. The Irish vote's irrelevant everywhere else. They
have agreed to put a Tory into St George's ward, a Liberal into St Cuth-
bert's and a Liberal into ours. It's been kept a dead secret. 'Don't you
know, the poor Irish will never realise what we're up to – bless my soul
they never look beyond their bottles of stout!'

Connolly Unless we can explain to them – –

Leslie And who in the face of the priests and the Liberals would believe a
godless Socialist? Unless the Socialist himself were an Irishman, and a
Catholic . . .

Connolly You mean me.

Leslie Good man! I knew you would!

The meeting breaks up and they all go out except CONNOLLY, *and* LILLIE,
who has overhead the last exchanges.

Connolly There was one other reason I was unwilling to stand
        And I speak it alone behind my hand
        Ashamed it should be heard by anyone but my wife.
Lillie if we don't win, we may very well be finished. I shall have to give
up my job for the period of the election. With unemployment as it is, I
have no hope of getting it back.

Lillie So even if you do win, we may very well be finished.

        In order to provide for two small daughters in a wee dark flat
        Lillie Connolly must take in washing, mending clothes, and that's
        that.

Connolly See the slave of a slave taking orders from her boss
        So that *his* boss may be toppled with the minimum of loss . . .
        She here puts her finger through the biggest hole in my coat,
        Let her give but one pull downwards, my whole torso is stripped
        bare.

Lillie Let the question of that lie, till you've found out who will vote.

Connolly None too many. The men whose votes I need are not even on the
register – with their addresses on a public list they are in fear that the
debt-collectors will discover the new tenements they have moved to as
the result of a midnight flit . . . yet somehow in some manner the circle
must be broken. And if I don't do it, who will?

SCENE 14

The Election is seen as a tag-wrestling match. GRABITALL *comes in with a
rope to make the ring.* LILLIE *takes hold of the other end of it and stretches*

it across the stage. Supporters of the different parties take their places with placards and banners, etc. GRABITALL *in the middle of the ring assumes the office of referee.*

Lillie So out he goes upon the town:
He stands alone, a working man,
To challenge with his hand and brain
The power of property and gold.
The Catholic Irish have been told
That their decisive vote will sway
The contest in St Giles's ward today.

Grabitall If Connolly can catch hold of that
Inevitably he sweeps the board –
Red, red will be his council seat
And Karl Marx in St Giles's ward
Will set his guillotine to work
Upon the steps of Giles's kirk!
Blood in the gutter, rape at the back door,
Larceny in the counting-house, starvation for the poor!
Step forward then the candidate
Who boldly dares to terminate
Both root and branch this evil thing!
The Liberal MacCrook now takes the ring!

CONNOLLY *is ready in the ring.* 1ST EMPLOYER (*as Liberal*) *prepares to enter and challenge him.* 3RD EMPLOYER (*as Tory*) *lounges at one side, confident that he will not be called upon. Suddenly* 2ND EMPLOYER (*as unofficial Liberal*) *vaults over the ropes. The four candidates all wear singlets with their party-titles and colours.* (*Labour: red; Liberal: yellow; Tory: orange and blue; unofficial Liberal: green.*)

2nd Employer (*knocks* 1ST EMPLOYER *aside*)
Not yet! For first *I* lay me claim
With me blackthorn stick to take good aim:
I've seen such tinkers as MacCrook
Made mincemeat of at Donnybrook –
James Connolly, you apostate,
Will ye say your prayers before you're bate!

Grabitall (*tries to regularise the situation*) Get out this you bloody fool!
2nd Employer (*knocks him aside*)
Who is to stop me – the bould O'Toole – ?
I'm as Irish as the Cross of Cong:
I invoke the Pope the whole day long!
It is a sin to be a socialist:
The very word of the parish priest.
Stand firm for the faith and the ould Irish sod:
A vote for James Connolly is a vote against God!

Connolly The only God that's worshipped by O'Toole
       Is the poor man's penny in his shop-till.
       I'll deal with you both short and sweet.

He throws 2ND EMPLOYER.

Grabitall The Liberal vote may well be split.
       Who is the next upon his feet?
       MacCrook, MacCrook, where are you man?
       Destroy James Connolly while you can!

1ST EMPLOYER (*who has been hurt by* 2ND EMPLOYER) *limps across to cope with* CONNOLLY.

1st Employer My record as a councillor
       Is well remembered year by year –
       I stand for Gladstone and Home Rule –
       Don't waste your vote upon O'Toole:
       I am the only proper Liberal!
       My friends, you always vote for me:
       I put the sugar in your tea:
       I put the money in your pocket –
Connolly And with the Tories run a racket:
       Tweedledum and Tweedledee
       Slice up the town 'twixt one and t'other
       Each one crams his stolen cake
       Into the greedy gob of his brother –
Grabitall Alack and well-a-day, he'll take
       The entire election from MacCrook!
Lillie All over town the Irish armed with chalk
       Write CONNOLLY on the walls and on the street:
       Five hundred dustmen come to hear him speak –
Grabitall This must not be permitted any more:
       Where is the Tory? I want him on this floor!

CONNOLLY *has now got* 1ST EMPLOYER *down.* 3RD EMPLOYER *sulkily comes into the ring.*

3rd Employer Here come I, McHook by name –
       I had not thought to play this game.

He throws CONNOLLY *off from* 1ST EMPLOYER, *and then proceeds to twist the arm of the latter.*

1st Employer McHook, did we not have a pact?
3rd Employer We did: but when you faced attack
       So furious from that vile dung-carter,
       I thought if you were put to slaughter

By the ancestral Orange foe,
The Irish would unite and show
The world once more in your defence
Their ancient valour . . . Make pretence
Of being almost overcome –
Oh will you not do what I ask – ?

Grabitall (*in* 1ST EMPLOYER'*s ear*)
Be saved, be saved in the nick of time
By the faceless killer in the true-blue mask!
Will no-one help to let the Liberal live?
Must Edinburgh turn Conservative?

1st Employer For God's Sake, both of you, leave me alone!

He and 3RD EMPLOYER *are now directed on to* CONNOLLY *by* GRABITALL.
They beat him heavily.

Connolly A shower of rain upon the pavement-stone
Washes away my slogans. No church-hall
Is made available for Connolly at all –

Lillie No, that's discrimination, that's not fair!

Connolly Oh Lillie, what is that? Is *fair* a word
You think a capitalist may have heard?
And then again we bear in mind
The right to vote has been confined
To householders alone. Our potential Labour strength
Lives in a dirty tenement and pays rent
To Liberal landlords, and therefore
He is disfranchised at the poll-booth door . . .

1ST *and* 3RD EMPLOYERS *are now slowly forcing* CONNOLLY *to the floor.*

I yet contrive to stand before I fall:
Here is my last defiance to you all!

I stand against slum landlords, against one-room rotten apartments, and
against the ruling class of property that makes such evils possible. All
the rest related to it. The same Liberal Government which supplies the
troops to Irish landlords to aid them in their work of exterminating the
Irish peasantry, also imports police into Scotland to aid Scots mine-
owners in their work of starving the Scottish miners. Until this is understood, we shall remain where I am now – down: oh the great appear
great because we are on our knees. If we all got up together – then – ha
ha! – then –

His last effort fails and he collapses to the ground. 1ST EMPLOYER *then lays
out* 3RD EMPLOYER *on top of him, and stands triumphant above both of them.
At the very bottom of the pile is* 2ND EMPLOYER, *upon whom they have all
tumbled without noticing.*

Grabitall Upon the final count of the votes polled in St Giles's ward, the figures are as follows. The Liberal candidate: one thousand and fifty-six. The Conservative ditto: four hundred and ninety-seven. (Good God, is that all? We should never have repudiated the electoral pact!) Connolly, the subversive Red: two hundred and sixty-three – *at* the bottom of the poll, *as* he well deserves, *and* we hope he learns his lesson . . .

He has pulled each wrestler up as he reads out the respective figure: he now turns to walk away, and trips heavily over the body of 2ND EMPLOYER.

Oh no – wait a minute – the unofficial Liberal – fifty-four!

2nd Employer (*scrambles to his feet*) Sure and begorrah, your honour, 'twas indeed a great honour to be of any sort of service to your honour in this business, at all, at all, at all . . .

GRABITALL *beats him out of the ring and off the stage. Everyone disperses except* CONNOLLY *and* LILLIE.

SCENE 15

Lillie At least, one seventh of the total vote was cast for you.
　　　　Both Tweedledum and Tweedledee next time
　　　　Will know to dread the printing of your name
　　　　Upon the ballot, and the voters too –
Connolly Will read the word of Labour and will mark
　　　　Their cross for us with confidence! Aye, we have struck a spark!
　　　　In defeat, indeed, a shout is better than a sob . . .
　　　　But nonetheless I've lost my job.

Lillie, I am becoming not a little bit cantankerous . . . Perhaps I should be alone . . .

He kisses her and she goes away, worried.

One of the worst winters in Scottish history . . . Completely unemployed, I had no alternative but to make myself independent and pursue unhindered my main interest – socialism. In February eighteen hundred and ninety-five I found a small shop where I set up as a cobbler. I got a little ad written out and inserted in the *Labour Chronicle*. Bit of a laugh and a joke while I was at it – for what it was worth . . .

'Socialists support one another. Connolly, seventy-three Buccleuch Street, repairs the worn-out understandings of the brethren at standard rates. Ladies' boots one and sixpence: Gents' two and sixpence.'

I suppose it did twist a wry smile here and there in some quarters. I actually collected from it a certain amount of business. The entire footwear I have here of a decent-minded radical family: the father is a Professor at the University, I believe. And the daughter – she's a sweet young lassie, offered to join the SSF at the age of sixteen. Of course I told her she couldna come unless she had her dad's leave: but he gave it: and sent the shoes.

A STUDENT *enters.*

Student Have you mended them, Mr Connolly?

Connolly I have, Annie, I have. At least, I put them on the last, and hammered a few nails and sewed a bit o' thread. They've been walked upon for rather longer than is usual for shoes of even this good quality . . . I doubt your father is a thrifty man . . . It's possible forbye, there is but little wearing left in them . . .

He brings out several pairs of shoes and boots from under his table.

Student (*looks at them, appalled*) Well, at all events, you did your best . . . How much do we owe you?

Connolly Oh – for a job like that, my dear, the charge is – er – gratis . . .

Student Gratis? Indeed not. Why, it wouldn't be right. There are eight pairs altogether: Mr Connolly, I insist upon paying.

Connolly Annie, it is me that should pay you, for I've ruined every shoe in your house. I tell you what, we'll split the difference. If you take your father two dozen copies of the newspaper to distribute in the University senior common room, I'll charge him half-price for the newspaper and half-price for the shoes. And any profit he should make on the sale of the paper – –

Student Which will be none, Mr Connolly. You don't know those professors.

Connolly I can guess at them. At any rate, let him keep what he can get and put it to the purchase of new footwear for the family. Sure I'd as soon have the paper looked at as make money out of it. That's the trouble, I'm afraid. Socialism has but small commercial value . . .

Exit STUDENT.

SCENE 16

Enter LESLIE.

Connolly And even on the grounds of comradeship it is sometimes sadly lacking . . . John, I want a word with you.

Leslie Hello, Jim, there you are . . . Can it not wait till tomorrow, Jim, I'm on my way to see a man about a leaflet I'm having printed.

Connolly It can *not* wait till tomorrow, John, and as it happens it concerns just that.

Leslie Just what?

Connolly Just a leaflet I'm having printed. Me: not you. Now look here – –

Leslie Jim, I'm well aware of what you're going to say.

Connolly I know you're well aware. And that's why I'm going to say it.

Leslie You are Secretary of the SSF.

Connolly Right.

Leslie You are not in any way an officer of the Independent Labour Party.

Connolly I'm not. But our relationship with the ILP is – as you know – fully fraternal.

Leslie The ILP – as you know – would like to take us over completely. They resent our separate identity.

Connolly Do we really need a separate identity?

Leslie Perhaps not: but it's what we've got. And I think we should hold on to it: at least until the ILP have given a satisfactory explanation of the stand they take on certain issues. Now: that document you have there was sent to the printers by your orders alone.

Connolly Aye.

Leslie It's a manifesto for the ILP.

Connolly Aye.

Leslie Their committee have complained to me that you have overridden their authority: you have absolutely no business undertaking their business for them.

Connolly It was only to save time. For God's sake, John, look here, I ran into Keir Hardie on a railway station in the pouring rain – he was late for his train – he says to me, 'Jim, would ye put this in to the printers. It needs to be distributed as quickly as possible in Edinburgh and Leith.' So I did, and that's all.

Leslie And the result is they all think that we are trying to take them over. And we think already they are trying to take over ourselves. There's a great deal of bad blood, Jim, and the sooner it's wiped up, the better. After all it's not the first time this kind o' thing's happened.

Connolly Do you want me to resign?

Leslie Don't talk bloody havers. But just make certain we don't have any more of it! And where the hell are you off to?

Connolly (*who has turned savagely on his heel*) I'm going to a hardware store to buy meself a wee mirror.

Leslie A mirror? What for?

Connolly For an experiment, John Leslie, in scientific materialism. I'm going to sit with a pencil and notebook and watch meself starve to death. Look, I can't mend shoes. It appears I am not capable of transacting political business without quarrelling with the entire world. So it's either death – or emigration.

Leslie Emigration? To America?

Connolly South America. They tell me, Chile. There's a deal of opportunity for bloody fools in that country.

Leslie Chile ... You'll be lecturing, I suppose, on socialism to the red indians or whoever you find there?

Connolly Why not? It applies to them just as much as it does to us.

Leslie You can do better than Chile. And when I said lecture, I meant no joke.

You're already well-known in local circles in Scotland. Why don't you turn professional?

Connolly Because no-one has ever offered to pay me a fee.

Leslie They might, if you advertised.

Connolly Oh, get away with ye – –

Leslie No. The movement is now big enough to accommodate officials with a regular salary. There are new branches starting up all over the British Isles. We'll put an ad for you directly, in the pages of our newspaper.

Connolly I did that for the cobbler's shop.

Leslie This one will be different. Here, give me a pencil. We've got to make you sound attractive . . . 'Married, with a young family: and as his necessities are therefore very great, he may be had cheap . . .' How about that?

Connolly Oh my God – John!

Leslie No there's more to it yet. 'No man has done more for the movement than Connolly – if they have done as much. Is there no comrade anywhere who can secure him a livelihood? He is today,' – I'll underline this – 'On the verge of destitution.'

Connolly (*as Leslie hands back the pencil and moves to go out*) John – just a moment – –

Leslie No – I'm on my way to see a man about a leaflet – I can't stop!

Exit LESLIE.

Connolly The advertisement was published and read in many quarters.
　　　　　The answer came soon after, from over the water.
　　　　　From Ireland of all places they wrote to me of a job:
　　　　　Paid organiser, no less, to the Dublin Socialist Club . . . !

Exit.

END OF PART TWO

Part Three: Professional 1896–1903

Act One: 'A Movement with some Purpose'. James Connolly becomes a political organiser in Dublin and founds the Irish Socialist Republican Party. He meets the new Ireland of the literary renaissance and disrupts the royal jubilee.

List of characters:

JAMES CONNOLLY
LILLIE CONNOLLY

WILLIAM O'BRIEN
DORMAN
TOM LYNG
JACK LYNG

Trade-Union ORGANISER
Independent Labour Party CANVASSER

3 WORKERS, one a young woman

NATIONALIST QUESTIONER
UNIONIST QUESTIONER
FABIAN QUESTIONER
PURE SOCIALIST QUESTIONER

MAUD GONNE
W. B. YEATS
ALICE MILLIGAN
ERNEST MILLIGAN

GRABITALL
3 EMPLOYERS
MAGISTRATE
POLICE CONSTABLE

A STRIKER, Leader of a strike picket
Local Government OFFICIAL
LIBRARY ATTENDANT
workers, strikers, unemployed, beggars, police, citizens, etc.

Act Two: 'Alarums and Excursions'. James Connolly, in Dublin, leads the Irish Socialist Republican Party in militant opposition to British imperialism and the Boer War. He is criticised by Keir Hardie of the British labour movement.

List of characters:

JAMES CONNOLLY

WILLIAM O'BRIEN
TOM LYNG
JACK LYNG
ALICE MILLIGAN
ERNEST MILLIGAN
STEWART

MAUD GONNE
W. B. YEATS

GRABITALL
3 EMPLOYERS
CIVIL SERVANT
JOE DEVLIN
ORANGEMAN
PRIEST

POLICE OFFICER
JUDGE

AFRICAN BEARER
BOER
GERMAN ARMS MERCHANT
FRENCH ARMS MERCHANT

PRIME MINISTER
2 Liberal MPs

KEIR HARDIE
BERNARD SHAW
BEATRICE WEBB
SYDNEY WEBB
ARTHUR GRIFFITH
citizens, demonstrators, police, Members of Parliament, etc.

Act Three: 'Outmanoeuvred'. James Connolly is rejoiced to find the Irish Socialist Republican Party recognised by the Socialist International. Rosa Luxemburg – in controversy with Kautsky – throws doubt upon Connolly's views of Irish nationhood. The ISRP throws doubt upon his views of political priorities. He determines to go elsewhere.

List of characters:

JAMES CONNOLLY
LILLIE CONNOLLY
NORA CONNOLLY (their daughter)

Mr RIORDAN (their neighbour)
OLD MARKET-WOMAN
BEGGING CHILD

WILLIAM O'BRIEN
TOM LYNG
JACK LYNG
STEWART
BRADSHAWE

GRABITALL
1st and 3rd EMPLOYERS
PRIEST

CHAIRMAN of International Socialist Conference
ROSA LUXEMBURG
KAUTSKY
2 French DELEGATES
2 Polish DELEGATES
Bulgarian DELEGATE

American Railway CONDUCTOR
Chorus of American TRAVELLERS
Socialist Conference DELEGATES

Part Three: Professional 1896–1903

ACT 1: 'A Movement with some Purpose'

SCENE 1

A bird's-eye view of Dublin around its bay, with the Georgian buildings rearing up amongst the slums. The whole guarded by redcoat soldiers and police. (Back-cloth 3.)

Enter GRABITALL. CONNOLLY *and* LILLIE *enter with baggage and children. There are beggars pestering all passers-by.*

Grabitall Mona and Nora and Aideen and Lillie and James—
     Yes, three children now – no doubt very soon there'll be four –
     Improvident as always – it's not *me* puts the wolf at their door –
     They pack up their poor luggage and travel by boat and by train
     From Scotland to Ireland, from a country of hunger and cold
     To a country of cold and of hunger as indeed might have well
         been foretold.
     This man has not come here to work
     And keep his wretched family – no mistake:
     He's come to spout and agitate,
     Declare, demand, all in a heat
     Disturb the apathetic peace
     Which, since the death of turbulent Charles Parnell
     And since the last defeat of Gladstone's Liberal power,
     Chokes the united voice that thundered for Home Rule.
     Lord Salisbury's Tory Government has a plan –
     Lest separatism, independent aspirations, once again
     Rear up their strength and break the empire's bond,
     Coercion now is done with: we are *kind* . . .
     More liberal than the Liberals – we will grant
     Reform of land, local elections; oh we will freely plant
     Hope of commercial growth to stultify
     All racial disaffection amongst the middle class.
     The anarchic rumble of the ignorant mob will pass
     Into oblivion – trade unions and the Labour Party, dust in a
         half-blind eye,
     Are both controlled from Britain and therefore pose no threat.
     For complete imperial unity we have achieved the best chance yet!

Mr Crookey, Mr O'Hookey – where's O'Toole?

Enter 1ST, 2ND *and* 3RD EMPLOYERS.

Chorus, gentlemen, please!

Employers (*singing*)

>   We will now encourage and cause to flourish
>   The native knowledge of our ancient land!

3rd Employer

>   I'm setting up a factory for the baking of biscuits and bread.

1st Employer

>   I'm setting up another one for the making of boxes of wood
>   For the package and storage of biscuits and bread.

2nd Employer

>   I'm setting up an all-Ireland transport concern
>   For the conveyance of Hibernian boxes of wood
>   Full of native-baked Gaelic biscuits and bread
>   To all parts of the country be canal and be road and be train –

1st Employer We need men –

3rd Employer We need women –

2nd Employer We need men –

Employers

>   Because of British domination
>   Upon the trade of our poor nation –

Grabitall Ssh – you don't mention Home Rule! You forget yourselves, gentlemen!

Employers Ssh – ssh – we forgot ourselves . . . But Mr Grabitall, nonetheless, sorr . . .

>   Because of *da-da* domination
>   Upon the trade of our poor *da-da*,
>   Creating ruinous competition
>   We're put into the sad position –

1st Employer Of having to say to every man we hire –

3rd Employer The wage is small, we can give you no more!

Exit GRABITALL, *with a patronising pat on their backs.*
UNEMPLOYED WORKERS *enter.*

2nd Employer Take it or leave it, do you refuse the job?

1st Worker

>   Sure between this and Ballydehob
>   There is no other work that I can find.
>   I have a mind
>   To go to England and do better there.

3rd Employer

>   So go! Where you come from there's plenty more. Next!

2nd Worker

>   My farm has failed. My family are poor.
>   I'll work for what you give me and endure.

1st Employer

You have your grateful patriotic reasons? Good.

2nd Worker

I can't afford the fare

Across the water. I want food.

3rd Employer

And food for Irish bellies in my factory is produced.

Young woman, you were all but seduced

Into the British brothels, were you not? Come, work for me

And live your frugal life in catholic purity!

3rd Worker (*a young woman*)

From worse than death they rescued me indeed –

Jasus, for all my lifetime do I need

To look for rescue day after bloody day?

I'd rather have a decent rate of pay . . .

Maybe I should be careful what I say . . .

Employers Come work work work . . .!

Those who have obtained employment begin working very hard to a fast rhythm clapped out by the EMPLOYERS. *The others stand around in a weary group.*

SCENE 2

Enter DORMAN *with his leaflets and a placard clearly printed 'The Socialist Answer' – not very successful in getting anyone to take them. A* TRADE UNION ORGANISER *bounces in.*

TU Organiser

There are, you know, trade unions:

We cannot help you all at once –

But for craftsmen, tradesmen, carpenters, engineers,

Solidarity and combined action will relieve so many fears.

Pay a subscription, take a card:

Remember, we must push hard

If our British parent-body is eventually to agree

That we too have an important voice

In their counsels from beyond the sea.

Of course, if your work is labouring, casual, unskilled,

We have no place in our congress where your hopes may be
    fulfilled.

Those working turn away from him, disappointed. He speaks to DORMAN:

And of course, if your main interest is political agitation,

We regret we are not prepared to discuss the state of the nation:

> In due time, very possibly, but at the moment we must say to you
> It is not very wise to bite more than you can chew . . .!

Exit TU ORGANISER.

Employers (*still clap the time*)
> Work work work . . .!

They lead their WORKERS *out.*

Unemployed Worker
> And they do work until each arm and leg
> Buckles and cracks. They are the fortunate.
> For us: sure we can emigrate
> Or tout for short odd jobs upon the corner of the street,
> Or, failing both of these, hold out our hand and beg.

Enter Independent Labour Party CANVASSER, *with a placard and leaflets*

ILP Canvasser
> The Independent Labour Party, responsive to the bould Keir
> Hardie,
> Looks for votes in the election to the Dublin City Corporation.
> We hope next year beyond in Belfast
> Our men will sit on the council at last!
> For water, gas, and sewage disposal
> We have many and many a brave proposal –

Dorman Socialism . . .?

ILP Canvasser Now don't let's try to run until we can learn to walk . . .

Exit ILP CANVASSER. *One of the* UNEMPLOYED, *begging, approaches* DOR-
MAN.

Dorman (*gives him a small coin*) I shouldn't really be doing this, you know. It won't help, you know. Socialism . . .! Have a leaflet.

Connolly (*approaches* DORMAN) Excuse me – I'm looking for the Dublin Socialist Club, can you tell me where it is?

Dorman Yes: in point of fact: here.

Connolly Here?

Dorman Yes, myself. Me. I'm practically the only member at the moment, I'm afraid. Can I help you?

Connolly My name is Connolly.

Dorman How d'you do? What can I do for you? Would you care for one of our leaflets . . . good heavens! Connolly! From Edinburgh! James Connolly! Oh dear me, I'm so sorry, Mr Connolly, you quite took me by surprise. Did you have a good trip? Why don't we go to the club-room – oh we do have a club-room, despite all appearances – my name, by the way, is Dorman. I'm so glad you've been able to come – this way, Mr Connolly, through the door marked *Public Bar*, we *call* it our club-room, though really it's only the snug, the landlord lets us use it on Tuesdays and Thursdays . . .

Lillie (*catches on to Connolly*) James, I am not bringing the children into any public bar. There's a notice over there that says there's a room to let. I'll go straight across and see about it. Come on, girls, come on . . . I suppose I had better look out for some washing or sewing to take in . . .

She takes the CHILDREN *out one way, and* DORMAN, *leading* CONNOLLY *out the other, brings him straight back again as though into the club-room. They are joined by the members of the club.*

SCENE 3

O'BRIEN, TOM LYNG, JACK LYNG *sit down.* DORMAN *introduces* CONNOLLY *to them.* (O'BRIEN *has a limp and walks with a stick throughout.*)

Dorman We meet in the snug of a pub, though most of us prefer to
        abstain:
        We find it difficult for all of us to be together at any one time:
        We are, as I said, very few: the brothers Lyng, William O'Brien –
        Mr Connolly has come as invited, to endeavour to sort us all out –
        Here he is, brimming over with fruitful suggestions: no doubt . . .!
Connolly The first remark I have to make
        Brings a blush into my cheek:
        But had we not best start as we mean to go on –
        What sort of wage can I expect to earn?
        The fact is, I can't imagine –
        However large your subscription –
        This club is in any way capable
        Of employing a full-time official?
        To do what work,
        For how many days each week?
        What facilities, what expenses, and basically for what hope?
        This is a matter before which nothing else can be disposed:
        As you know, I have a family to feed and house and clothe.
Dorman Good. Well: that's candid. Vice versa, why not?
Tom Lyng We are a very small club –
Jack Lyng Not even a club –
Dorman A collection –
Tom Lyng Of all manner of individuals, all loosely devoted to the general principles
Jack Lyng Of socialism –
Dorman Right! But our activities –
Tom Lyng Amount to practically nothing –
Jack Lyng Except a meeting once a week on the steps of the Custom House –
Dorman To which hardly anybody comes – and of course we issue leaflets –
Connolly D'you get them out yourselves?

Tom Lyng No. They're printed in England by various fraternal groups.

Jack Lyng So we haven't got much money.

Dorman We could pay you a regular wage or on a job-by-job basis, or out-of-pocket expenses –

Connolly It'll amount to no great income if all I have to do is the kind of thing you're already doing.

Tom Lyng We don't want you to do that.

Jack Lyng We would like you, if you can, with all your experience from Scotland –

Dorman To transform us, if that is possible, into a movement with some purpose . . .

Connolly Purpose . . . It means what? I will tell you what it means. It means a properly organised revolutionary party – nothing less, or I am done with it. And the concomitants are as follows: regular subscriptions, a weekly or a monthly newspaper, a permanent working committee, a rank-and-file membership that is actually prepared to do some work when it is wanted and, of course, a manifesto. We get together an ad hoc working-party, we can draw one up without delay: and we can take the opportunity of exploring each other's political views – right? Then we present the manifesto to a general meeting of the entire club, any friends, any sympathisers, invite them all in, from Dublin, Cork, Belfast – throw it open to the widest controversy! And already we have made a name!

They all huddle together as a working-party with their backs to the audience – except O'BRIEN *– who comes downstage to speak.*

O'Brien Before they fetched him over here they were talking about him continually – Connolly will say so-and-so, his point of view will be this and that – I asked, who was this Connolly? 'He's a very smart fellow', I was told. 'And what is he?' 'Just a labourer.' 'A labourer?' said I, 'How could a labourer know all these things?' 'He went to the Library in Edinburgh and he studied.' This was not very convincing to me. I could not understand how a labourer should be so important as all that. The labourers I am acquainted with are people who drift around the roads and take up casual jobs and are almost entirely illiterate. However, I had to accept what was stated . . .

> And here today I see this labouring man stand up and take
> His tablets to the multitude like Moses on the rock . . .

SCENE 4

The CLUB-MEMBERS *take their seats as though on the platform of a public meeting,* CONNOLLY *in the middle. He holds the manifesto.*

Connolly The announcement of the formation of a new revolutionary party.

Which calls for the establishment of an Irish socialist republic. Which will be based upon the public ownership of the land and of all instruments of production, distribution and exchange. Which demands the nationalisation, under the control of properly elected boards, of both agriculture and industry, a minimum wage and a forty-eight-hour week, free education under the control of popularly elected committees, pensions to be paid for out of a graduated income-tax: and universal suffrage. The party to be known as the Irish Socialist Republican Party. In accordance with our belief that the subjection of one nation to another, as of Ireland to the authority of the British crown, is a barrier to the free political and economic development of the subjected nation, and can only serve the interests of the exploiting classes of both nations. We want to set up branches everywhere. The minimum weekly subscription is one penny per member, and the entrance fee is sixpence. A weekly newspaper to be known as *The Workers' Republic* will be published as soon as our financial circumstances allow. Any questions?

Questions come from the floor of the house:

Nationalist Questioner Does not the Catholic Church teach that private property is ordained of God?

Connolly The private property of the money-changers who were driven out of the temple – what does the church teach as to the rights and wrongs of that?

Nationalist Questioner The socialist ideology is alien to the Gaelic race.

Connolly And what d'you think St Patrick brought here but an alien ideology? Why, you argue like a pagan druid! And moreover from the same premises – the ultimate identity of church and state.

Exit NATIONALIST QUESTIONER.

And there you see the potentiality of your middle-class revolution. Oh they will talk until the moon turns green about freedom for the people – but the moment they feel their own property is threatened, they will abandon you and run, crying out on the name of God. Next?

Unionist Questioner The beginning of social revolution in Europe was the protestant reformation of the sixteenth century: the trade union movement of Great Britain is the legitimate inheritor of the puritan conventicles of the seventeenth century: and only by securing ourselves firmly to that movement can labour organisations in Ireland expect and enjoy the solidarity they require. Republicanism is a red herring.

Exit UNIONIST QUESTIONER.

Connolly And there ye see the potentiality of your unionist revolution. Defensive and sectarian: and in the end amalgamated with the Tory bosses of the City of London. Next?

Fabian Questioner Excuse me: I was most impressed with the general grasp of political reality conveyed in your programme: but I wonder, as a stranger from England, if you have altogether appreciated the *abrupt* nature of the reforms you have so sensibly outlined? Would it not be possible to reach equally desirable goals by means of evolution rather than revolution? By permeating, perhaps, the existing democratic structures, upon a long-term electoral strategy: and by laying for the time being more emphasis upon, say, your schools project, rather than upon the more divisive political theme of a republic?

Connolly If reform was all we wanted, we could get it, from Lord Salisbury, by means, as you say, of the existing democratic structures. He has a man over here already, in Dublin Castle, paying bribes to the Irish people in the shape of school projects and other such-like benefits, exactly for the purpose of preventing revolution and encouraging evolution. And making sure that evolution will in the long run never be socialist.

Fabian Questioner Yes I suppose so . . . I do think, however, you ought not to condemn the existing administration without a thorough grasp of the statistics involved. The whole question of getting rid of the hidebound capitalist-bureaucratic system can only be undertaken with extensive research, and – dare I say it – *experience* in the ramifications of local government? Thank you so much.

Exit FABIAN QUESTIONER.

Connolly Aye: the potentiality of your fabian revolution. Experience and research in the existing hidebound system till no-one can tell whether 'tis you or the system are bound up with the strongest hide! Next.

Pure Socialist Questioner I would, as a convinced atheist and internationalist of long standing, put these points to the speaker, as follows, viz: we start with materialism . . . and thus, dialectically, arrive at revolution. Karl Marx has made abundantly clear the impossibility of revolution in primarily peasant economies such as Russia – and therefore, by extension, Ireland . . .

Connolly And your question?

Pure Socialist Questioner Question? Oh yes . . . you are premature. In this country, it can't be done.

Connolly But your question?

Pure Socialist Questioner Well: I mean – can it? The very existence of this new party is simply playing into the hands of the imperialist, chauvinist, capitalist cliques: comrade, let me tell you, if you want a revolution you've got to sit down and bloody *plan* for it. You can't just write it out on a little bit of paper and expect us to take it on trust . . .

Exit PURE SOCIALIST QUESTIONER.

Connolly Do I really need to sum up the purist revolution? All theory and damn-all else. Thank you very much.

The meeting breaks up.

Well –

>The brambles and the briars are clean cleared away and cut:
>The green of the young tree will drink up life from every root.

Tom Lyng We have a membership of eight.

Enter GRABITALL.

Connolly We will soon get more than that.
O'Brien Oh we won't if we stay here:

>We must work, we must go out –

Connolly (*to* O'BRIEN)

>I saw your eyelid on the droop –
>You experienced some short doubt?
>Does it bother you yet?

O'Brien It does not.

>I am quite sure.
>When I see the class of man that your words have turned away
>I am convinced absolutely that yours is the straightest way.

Connolly So we go out and we do it.

>We are young enough and strong enough to lose nothing if we
>   attempt it.
>The small clear statement – if indeed it be correct –
>By being so small has no choice but to talk direct.

Grabitall Direct small speech in this cantankerous noisy town

>Nine times out of ten is not heard or is shouted down.
>Drink from a thousand taprooms ends up down the drain,
>Urine and vomit drag each Dublin dream
>In sodden fragments to the Liffey's brim –
>Against this tide who strives but bold undaunted Jim?
>How long before he finds he has not yet learned how to swim . . . ?

SCENE 5

CONNOLLY *becomes aware of some difficulty engaging the members of the*
ISRP. *He looks inquiringly at* DORMAN.

Dorman The subscriptions to the new party should easily have provided

>One pound for you per week after all expenses divided –

Connolly But they don't?
Dorman Dear me, they do not.
O'Brien D'you see, we were expecting the great part of our rank-and-file
support to be from the lads in the building-trade: but they're all out on
strike.
Tom Lyng It's not apathy, it's bloody poverty.
Connolly So don't insist on subscriptions. Chalk 'em up and let 'em in. We are
not making a business out of this business, d'ye get me?

O'Brien But where does that leave *you*? Sure the first question you put to us
was how much you would get paid.

CONNOLLY *shrugs. The* ISRP MEMBERS *leave him.*

Connolly Was I not wise when I was a young man
Neither to drink nor smoke, for now I find
Just so much money in my hand
As will keep me and mine for just one week.
Seven days therefore I have to look for work.

The EMPLOYERS *enter, each with a placard reading 'Situations Vacant'.
During the song,* CONNOLLY *approaches them one by one to ask for work,
but each time the placard is turned round and he reads the inscription on the
reverse: 'No Vacancies'. This becomes a kind of* danse macabre, *the*
EMPLOYERS *enticing him on deliberately to enjoy his disappointment.*

Grabitall (*sings*)
There is no doubt that even though
The trade of Dublin is depressed
If confidence can be maintained
All things will turn out for the best.
Employers (*sing*)
We have no work for you any more
That sign should be taken off the door.
Grabitall (*sings*)
America, I grieve to say,
Across the ocean starts to pose
A serious threat to world-wide trade:
Some British firms may have to close.
Employers (*sing*)
We have no work for you any more
That sign should be taken off the door.
Grabitall (*sings*)
And in the German empire steel
Is being produced at such a speed
Unless there is an enormous war
For Sheffield there'll be no more need.
Employers (*sing*)
We have no work for you any more
That sign should be taken off the door.
Grabitall (*sings*)
Therefore it is incumbent on
All Dublin men to show restraint
In wage demands at such a time –
I will not hear your cheap complaint!

Employers (*sing*)
>   We have no work for you any more
>   That sign should be taken off the door.

Enter BUILDING STRIKERS *on picket.*

Grabitall I address myself particularly to the members of the building-trade
>   (*Sings*) How can you think that we can spend
>   Unheard-of sums on brick and stone
>   When in productive industry
>   Our profits hardly hold their own?
Employers (*sing*)
>   We have no work for you any more
>   That sign should be taken off the door!
Grabitall And I tell you if this strike goes on
>   There'll be no work for anyone ever again!

Exeunt GRABITALL *and* EMPLOYERS.

SCENE 6

Re-enter 3RD EMPLOYER (*as Nationalist MP*).

A Striker And here comes our member of parliament, me boys, to support
   us in our strike! Three cheers and a rouser for the party of Parnell!
3rd Employer (*acknowledges the cheers*) Now look here, men, I have to tell
   you you are grievously misled. This strike is an anti-national strike, it is
   fomented in the interests of British big business and it has no other purpose than to bring the Irish economy down upon its bleeding knees!
   You must all go back to work.

Exit 3RD EMPLOYER.

Striker Jasus – is that what we voted for!
Connolly (*comes up to picket*) On behalf of the Irish Socialist Republican
   Party I have a formal proposition to put to you.
Striker What? Who are you? Aren't you the feller was round this morning
   spying out for a job of work?
Connolly My suggestion is this: the Dublin Trades Council and the ISRP set
   up a joint committee to put forward a candidate for that waster's con-
   stituency the very next election. A Labour candidate. It can be done.
Striker It's not on.
Connolly Why not?
Striker Premature. We don't know you. Oh yes, we've read your leaflets.
   We've also heard that seven-eighths of the active trade unionists in
   Dublin walked out of your first meeting.

CONNOLLY *turns away, disappointed.*

Hey – brother – about that question of a job you were looking for: corporation new drainage scheme – they want all manner of unskilled labour – but bring your own shovel and I'd recommend you to put the word out for some waterproof clothing . . .

Exeunt STRIKERS.

SCENE 7

Connolly I will knock once more
Upon this final door –
To the Dublin Corporation
I put in my application
For an unskilled situation
Digging drains for sanitation . . .

He knocks and an OFFICIAL *appears.*

Official The relevant department
Regrets to have to say
That its progressive drainage project
Is subject to delay –
Due to, as the public
Officially have been told,
Untoward technical circumstances
Outside of our control:
Due to, as in private
Unofficially I can make it known,
Bureaucratic obstruction
That has clogged its way down
From the government in Westminster
To Dublin Castle and the City Hall:
We will never get this town cleaned up
Until we get Home Rule.

Connolly No, no, that's a delusion. Can I give you a leaflet? The ISRP holds meetings outside the Custom House every Saturday afternoon and on Sunday evenings, and Tuesdays at – –

Official Here – I'm a civil servant! D'you want to put the heart across me with the likes of that handbill! Unemployed labourers advocating a godless republic!

Connolly Is there a chance of a job or isn't there?

Official Indeed there is not. Merciful hour, whatever next . . .!

Exit OFFICIAL.

Connolly Whatever next, there is no question now
        The state we live in is a monarchy indeed.
        Our sovereign ruler wears a threefold crown:
        The three brass balls above the pawnshop door . . .

Enter O'BRIEN.

O'Brien Jim – ! Did ye hear, the building strike is over!

Connolly And who won?

O'Brien The carpenters have settled without consulting the labourers. The labourers have disaffiliated from the trades council in consequence. Proletarian solidarity comes home from the pump like water in a sieve.

Connolly We'll get out a leaflet.

O'Brien I thought we should call a meeting. This time we may be able to collect a few subscriptions? Sure the labourers are bound to be bloody livid at the whole business – their situation at this moment is not one to be envied – –

Connolly Oh yes it is.

O'Brien Jesus-and-Mary: I forgot it altogether . . . the work on the drainage is beginning at last.

Connolly They have me marked as a trouble-maker.

O'Brien Well: you have been observed in and out of the library, round the bookstalls on the quay . . . which does mean you make trouble. But it also means this: the foreman's been forewarned that if he doesn't treat ye decent ye'll write him up every word in your forthcoming encyclopedia – the foreman's an ould butty of an ould butty of a friend of mine – so get hold of some waterproof gear. Five o'clock tomorrow morning . . .

Exit O'BRIEN.

SCENE 8

Enter LILLIE.

Lillie Oh James, I am so glad, so glad, after all this long time! I must brush up your clothes and you must mend your shoes tonight. I have a bit of leather put by for you but you looked so tired I didn't mention it.

Connolly Aye, I was tired: but you know, I don't believe I shall ever be tired again! To have no work is more exhausting than the hardest labour in all the world. So where's the leather . . . ? And let's hope I make a better fist of it than I did in Edinburgh, hey?

He sits down and starts mending his shoes. LILLIE *looks after his coat.*

Oh my God . . . !

Lillie What's the matter?

Connolly My boots. I've just ruined them. The wet today has made them rotten and will you look at them – I've pulled them apart! I can't dig a drain without boots.

Lillie Oh, James – now let me think. You have your slippers. They've got good strong soles, and the top comes right up to your trousers – if they could be tied with a bit of string – here –

She adjusts his slippers for him.

Do you think you could manage with these for one day? We could buy you a second-hand pair of boots in the morning – sure won't we be able to afford them now you've got work? You could do with the slippers for one day, couldn't you, James – couldn't you?

Connolly Aye, aye: they have strong soles. And the trousers hide the string. Why, surely, unless I was to work in a ten-foot pit of mud, you couldn't find a better pair from Glasnevin to Deansgrange. They'll do – by God we'll make them do!

Exit CONNOLLY.

Enter GRABITALL.

Grabitall It was not in a ten-foot pit of mud
But one so deep that even with a rod
You could not measure it in the pouring rain.
And here your bold man has to work from five a.m. till nine
O'clock at night. His humble home
Awaits him in an apprehensive gloom . . .

Exit GRABITALL.

LILLIE *paces about anxiously. The clock strikes ten.*
CONNOLLY *staggers in, absolutely dead-beat.*

Connolly (*sits down*) It's all right . . . It's all right, Lillie . . .

Lillie Oh James, my poor James . . . don't try to eat anything. Drink this, it will do you good.

Connolly I haven't the strength, Lillie, I haven't the strength . . .

He pushes the tea away.

Oh God, Lillie, I'm no good. I'm no use to you and the children. The wheelbarrows, all day: cement in the big barrows: all day long and nothing else. I'm no use to you and the children. I cannot do the work! And as for the revolution . . . ! Oh James Connolly will *talk* the strongest man in all of Dublin into the deepest hole was ever dug! Lillie, I disgust myself.

Lillie After months of starvation, how *could* they expect you – sure, disgust is the right word: but I wouldn't stick it on *you.*

She puts his feet in warm water, eases his braces, etc.

Now, James, you are to rest there till I come back from a message . . .

She slips out.

Connolly (*to audience*)

> The work I do for all of *you*
> Will not be done in time
> Unless I find
> Some other way to do the work
> I do for those within my home . . .
> How many lives can I keep living,
> And how much life can I continue giving?
> I thought, when I came home tonight I'd read a book:
> But every letter in the book is running from me
> Like the pull of a flooded brook –
> The waves of words float hopelessly in and out of my skull –
> How strange I have had no patience ever
> With any man that I thought was a fool . . .

LILLIE *re-enters.*

Lillie (*softly – he is too tired to turn round to her*) James . . . James . . . You need not go back again to be killed again tomorrow.

She shows him money.

Connolly Where did you get this? Where'd you get it, Lillie? Lillie. Lillie!

Lillie Sure 'twas only my little gold watch. Didn't you give it me in Edinburgh – I couldn't bear to part with it! But just now when I saw how you were – James, for the first time ever you were losing your faith in yourself: I knew it would have to go.

Connolly I'll make it up to you, Lillie. God help me, I'll make it up to you. The very first thing in the morning, I'll – –

Lillie You'd do better to stay in bed.

Connolly No. I must go to the National Library. I know well it's not *work*. Book-reading, that's all: and bought for, minute by minute, at the cost of your gold watch. But it's work. I've got to do it.

Exit LILLIE.

SCENE 9

Connolly (*sings*)

> Every day in the National Library
> The same book I take out of the shelf
> In no bookshop have I ever found it
> Heard its name upon nobody's mouth.
>
> Half-a-century since it was written
> By a cripple, a feeble poor man

Who in prison did die of a blood-bursting lung:
If he hadn't, no doubt he'd have hanged.

If they'd hanged him a national martyr,
Unbounded his glory and fame –
But writing a book for this people is not
Any way to preserve your good name.

Yet he wrote it and here I have found it
I copy it out slow and sure –
James Fintan Lalor, *The Faith of a Felon*:
I will shout it in each Irish ear – !

At all events, whisper it . . .

Copy it out and make sure it is printed
Pass it on then from hand to poor hand –
Let it not be forgot, before Marx grew his beard
Fintan Lalor put forth this demand –

'The entire soil of a country belongs of right to the people of that country.
To be let to whom they will. On condition that the tenant shall owe no
allegiance whatsoever to any prince, power, or people – other than those
of the nation whose lands he is permitted to hold . . .' Which means that
the unionist landlords in Ireland, and the unionist administration in
Dublin Castle which supports them, have defaulted in their obligations to
their *own* proper landlords. That's *us*! And we, being thus defrauded,
have no alternative but to evict!

My Lord Lieutenant, are you there?
Here's Captain Blazer before your door.
You are ordered by the Irish people this very day
To vacate your rented premises without hindrance or delay.
Queen Victoria, do you hear?
Or do we have to break the door?
Distasteful but it must be done:
Cathleen ni Houlihaun, break it down . . .!

Who dares to stand and tell me that republicanism and socialism are in
no way compatible!

In the academic exactitude of this funereal reading-room
The lie has been refuted: the truth at last comes home!

LIBRARY ATTENDANT *slides up to him.*

Library Attendant Ssh, you are disturbing Madame Maud Gonne . . .

MAUD GONNE *comes over to* CONNOLLY *and looks at the book he is holding.*

Maud Gonne You are not only reading him – you are copying him out.

Connolly I am so sorry – did I distract you?

Maud Gonne The point about Lalor is this: nothing in the rural areas has changed since he wrote that book. Do you realise that in the western counties at this moment there is the onset of a potato-famine nearly as bad as eighteen forty-seven? Oh, I know who you are – you are the red Scotchman from Dundee.

Connolly Edinburgh. And I'm Irish.

Maud Gonne Keir Hardie told me about you.

Connolly Keir Hardie – you know him?

Maud Gonne I don't know him, but I've met him. He wanted me to pull his chestnuts out of the fire for him in London. He said the socialists of Britain ought not to allow the Famine Queen to be given sixty years of jubilee through the streets of her capital when there were poor men and women starving within a mile of Buckingham Palace, and the strikes, and the unemployment, *et patati et patata* . . . and would I help? *Et par consequence, je lui ai dit*: if the socialists of Britain are going to prevent it, let them do so, why ask me? *Je suis Irlandaise, bien sûr* . . . Oh I knew what he had in mind – if anything should go wrong, like a riot in Trafalgar Square, one or two men dead perhaps from the cudgels of the police – there would be no-one to blame for it but a wild woman from the Celtic west whose inflammatory speech had passed all the bounds of proper British convention. If I am to resist the jubilee, here is where I do it. For the sake of Sligo and Mayo and Galway – before Pimlico. Do you know that this happened in Cahirciveen, this year: a widow-woman, her rent six-pound-twelve-and-six upon her one small field, she lifted but three baskets of potatoes, all worthless as food or as seed. Her only other income: the butter she would churn herself – six pounds in the whole year. Her landlord demanded rent, let her pay or he would evict. She gave him the money. It was everything she had. Everything. What will she do now? What will they all do?

Connolly America?

Maud Gonne Where the speculators and the Tammany politicians tell them lie upon lie – they want them there for one reason –

Connolly That they work for small wages, they know nothing about trade unions, and any crook that can once get them in to the country has their vote for evermore. Dublin Castle forbye is as glad to have them go as the Americans are to receive them. Well, some of the Americans.

Maud Gonne Certainly not those who are put out of work by their arrival. *Mais c'est correcte, la verité*. Did you know famine-fever has broken out at Crossmolina? I have been there, I have seen it. I have myself, alone, confronted the Board of Guardians in the town of Belmullet and demanded that they issue some relief to the poor people – of whom at least ten thousand stood behind me in the street – I was wearing, *par chance, par bonne chance*, my robe and cloak of green. An old man at the back cried out in Irish – 'She is the Queen of the Shee come to Mayo to save the people!' – the Shee, you know who I mean, they live secretly under the hills –

Connolly You mean they thought you were a *fairy* – ? Oh, come now –

Maud Gonne It was convenient for them to tell each other they thought I was a fairy. For how else would they have found the courage to defy the armed police? At all events they did so. They got what they cried out for. Six shillings per week. Seed potatoes from Scotland at the government expense. I told them: 'You have won these things by your numbers, your united strength. By your strength and your courage you must win the freedom of Ireland.' But I am not sure they followed me quite so far as that . . . Will you help me create in the city of Dublin a Queen Victoria's jubilee beyond all jubilees that were ever thought of?

Connolly If the Queen of the Shee indeed were to have come from under her green hill,

> She could not with greater speed subject me to her will.
> May I tell you: I've not been well?
> I'm in no state for the sudden glamourie
> Of the silver voice of a well-dressed lady . . .
> Will I dispel it with a charm?
> I hold it up so, between finger and thumb.

He moves away from her, holds up his hand towards her, with thumb and forefinger crooked, and speaks very rapidly and aggressively.

Understand the reality of soundly principled class struggle. Unite British and Irish workers. Recognise capitalist nature of exploitation. Unmask both monarchical and nationalist mysticism. Identify the enemy, identify the enemy, identify the enemy upon lines of correct analysis. Strengthen the position of the Irish Socialist Republican Party . . . Can I interest you, while we're at it, in becoming a member? Now you can't go answering *that* with a kind of deceptive poetry.

Maud Gonne I hope not.

Connolly Oh: you don't like poetry?

Maud Gonne Potatoes are what matter.

Connolly My God, yes: but from what I had heard of you I would not have thought –

Maud Gonne

> That *I* would have said so?
> Lalor wrote a book, he fell sick, he fell dead.
> They should not look at *me* until that book has been read.

She takes CONNOLLY *and leads him round the stage.*

> The most beautiful woman in the whole of Dublin city

Takes hold of the short squat labouring man and brings him in
to her committee . . .

SCENE 10

Maud Gonne Willie – !

Enter YEATS, *followed by* MILLIGAN *and* ALICE MILLIGAN. *She introduces them to* CONNOLLY.

W. B. Yeats, the greatest poet in the English tongue:
Though this is not yet known, he is still too young.
Alice Milligan and her brother from the sour town of Belfast:
She publishes a political paper and he is confused and lost
Among the myth and legend of the ancient Gael.

Milligan We the Irish will be fighting for ever and ever again we faint and
fail . . .

Yeats I hear the shadowy horses, their long manes a-shake
Their hoofs heavy with tumult, their eyes glimmering white –
We have proposed, that in order to counteract the philistine jingoism of
Queen Victoria's jubilee, we should set afoot copious and nation-wide
celebrations of the centenary of the rebellion of seventeen ninety-eight . . .

Connolly Very good, that's for *next* year. But by then the Queen's jubilee will
have made its effect. If the organisers for that event do succeed in whip-
ping up more enthusiasm for the monarchy than has been known here for
years – how will you manage in twelve months to reconvert the population towards a bunch of defeated rebels?

Yeats We have proposed – –

Alice Milligan Mr Yeats has proposed – –

Yeats Shouldn't we take it as a committee-decision, Miss Milligan? I prefer
the associative *we* –

Milligan Conveniently ambiguous: could be confused with a speech from the
throne . . .

Yeats We have proposed that this committee should take part in the jubilee
too: but in order to *mourn* the event rather than *celebrate*.

Maud Gonne (*to* CONNOLLY) Will you help?

Connolly (*to audience*)
You will tell me these are no socialists, you will tell me I should
not join
With the idealistic middle classes: they will drop away from us
one by one – ?
We have a membership of *eight*! The pale hand of the English
Queen
Plasters over the whole of Ireland with complacency and deceit:

> I will join my voice with anyone who has the spirit to cry out
> And say: NO – we are alone
> We are Irish and our own men!
> We must be heard, we must be seen
> And we must not be forgotten.

Make your plans: I'll go along with them. And the ISRP will be proud to participate.

Alice Milligan (*takes* CONNOLLY *aside*) Anything you want to write about Lalor, Mr Connolly, I'll publish in my paper.

Connolly It's understood there'll be no poetry? Relate Lalor to Karl Marx. Develop the concept of primitive communism as the basic original arrangement of land-tenure in this country.

Alice Milligan We may have to print your article with an editorial disclaimer.

Yeats Mr Milligan, come here. Who is this dangerous man
> Slouching, as it were, towards Bethlehem to be born?

Milligan I think we should all listen to him: I think it is his turn.
> Already things have been spoken I have never before heard said.

Exeunt.

SCENE 11

Enter GRABITALL *and* EMPLOYERS. *The latter are hanging up strings of bunting and erecting coloured lights and heraldic devices of the royal arms, etc. A big banner at the back with the message 'Victoria Regina: 1837–1897: Sixty Glorious Years!'*

Grabitall The British Empire roars and cheers
> World-wide for sixty glorious years.
> Australia – there it goes!*
> New Zealand* – Canada, the far-flung northern snows* –
> The African, the Indian, black as night,
> Bellow and yelp their loyal royal delight† –
> As drums and guns and gongs and singsong girls declare
> The joyful pandemonium of this great imperial year . . .!
> From Ireland too we want to hear a cheer.

Employers God Save the Queen!
> And let it be made known
> That loyalty, independence and Home Rule
> Can all together ring the Dublin bell!
> We here hang out our bunting, row on row
> From Dublin Castle to the Phoenix Park,
> Illuminate the lot when it gets dark,

> * Cheers (offstage)
> † Cheers and some booing (offstage)

> While up and down the mounted troopers go
> Deterring all intruders: this is a show
> We are determined to keep safe and sound:
> No sacrilege today on loyal Irish ground . . .

Grabitall Let there be light!

The illuminations begin to go on: amidst gasps and cheers from the crowds who have drifted in. CONNOLLY *appears at one corner and addresses the audience:*

Connolly A certain member, who shall be nameless, of the ISRP, being employed all unsuspected by the Dublin Electricity Company, has his hand upon the switch that has just made this crucial connection. To him alone the responsibility of turning nightfall into a simulacrum of the aurora borealis: to him alone the responsibility for what happens next!

More and more lights go on: and the cheers are redoubled. Suddenly: complete darkness.

Ha ha, me bould Barney: you're dead on the minute!

Lantern slides appear on a wall surface as the crowd groans with disappointment. They illustrate statistics and scenes of famine and emigration. The crowd, astonished, giggles, laughs, and in places gives yells of outrage.

Implacable as Queen Jezebel in an upper window of Rutland Square Miss Maud Gonne applies her timeless beauty to the ephemera of modern science. Sure 'tis no more than a smokey old magic lantern –

> But not the finger of God on the wall of Belshazzar the proud
> Wrote for his doom and foreboding one word so much to be
> feared.

The illuminations come on again.

Ah: well, we didn't think Barney could keep his hand on the switch for ever. But don't go away now – we're not finished by a long way.

Vulgar music playing a funeral march is heard – kazoos, etc. A group of demonstrators enter slowly, carrying a coffin with a black pall reading 'The Corpse of the British Empire'. Yeats is in the lead, and they sing:

Coffin-bearers

> Here comes the empire, carry it away
> Throw it in the river, tip it to the sea:
> For it is dead and rotten it is dead and rotten –
> Here comes the empire carry it away . . .

POLICE *rush in to intercept.*

Grabitall Break every head: they shall not cross the bridge!

Connolly (*puts himself beside* YEATS) Get it to the river – tip it over the edge!

After a scuffle the coffin is got to the edge of the stage and thrown over.

> Here goes the coffin of the British Empire!
> To hell with the British Empire –
> Into the Liffey and out into the sea – !

The POLICE, *outmanoeuvred, now attack the demonstration with savagery.
At the end of the fray, they are left holding* CONNOLLY.

> After all that, it was not surprising they put the handcuffs upon
> *me*.
> And yet, the following morning, after one cold night in gaol,
> When I came up before the magistrate, he did not want to look a
> fool.

Enter MAGISTRATE: CONNOLLY *is placed before him.* MAUD GONNE *and*
YEATS *re-enter.*

> They could not prove I had incited anyone to rape, burn, or kill –
> The more fuss they made about it, the more it would be talked of
> abroad,
> And in India, Ceylon, Africa, men and women who had roared
> God Save the Queen as loud as any would maybe wonder had
> they done wrong:
> Seeing their views were not shared by the greatest poet in the
> English tongue . . .

Maud Gonne Mr Yeats was not arrested, being a member of the middle classes.
Yeats Nonetheless it was well-known that from behind these gleaming glasses

> The inspiration for the demonstration had originally shot out like
> fire.

Magistrate

> I shall fine you one pound and I also require
> You give recognisances for good behaviour or whatever else needs
> to be said . . .

Maud Gonne

> Whatever else means this much: an old woman today lies dead
> Because the metropolitan police of Dublin cracked open the skull
> of her head
> When all she was trying to do was get away home out of the
> crowd.

Magistrate Clear the court!

Prompted by MAUD GONNE, YEATS *pays money to a* POLICEMAN *and gets a
receipt.*

Connolly I remain here to make the statement that I do not intend to pay this
fine –

Policeman It's paid, we have the money, there's the receipt.

Maud Gonne (*to* CONNOLLY) Don't argue – go home – come along . . .

He looks inclined to dispute it: but everyone else goes away and he is left alone, with MAUD GONNE, *who leads him away.*

SCENE 12

Noise of a child crying all through the scene.

Connolly Lillie – where are you, Lillie? Safe and sound, my love – we are here – !

Enter LILLIE, *with a baby wrapped up in her shawl, very worried.*

Lillie Your daughter Nora has been sick all day:

    I asked the doctor what was wrong

    And all he said to me was that he could not say.

    I asked him did he think there could be any danger:

    He told me he could not tell, that in the end I would discover

    That all sickness in these streets is as dangerous as yellow fever.

    He gave me some medicine that would do nothing but keep her quiet –

    Which it does not as you can hear, she makes more noise than your last night's political riot –

    And *I* am left to do nothing but sit by her bed and wait.

    And holding *this* one: how about that . . . ?

She is angrily trying to do housework and nurse the baby at the same time. GRABITALL *enters at one side.*

Connolly My God will she do nothing but thrust up her backbone and greet – ?

    Here, Lillie, let me take her –

Lillie In God's name, which is worse:

    A rake of a husband rolling all hours in and out of the public house

    Or this wilful political libertine who prefers his own pride and a Bridewell cell?

Grabitall Secure in the knowledge that his fine will be paid

    By an elegant educated unmarried lady – oh she never scrubbed a floor in her life:

    From the breeding and burden of children such loveliness we suppose is kept safe . . . ?

Maud Gonne

    He bites his lip, is well aware,

    He does not dare

    To speak one word.

Lillie You need not tell me you believe
    That man has not been born to lead
    Nor woman from his lazy rib-bone built up only to serve.
    You need not tell me when we are so poor
    That by my strength behind this tenement door
    Yourself are strengthened all the more
    To stand out in the street and state
    That you at least alone will not accept defeat.
    If I stand out with you our children could not eat.
    All last night I filled my empty arms with hate.
    I now declare it.
    James, what I have said, you need not say again.

Connolly You know and I know we must do what we have always done.
    But I was not in the street alone:
    Not only Mr Yeats and Miss Maud Gonne –
    You also I saw walking when we threw that coffin down.

Maud Gonne
    I saw Eire the goddess walking and she wore a robe of green.

Connolly And *I* saw a large element of a large class of the ragged riffraff of
    Dublin,
    Their potato-faces split with a very dirty grin . . .
    There is no recrimination over what is best to be done.

Maud Gonne
    No recrimination, and no *doubt*, surely, over what is to be done:
    We must immediately get ready to raise the ghost of bold Wolfe
    Tone!
    The centenary is very near
    We have no more than a year
    We may be sure that if last night there were heads broken in
    Next year they will crack all bones between kneecap and chin:
    Mon Dieu but we have them rattled,
    The great wolf-hounds have picked up the scent . . .

Lillie Miss Gonne, I mean Madame Gonne, came round here, James, while
you were in prison this morning.

    She paid for the doctor
    She paid for the rent
    She did almost everything for me it was possible to resent:
    And now both of us are so grateful
    She was so offhand and so cool –
    Had either of us said anything
    We would have felt such a churl and a fool.

Exeunt.

END OF ACT 1

ACT 2: 'Alarums and Excursions'

SCENE 1

A bird's-eye view of Dublin around its bay, with the Georgian buildings rearing up amongst the slums. The whole guarded by redcoat soldiers and police. (Backcloth 3.)

Enter GRABITALL *and a* CIVIL SERVANT.

Grabitall How does it happen that the man Connolly was fined no more than one pound? Confound it, sir: he completely disrupted the Queen's jubilee!

Civil Servant Yes indeed, one pound . . . Not altogether so small a sum as it sounds. I understand he's out of work.

Grabitall He did not have to pay it himself. His impudence has not been quenched, rather is it aggravated. To commemorate the insurrection of seventeen ninety-eight is potentially a most serious challenge to the entire concept of the political union between Ireland and Britain. I am well aware these street demonstrations are the work of no more than a trivial minority – but we must understand that they not only occur – they are *seen* to occur by a significant body of persons – within a very short time they will become the accepted thing. There is only one thing to be accepted in Ireland at this time: and that is the continued benefit to all of her people of the Imperial system. I will only believe that that is believed when the Dublin mob itself puts paid to this man Connolly and these renegade gentlefolk who encourage him to his nonsense. The jubilee crowds were distinctly heard by the police to be cheering and laughing and egging him on.

Civil Servant Do you suppose if Her Majesty herself had been in Dublin –

Grabitall Are you mad? Would you have her insulted to her face?

Civil Servant I don't think she would have been. The face was far distant, the concept is abstract – so nobody cared. But if Her Majesty were to show that she cares for Dublin – I mean a personal relationship, a direct communication – she is a very gracious lady –

Grabitall Out of the question! Of course . . . we could get hold of a Duke . . . The Duke of York!

Civil Servant Sir, the very man! Happily married, entirely non-political. The Duchess as well. They say she is most popular.

Grabitall Doesn't matter what she's *said* to be – we have to prove that she *is*. Leave nothing to chance. Assemble a suitable crowd for the occasion – people in government service would be best –

Civil Servant And their wives –

Grabitall Soldiers off duty –
Civil Servant Policemen –
Grabitall Castle officials –
Civil Servant Military pensioners –
Grabitall And their wives!

> *A crowd assembles, with the* EMPLOYERS, *who distribute small union jacks to wave.*

Are we ready?

A POLICE OFFICER *button-holes the* CIVIL SERVANT *and whispers in his ear.*

Civil Servant Just one moment . . . Good God, we can't have that!
Grabitall What's the matter?
Civil Servant: The Irish Socialist Republican Party has announced a special meeting of the most radical of the seventeen ninety-eight commemoration committees to coincide with the arrival of the Duke and Duchess.
Grabitall We can't have that!
Civil Servant I have said so. The police are taking action. Wait a moment –

> POLICE *start moving across the stage. The* CIVIL SERVANT *intercepts them:*

– now be very very careful!
Grabitall (*snatches a drawn sabre from a* POLICE OFFICER) Action – what sort of action? Good God, we can't have *this*! Get me the superintendant!
Civil Servant No no, sir, it's too late – the Duke of York is already here!
Grabitall Cross your fingers, touch wood, say a prayer, we've got to go through with it! Bring on the Duke of York!

> *To the tune of 'The Grand Old Duke of York' puppets representing the* DUKE *and* DUCHESS *are trundled across the stage. The crowds wave and cheer. From the middle of the crowd* CONNOLLY *bursts forward with a green banner unfurled which reads 'Truth Freedom and Justice in Ireland'. The* DUKE *and* DUCHESS *are hustled away in panic, the* POLICE *set upon the crowd, trying to reach* CONNOLLY, *but hitting all sorts of people in the process.* CONNOLLY *escapes, and the stage is cleared of all save* GRABITALL *and the* CIVIL SERVANT.

SCENE 2

Civil Servant Do you want to see the newspapers?
Grabitall I do not.
Civil Servant The Germans in particular were extremely amused.
Grabitall There were no arrests. Why not?
Civil Servant I don't think the police were able to catch anyone . . .
Grabitall Twice . . . in two months! And you were the clever fellow who told

me it might be possible to 'pre-determine' the tone of the commemoration of Tone . . . I was not making jokes for you to laugh at, you fool. Wolfe Tone was a republican; had his rebellion been successful, he would have set up in Ireland a secular, egalitarian, revolutionary state which would have joined with Napoleon in the total destruction of the kingdom of Great Britain – my God, in the scales of history that man would have outweighed Nelson – Trafalgar would have been reversed, Waterloo could never have happened. You and I would be on one level: and a rude labourer like James Connolly would hold the power of life and death over both of our heads!

Civil Servant But Wolfe Tone was not successful – he died a martyr, he is revered by both labourer and industrialist –

Grabitall Catholic and protestant –

Civil Servant Creditor and debtor . . . He is all things to all men. And therein lies his danger. Any one group among all those groups can take him over and exploit him.

Grabitall It is up to us to ensure that *we* determine *which* group.

> The old old tale
> Divide-and-rule
> If the workers push
> Then the bosses must pull . . .

We'll start with religion. Wolfe Tone was a protestant, therefore in the north the sacred memory of the damned cut-throat must be made the exclusive property of the most bigoted catholic faction! Call down to me Wee Joe Devlin!

Civil Servant Mr Devlin, we want a word!

Calls for 'Mr Devlin!' receding offstage. After a pause, enter DEVLIN.

Devlin I heard ye say cut-throat . . .
> It's a lie and a damned lie.
> Never never never could a brave Irish lad
> By his own hand come to die.
> For if he did he would go to hell.
> He was murdered, in his cell.
> He shot straight into the arms of God –
> How can we describe such a one as a dirty prod?

Civil Servant
> Can you make it clear to all Belfast town
> That gallant young Tone
> Was one of your own?

Devlin You give me the word – it shall be done!
> With priest and bishop and bell and book
> We hang him up high on our Roman hook!

As he goes out an ORANGEMAN *enters with a drum.*

Orangeman Do we hear Wee Joe Devlin hail the name of Wolfe Tone?
Then we drown him with the drumming of the Battle of the
Boyne!

He goes out after DEVLIN, *making a dreadful noise on his drum. Enter* ALICE
MILLIGAN.

Alice Milligan That clear enough marks the end of any republican commemoration in the north. Where on earth is Maud Gonne? If she doesn't
take care, an equivalent dirty trick is about to be played in Dublin.

Grabitall In Dublin mad Maude Gonne
And James Connolly all on their own
Have prepared a celebration
Directly linked to revolution.
If Crookey and O'Hookey can be got on their committee
They will split, they will split
And the world will weep for pity . . .

Enter EMPLOYERS.

Who is the man to get them there?

Enter YEATS, *dreamily.*

Civil Servant (*looks at him*)
Mr William Butler Yeats, with his long poetic hair . . .
(*To* YEATS) Mr Yeats, you are a protestant – don't you think it would be
desirable, in the interests of the education of the soul of the whole
nation, if these well-meaning but perhaps fumbling decent catholic men
from shop and counting-house –

1st Employer We're more than that, we're more than that –

3rd Employer
In the parliament of Westminster
We each one of us hold a seat!

Civil Servant Just so . . . don't you think, Mr Yeats, it is your duty as a leading
cultural figure to reject nobody from the arrangements of this patriotic
epiphany?

Yeats The word *epiphany* is very nice.
I am happy to lend my best efforts to splice
In the rope of national unity every frayed and broken strand.
Mr Crookey, Mr O'Hookey, I rejoice to shake your hand . . .

GRABITALL *and the* CIVIL SERVANT *withdraw discreetly.* ALICE MILLIGAN
goes out, shaking her head ominously. The EMPLOYERS *examine the decorations which are still hanging where they were put up for the Jubilee.*

3rd Employer A question of economy on the public manifestations – we can

make a job of it here with this yoke and keep all th'expenses down –
YEATS *starts removing imperial symbols from the decorations.* 3RD EM-
PLOYER *stops him: and takes from him a large shield of the royal arms.*
Merciful hour: ye'd think these bloody poets had never handled a petty
cash return in their lives at all at all . . .

He reverses the royal arms and reveals the Irish Harp on the back.

Don't ye see, two in one – sure, th'underside of th'skirts of tyranny
reveals th'intimate garments of th'goddess of God-given Liberty!

*They turn all the shields round in this way. The biggest one, in the middle,
proves to have the royal arms on both sides.* 1ST EMPLOYER *studies it in
perplexity.*

No no no – turn it round, man, turn it round, have some sense of chro-
matic relevance!

1st Employer Sure, amn't I after turning it?
3rd Employer I think we have a tentative problem here . . . so what'd we do?
1st Employer So what's to prevent us from modifying it, so?

He drapes a band of green ribbon transversely across the shield. MAUD
GONNE *enters and watches what is happening.*

Maud Gonne Willie, in the Name of God, what do you think you are doing!
Yeats (*up a ladder with his mouth full of tacks*) Hallo there! I'm only –
Maud Gonne (*points to the 'modified' shield*) Good heavens, that's out for a
start! Will you please take it down.
3rd Employer

> Excuse me, Miss Maud Gonne –
> The good work which you began,
> By our own efforts and contribution
> Is now brought to its fruition.

1ST EMPLOYER *brings in a large medallion of the Wolfe Tone profile, which
is hung underneath the 'modified' royal arms. Music begins: 'The Wearing
of the Green'. A crowd assembles with green flags.* GRABITALL *and the*
CIVIL SERVANT *join the* EMPLOYERS *in a formal group in front of the medallion.* CONNOLLY *enters near Maud Gonne.*

> Mr Devlin out of Ulster
> Has come to help our function prosper.

Enter DEVLIN *with a* PRIEST *and they join the central group.*

Devlin Mr Devlin from Belfast
> Has brought with him a holy priest.
Priest (*deferred to by all, takes pride of place*) Wolfe Tone, we must remember,
was a man of his own time, and much of what he said and did has of
course been rendered redundant by the progressive spiritual enlighten-

ment of the modern age. Had God made it possible for him to have
received his education at the catholic college of Maynooth – he surely
would never have – –

Connolly Enough, enough!
    This dreadful stuff
    Can never be endured!
    Miss Gonne, my party will have no part
    Of *this*!
    Are we assured
    As we walk out
    That you as well walk out with us?

He stalks out with some ISRP members who have joined him.

Maud Gonne
    I do not know, I cannot say
    It breaks my heart to play no part
    Upon this great centenary day.
    Willie, what have you done?

Yeats My love, my heart, my dear Miss Gonne,
    I did it for the best . . .

Maud Gonne
    All finished, disintegrated –
    What will they think of us in the west . . .?

The PRIEST *has now completed his eulogy.* GRABITALL *comes over to* MAUD
GONNE.

Grabitall Because the clergy participated
    They will think it both meet and fit.
    So do I. I take off my hat.
    Dulce et decorum est pro patria mori . . .

Priest My friends, this pregnant sacramental story –

1st Employer This supreme sacrifice –

3rd Employer Of sugar and spice –

Devlin And all things nice –

Priest *Requiescat in pace* for the honour and glory –

1st Employer Of national Irish biscuits and bread –

3rd Employer
    Patriotically packed in boxes of wood –
    There's a little leaflet handed round we'd be glad to have read –

The EMPLOYERS *distribute advertising literature to the crowd:*

1st Employer Advertising our products with decency and taste –

Devlin Appropriate to the solemnity of the present occasion –

Grabitall And thank God we've got rid of all thought of revolution!

Everybody claps politely. CONNOLLY *suddenly appears through the crowd selling newspapers.*

Connolly (*very raucous*) *The Workers' Republic* – buy *The Workers' Republic*! Buy the first socialist newspaper to be published in Ireland! Buy the *only* socialist newspaper to be published in Ireland! Buy *The Workers' Republic*! Read *The Workers' Republic*!

> Ha ha ye did not think we'd have this ready quite so sharp!
> Aye there's more than one string to the old minstrel's broken
> harp . . .

GRABITALL *and all the Wolfe Tone celebrants leave rapidly.* MAUD GONNE *remains.*

Maud Gonne

> Well enough: but I am afraid it will do little good.
> I see no course but to revert to the old oath-bound Brotherhood.

Connolly Conspiracy? Secret terror?

> You walk blindfold in a bog of error.
> Liberty and justice should not need
> Like criminals to hide their head.
> Cry socialism aloud in the open field
> And let its logic be revealed
> To all for all for ever . . .

Buy *The Workers' Republic*, read *The Workers' Republic*!

> And yet I must admit it true
> That had this Brotherhood not worked concealed
> Known only to a few
> Year after year
> The weight of slavery in our long dark night
> Would have crushed us utterly with despair.

Maud Gonne I wish I could believe that you were right . . .

Exit MAUD GONNE.

SCENE 3

Connolly Buy *The Workers' Republic*, read *The Workers' Republic* –

He sings:

> Every Friday once a week
> Keen in the claw and long in the beak

Fierce as an eagle overhead
It costs ye a penny, it's worth a whole quid!

They said that we were very small
They could not hear us, not at all,
They mocked us and they'd shout us down,
They watched us sink and they hoped we'd drown.

Sure it beats in my hand, the sap in the wood,
The root in the ground and the pea in the pod,
The egg in the hen, the salt in the soup.
You start from nothing, it's your only hope . . .!

He passes up and down among the audience, offering them the papers and making as though people have put questions to him.

A few simple answers to a few simple questions. Congratulations, Jim, we never thought you'd get it out, and where in the name of God did the money come from? In the heel of the hunt from yourselves, subscriptions, collections, beg, borrow, scrape it and save – and fifty pounds in a lump sum from Keir Hardie over in Britain. Who prints it? A small man in a back street. And he doesn't overcharge. But have we got enough money to carry on paying the bills? The answer to that one is definite: no. Unless more people buy it next week than are buying it this week and more the week after that than are buying it next week. What's in it? So let me tell you: eight pages; with a poem by my old friend John Leslie, very appropriately upon Wolfe Tone; an attack upon sectarianism; a few articles by yours truly upon the origins of modern war, which I attribute to the struggle of the capitalists for more markets for their produce; the inevitable instability of land-ownership in rural Ireland leading to the present disastrous famine in the west; a demand for political action by trade unionists: and a vigorous opinion upon the revival of the Gaelic language.

Enter ALICE MILLIGAN.

Alice Milligan Which is what?
Connolly That in general and isolation it's an admirable idea: but also it is quite impractical to teach a starving man *any* language.

She shakes her head ominously.

Enter MILLIGAN. *He is followed by* O'BRIEN *and other ISRP members.*

Milligan I have already heard that in Belfast
By the very title of your paper an entire market has been lost.
Connolly How's that?

Milligan Socialism in the north can never be republican.

Connolly Republicanism in the south can never be socialist. I've heard both notions *ad nauseam*. I don't believe either. I have set forward my arguments: and I'm happy to inform you that my point of view is supported from an unexpected area of the highest authority. I have here a letter from Mrs Eleanor Aveling, in London. Her husband has decided to take up associate membership of the ISRP for which purpose she encloses a postal order for one shilling. Now that's not a laugh. It's good news of enormous potential consequence.

O'Brien Mrs Eleanor Aveling?

Milligan Who the deuce is Mrs Aveling?

Connolly Ha ha she is none other than the daughter of Karl Marx!
    According to her father's word, the English working class
    Will never accomplish anything until it has first got rid
    Of the problem of Ireland. Now surely, surely what he said
    Is proof enough for the thickest head
    In Ulster that national independence must come first!

Milligan There's more to it than that. An Ulster catholic bishop has condemned the new newspaper.

O'Brien Isn't that what we want? So the protestants after all will buy the unfortunate rag?

Connolly Will they not? Not? Then why not?

Milligan Don't you see that they will see it as a particularly subtle jesuitical trick by the bishop designed to promote the paper by stealth?
    Mr Connolly, it's very clear
    That the full ramifications of the Ulster complication
    Are so remote from you down here
    That you cannot yet have the remotest conception
    Of our Belfast capacity for self-mutilation.

Connolly H'm . . . but on the other hand with such a newspaper we must expect and welcome controversy. It cannot be a bad thing that on both sides of the religious-political divide –

Alice Milligan Mr Connolly, in Ulster, the controversy has not even begun to take place! The paper has not been purchased!

Connolly How many Irishmen live in America? I have here a letter from Daniel De Leon, chairman of the Socialist Labor Party of the United States.

Milligan He can't be an Irishman.

Connolly He's a Jew. And in his party there are Italians, and Irish, and Germans, and Greeks; protestant, catholic, orthodox, hebrew – who cares? They're all socialists: and they have *heard* of us, d'you see! De Leon has a weekly newspaper – he asks me for a series of articles on the famine in the west – Maud Gonne has gone to Mayo – I go out there to join her and I write upon what I see. De Leon also tells me that he has made use of our manifesto to get Irish-Americans to vote for the socialists in the municipal elections. We must send him a letter of solidarity – can you draft one?

MILLIGAN *makes a note.*

And do what you can for God's sake in Belfast – if the working class won't read it, at least get the damn thing circulated among your literary intelligentsia – I daresay in those quarters you're not intimidated by the bishop or disturbed in your dreams at night by mad Fenians with bloody pitchforks . . . ?

Exeunt MILLIGANS

O'Brien We have municipal elections of our own for the first time next year.

Connolly With the benevolent Tory intention of keeping us quiet in our own wallow. Well, we must take advantage – put up at least one candidate – bark, howl, break our teeth upon the bars –

Tom Lyng I don't know that we can afford it.

Connolly It's sheer waste to put out political print without a living man at the election to embody what we call for. Very well: we need a candidate. The North Dock ward of Dublin, the paper has sold well there – particularly because of our articles attacking the liquor-trade. Comrade Stewart?

Stewart Now I did warn you if you asked me I could guarantee you no success . . . But I daresay on the relevant subjects such as schools, unemployment relief, hospital services and cetera, I can throw together something to make some of 'em sit up. I have taken pains to make a comprehensive study.

Connolly I've advised Stewart his main platform should be a straightforward statement of the incontrovertible fact that the public welfare of Dublin is a European disgrace . . . Any questions?

O'Brien I have. There's a whole bagful of candidates calling themselves Labour being put up not only in Dublin but in all corners of the country. Our attitude towards 'em?

Connolly Watchful in the extreme. Any candidate that says Labour, let him prove it by his policy. If he's able to do so, the columns of *The Workers' Republic* are thrown open to him free of charge. The paper will make the candidate, the candidate will make the paper: with the newspaper and the candidate and the electorate all together we will construct the political party – and then . . . !

They all disperse, except CONNOLLY.

SCENE 4

Connolly And then indeed – then, what? Success . . . ?

Such was the confidence I did profess
In this, the mighty engine of the press.
Pride, pride – however hard we tried, we could not sell
Sufficient newspapers to pay the printers' bill.
No bourgeois newspaper, no public hall
Was open to our revolutionary call:
Just as in Edinburgh, the parties of the rich and fat
Took care of that.
The spokesman for the lean and poor
Knocked every day upon an iron-barred door.
Sackcloth and ash! We took a bash:
And in the end we ran clean out of cash . . .

The PARTY MEMBERS *straggle in again, dejected.*

Is there nobody in this farcical organisation that knows how to keep an account? Look at this for Godsake, d'you call this an expenses-return!

Tom Lyng Now there's no call to be blackguarding us – them expenses was called for in a hell of a hurry to get the candidate home from a particularly rough meeting – with the priests that was in it driving the mob on to us with sticks from the porch of the pro-Cathedral – do you expect me to ask the cab-driver to take the time to give a receipt?

Connolly Aye . . . This torn-up cigarette-packet, when we examine it properly, is the root of the entire problem. Dressed, as it were, in an envelope of obscure rags, we conceal in every fold and turn-up a penny here – a ha'penny here – and God preserve us, here's a shilling!

He is making a pantomime of searching his clothes. The coins are real.

Who'd ha' thought it – in the hem of a waistcoat-lining! No, it's not: it's a tin-plate button! Indeed, we have the mentality of a street mendicant, a professional at that. And we're a bob down on the final score unless we can find one in our sock. It won't do.

O'Brien It's just ridiculous.

Connolly So what did I tell you?

Jack Lyng So what next?

Connolly Under no circumstances whatever can we abandon the notion of a newspaper.

Tom Lyng All right. Once we've had it, we can't do without it.

Stewart If I'd have had the cash that's been sunk into that newspaper, I could have hired halls all over Dublin for the conduct of me meetings.

Connolly You know perfectly well it was not the *cost* of the halls that stopped it –

O'Brien Overt political censorship by the committees that controlled them.

Stewart I'm not persuaded of that.

Connolly Well I am. So let's have less of it, putting the whole blame on the bloody paper. For which at this present moment, we are not able to afford a printer. So we print it ourselves.

O'Brien Us? Who?

Connolly If necessary, me. At eleven years old I was handling type in a printing-office.

Stewart Sure, this'll all take ages. To get even one edition printed – let alone every week –

Jack Lyng And we're still not going to be able to distribute in Belfast . . .

Connolly A weekly paper is impossible. Already the damn thing got to be so *weakly* that it lay down and died – what we will have to settle for is one that will appear whenever it becomes strong enough to put itself out . . . Joke . . . All right, lads, find some money. Find a press. Type. Ink. Paper. Why don't we find it today?

They all go off, busily. O'BRIEN *and* CONNOLLY *remain behind.*

SCENE 5

Connolly William, you're the treasurer. Now that's it . . .

He hands O'Brien all the money he has found in his suit.

That's my contribution.

O'Brien But this is –

Connolly Everything. Empty pockets. What am I to do? Oh, I get paid well enough for organising the party – seven shillings every week . . .

O'Brien When it ought to be twenty.

Connolly Aye, it *was* – for a while . . . I've tried all different classes of work – when I could get them. The heavy work destroys me – I mean, literally: I can't think. And for anything else the hours are all wrong, I'd have to give up the politics completely. William, what I really need to be is an independent capitalist. Your brother . . .

O'Brien He does have a little money, yes.

Connolly Look – if he could – just this once, mind – stake me out, say a matter of no more than two quid – I can get hold of a pedlar's pack and a stock of bits of nonsense – holy pictures, needles and thread – you know the kind of thing that old wives buy at the back door . . . ?

O'Brien Together with a pair of trousers that don't exhibit what's normally hid . . .

Connolly What – ! Where – ?

Twisting himself round, he discovers a large hole worn in the seat of his pants.

Oh my God, no! It was not like that this morning!

O'Brien It is now. You turn up at a back door, so: you'll be in the Bridewell in five minutes. At all events, here's two quid. I'll get it back from the brother. And – moreover –

Like a conjurer, from the inside of his overcoat or somewhere he produces a new pair of trousers.

Connolly And where the deuce did you get those?

O'Brien There's a feller in my own trade – a little tailor's apprentice who works next door to the party-office – he sees you climbing the stairs every morning from below. The state of your backside has created him professional pain. Put them on.

Connolly But I can't afford –

O'Brien It's a gift. Put them on.

CONNOLLY *does so.*

Connolly It lowers me sufficiently in my own opinion, this whole business – I would be glad of an explanation of what you find in it so damned funny?

O'Brien Jasus, he's read your pamphlets but he's never really looked at *you.* I'm afraid he's gone and made them for a man with *straight* legs.

They both laugh.

Connolly Thank you. Thank you, William. William, you're a good man . . .

O'BRIEN *goes and fetches a pedlar's pack and a tray for* CONNOLLY *and then goes out.*

Connolly (*sings*)
> With a song upon my lips
> And a pack upon my back
> I wander through the wilderness
> Upon my weary track.
>
> O do you want a button-hook
> Or do you want a stay
> Or a pair of laces for your boots . . .?
> And if you want them, can you pay?
>
> For all is rock and stone
> And barren all around:
> I once was told a story
> There was gold beneath the ground.
>
> It won't be found by digging
> Nor by searching on a chart:
> But maybe when you're three parts dead
> You'll fall and burst your heart.

> Then if you could but see it,
> The place wherein you are
> The rocky reef you lie upon
> Would glitter like a star . . .!

Exit.

SCENE 6

A landscape devastated by war – broken trees and buildings, wrecked vehicles, dead men and horses, etc. (Backcloth 4.)

Enter 1ST *and* 3RD EMPLOYERS *in safari gear (English colonial accents). They are in the last stages of exhaustion and collapse on the ground. They have an* AFRICAN BEARER *with them, loaded down with baggage.*

3rd Employer (*after a pause, scrabbles in front of him*) My God – ! Crook, look here – ! My God, Crook, we've found gold! We are rich – rich – rich – !

1st Employer Too late . . . no good . . . water . . . Hook, we must have water!

Bearer (*stands like a statue*) Bwana – I smell water.

Enter a BOER.

Boer (*aggressively to* 3RD EMPLOYER) Man, do you dare set your profane feet upon the sanctified pastures of the people of God?

(*To the* BEARER)

You, you damn Kaffir – stand away when a white man's talking or I'll take the hide off your black back!

He beats the BEARER, *who does not offer resistance or flinch, but moves slowly back a couple of steps. The* BOER *holds out a water bottle to the* EMPLOYERS.

Now – you – I give you water that you may not perish in your affliction: you have drunken it: you will depart. The husbandry of these fields is for the people of God alone and no outlander of the unregenerate shall enter it unto them nor covet them, upon pain of mortal chastisement. Go!

3rd Employer Just one moment, sir, if you please . . .

He is scooping something up from the ground into his helmet.

Boer Ha! You find gold. You find death. It has been written: in the scriptures. Therefore, we do not dig. We shall not prevent *you* – if indeed you are an-hungered for your own self-destruction. But of course you will pay. And of course in our congregation you will not lift up your voice. So there you are. Dig.

He stands back, and they dig furiously, shovelling up and piling gold. The
BOER *then siezes a large amount of it.*

My percentage. I assess this according to the laws and commandments of
the people of God.

1st Employer Mr Hook?

3rd Employer Mr Crook?

1st Employer I say, Hook, this is not right. Find a phrase.

3rd Employer 'No taxation without representation'?

1st Employer Yes: we demand democracy!

Boer Outlander and unregenerate – get off my land *now*! I said put down that
spade!

Scuffle. The BOER *knocks* 3RD EMPLOYER *down and puts his foot on him.*
1ST EMPLOYER *fires wildly, misses; and in turn is wounded by a shot from*
the BOER. *The scuffle develops into a regular battle. The fighting should*
be suggested symbolically by the hurling of rolls of toilet paper and the
like. The BOER *has the advantage. The* BEARER *remains on the stage*
throughout this episode – the combatants ignore him most of the time:
but also use him as a shield, an aiming-rest, etc. . . . .

1st Employer Help help. Help help. Discrimination. Help!

Enter GRABITALL.

Grabitall This gold was found for me to lift up my shares and stocks:
No choice but to deliver these incompetent cowardly blocks –
Their cry resounds upon the arid plain:
It is not heard in vain.
You greedy bigot – back! Before the army of the Queen
With gun and drum and bugle turns
Your God into a thornbush and your promised land
Into a valley of dry bones . . .

Boer If I run out of bullets I will repel you with thrown stones.

The battle rages. MAUD GONNE *crosses the front of the stage.*

Maud Gonne (*en passant*)
The Boer Republic sets its back
Against the rock
And stands the shock –
It is not right
Such noble independence all alone should fight
Without assistance and support . . .

She goes. Enter GERMAN *and* FRENCH ARMS MERCHANTS *with loads of*
symbolic ammunition, which they load upon the BOER, *glaring in rivalry*
meanwhile at each other.

German Arms Merchant

> My friend, by way of lawful trade,
> My pleasure now to offer aid:
> From Germany from the firm of Krupp.
> *Gott in Himmel:* do not give up!

French Arms Merchant

> The power of death from *La Belle France*:
> Perfidious Albion must not advance!
> With cartridges and French cold steel
> Such capability to kill . . .!

Grabitall (*fetches ammunition for the* EMPLOYERS)

> For Vickers-Armstrong and Lee-Enfield I am an accredited agent –

He goes up to the other two MERCHANTS

> Gentlemen, don't you think we can come to some agreement:
> Let me whisper in your ear –
> We don't want anyone to hear . . .?

He gets into a huddle with the ARMS MERCHANTS *on the fringe of the renewed fighting.*

German Arms Merchant

> Dreadnoughts, howitzers, dirigible zeppelins, machine-guns,
> TNT –

Grabitall Submarines, torpedoes, dynamite, gelignite – of course for my usual fee –

French Arms Merchant

> Counting three hundred *mitrailleuses* for the value of one long-range gun.

Grabitall Subtracting from the cost of a first-rate ironclad cruiser –

French Arms Merchant

> Sixty per cent –

German Arms Merchant

> Seventy –

Grabitall Seventy-five?

All Three *Done . . .!*

They clasp hands on the bargain. The FRENCH *and* GERMAN ARMS MERCHANTS *slip away.*

Grabitall My God the British army will too easily be beaten
> And the fighting brought to an end . . .!

3rd Employer

> You can find someone else to bloody well send!

German Arms Merchant (*as he goes out*)

> All this metal to manufacture . . .

French Arms Merchant (*on his way out*)

> And no use for it at all . . .?

Grabitall Bugler – sound the call!

The battlefield clears, the EMPLOYERS *and the* BOER *fighting each other off out
of sight.* GRABITALL *takes hold of the* BEARER *and thrusts him out of the
way of the characters entering for the next scene . . .*

A fanfare.

You bloody dog, clear off, get out –
We're dealing now with affairs of state!

SCENE 7

Enter PRIME MINISTER, TORY MPs, LIBERAL MPs, KEIR HARDIE.

Grabitall The Conservative government in parliament assembled, explains
with some embarrassment the failure of its preliminary military campaign: and promises to do better.

Prime Minister We will do better.

Grabitall (*prompts him*) We will win!

Prime Minister Indeed we will win. Already we are introducing our for-
midable new weapon – the internment camp for civilians! But we demand an outright effort by the entire British Empire on behalf of the
British Empire.

A pause.

Well . . . Can we not hear from the Liberals, if you please . . . ?

1st Liberal Fervent response to the Prime Minister's fervent hope.

2nd Liberal Fervent denunciation of the fervent response.

1st Liberal Sit down.

2nd Liberal Shan't.

1st Liberal Traitor!

2nd Liberal Imperialist!

1st Liberal Why not? All the better for trade.

Grabitall Split. But as for Labour . . . ? No doubt firm to its fraternal idealism –
Labour . . . ? Come, gentlemen, look sharp! The Prime Minister is waiting to pass the army estimates – enormously increased – Mr Keir Hardie,
will you kindly make up your mind?

Keir Hardie The Independent Labour Party will not and cannot approve the
forcible coercion of small and helpless nations.

A group of Labour supporters now thrust themselves forward.

Bernard Shaw Boers are backward!

Grabitall Mr George Bernard Shaw – of the Fabian Society.

The Webbs Even a Conservative government is more civilised than the Boers!

Grabitall Beatrice and Sydney Webb – of the Fabian Society.

Bernard Shaw If the Boers are not defeated they will oppress the black African –

The Webbs With mounting intensity, year after year, until our grandchildren and great grandchildren will be totally unable to do anything about it!

Bernard Shaw We ought to beat the Boers – here and now!

Keir Hardie Traitor.

Bernard Shaw Idiot.

The Webbs White supremacist.

Keir Hardie Paternalist.

Bernard Shaw Bigot!

Keir Hardie Imperialist!

Bernard Shaw Why not? All the better for the life-force of the human race.

Grabitall One war in the southern hemisphere
And another war over here –
The Conservatives alone see their object quite clear –

Exeunt all (save GRABITALL *and the* PRIME MINISTER*) scuffling and shouting mutual abuse.*

SCENE 8

Prime Minister
While they thus wrangle up and down the hill
The bugles call
The ranks begin to fill –
Grabitall The unemployed prepare to kill.
The fighting Irish manifest their well-known zeal
For foreign blood; and flood
Both north and south
Into the gaping cannon-mouth . . .

Drums and bugles, etc. SOLDIERS *with colours pass and re-pass, marching with panache.*

Crookey and O'Hookey know full well
What drum to thump today, what tale to tell.

Enter 1ST *and* 3RD EMPLOYERS.

1st Employer (*sings*)
The loyalty of Irishmen to the Queen of England's need –
3rd Employer (*sings*)
Will prove to the Queen of England that the Irishmen indeed
Are worthy of an independent parliament of their own:

1st Employer (*sings*)

>And graciously she'll grant it them when once it has been shown
>How be hundreds and be thousands they will fearlessly advance –

3rd Employer (*sings*)

>To the forefront of the battle, boys, with never a backward
>glance!

Employers (*sing*)

>The war, the war, come forward to the war
>And reap the reward of glory and gore . . .!

Prime Minister (*about to leave*) Thank you very much – good morning.

Enter CONNOLLY, MAUD GONNE, *and* O'BRIEN.

O'Brien Not so James Connolly. The Government

>Assumes its rigorous attitude and declares –

Prime Minister

>'THIS'.

O'Brien At once, with calm and dark intent

>He claps upon his head his four-square hat,
>Fixes his four-square features, and declares:

Connolly 'THAT'.

>GRABITALL *and the* PRIME MINISTER *contemptuously go out.* CONNOLLY *and* MAUD GONNE *take their places on a rostrum. People assemble to listen to them.* O'BRIEN *unfurls a red banner reading 'ISRP opposes imperialist war!'*

The meeting today of the Irish Socialist Republican Party is, as far as I know, the first public protest to be held against the war anywhere in the British Empire. This is a war that will undoubtedly take rank as one of the most iniquitous wars of the century. Both the war itself, in South Africa, and the condition of this country, are the work of a beast of prey that is not to be moralised, converted, or conciliated. It can only be destroyed!

Cheers.

England's difficulty should be Ireland's opportunity! For every soldier required in Ireland to keep us from our true destiny is one less man to prevent the Boers from determining their own future. Comrades, if we can act upon our understanding of that fact, a very considerable portion of the British army will not be sent to the Transvaal. Agitation for ourselves, and against the war, and against the Home Rule-Unionist twin brethren who keep us apart in order to rob us, must begin, it must continue, and it must increase every day until victory is achieved! Miss Maud Gonne, whom you all know, has a resolution she wants to move.

O'Brien The resolution condemns –

Maud Gonne The criminal aggression of the British government.

O'Brien The resolution proposes –

Maud Gonne Meetings of protest to be held all over Ireland.

O'Brien The resolution urges –

Maud Gonne That every Irishman who has emigrated to South Africa should immediately take up arms against Her Majesty's Forces and in defence of the Boer Republic! The first man to do that – *par l'amour du bon Dieu* – I swear that I will marry him!

Enormous cheering.

O'Brien The resolution is unanimously passed. The resolution is overtly seditious – the police do not interfere.

The meeting breaks up. Exeunt all save GRABITALL. *As the stage clears* O'BRIEN *showers leaflets all over like confetti.* GRIFFITH, *who has entered during the speeches with a green banner reading 'Sinn Fein opposes British war in South Africa', throws his literature about, too.*

SCENE 9

Enter a breathless POLICE OFFICER.

Grabitall And *why* did the police not interfere?

Police Officer Insufficient men on the ground at the time, sir.

GRABITALL *picks up one of* GRIFFITH'*s papers – the* OFFICER *one of* O'BRIEN'S.

Grabitall How the devil is he printing it?

O'BRIEN *re-passes across the stage calling 'Read* The Workers' Republic . . .'

O'Brien (*to audience, as he goes out again*)
　　　All on his own, as he said he would do it: he says it and he does it.

Grabitall Find it out then and suppress it.

The OFFICER *shrugs helplessly.*

　　　There's a printer's name at bottom of this sheet
　　　Emblazoned clear as paint: do you dare claim
　　　You do not know the premises whence it came?

Police Officer (*looks at the paper* GRABITALL *holds out to him*)
　　　You are too hot, sir. This is not the same.
　　　This is a paper published by Sinn Fein.

Grabitall I'm reading it!
　　　Not an infinitive that is not split.
　　　So typical. But listen! 'Irishmen:
　　　The freedom-loving patriotic Boer must win!
　　　If Saxon crudity in Africa prevail

Farewell farewell the liberty of the Gael!'
Why, this is twice as bad as is the other –
Suppress them now, suppress them both together!

Exit POLICE OFFICER. CONNOLLY *and* GRIFFITH *re-enter with their bundles of newspapers.*

Connolly Come buy *The Workers' Republic*! Buy it today!
Tomorrow it may have vanished clean away!
Griffith Thus I defy the governmental ban –
Come buy, come buy *The United Irishman*!
Connolly (*looks sideways at* GRIFFITH)
Who pays to pave
The way for your brave paper – master or slave?
Grabitall So Connolly puts the question –
Arthur Griffiths thinks it comes from the wrong direction:
He was anticipating on his neck
A policeman's truncheon – answers with rebuke:
Griffith All of the Irish bend beneath subjection
And every man in Ireland without restriction
Has the right to pile such wealth as he is able.
What else is meant by freedom for the people?
I think, sir, we had better walk apart . . .
Connolly I think we had, my lad, with all my heart . . .

(*To audience*)

Good heavens, this is no time to be quarrelling with Arthur Griffith.
Just so we know where we stand – that's all.

Exit GRIFFITH.

SCENE 10

Enter O'BRIEN.

O'Brien Jim – Jim – Joseph Chamberlain –
Connolly Joseph Chamberlain – chief short-order-cook in Queen Victoria's
imperial chop-house – well?
O'Brien They've invited him to Trinity College, Dublin, to receive an
honorary degree. Now, Jim, this can be no coincidence!
Grabitall (*to audience*) Indeed it is not – we are losing the war: support for the
troops in the Transvaal must be drummed up – Joe Chamberlain in
Dublin will rally the loyalist cause!
Connolly (*formally, to audience*) The inevitable rally of protest that has been
organised receives nation-wide endorsement. Even Crookey and
O'Hookey are so alarmed they have consented to address it.

Crowds begin to come in again. O'BRIEN *unfurls a red banner reading 'No support for Imperialist Aggressors in Dublin'.* GRIFFITH *unfurls a green banner reading 'Reject British hypocrisy'.*

1ST *and* 3RD EMPLOYERS *enter.*

1st Employer Responsive as we are ever to the demands of our constituents –

3rd Employer And aware of the deleterious effect of the casualty-lists from South Africa on the ballot-box next time round, we have prepared a strong statement –

1st Employer Appealing to the British government –

3rd Employer To use its best endeavours –

1st Employer To patch up a peace with the Boers.

Grabitall Dissent must be destroyed – policemen, are you ready?

POLICE *assemble under his wing.*

Grabitall By order of the Lord Lieutenant, the rally of protest is forbidden!

The POLICE *deploy.*

The people are on the street, the police are on the street, the speakers –

3rd Employer (*slinks away from rostrum*) Have not arrived –

1st Employer Or if we did – we've all gone home . . .

Exeunt EMPLOYERS.

Grabitall So the crowd has no leadership, no focus, a herd of goats, break it up!

O'Brien James Connolly and Maud Gonne upon two wheels arrive:
The flag of the Boer Republic flying in the breeze –
An old experienced dust-collector knows how to drive,
Dodges with ease,

CONNOLLY *and* MAUD GONNE *move rapidly through the crowd as though he is driving a cart with her mounted behind him. She waves the Boer flag and holds a speech. The* POLICE *try to stop them but are hampered by the speed and movement of the crowd.*

The lady stands and sways and reads her –

Maud Gonne (*as she and* CONNOLLY *stop still for an instant*)
Treasonable speech!

O'Brien And then sits down –
James Connolly steers his reeling juggernaut
Three-quarters round the town –
Now he's arrested, now he's not –
The lady reads her –

Maud Gonne
Treasonable speech – again!

O'Brien To another crowd in another spot:
And then they all go home.

CONNOLLY, MAUD GONNE *and* O'BRIEN *go out. Everyone else disperses except* GRABITALL *and* POLICE, *who are left completely baffled – their helmets, knocked off in the scuffling, are strewn all over the stage.*

Grabitall I do not regard this evening's work as much of a success.

SCENE 11

Enter POLICE OFFICER.

Police Officer

But sir, but sir, we've found his printing-press!
What shall we do with it?

Two CONSTABLES *stagger in with a press*

Grabitall Batter it into scrap!

The POLICE *destroy the press.*

Police Officer

The other chap?

Grabitall Griffith?

Police Officer

I think, sir, when he hears of the rival journal's fate,
His style of article will moderate –
I think, sir, with a liberal wink, we could let pass
The theoretical offerings of the middle class . . .?

Grabitall Sinn Fein: 'Ourselves Alone' . . .? Leave them alone.

Police Officer

And yet, sir, I have heard it said
That the old occult Republican Brotherhood
Collects the cash for and has members in
Your shapeless something of a vague Sinn Fein . . .
'Twould be grave implications were them two linked?

Grabitall Defunct – extinct –

I am assured the Brotherhood is no more:
It fell to pieces in the Land League War.
It does not bear
Upon the one political hard fact
That recruiting for the army has hit rock-bottom
With all this riot and vulgar ruction –
There is the trend we have to counteract.

For a very sufficient reason. I have overdone it yet again. I have ground, according to my nature, the faces of the English poor so hard, and exploited them so mercilessly, that the military medical officers reject them as unfit. But Paddy – now – our rural Paddy, with his bacon and his cabbage and his buttermilk and strong potatoes – there is the material for interminable war – and I swear that I will have him! For if I don't – by God, I'm finished . . .! Political, electoral – have we done it – what's the news?

Enter 1ST *and* 3RD EMPLOYERS.

3rd Employer I am glad to report, sorr, that the moderate party of Home Rule in its various shapes and disguises has won the greater part of the votes upon all the local councils it contested. As for Labour –

1st Employer Devil a bit, sorr – banjaxed altogether – in the heel of the hunt not a socialist revolutionist got a seat in the entire country!

Enter CONNOLLY.

Connolly Brief statement from James Connolly explaining his defeat . . . I warned you last year and I warn you again this: that a Labour candidate who is no socialist is no good to the working classes. I am, however, more concerned – I would go so far as to say embittered – by the treatment we have received from the labour movement in Great Britain. I did not believe that they too would have cast us out: but from the throat of Keir Hardie we have heard the hue-and-cry . . .

Enter KEIR HARDIE – *he stands some way from* CONNOLLY *and they both speak to the audience.*

Keir Hardie I am exceedingly disappointed with the ISRP. There has been, of course, much sound and fury – Comrade Connolly for example at the head of a mob, brandishing a Boer flag and shouting, not only for an Irish Republic, but for the defeat of the British army! Why, what *is* the British army, what else but working men? In Britain, we have been struggling, year after year, for the formation of a strong and effective Parliamentary Labour Party . . . I was under the impression Comrade Connolly shared that struggle.

Connolly Who said I did not?

Keir Hardie By withdrawing as it were the socialists of catholic Ireland –

Connolly We are totally non-sectarian –

Keir Hardie That's what you call yourselves. But how many protestant workers in the north subscribe to your newspaper? By withdrawing as it were the socialists of catholic Ireland from the potent working-class community of the rest of the United Kingdom, and placing them as it were upon the same footing as the exploited but alien Boer –

Connolly Aye, or the Hindoo – or the rebellious Chinese Boxer –

Keir Hardie (*turns to face* CONNOLLY, *and indicates his own cloth cap*) This hat, I'd have ye know, was the first true workman's roof ever to have been seen proceeding into the portals of the House of Commons. You can match that, you can answer me: if not, you'd best bide quiet . . . So . . .

Labour in parliament can only achieve anything if part of its programme is adopted by the Liberals who in turn are dependent upon the votes of the Irish Party. The Irish Party demand that the Liberals, when in office, bring in a bill for Home Rule. QED – Labour must give support to Home Rule. Indeed we would prefer in the long run an Irish Republic, but –

Connolly D'ye think we could have that in writing, Mr Keir Hardie?

Keir Hardie The long run being not before we have built a majority party of our own. The recent results of the municipal elections have proved that the basic desires of the Irish working class, as expressed through the ballot-box –

Connolly Forty per cent of the adult males cannot vote – and that forty per cent are entirely working class.

Keir Hardie The basic desires of the Irish working class have nothing whatever to do with the dream of a republic! Municipal administration – gas-board, water-board, housing – as already in large measure achieved in protestant Belfast – and of course the development of trades unions in industry. Until you are prepared to devote your energies to that, the policy of the Independent Labour Party of Great Britain – I am sorry, but there's no help for it, it's a matter of common sense – will be to co-operate and to consult upon Irish affairs with the Irish Parliamentary Party under the leadership of John Redmond.

Grabitall (*sings*)
> Crookey and O'Hookey shake on that
> It is indeed a feather in their hat –
> (Exchanges the hat)

A general swap-around of hats, between GRABITALL, *the* EMPLOYERS *and* KEIR HARDIE. *The latter has been approached by the* EMPLOYERS *from behind, and induced to shake hands. At the end of the hat-changes* KEIR HARDIE'*s cap is on* GRABITALL'*s head,* GRABITALL'*s topper on* KEIR HARDIE, *and the two* EMPLOYERS' *hats are mutually exchanged . . .*

1st Employer (*sings*)
> That our friends across the water –

2nd Employer (*sings*)
> Lead their own friends to the slaughter –

Grabitall and Employers (*sing*)
> And our profits are safeguarded, tit-for-tat!

HARDIE *discovers what he is wearing and indignantly swaps back again with* GRABITALL. *He turns his back on the trio.*

Keir Hardie (*to Connolly*) I'm afraid your socialism in Ireland is up the creek both oar and paddle: Jim, pull yourself to the ground, man, before you're blown beyond the moon!

Connolly I demand an opportunity to make a full and reasoned reply to this disastrous misjudgement –

Keir Hardie Get some votes in, laddie, and then we'll listen. I'm not interested in piss-and-wind . . . !

Exit KEIR HARDIE.

SCENE 12

CONNOLLY *suddenly leaps off the stage and runs up and down among the audience shouting.*

Connolly I will not be dictated to! Victory for the Boers and an Irish Republic – Victory for the Boers and an Irish Republic – Victory for the Boers and an Irish Republic – !

GRABITALL *sends the* POLICE OFFICER *to try and catch him. There is a chase: but* CONNOLLY'*s cry is taken up by a crowd of people who come in and all mill about yelling. Finally* CONNOLLY *leaves the hall, with his supporters, still to be heard shouting offstage.*

Grabitall (*to* EMPLOYERS)
>Crookey – O'Hookey – ! – a job – a job
>Contrived to drown the deafening of this mob!

The crowd comes in on the stage and this time chases GRABITALL *who runs about for a while. Finally he leaves them behind and re-enters on stage to the cowering* EMPLOYERS.

>They're after you, you know, as well as me⸱
>So, save yourselves by putting in your plea . . .?
>I say save yourselves by putting in your plea!

The EMPLOYERS *for a moment are nonplussed.*

3rd Employer (*gets it*)
>I have it, sorr, I take your drift – why don't we all invite the Duke of York?

1st Employer Too small at all at all – he didn't work . . .

3rd Employer Ah sure, what's the Duke of York?

1st Employer A little whipper-snapper of a diffident grandson that couldn't say boo to a goose – no no, sorr, 'tis inevitable –

3rd Employer Sure, it can't be delayed any longer –

1st Employer The old lady!

3rd Employer The old lady!

1st Employer We must have in the old lady!

Employers Sure, nothing will go wrong.

Grabitall Fill the town with loyal protestants from Harland and Wolff of Belfast – all the school children get a holiday and be marshalled with their teachers – the Lord Lieutenant will provide them with a treat in the afternoon. The employees of Guinness's brewery will get a holiday and a shilling bonus, and be marshalled, with their supervisors. Civil servants –

3rd Employer And their wives –

Grabitall Soldiers off duty –

1st Employer And their wives –

3rd Employer Policemen –

Grabitall Castle officials –

3rd Employer Military pensioners –

Grabitall And their wives. – The wives will bring the children, and the children will be given flags . . .

A loyal crowd assembles and are given union jacks to wave. POLICE *assemble in large numbers.*

Are we ready?

CONNOLLY *appears at a distant corner.*

Connolly Monarchy is a survival of the tyranny imposed by the hand of greed and treachery in the darkest and most ignorant days of our history –

Grabitall We can't have that!

GRIFFITH *appears at another corner.*

Griffith The Famine Queen of England, had she had her way, would have starved every Irishman out of this world in eighteen forty-seven – she is nothing more than a living symbol of the permanent hatred felt by the dull Teuton for the free poetic Gael –

Grabitall The police must take action!

Police Officer What sort of action?

Grabitall By no means the same sort as you took for Joe Chamberlain and even less for the Duke of York! Just keep them off the streets. I said fill the streets with children. I don't see any children!

Police Officer If you please, sir, there appear to be no children to be found . . .

MAUD GONNE *enters, leading a file of children.*

Maud Gonne (*sings*)

> O all you little children come follow after me
> And in honour of your native land I will give you cake and tea:
> Don't go with the Lord Lieutenant: don't go up to Phoenix Park –
> He will put you in his big black pot for his dinner in the dark.

> Come with me, come with me, where the shamrock leaves are
> green
> I will save you from the dragon teeth of the hungry Famine
> Queen . . .

She leads the children round the house and out.

Grabitall (*to* POLICE, *who are about to chase her*) No, stay where you are, we haven't got time! Cross your fingers, touch wood, say a prayer – we've got to go through with it! Bring on the Queen of England!

Connolly (*shouts above the cheers and music*) The mind accustomed to political kings can too easily be reconciled to social kings – capitalist kings of the workshop, the mill, the shipyard and the docks . . .

To the tune of 'God Save The Queen', a puppet representing QUEEN VICTORIA *is trundled across the stage before the excited crowd.* GRIFFITH *and* CONNOLLY *come running down towards her – both of them are struck simultaneously to the ground by police batons.*

Grabitall Now get her back to England – quick!

The QUEEN *is hurried out and the crowd disperses.*

> Nobody in Ireland, from now on, is going to be allowed to do anything at all – if I don't like the look of it! Enforce that at once!

Police Officer Yessir, at once, sir! Where shall we start, sir?

Grabitall (*indicates* GRIFFITH) With him. Seize his newspaper.

Police Officer Smash up his printing press?

Grabitall We do not want to start another riot!
> Our only purpose now is keep things quiet.
> Forbid all public meeting and procession.

Police Officer
> That ban will be broken.

Enter CIVIL SERVANT, *with newspapers.*

Civil Servant
> No – no – it won't! The stock exchange has spoken!
> *The Wall Street Journal* and the London *Times* –
> 'Severe depression
> Affecting trade and all employment – !'

Grabitall Saved! We are saved! At the very last moment!
> But yet we must make haste to circumvent
> Trade union opposition to our firm-principled intent.
> The employer here pays off a very old grudge,
> Assisted by his friend, the high court judge . . .

SCENE 13

A JUDGE *in his wig and robes comes in.*

Judge 'Quin versus Leatham . . .'
Grabitall An Irish lawsuit started in Belfast:
>   Most salutory that Ireland should come first.
>   And after – to South Wales:
>   No trains upon the rails –
>   Judgement, if you please, before the company should fail!

Judge 'The Taff Vale Railway versus the Amalgamated Society of Railway
Servants . . .' In both of these cases the judgement is as follows: trade
unions are held liable for all damages and loss incurred by industrial
action. So therefore the man Quin, and his so-called Butchers' Union,
must pay to Mr Leatham, a slaughterhouse proprietor, the sum of two
hundred and fifty pounds: while the Amalgamated Society of Railway
Servants must pay the Taff Vale Railway no less than forty thousand.
That will teach them to withdraw their labour upon the whim of a fanciful
grievance and hold the whole community to unauthorised ransom.

Grabitall If the unions are left
>   Without a penny to their name
>   They have none but themselves to blame.
>   There is nothing they can do –
>   But pay the bill –

Judge And pay the lawyers, too!
Grabitall We'll find their money-bags from now not quite so full
>   Of proud disruption and democracy abused.
>   Prices will rise, wages will fall:
>   With no-one permitted to do anything at all,
>   Nothing will happen. People will be so confused
>   The very vote itself will not be used.
>   Unless in favour of Conservative . . .
>   For when a man can hardly stay alive,
>   What greater blessing can he know
>   Than to conserve the status quo?
>   Hungry folk are rarely over-bold:
>   Rather than starve, they do what they are told!

Exeunt all but CONNOLLY.

Connolly (*gets slowly to his feet and addresses the audience*)
>   I would prefer to prove him wrong.
>   We filled the streets and sang our song:
>   We thought we heard ourselves applauded.
>   Our short sharp entertainment is concluded –
>   Those we thought

> Joined in with us on every note
> In fact throughout
> We now so ruefully can have no doubt
> Had kept their mouths tight shut . . .

Exit.

END OF ACT 2

ACT 3: 'Outmanoeuvred'

SCENE 1

Converging processions of demonstrators representing socialist and nationalist ferment from different parts of the world, in a variety of costumes and with a variety of slogans on their banners in many languages. The whole contained within a border of watchful police of no particular nationality. (Backcloth 5.)

Enter CONNOLLY, *very depressed, and an* OLD MARKET-WOMAN *with a basket of Christmas holly, etc., to sell.*

Connolly (*sings*)

> For weeks and months I've been so tormented
> With agitation for the public weal –
> Blood in my face and my bold brain beating
> Against the base of my angry skull.
>
> I have had no time for wife nor family
> I have had no time to speak a civil word
> To friend nor neighbour – like a wild red Indian
> I have prowled through the town without sleep or food.
>
> I am hardly aware of the date or the day of it –
> What is the month . . . ?

Old Market-Woman

> December.

Connolly (*sings*)

> What day . . . ?

Old Market-Woman

> It is the twenty-fourth: your chiselurs are expecting you.

Connolly (*sings*)

> Nothing I can bring them, there is nothing I can say . . .

Exit OLD MARKET-WOMAN. *As she goes a bit of greenery falls from her basket.* CONNOLLY *picks it up, is about to call after her, then looks at it – it is only a fragment – he rather guiltily shoves it under his coat. A* BEGGING CHILD *accosts him.*

Begging Child Hey, mister – a merry Christmas – d'ye have a wee penny for us –?

Connolly (*cornered, after he tries in vain to hurry past*) Aye . . . merry Christmas. But I'm afraid I've got no penny.

Begging Child Please, mister, please – me da broke his leg and there's nothing in the house and me mammy said –

Connolly Nothing?

Begging Child Me mammy said I was to go out and ask for pennies in the market or else there would be nothing.

Connolly Here – here's a ha'penny – no, wait a minute, I can just make it two – here's three ha'pennies and that's all.

The BEGGING CHILD *scampers away.*

In my own house, what will there be?

He sings:

> On Christmas eve, in a house without festivity
> Where is the pudding should be boiling in the pan?
> Christmas eve and no money in my pocket –

SCENE 2

ÇONNOLLY *arrives home and* LILLIE *and* NORA *greet him.*

Connolly (*sings*)

> But two shillings for a gift, Lillie, spend them how you can . . .
>
> It is not that I forgot, Lillie . . . but . . . No: do you see these!

Out of his pedlar's pack he takes a suddenly remembered bit of coloured and gilt ribbon.

I sold two of them in two days and one of them was charged to credit.

Lillie James, do you really think you ought to accept credit?

Connolly There was ten children in that tenement and the father in Mountjoy gaol . . . Hang them up for us – on the tree.

Lillie Do you know that in Moore Street they were charging a whole half-crown for a splinter of wood and a splutter of branches like a brush you'd use to sweep the chimney? So you see: there's no tree.

CONNOLLY *looks grave, shakes his head: then suddenly as though by magic whips the bit of green stuff from out behind him.*

Connolly (*sings*)

> Ding-dong merrily on high
> In heaven the bells are ringing
> Ding-dong merrily on high
> On earth the quires are singing –
> Gloria in excelsis!

Put it up on the mantle-piece, put the gew-gaws on it: so!

His improvisation is received with great excitement and delight.

There ye are then, that's a tree!

Lillie For behold I bring you good tidings of great joy which shall be unto all people . . .

Connolly As for that, we do have the newspaper being printed once again. No subscriptions – or hardly any.

Lillie For ourselves to have nothing, there must be others who have far less.

Connolly And is that a consolation . . .? Lillie, what's less than nothing?

Lillie Now, James, in front of the children . . .

Connolly All right: let them answer. Nora, what's less than nothing?

Nora Less than nothing would be if Daddy had forgotten to pick up a branch from the gutter.

Lillie Less than nothing is to have nothing and no way of knowing why, and no comprehension as to how things might be changed. You gave me that comprehension. You have given it to many others.

Connolly Many others? A few others. One or two: no more than that.

Lillie In the old days, in Edinburgh, you were a big success – as a lecturer, I mean.

Connolly Better audiences than I've ever had in this reproachful country.

Lillie Had you not best go back again?

Connolly What? All of us? The whole family – and you yet once more with a baby on the way? Lillie, are you mad?

Lillie No, of course not the whole family. But you are well enough known now to get engagements to lecture in all manner of places in Scotland and England – all you need do is put an advertisement in one of the socialist newspapers – surely that is not going to cost us more than two bob? Go on now, go and do it.

Connolly And leave you here alone? Lillie, that is not a risk I am at all inclined to take. God knows what could happen – suppose I fell ill in England, or the fees for the lectures never came through – or the children were ill or an accident – and besides, in this neighbourhood: it's a very rough area for a mother without a husband – and the conditions of these houses –

Lillie I had words with the rent-collector on that subject yesterday.

Connolly Aye?

Lillie I pointed out to him the hole in the tread of the staircase just below our landing – I said any child could catch her foot in that without thinking: and then himself and his master the landlord would have a death on their hands.

Connolly And he said . . .?

Lillie He said 'Missus – you already have an *agitator* on *your* hands' – he meant you – he said I ought to think meself lucky to be allowed to stay in the place at all, the way the newspapers put names on you when you rose up against the Queen's visit.

Connolly That's exactly what I mean – with me here, they're afraid of me, but if I were to go to England –

SCENE 3

Enter a NEIGHBOUR.

Neighbour Oh – excuse me – Mrs Connolly – is your husband at home?

Connolly Why, hello, Mr Riordan – come in, sir. A merry Christmas to you, Mr Riordan! Lillie, have we got anything we could offer to Mr Riordan to –

He makes a drinking gesture to LILLIE, *who shakes her head, embarrassed.*

Neighbour Oh don't trouble yourself at all, Mr Connolly, sure I only put me head in on me way home from work, being asked to deliver a small message if it's quite convenient . . .

Connolly Yes, yes . . . by all means . . .

Neighbour It's the tenants, Mr Connolly, in O'Sullivan's Buildings, you know the place – in the Coombe? Well me sister's husband Terry is a member of the committee they're after forming over there to defend themselves against eviction – there was th'increase, y'see, of rent: and sure to God they can't pay it: so they made up their minds to resist –

Connolly They did!

Neighbour They did so, sir.

Connolly Good for them. Can I help?

Neighbour Sure wasn't that the very message? They have a meeting in the square the evening after St Stephen's, and they wanted to know, if it was altogether convenient, would you be so good as to address them, Mr Connolly? It would help them a power of good, sir, if they had a speaker like yourself; one of their own, as it were, that could advise them and they could trust . . .

Connolly Mr Riordan, tell the brother-in-law I shall be only too happy to come!

Neighbour Mr Connolly, thank you. You're a good man in time of trouble.

Exit NEIGHBOUR.

Lillie Was that wise?

Connolly If we're in queer street with our own landlord it certainly is a bit of a risk, but –

Lillie But it's a risk you are inclined to take . . .? But take the other one, as well. James, you need new places, you need new people –

Connolly And above all we need some cash.

We filled the streets, we sang our song:
We thought we heard ourselves applauded . . .
Dublin it seems is dead, or deaf – I cannot push
A tune into the drums of ears that will not ring – !
No doubt my music must be made elsewhere.
What shall I play? I will declare

The one tune needful for the present day:
True revolution is the enemy of reform!

Lillie Every time you say that, James, I think of meself out shopping: and I
wonder is it true or false, half a loaf better or worse than no bread?

Connolly For little more than half a loaf of bread
The open razor shaved great Samson's head
Clean to the bone till all his strength had fled.
We need to pull both tower and temple down –
Our hair of power must be full-grown:
In Scotland and in England I will tell them so –

Enter TOM LYNG.

Lyng (*holds out a letter*)
To Paris, France, you must prepare to go!
The International Socialist Conference have written to invite
Our party, on its own, to send a delegate –

Connolly Ireland is recognised in her own right
Apart from Britain, at this conference?
For the first time ever our true historic place
By socialists is granted us in the face
Of all the world . . . ? God, Tom, for this alone we're still alive!

Tom Lyng
Here is the letter. It seems to say
That if we go we must pay our own way . . .

Connolly That rules out me, I am afraid . . .
Yourself and Stewart, though, could afford
Your third-class passage and your bed and board?
I'll brief you briefly – 'Revolution or Reform':
That is the theme that takes this conference by storm!

SCENE 4

LILLIE *and* NORA *go out;* CONNOLLY *walks up and down instructing* TOM
LYNG. STEWART *comes in and joins them.*

Connolly The French Socialist Party is split down the middle: one of their
members has accepted a seat in the bourgeois liberal government, which
also includes the notorious General Gallifet – the man who is known as
'The Butcher of the Commune', for the cruelty with which he put down
the great Paris rising of eighteen seventy-one. The justification? They
have at least one socialist in a place of power . . . he will be able, if he is
lucky, to carry out a few reforms. So, little by little, revolution, and its
inconvenience, will be rendered unnecessary . . . Do you need me to tell
you why this must be opposed? To the extent, if it goes so far, of ap-

parently entirely wrecking the international socialist movement . . .? Consider the possibility of an Irish delegation, for the first time ever at such a conference, making its weight felt, where it is needed, in the condemnation of these French hypocrites. If we are able to do that, then perhaps we may be able to avert the day in Ireland, when the same thing happens here – in my worst dreams I can foresee how our children and our childrens' children will awake to discover a party of the working class has joined, without protest, in an independent Irish government composed of every gombeen man and grabitall-financier from Killiney to the Hill of Howth! On your way, lads, do your best.

CONNOLLY *retires to one side of the stage. A large red banner reading 'Paris Conference Socialist International 1900' is brought in at the back: and the stage fills with* DELEGATES, *squabbling and hurling abuse at each other.* GRABITALL *strides amongst them, dividing them almost by force, so that they fall back into two clumps. The conference* CHAIRMAN, *equipped with a speaker's desk in the middle, beats with his gavel for silence.*

Grabitall This five feet that I pace across the floor will separate
Fraternal comradeship from intestinal hate –
Each individual socialist delegate
According to ideology takes his stand
Splitting the vote of nearly every several land –
Upon my right-hand –

French Delegate (*right-wing*)
France!

Grabitall Upon my left-hand!

French Delegate (*left-wing*)
France!

Grabitall Throw down the biting bones, my boys, and make them dance!

Connolly Application from the French left for a vote of condemnation against the action of the French right in permitting their associate Millerand to take his seat in the bourgeois government.

French Delegate (*left-wing*) They are renegades – expel them from the movement! Revolution!

Grabitall (*who has now gone to the opposite side of the stage from* CONNOLLY) Justification by the French right of their attitude towards Millerand.

French Delegate (*right-wing*) Millerand is the first French socialist ever to be awarded a ministerial portfolio. He is the foot in the door, the spark in the dry haystack, the spout of water from the rock in the middle of the desert. Fellow-delegates, we must all welcome the opening of a new chapter in the reform of social policies!

Uproar

Connolly If the Chairman cannot decide who to call upon next, there may never be another speaker – ever –

Grabitall He looks around to catch a rescuing eye – ha-ha he is there:
Distinguished comrade Kautsky, intellectual heir
Of mighty Marx and Engels, he will dare
To peer round this obstructed corner . . . With jesuitical device
Each simple word he speaks, he will interpret twice or thrice . . .

Kautsky Comrades: let us examine very very carefully the exceedingly complex ramifications of this profoundly important crux . . .

Connolly Like wool upon a spindle
He winds and winds his argument:
It is all a kind of a swindle –
But this is comrade Kautsky's bent.
He approaches his conclusion, he is now about to ask
The delegates to help him define their collective task . . .

Kautsky (*who has been speaking inaudibly with baroque gestures*) . . . so I offer to this conference the question whether or not it is our historic collective task to resolve the contradictions and obtain a correct compromise . . .?

The IRISH DELEGATES *are in the body of the hall, to one side.*

Stewart Now that's not what Jim Connolly told us.

Tom Lyng Jim Connolly said – make our weight felt.

Stewart (*as* KAUTSKY *goes on and on*) I don't see how we can argue with a continental of that class. By God, the man's a polymath. I tell you, he scares me rigid . . .

Grabitall Comrade Kautsky's dialectic has already probed so deep
That two-thirds of the assembly have fallen fast asleep.

Connolly The longer he keeps them stupefied, the more certain it will be
When he reaches his conclusion, they can do nothing but agree.

Kautsky May I suggest, therefore, fellow-delegates, that we do not *condemn* the French Socialist Party: nor, fellow-delegates, do we make the crucial error of *supporting* their procedure. We consider, very carefully, whether or no the French party were actually *responsible* for the elevation of Millerand to the cabinet of France. I cannot find, upon studying the documents in this case, that at any time were they consulted. The party, as a party, had nothing to do with it. So: the resolution before this conference should, in my opinion, read as follows: 'We criticise the individualist action of comrade Millerand, and recommend the French Socialist Party to impose in the future a more precise discipline.' Do we not think that solves everything . . .?

Rosa Luxemburg (*jumps up in the body of the hall*) You deliberately evade the entire point that is at issue! We exist here for one purpose: to overthrow capitalism. To tinker with it in the shape of reactionary coalitions is objectively to offer it our support! Whether or not Millerand consulted the French party has nothing at all to do with it. Members of his own party in this hall have defended his action and have called on us to welcome it. Therefore they deserve to be utterly condemned and expelled from the International. To offer them this compromise for the sake of reuniting their very properly divided party is in itself a blatant gesture of approval towards Millerand!

Chairman Delegates will only speak, please, when called upon by the chair. And we require those who speak from the body of the hall to state their names and affiliations as a preface to their remarks.

Rosa Luxemburg Rosa Luxemburg, member of the German Social Democrats.

Grabitall From the party of comrade Kautsky . . . Yet another group with a split in it!

Connolly Comrade Kautsky is aware of her – and of the book that she has written –

Kautsky *Reform or Revolution* was the title, was it not . . . ? We are all of us beholden to the erudition of comrade Luxemburg. But in matters of practicality she has perhaps a little to learn. She comes, I understand, from Poland, where the tradition has not always been to put all things in their proper order . . .

Tom Lyng Seems to me she's put it very much in the proper order.

Stewart Keep your eye upon her, so: when she votes, we vote with her. Why, she speaks with the very voice of Jim Connolly himself.

Chairman Votes. Those in favour of comrade Kautsky's ingenious compromise?

Grabitall Austria . . . Great Britain . . . Germany . . .

Tom Lyng Why dammit, she doesn't have a vote! She's not an accredited delegate.

Stewart She didn't have the right to put in her opinion at all! But she put it – she's a great girl!

Chairman Those opposed to comrade Kautsky's ingenious compromise?

Polish Delegate (*right-wing*) One moment please! The Polish delegation is unable to reach agreement within itself as to which way it intends to vote! The debate must continue until all delegations have reached unanimity!

Polish Delegate (*left-wing*) By no means! I demand the right to have my dissenting opinion recorded. He wants to vote *for*: I am against! I will never never never be unanimous with him!

Chairman Delegations that are divided will be recorded as such. Those divided?

Grabitall America . . . Italy . . . Poland.

Chairman Finally: those opposed.

Connolly Bulgaria.

Grabitall That's all.

Connolly No no –

Observe: the Irish are standing for the count!

My delegates have their own interpretation of the point . . .

Tom Lyng (*up at the centre of the platform*)

We in Ireland know our Millerand, who he might well be:

        The socialist whom Keir Hardie longs to see
        Clasping the hand of Redmond and Home Rule!
        If we should follow him, our entire life's work would fail.
Grabitall The point is made, but yet it is not taken.
        Provincial Irish slogans are not spoken
        In such a cosmopolitan atmosphere
        Unless you want to get a frozen stare
        Of scandalised incomprehension.
        Poor Lyng regrets his vulgar intervention . . .
Chairman Delegates voting should refrain please from any comment upon their vote. The debate has been closed.
Bulgarian Delegate No no, excuse me, upon a point of order, comrade chairman: Gromek, Bulgaria. The question already raised by the Polish delegation. If a delegation is divided and has recorded itself as such: then how can this conference recognise both factions of that delegation as truly representative of the country that has sponsored it? For instance – who is Poland? That gentleman: or that one?
Rosa Luxemburg Does it matter?

General cries: 'Of course it matters!'

Rosa Luxemburg (*gets up on to the platform despite the* CHAIRMAN) At an international socialist conference it is important whether *Poland* is truly represented by him – or by him – ? Nonsense! What do we suppose Poland – as a concept – has to do with scientific socialism, which extends beyond frontiers and recognises only *classes* as the fundamental structure of the present state of the human race? Why, Poland, as a concept, does not even exist! The nation, as we all well know, is divided out and ruled by Germany, Austria, Russia, as subordinate provinces of their three respective empires. Why else have I come here as a member of a *German* party?
Stewart Now wait a moment: I've come here as a member of an *Irish* party! By your argument, ma'am, 'tis the *British* delegation that my friend and meself had ought to be attached to?
Rosa Luxemburg That is so: yes.
Tom Lyng But – but – but here, wait a moment – it's for that very reason that we voted against Kautsky!
Rosa Luxemburg I hope not. If you think that revolution can best triumph over reformism by invoking these national differences, then let me caution you both to examine your position. . . .
Grabitall The chairman calls for order: the digression is cut short:
        The conference adjourns: the Irish delegates feel quite hurt.

Exeunt all save STEWART, TOM LYNG, *and* ROSA LUXEMBURG: CONNOLLY *stays at the extreme side of the stage, and* GRABITALL *busies himself con-*

temptuously clearing up the debris – tearing down and rolling up the banner, etc.

Tom Lyng (*catches* ROSA LUXEMBURG *as she makes to go out*) Excuse me, ma'am: ye have us both extremely bothered.

Stewart We feel obliged to take you up on the things that you said just now.

Tom Lyng Our party is republican, you see: the complete separation of Ireland from Great Britain is an essential part of our – –

Rosa Luxemburg And so it is with many of the Poles. We have our own socialists who cling to a utopian and fantastic plan for the reconstitution of the country. But is not this dangerous heresy, comrades, exactly what we struggle against? We who are convinced that the proletariat is not in a position to change political geography, nor to reconstruct bourgeois states, but that it must organise itself on existing foundations, historically created, so as to bring about the conquest of socialist power and the ultimate socialist republic, which alone will be able to liberate the entire world! *There* should be the true meaning of this word you use – republican.

Stewart Sure she talks like an Orangeman out of Belfast . . . I've heard the very same argument put forward by labour organisers in the North who are after nothing more than the supremacy of their own religious sect over everyone else in the province!

Rosa Luxemburg Ah, religion . . . ! It goes hand-in-hand with national sentiment, as always! Why, christianity and socialism have nothing in common. The subordination of the material welfare of mankind to the will of the supreme deity . . . ? No no: keep well away from it . . . Do not think of yourselves as catholics, nor of others as protestants, nor of any of you as Irishmen: you are proletarians or you are nothing: and your interests are identical. And let me add: that to set one so-called national interest in competition against another – in itself, you will observe, a capitalist activity – inevitably involves militarism: the greatest danger of the present age. The powers of Europe are expending twenty per cent, thirty per cent more of their national budget upon armaments than was the case five years ago. The man who is half a nationalist will always join a national army when his patriotism is invoked. Remember that . . . But you did well, in your vote against Kautsky.

Tom Lyng And you did well, yourself, ma'am, in your interruption of that feller. Congratulations, comrade.

ROSA LUXEMBURG *shakes hands with them and goes out.*

Grabitall Not a little bewildered, they come home, they see their chief:
Do we suppose he can resolve for them the confusion of their belief?

Exit GRABITALL. CONNOLLY *comes to meet* TOM LYNG *and* STEWART.

Connolly You don't want to take too much notice of that Luxemburg one. On reformism, from what you tell me, she's very sound. But as regards the national question: don't forget she's a Pole, and Poland at one time had an empire itself. Did ye never hear of a king of theirs called John Sobiesky? Conquered left right and centre. She's quite right, if she doesn't want any more o' *that* coming up . . . She's also, I believe, a Jew: and the Jews have been persecuted the way you'd hunt rabbits by both the Poles and the Russians. So you wouldn't expect the girl to be particularly concerned which one of the two gangs was in charge – if anything she prefers Germany where the Jews have no problems: fellow-citizens with their own religion and no nonsense about it. In her place, quite clearly, national sentiment is of small value: but the Irish question's different and we judge it by different rules. The next time we go to one of these international affairs, we are going to have to work out much more thoroughly our particular philosophy and explain it with great care. But there's time for it. The important thing is: we made a principled stand. And they know now who we are. In due course they'll know us better . . .

Exeunt TOM LYNG *and* STEWART.

SCENE 5

Connolly Through the years of nineteen hundred and nineteen hundred and one

It seemed that my travels would never be done.

Around Scotland and England, east and west

In third-class carriages without any rest,

Cheap temperance hotels with damp and cranky beds,

Audiences in draughty halls invariably at odds:

And myself on the platform trying to explain to their grotesque heads

The complex clarity of the clear-cut world I dreamed I could foresee . . .

I must forbid myself to think that they are bigger fools than me . . .

And yet in the name of God what else must I call them . . . ? Shall we take for an example this ridiculous Kautsky compromise – the British socialists in Paris voted for it to a man: and yet, in their newspapers, they turn around and abuse Millerand! In Glasgow and Falkirk, Aberdeen, Leith, Salford – inevitably at every lecture I give, it comes up – and inevitably I prepare for it. . . .

Shall I show you how it goes each weary day:

It always goes the self-same way . . .

I dismount from the railway-train, I am met upon the station platform by the inevitably serious young man . . . 'Comrade Connolly? How d'ye do, sir, I'm so glad you were able to come – now I can't honestly tell you we expect a *huge* meeting tonight, unexpectedly the date has coincided with the all-in wrestling at the Municipal Free Trade Hall – ha ha – but we have managed to secure for your lecture the Saxe-Coburg Terrace Unitarian Meeting-Rooms, no it's not actually in the *church*, round the back down this small passage-way, through the wicket-gate, mind the step . . . oh dear, I'm afraid the lamp's broken – let's hope the old care-taker hasn't forgotten to leave the key in the thing-a-majig! Aha, here we are! I feel highly confident that those who have prevailed upon themselves to turn up will be a really keen and interested, indeed I might say *devoted* section of the socialist movement in this area – not perhaps entirely *representative* – but we couldn't really expect that, could we, with the situation . . . I mean, socialist politics these days look pretty thin and feeble when our lads at the Boer War are pouring out their hearts' blood for the cause of the cash-nexus. I predict you are going to get a fair amount of heavy questioning on *that* score tonight – but you won't mind . . . ?' And Jasus but he's not wrong! So size up the audience. Launch into it, keep it cool, keep it logical, try to anticipate all objections in the body of the discourse, so that heckling towards the end will find little to take hold of . . . There we are, forty minutes' worth: thank you very much, ladies and gentlemen . . . 'I'm sure if any member of the audience has any questions the speaker would be only too happy to . . .' Wait for it. Here it comes. Number one, from the far left. There's some-one who's been reading something starts quoting Rosa Luxemburg. Irish national aspirations, how to reconcile with socialism.

> Pat-a-cake, pat-a-cake baker's man:
> I've rolled him and wrapped him and put *him* in the pan . . .

No great difficulty so far. Number two, from towards the centre . . . 'Can the speaker explain please how an Independent Labour Party can be expected to function entirely free from all Liberal ties, when the trade union movement is presently hamstrung by the Taff Vale legal judge-ment?' That's a wee bit more complicated. I try to explain that so long as the Liberals remain confident of the Labour vote in parliament, so long will they deliberately delay any action upon Taff Vale – we are therefore dependent for our very political existence upon paying blackmail to our masters. If there's Irish in the audience, I can work a way round this one: for the Liberals are as bound to the Irish Party as Labour is to the Liberals and the answer must clearly be for the Irish voters to transfer support from the Liberal Home Rule policy to Labour and republican-ism – 'ah but, comrade, the British Labour Party is in no way republican' – so make it so, you have the numbers, you have the voice, you have the power – all you lack is the bloody will!

> I've to remember meself damn quick
> Before I call him a stupid Mick:

Watch it, Connolly, watch it, you're going over the brink:
You once start abusing them and by God, boy, you are sunk!
Nearly done, look at my watch,
Ten more minutes and my train to catch –

God, here it comes: Number three from the pig-ignorant right – 'How can you justify your pro-Boer stance?' Fairly polite – before I can answer – 'Pro-Boers is bloody murderers, my brother is shot dead these three weeks in the Argyll and Sutherland Highlanders!' Hold it – where's the chairman – this looks like a put-up job . . .! 'Treason' they shout, 'What about Ladysmith! What about Mafeking! Fucking foreigner get home to where you fucking well came from!' . . . Oh certainly not every night: not inevitable: just often enough to make me nervous as a kitten. At Oxford the undergraduates threw stones at me and drove me out. Oh I went for them and no mistake with the broken handle of the old red banner –

Four of them I laid out flat
But they knocked off me my one good hat –
So much is the worth of a university education
To men who defend the backbone of the great British nation . . .

And oh such confusion about what the British nation even *is*! The Irish Socialist Republican Party must set up branches in Britain: thank God I am not altogether without success at this . . . so far so good. But wherever and upon what issue, it always boils down to the same old perennial – half-a-loaf-or-no-bread – Aye, it's not only the whole loaf we are demanding but the entire baker's shop! And I warn you it is more than stones will be fired at you to keep you out of it – they'll throw *loaves*! You don't eat them . . . throw them back!

And every day upon the train or in the station waiting-room
I sit huddled in my overcoat and I write my letters home . . .
Money and love for my family, that comes first:
For the party, instructions – and money – and every week such a
    burst
Of exhortation and suspicion and mistrust,
That when I look over what I've written I am forced
To believe that they will believe that I have taken leave
Of the balance of my intellect:
But what else can they expect?
They barely ever write to me to tell me what they are about –
How the devil am I to know if I do not find out?

For example . . . To Tom Lyng: 'Dear Comrade, The meetings here are awful, the smallest I have had in England. I don't much like the idea you put forward in your last letter about establishing a *drinking club* in the party headquarters . . . Please thank O'Brien for being so helpful to me yet again in the matter of money and clothes: I felt so ashamed about having to ask him, it nearly made me resolve never to go back to Dublin again . . . I am still left completely in the dark about the arrangements for printing the newspaper. Please write to me and tell me these things: it's most important . . . The enclosed article about Kautsky and his relevance to the Home Rule Party, will you print it, if you can, in the next number of *The Workers' Republic*? . . . Ah, yes, thank God, some good news! It is truly splendid to hear that the Union of United Labourers have elected me in my absence to the Dublin Trades Council. Even more that they should be pressing for my personal nomination as a candidate for the city elections. I will certainly accept!' And I did . . .

SCENE 6

Enter GRABITALL.

Connolly Three candidates for socialism and against Home Rule
      We put into the field: and truth to tell
      My hopes once more were high – the more so, I daresay,
      That I myself in person stood forward to display
      The full extremity of our doctrine – take or leave.
Grabitall They left.
Connolly I now am told that many would have voted for us if only they
      could believe
      That others would as well.
      But very few were brave enough to tell
      Each other this, so therefore they all thought
      The party of their choice had no support:
      Therefore they placed their votes elsewhere . . .
Grabitall Here is one reason why they did not dare.

Enter a PRIEST. (EMPLOYERS *behind him.*)

Priest My dear children, as your parish priest, I inform you that James Connolly is an atheist: and of course, a baptised catholic who willingly and wittingly votes for a known exposed atheist renders himself liable to automatic excommunication.
1st Employer Very much obliged to you, Father . . .
3rd Employer That covers it very nicely . . .

Exeunt GRABITALL, EMPLOYERS *and* PRIEST.

Connolly Four hundred and thirty-one votes may appear to be very small:
      In the circumstances, 'tis a wonder I got any at all . . .

SCENE 7

Connolly Nothing for it: turn my back,
Divert across the ocean my zig-zag lonely track –
Drive my furrow to America, the soil there at least is thick:
And that which can be planted may well contrive to grow.
Without I try it out I cannot know.
I go.

The invitation came from Daniel De Leon and the American Socialist Labour Party. They are anxious to have an Irish lecturer to speak
principally to audiences of working-class emigrants: and to convince
them that the national independence of Ireland is better served by socialism than by the Home Rule nationalist cliques, which already control
large areas of industrial America. Tammany Hall, in fact. Gangsters.
Catholicism and corrupt patronage. Well, there's one thing about
America – whatever your politics, they are stark mad about public lectures!

Enter an American CHORUS-LINE (*men in bow-ties and flat straw hats, with
canes: girls in fishnet tights with bunches of feathers on their buttocks: one
man representing a* RAILWAY-CONDUCTOR *with a peaked cap, a whistle to
blow, and a flag.*) *They dance a routine in the manner of a travelling train,
stopping between the stanzas of the song.* CONNOLLY, *with a battered suit-
case and his lecture notes, trots along with the dancers, miming speeches at
each pause: gradually becoming more and more exhausted.*

Conductor (*sings*)
From New York State via Salt Lake City
To San Francisco Bay
This is no trip that a man can take
In a matter of a night and a day.
Chorus (*sings*)
Oh the wheels they spin and the train-bells ring
And the engines blow and blow
Across the plain and over the range
Six months upon the go.
Conductor (*after pause – sings*)
All aboard . . .!
To Yonkers, Tarrytown, Boston, Buffalo,
Minneapolis and St Paul:
This wandering man traversed the land
with his words like a waterfall.
Chorus (*sing*)
Oh the wheels they spin and the train-bells ring
And the engines blow and blow

> Across the plain and over the range
> Six months upon the go.

Conductor (*after pause – sings*)

> All aboard . . .!
> California where the orange groves
> Are ripened into gold
> Colorado where the miners' lives
> Are cruelly bought and sold.

Chorus (*sings*)

> On the wheels they spin and the train-bells ring
> And the engines blow and blow
> Across the plain and over the range
> Six months upon the go.

Conductor (*after pause – sings*)

> All aboard . . .!
> By dark Detroit to the eastern sea
> How the crowds come round and cheer
> Are the rebel hands that built this land
> Now ready to rebel once more?

Connolly (*breaks away from the movement and singing down front as dance goes on behind him*)

> Or the goon and the gun and the lawyer's tongue
> Are they stronger than ever before?
> There is nothing I can do but tell it true
> And hope that someone will hear.

Taken me half a year – I've travelled six thousand miles – and thank God, that wraps it up . . .

The CHORUS *now dances undulating as it might be ship at sea –* CONNOLLY *at the rear waves good-bye to the USA . . .*

Chorus (*sings*)

> Oh the screws they spin and the ship-bells ring
> And the ocean gales do blow
> Astride the tide to the Irish side
> Now homeward I must go . . .

Connolly All that I earned I sent forward before me – so much for Lillie and the children – so much for the newspaper – so much for the general funds of the Party. It will have been well spent.

SCENE 8

Enter O'BRIEN, THE LYNGS, STEWART, *and* BRADSHAWE. *They sit as for a committee meeting: then seeing* CONNOLLY, *they stand and welcome him with a song.*

ISRP (*sings*)

>Here's a welcome to Old Jim
>Far and wide he had to roam
>Oh we missed him when he was gone
>And we're glad to have him home.

>Oh we're glad to have him home
>There is so much work to be done
>And the only man to do it
>Is the noble hero Jim!

>Notwithstanding we are socialists
>And we work all as a team –
>The success of such a party
>Cannot depend upon one man.

>Jim is useful, that's well known
>And we're glad to have him home:
>But we got on very nicely thank you
>All upon our own . . .

Connolly Something's gone wrong. No clue to it in your letters. Tell me.

O'Brien No no, Jim, there's nothing . . .

Jack Lyng (*after a pause*) The Municipal Elections.

Stewart We had to get going with the arrangements on our own.

Tom Lyng We thought we should make a change.

O'Brien We lost heavily last year at Wood Quay.

Connolly Where myself was the candidate.

Stewart We should select a new ward to put up our candidate this time.

Connolly Select a new candidate . . . ?

Tom Lyng Now we didn't say that.

Jack Lyng Tom, you're handling this all wrong. Jim, listen to me, there was never a suggestion whatever that you as candidate should be replaced! But the electorate at Wood Quay –

Stewart Will have nothing to do with us.

Connolly So you suggest we shift our ground? Altogether a novel political principle – the nomadic conception. Very well then: where?

Stewart (*after a pause*) We thought maybe Ringsend.

Another pause. CONNOLLY *gets up and walks away from them, thinking. While his back is turned,* TOM LYNG *does something with a lemonade bottle from which* BRADSHAWE *has been taking refreshment.* STEWART *watches this by-play and he and* TOM LYNG *wink at one another.* CONNOLLY *suddenly turns round on them.*

Connolly Ah! Good! Ringsend. I wonder why?

Tom Lyng There's a good deal of support there –

Connolly There certainly wasn't before I went to America.

Stewart We're after selling a crowd of copies of the newspaper down there –

Connolly And how many is a crowd?

Stewart Harry Brady lets us hawk them to the customers in his bar on a Friday night – I can get rid of a dozen a week there: now I think we should try to be building on that.

Connolly Build votes on twelve copies flogged to drunks who can hardly read? You're out of your mind. Wood Quay or nowhere.

Stewart Look, the publicans and the slum-owners have come together with the clergy to put a very black name upon socialism in Wood Quay. Haven't they threatened to raise up the rents of the tenants if our vote is increased?

Jack Lyng Jim, it's a matter of tactics – we must move into a district where we're not already known –

Connolly Ha, yes, not known? I thought you told me the Ringsend boozers were flooded out with our newspaper?

Stewart There have been no articles in the paper lately attacking the sellers of drink. So long as we can contrive not to antagonise Harry Brady with the class of manifesto you put out last year in Wood Quay, I would imagine that we could have the freedom of his bar –

Connolly Just what in the name of God have you been printing in that paper? Will ye give me at once a copy of the latest edition!

O'BRIEN *hands him a newspaper.*

I read this one in Detroit, six weeks ago. I said the latest –

O'Brien The fact is, that paper there is the last one to come off the press. The fact is, the fact of the matter, there's been a proper financial fuck-up.

Bradshawe (*who has suddenly got drunk*) Fuck-up, says your man. You can't *get* a fucken paper without ye first get your paper to print it on – right? So the stationers won't sell us the fucken paper, nor yet ink. These brainless fucken gawms here, Jim, d'ye realize what they've gone and done? They've put the fucken printing-press – *our* press, belongs to *us* – they've put the fucker into hock to pay the bills of the paper-merchants . . . and yet still the bills aren't paid . . . If I didn't know that I'd never been anything else than a totallyteetotaller . . . I would tell youse stupid bastards that I had got meself fucken drunk . . .

Connolly You had better go home.

BRADSHAWE *staggers out.*

What kind of game have you been playing with this – member?

Tom Lyng Now look, Jim, 'twas no more than a harmless prank of a joke –

Stewart Sick to death of his crawthumping about the evils of drink, that's all . . . A lad that can't tell gin from fizzy lemonade ought not to be in bloody politics.

Connolly (*picks up the lemonade bottle*) I suppose this belongs to Harry Brady.

Stewart Indeed it doesn't – it belongs to us. And there's a deposit on that bottle – you don't just throw it away!

Connolly Deposit? Belongs to us?

Tom Lyng In view of the lack of interest you showed in your letters when I put the project forward, we were compelled to take a decision in response to the situation. Quite normal in societies and clubs of any sort to apply for a beer-and-spirits licence: I mean, for heaven's sake, man, we haven't opened a *saloon* – there's a small cupboard in the back office and we buy the stuff outside and bring it in by the crate.

Connolly Who buys it?

Stewart I do.

Connolly Who from?

Stewart All sorts of places.

Connolly Harry Brady?

Stewart Why not? If he has fair prices?

Connolly It is apparent to me he has very far from fair prices! Because, Jasus, if he had, we would not now be insolvent! And all the money that I earned, through six months in America, would not now be poured away – for what? A licensed bloody bar, a prank of a joke, and a printing-press in hock!

They all sit silent, ashamed.

I shall say and think no more of it. I hope to God you will do likewise. The election will test all. Wood Quay!

Enter GRABITALL.

Grabitall Last year James Connolly got four hundred and thirty-one votes. This year James Connolly gets two hundred and forty-three.

Exit GRABITALL. *The* ISRP MEMBERS *go out, despondent.*

SCENE 9

CONNOLLY *sits at a table and starts writing.*

Connolly James Connolly sat down
And pen and paper he took
Without a word he set to work
Writing his history book.

Enter JACK LYNG.

Jack Lyng Jim: the printers of the newspapers have not yet been paid. And we're going to lose the printing-press for good if we can't pay back the money we were loaned on it. Jim, for God's sake – leave your writing for one moment – Jim, what are we going to do?

Connolly Hold a committee-meeting.

The other members of the ISRP enter – BRADSHAWE *is now sober, and even more self-effacing than before.*

Everyone present? Right. Motion before this meeting: all money in the kitty goes direct towards the payment of outstanding debts incurred by the party-newspaper. All the money. All. Anybody second that . . . ? Oh come on: we are a revolutionary political party. Financially we're bankrupt – our organisation is in fragments – and we have nothing whatever to restore ourselves with. Except ideas. Except, comrades, the quality of our political ideas. Those ideas have been permanently expressed on the pages of our newspaper. And also, as you know, in the pages of my half-finished book *Labour in Irish History* which – as you know – has been regularly appearing as a serial in the newspaper. I have my name on the title-page: but only because it is customary. The real author of the book is the Irish Socialist Republican Party. The book, in fact is us: and if we cannot get it printed, our voice has been struck dumb. Add to that the question of reliability and trust. Are you not aware that there are literally hundreds of subscribers in America, who have paid up their money and who expect to receive their copies? Upon what else, therefore, do you suggest that we expend our resources?

O'Brien There's the rent for the committee-room.

Tom Lyng There's a whole lot of expenses that have to be settled first. Oh we've had to put out money out of our own pockets, I'd have you know! Stewart has the list.

Stewart I have here a wee chitty, every penny of it's on it. There was three-and-sixpence for the cardboard for the placards for the picket . . .

Connolly Any reason why ye shouldn't have got your old pal Harry Brady to have *given* you the bloody cardboard? Go on, read the next one.

Stewart The next item's rather large. But we held it to be justified. It's twelve shillings and eightpence – the return fare to Athlone.

Connolly And who was the excursionist?

Tom Lyng Gerry O'Malley.

Connolly Who?

Tom Lyng Ah sure you know Limping Gerry. He helped us out many's the time delivering the leaflets. Of course he's been unable to come forward openly as a member, on account of his brother being a sergeant in the constabulary – but –

Connolly If it's the Limping Gerry *I'm* thinking of, his distribution of leaflets was usually confined to leaving them in a lump in the gentlemen's, for whatever purpose. Why Athlone?

Stewart Didn't his mother want him home for Christmas, and she with a bad leg?

Connolly I thought it was himself was after breaking his leg . . . Read your list.

O'Brien I don't think there's any point. It seems to me you are determined to make mockery and scoff of every piddling bloody thing. You have a motion you have put before this committee. We spend everything we've got upon the publication of your book – or we endeavour to space it out upon regular political needs in a reasonable proportion.

Connolly I did not say *my book*! I said the newspaper . . .!

Stewart Which *is* your book – look at it! There's nothing in it but your book! For God's sake let's have a vote upon the motion of comrade Connolly . . . Those in favour . . . ? Hardly any. Those against . . . ? Aye, nearly everyone. So what are you going to do?

Connolly Resign.

Jack Lyng Man, you cannot resign!

Connolly Can I not, Jack? Why, I have.

Jack Lyng But we don't have to accept that –

Stewart I propose that this committee should accept the resignation of comrade Connolly forthwith. Those in favour . . . ? It's a majority.

The MEMBERS *get up to go*.

O'Brien (*turns back as he goes out*) Jim, when all's said – you did lose two hundred votes . . .

CONNOLLY *is left alone*.

SCENE 10

Connolly Party or no party, I must continue to publish the paper . . .
   Why, sure, they will ask me back:
   They will beg me to reconsider.

Enter LILLIE.

Lillie James, I think you will have to let them make their own mistakes for a while.

Connolly For ever! By God: I've done with them! If it had been any other issue but the question of the newspaper –

Lillie You said you would continue to publish it yourself . . . ?

Connolly How? When? Where? It isn't possible . . . Not in Dublin . . . Suppose, Scotland. Now, here's a point. There's a good man called Matheson. I talked with him in Glasgow about the opportunity to set up a Scottish equivalent to De Leon's Socialist Labour Party. He also suggested that it might not be impracticable to print *The Workers' Republic* over there – what about that? Wait a minute – Lillie – think: I could go to the Edinburgh technical college, and I could take a proper course in linotype operation! Yet – oh confound it – not even Scotland and the socialism in Scotland is capable of a wage to keep me and you and all the children . . .! I imagine, in the entire English-speaking world, De

Leon alone has a socialist party-structure sufficiently large to afford employment and security to a family man . . . and we do have to think of that.

Lillie You approve of his party?

Connolly He has a strong, theoretical, permanent nucleus of very well-disciplined members: when I was over there last year I was enormously impressed – and their newspaper – it's not just a sheet, you know – it's as large and as competently produced as *The Irish Times*! You know he as good as told me if I ever went back to New York I could have a job for the asking on the editorial board? And failing that, if I learnt the linotype yoke, why wouldn't I walk straight in and take my place at his printing-press? Why, in New York, we could live like – I was going to say *kings* but *Americans* is good enough . . .!

Lillie We?

Connolly Would you not want to come?

Lillie Well, I don't want to stay here!

Connolly Scotland first, get together with Matheson, then from there to New York, and you follow me as soon as I'm fixed! What are you laughing at?

Lillie I was just thinking, how many emigrants have set off for America, weeping and all mournful because they were compelled there by their landlords – you must be the first one to be driven out by the socialists – and you're not mournful at all!

Connolly It's not villainy, it's stupidity – oh we can laugh at it, we can plot revenge!

> Like coals of fire heaped on them head and tail
> When they receive via transatlantic mail
> The newspaper, the pamphlet – and the book
> That I myself will print in 'God's Own Country' – they will look
> At what is written on the title-page: and it will read –
> 'Jim Connolly made this – you had better pay good heed!
> It tells you all you want to know –
> It was his wife, you see, showed him the way to go . . .'
> They'll say – 'Lord save us, I remember him!
> Them Yanks is welcome to the busy Jim.
> Do you suppose we'll ever get him back?'
> Then one of them – O'Brien perhaps – will think a bit
> And slowly answer – 'I am sure of it:
> But when he comes, he will have left behind
> The American-Irish finally of one mind.
> With their political voice, their dollars, they will give aid
> No more to the Home Rule hypocrites nor yet to the futile trade
> Of worn-out Fenian terrorism: but socialist one and all
> They'll rally to the sound republican call

        To liberate our nation not alone
        From foreign despots but also from our own
        Self-generated capitalistic maggots . . .'
        Ho – coals of fire, why, dammit, we'll pile up *faggots*!
        O'Brien will cry, in midst of the roaring flame:
        'To send Jim off, indeed we were to blame;
        But how much more to blame would we now be
        If he had never travelled across the sea?'
        Irish revolution will not come
        Unless the Irish in their New World home
        Prepare it, foster it, and so send it back:
        De Leon is the key to the Dublin Castle lock,
        And the hand to force him in, to turn the protesting latch
        Is the hand of poor Jim Connolly, whom all men think has met
            his match.

Lillie Holding his wife to his heart
        Awake, alive, defiant,
        He puts forward his feet once more
        In the seven-league boots of a giant.

Enter GRABITALL *as they go out.*

Grabitall He puts forward his feet without fear .
        Good God will he never be taught
        That the world both new and old
        By no-one but me is controlled:
        And when the message comes: 'You're through!' –
        That message, little man, is meant for *you* . . .!

END OF PART THREE

Part Four: The New World 1903–1910

Act One: 'Into the Party'. James Connolly emigrates to the United States. He joins the Socialist Labor Party, led by Daniel De Leon. He is frustrated by its doctrinaire sectarianism.

List of characters:

JAMES CONNOLLY
LILLIE CONNOLLY

EUGENE DEBS

DANIEL DE LEON
MANAGER of De Leon's newspaper office
PASSANO (Branch Secretary, Socialist Labor Party)
3 Socialist Labor Party MEMBERS (Troy Branch)
Socialist Labor Party Conference CHAIRMAN

WOMAN WORKER

WILLIAM HAYWOOD
MOTHER JONES
2 MINERS

SAMUEL GOMPERS

GRABITALL
3 BOSSES
MANAGER of Insurance Company
2 DETECTIVES
3 Immigration OFFICIALS

immigrant workers, newspaper-office staff, children, shirt-factory women, newsboys, Socialist Labor Party Conference delegates, etc.

Act Two: 'Out of the Party'. James Connolly greets with enthusiasm the Industrial Workers of the World, believing them to be the great new revolutionary force. He forms the Irish Socialist Federation among immigrants to the USA. Unable to accommodate himself to De Leon's control of the Socialist Labor Party, he determines to pursue his politics elsewhere.

List of characters:
JAMES CONNOLLY
LILLIE CONNOLLY
NORA CONNOLLY (their daughter)

EUGENE DEBS

DANIEL DE LEON
3 Socialist Labor Party OFFICIALS
Socialist Labor Party COMMITTEE SECRETARY

ELIZABETH GURLEY FLYNN
Irish-American PARTY WORKER (SLP)
Industrial Workers of the World ORGANISER
2 HOBOES

RUSSIAN REVOLUTIONARY EXILE
FENIAN REVOLUTIONARY EXILE

WILLIAM HAYWOOD
MOYER
PETTIBONE
MOTHER JONES

SAMUEL GOMPERS
2 AMERICAN FEDERATION OF LABOR (AF of L) OFFICIALS
AF of L OFFICIAL (Newark)

GRABITALL
3 BOSSES
MANAGER of Sewing-Machine Company
SECRETARY of Sewing-Machine Company
SUPERVISOR of Sewing-Machine Company
Irish-American PUBLICAN
POLICE OFFICER
PEACE-OFFICER
PINKERTON DETECTIVE

2 REPORTERS
LIBRARY ASSISTANT
DOCTOR

hoboes, socialists, demonstrators, Wobblies, police, Irish-Americans, newsboys, etc.

Act Three: 'Forward to the revolution . . . ?' James Connolly, as IWW Organiser, struggles against odds in New York. He helps the presidential election campaign of Eugene Debs. He becomes a paid worker for the Socialist Party of America. He determines to go elsewhere.

List of characters:

JAMES CONNOLLY
LILLIE CONNOLLY
NORA CONNOLLY (their daughter)

EUGENE DEBS
HILLQUIT
3 MEMBERS of the Socialist Party of America

DANIEL DE LEON
Socialist Labor Party OFFICIAL

WILLIAM HAYWOOD
ELIZABETH GURLEY FLYNN
CHAIRMAN of IWW meeting (New York)
CHAIRMAN of IWW National Convention
3 DELEGATES to IWW meeting (New York)
IWW OFFICIAL

JAMES LARKIN

SAMUEL GOMPERS
AF of L OFFICIAL (Construction Union)
AF of L OFFICIAL (Teamsters Union)

GRABITALL
3 BOSSES
Irish-American PUBLICAN
CARDINAL-ARCHBISHOP of Armagh
POLICE OFFICER
HOODLUM
BUILDING FOREMAN

2 Building WORKERS
2 REPORTERS
IRISH IMMIGRANT

A letter from Ireland

unemployed, hoodlums, female garment workers, tramway workers, police, Socialist Party workers, IWW delegates, US Marines etc.

Part Four: The New World

ACT 1: Into the Party

SCENE 1

Immigrants arriving in the USA from a ship; with the Statue of Liberty, watchful police, and skyscrapers filling the background, so that little or no sky is visible. (Backcloth 6.)

The wide open spaces of America, mountain, desert and farmland, with groups of workers with red flags confronting armed posses of sheriffs' deputies, Ku Klux Klan etc. (Backcloth 7.)

Enter BOSSES: *followed by* IMMIGRANT WORKERS, *who start building furiously.*

1st Boss We're gonna build, we're gonna build,
    We're gonna build these United States – –
2nd Boss We are in business, we're gonna build,
    We're gonna scrape the skies with steel and concrete – –
3rd Boss We're gonna build, we are in business, the whole New World is filled
    With the need and the desire to climb higher higher higher
    Till we walk the highest wire – –
1st Boss The highest wire the longest drop:
    Yet at all times at the top
    There will be one man standing tall –
Bosses And he stands there for us all!
1st Boss So let's get moving. Hustle. We got construction to complete. We got millions and millions of free citizens to complete it for us: and Jesus Christ we gotta deadline!
3rd Boss So let's look at what we got. We got Irish, we got Eyetalians, we got Polacks, we got Swedes – so according to their ethnic categories, let's arrange them into gangs – and for each gang we give a flag, and the first gang to hit the roof, the flag of their national origin flies over the completed structure! Say, how's about that for an incentive – come on – you *dummkopf* immigrants – move!

Improvised race between groups of workers to see which group builds to the top first. The winners greeted with enthusiasm and their flag raised. Songs of different nations sung all together: and the workers disperse exuberantly. Enter GOMPERS. (*During this scene he is constantly distracted by the telephone, he answers briefly, issuing instructions for strikes etc . . . business to be improvised.*)

Gompers (*to audience*) Hi. Say, folks, you know me – warm-hearted, generous-natured, cordial-spirited Sam Gompers, the very essence of the schmaltzy sympathy that puts America where it is! Do you want I should level with you, do you want I should ingratiatingly make the flesh on your backbone creep? Okay: I'll give it you straight. As of right now, nineteen hundred and three, I am constitutional president of the American Federation of Labor – a trade union organiser is all – elected thereto December eighteen hundred and eighty-six having heretofore presided over the New York branch of the Cigar Makers' Union, having heretofore made cigars, in a Lower East Side sweatshop at the age of thirteen. The New World, the golden pavements, my friends, you should be so lucky! Like I told you, I pack wallop. Like I told you, the American bosses don't like my name one little bit: yet with them I can sing and dance, yeah, with these guys I can go places . . . Hey, folks, just watch 'em sweat!

Sings:

> My name is Samuel Gompers and the American labour movement
> Depends on me for all its huge advancement and improvement.

If they don't accept me then who do they accept? Saboteurs, agitators, God knows what from God knows where – let 'em figger it out and hear them settle for the roach on the kitchen floor – yeah, sure they'd rather that than a tribe of alligators in the drains.

Bosses (*sing*)
> Gompers is the boy for us, Gompers knows his onions,
> We all rely on Gompers for responsible trade unions.

Gompers (*sings*)
> If the bosses all will undertake to recognise my outfit –

Bosses The AF of L. . . .

Gompers (*sings*) I promise in return that I –

> So make it sweet for 'em, why not? Pat their backs to burp their pap up –

> I promise in return that I will never hog the market.

So let's have some lousy give-and-take around here: gentlemen, state your needs.

Bosses (*sing*)
> We must have immigrants and blacks and dirty yellow dagoes
> To hire and fire at our own desire and moderate the payroll.

Gompers (*sings*)
> And Irishmen and Eyeties too – I keep 'em where you need 'em:
> I never question what you pay or how you choose to bleed 'em.
> I keep 'em out and keep well in the loyal white-skinned Yankee
> Whom I so firmly organise, there'll be no hanky-panky!
> No wildcat strikes, no lockings-out, discreet negotiations
> Ensure your peace and quiet to build –

Bosses (*sing*)

> Cartels and combinations.
> Wages rise but prices fall, production costs are stable –
> Sam Gompers does his work for us as long as he is able.
> United Steel, the Railroad Trust, the House of Rockefeller,
> All join together hand-in-hand to fill the nation's cellar:
> A chicken hot in every pot, good news for every organ –
> And don't forget the enormous debt we owe to Pierpoint
> Morgan . . . !

Enter GRABITALL (*as J. P. Morgan*), *and takes a bow as the* BOSSES *dance a brief reprise.*

Grabitall Who controls through interlocking directorates no less than one quarter of the nation's total corporate assets! Gentlemen, lift your hats!

They all lift their hats and stand for a few seconds in silence.

Mr Gompers, in my opinion, associations of working men in restraint of lawful trade are repugnant to the constitution.

Gompers Mr Grabitall, your great trading enterprises depend on purchase of raw materials in the best possible market. So the working men you hire to process those raw materials are a raw material themselves: and they have left it up to me to determine their own market. The skill of a trained craft worker is a commodity he puts a price on: you meet the man's price, you're entitled to the merchandise. If not – –

Grabitall In the market where I deal I fix my own prices.

Gompers So we strike you and we picket you and you lock us out, why not, and then there ain't no market on God's earth for you to deal in! So what do you do then? Look, in eighteen ninety-three in the AF of L, an attempt is made already to commit the outfit to a socialist platform: we defeated that attempt. Do you want we should be so alienated our rank-and-file would try it again?

Grabitall You'd have me believe that to recognise trade unions will consolidate private enterprise?

Gompers You'd better believe it. Mister, I don't want no more than what you want: – *more: here: now!* In a free market! So meet those terms.

Sings:

> Sure we came here to make it
> We came here to make it
> We came here to make it
> To make it to the top!

Grabitall (*sings*)

> If I don't cut your throat
> If I don't cut your throat
> If I don't cut your throat
> Then my throat's gonna be cut!

Bosses (*sing*)

   So I jump on your back
   So you jump on my back
   And I jump on your back
   We're all of us gonna be rich!

Gompers

   We call it pioneering
   We call it high-frontiering]
   We call it buccanneering
   Watch me slay the son-of-a-bitch!

His telephone rings.

Yeah, Gompers here, AF of L . . . yeah . . . yeah . . . so leave it with me, I'll fix it, in the meantime tell your membership you have strike-action authorised as from Monday week.

He rings off.

That's the boilermakers' local from the Roanoke shops of the West Virginia Railroad: seems like we have a problem. Rate for the job in accordance with our agreement of June nineteen hundred and two should be as from five dollars on a pro-rata basis – management there sticks hard at four dollars fifty. Demand must be met by seven days next Monday or we yank them boilermakers out. Okay, next business?

His phone is ringing again and he picks it up and answers it. Other phones ring and BOSSES *answer them.*

1st Boss We gotta problem. There's a pile-up of stocks of winter coal in the Blue Valley Mining Company's yards has gotta be shifted by October or production comes to a standstill. And without we have in action the new locomotives – –

2nd Boss That Blue Valley coal is on order to Consolidated Edison Electric Power, New York, demand for installation of new street lighting in East Brooklyn, if not met, threatens breach of contract with city authorities. We gotta problem.

3rd Boss We got more than a problem, we gotta goddam catastrophe. There's an Attorney General's Investigatory Board looking into the New York electrical contracts division right now: and all they want to clinch their case is evidence of kickbacks on the overall Con-Ed dealings. It could affect the election!

Bosses It could affect the election, it could affect the election, it could affect the election!!

Grabitall How's the share index?

1st Boss West Virginia Railroad, down down down.

2nd Boss Consolidated Edison, down down down . . .

Grabitall Gompers, you gotta *act*!! Them West Virginian locomotives has
gotta be rolling by – –

Gompers Monday week? Five dollars. Tell you what, boss, make it easy. Call
it four seventy-three and hold over the twenty-seven.

Grabitall Hold it over until when?

Gompers Till finalised formulation of an advanced agreement next year.
Retrospective, with inflation, sure, you'll bleed, but you'll never know it.

Grabitall Four-seventy.

Gompers Seventy-three.

Grabitall Seventy-three . . .

Gompers I'll tell the boys . . . (*On the telephone*) Hello, Roanoke? We had an
answer. Four dollars seventy-three. That's ten cents a man more than
you asked me to hang out for. Yeah, sure, we're doing business . . .

Grabitall (*to* BOSSES) I want them blueprints. Now look here, you see these,
there's an expert assessment here of a total re-run of the Roanoke shop-
layout – conveyor belts, mass production, every part of the locomotive
fixed into position by one man after another who need no special skill
beyond the elemental ability to slot a peg into a hole as the fabric is rolled
in front of 'em. Replace fifty bone-idle boilermakers with three hundred
Polack woodchoppers who never saw a steam engine in their lives before,
production of locomotives goes up five hundred per cent, the payroll is
cut by sixty per cent, and the grip of the goddam union is shaken off for
for ever. Don't you see, there ain't no stopping us!

They run out cheering.

Gompers So don't think I don't know what these guys are cooking up for me.
The logical conclusion of industrial mass production is the mass-basis
industrial union. I'm allergic. My unions are of craftsmen to protect only
their own craft, because, tell me, what does a man honour more than the
skill of his own hands? What else does he have that should make him a
man? Let them bring in their conveyor belts. Five hundred Polack
woodchoppers – oh I read that bastard's mind but good – but between
'em they'll produce no boilers unless there's one boilermaker on the job
to tell 'em how to do it. And by me that guy's protected! I yank him
outa the plant: the entire line runs into the ground. That one guy, an
employee, is the king of his production-line: pumpkin-pie and kraut-
and-wieners his goddam bosses'll have to feed him if they want to keep
him crowned for them. And Sam Gompers sees they do. That one guy,
in an AF of L Union, keeps all four hundred and forty-nine alongside
of him in employment – in good wages – so for what do they need a
union? It's logical, it's practical, it's American, it's democratic – –

He sings:

> I really cannot understand how anyone can imagine
> How anything is wrong at all with such a useful system?

Yet here they are, the theorists, the left-wing agitators,
Who do their best from east to west to undermine my status!

SCENE 2

Enter DEBS *and* DE LEON, *with placards indicative of their respective parties.*

Gompers Socialism . . . ! Thank God there's two of 'em. Thank God they don't agree. Thank God they hate each other's guts. Eugene Debs – the Socialist Party of America – rabble-rousers and roused rabble, cornfed mid-west revivalism mixed in with smoking axle-grease! Here's a slob that believed all the slobs should go together, an industrial union of every man in the railroad industry no less – 'cepting of course the niggers, not even Debs got room for them – forms his own national union, cuts right across the separate trades in the AF of L, and pulls 'em all out on strike in eighteen hundred and ninety-four: for a general national wage-hike for every railroadman in the land? Get wise. They struck in *sympathy*: for the men who built the Pullman cars their hearts bled and they struck. And they *were* struck – weren't they, Debs? The US Army, horse and foot, came down on Chicago like the locusts came on Egypt –

Debs Yes sir, that strike was broke. And we would not have been broke had the AF of L at the moment of need stood fast by our right hand and – –

Gompers Debs, don't talk to me. Go talk to Dan De Leon.

De Leon Why send him to talk to me? He talked to me often before, he could have learned his lesson before. He could have learned his lesson from me that Sam Gompers is no lost soul to be driven to remorse and penitence by appealing to his past transgressions: but a live and active enemy of the American working class: who deliberately set out to destroy the Railway Union in alliance with the federal army.

Gompers What he means, folks, is just this, that his Socialist Labor Party exists for one purpose – to establish a set of unions devoted to alien ideology and subvert the American working man from his natural way of life.

De Leon *My* unions, the Associated Trade and Labor Alliance, are informed at all stages by the scientific doctrine of the properly-constituted political party, measured and tested against the yardstick of informed international socialist opinion.

Gompers For *your* party, Eugene Debs, they got no better word than a pack of kangaroos.

De Leon *My* phrase, Brother Gompers –

Gompers Why not mine? They jump here, they jump there, among the AFL, among the Democrats, among the nigra-hating rednecks of the Deep South even: Debs, go take a jump right outta my yard!

De Leon And consider, Debs, before you do, just who is going to give the orders to the United States Cavalry the next time you jump so high.

Debs The only ones who should ever give orders to the United States Cavalry are the people of the United States for the furtherance and defence of their democratic rights. I am for socialism because I am for humanity. The time has come to regenerate society – I believe we are on the eve of a universal change! Comrade De Leon: so long as your Associated Trade and Labor Alliance remains unable to extend its membership beyond the bounds of last week's shipment of bigoted Silesian sectarian conspirators, you will stay as you ever have been, way outside the mainstream of the drive of this great nation towards the promised land of social justice!

Exit.

Gompers Yeah . . . he said the mainstream. Come on, Dan, tell the world that you and only you can diagnose the course of *all* streams, main and tributary.

De Leon The mainstream, of course, is the Socialist Labor Party because only the Socialist Labor Party is directly the product of the American section of the First Socialist International. I won't waste words on Gompers. In due course the development of the Associated Trade and Labor Alliance will overtake and break his collaborationist union-structure. As for Debs, he talks big: and his party membership is no doubt big. But do you know I don't believe you could find one single member of that opportunist organisation to talk the same way he talks? Thousands and thousands of dedicated worthy souls: the tower of Babel will be their monument. Now in *my* party, there is discipline, lectures, discussions, correctly-organised public activity: and the central organ of the party, my newspaper, *The Weekly People*, is the corner-stone of that activity.

Gompers (*singing*)

> Yeah, newspapers, any mug can read and write
> Let anyone who wants to, set his notions up in type.
> But it ain't no editorials of resounding high desire
> In the end will fire the flame upon the pyramids of power –
> No, Sam Gompers has a trickier way to go:
> When the working class knows nuth'n, boys, there's nuth'n for
>   them to know –

Know-nuth'n's where they were, know-nuth'n is where they will be, even *after* they read my newspaper: so to find out who they are, who to tell them but Sam Gompers? – Sam Gompers indispensable, Sam Gompers can never be toppled. Watch it.

Exit GOMPERS.

SCENE 3

De Leon We cannot afford to have the revolution conducted by amateurs. Where is Mr Lyon?

The full bustle of a newspaper office surrounds him, people passing papers, delivering proofs, dictating memos etc. The MANAGER *comes for orders.*

Frank, I want an article on the front page, if you please, condemning yet again the tendency of those ex-party members who split away from us in ninety-nine and allied themselves with Eugene Debs.

Manager Mr De Leon, you said all that in your article last month –

De Leon It has to be said again, Frank, if only to convince our readership that the retrograde anti-party internal conspiracy of eighteen ninety-nine is still alive in Debs's ranks and seeks every possible opportunity of re-infiltrating the SLP!

Manager Yessir, Mr De Leon, will you write it yourself?

De Leon Of course, I'll go right in, set to work on it now.

Manager Rabinovitch! Goddammit, man, will you hold the front page – Mr De Leon has decided to write a new leading article . . .

The general bustle of the office continues. DE LEON *retires.* CONNOLLY *enters, with his emigrant's luggage.*

Connolly (*sings*)

> With a song upon me lips and a pack upon me back
> I have travelled o'er the ocean upon me weary track.
> From the coast of Erin's isle to the harbour of New York
> Rambling Pat across the world comes looking out for work!

(*speaks*)

> And both me eyes opened wide with a round regard for opportunity
> I fetch the ferrule of me wee stick to the Socialist Labor Party!
> Not of course for the first time I've been in front of this door:
> Indeed, to tell the truth of it, I was here just last year.
> And every year there are men leave Ireland by the thousand and the thousand score.
> Driven out by their landlords, driven out by the police,
> Driven out very simply only because they are so poor
> Sure it's easy enough to tell that I too at the root of it am but one of these:
> I wonder could you also tell that in my case there is something more . . . ?

For am I not the man who created in Dublin the Irish Socialist Republican Party; devised, edited and personally sold the party newspaper *The Workers' Republic*; and in the year nineteen hundred sent no less than two delegates to the International Socialist Congress at Paris – and all this upon the quivering bog-rotten resources of the pre-industrial Irish peasant economy – what can I not do for the movement in *this* country – what can I not do in this newspaper? Hardly a job in these offices I will not be able to fill! And for party-work at last within a truly well-organised group – oh the ugly duckling indeed has left his puddle and found blue water! Hello – Frank . . . !

Manager (*rushes past and bumps into* CONNOLLY) What the hell are you doin' here, mac! You're in the way, get outta the way, we gotta deadline to beat!

Connolly But Frank, Frank Lyon, you know me –

Manager (*talks across* CONNOLLY'*s stammer*) Say, do I know you? Why, sure, Jim Connolly – Jim Connolly from Dublin, Ireland. Am I right? Glad to see ya again, Jim, how long will ya be in New York, say we oughta meet up some time, have a drink, swop some yarns, I got business just this moment . . .

Connolly Look, Frank: I want a job. I've come back to New York on a – yes, well – on a permanent basis. D'you suppose you could find me –

Manager Job? What sorta job? Oh no, Rabinovitch, no – willya tell the cartoonist Pierpoint Morgan as an octopus was in Debs's paper last week – the Kangaroos of the SPA are the assignment he was given – Godsake, he's a goddam artist, let him show some creativity!

Connolly I am a qualified linotype operative, Heriot Watt College, Edinburgh, and I hoped – –

Manager You're a qualified whatsit? Say, we printed the posters for your lectures last year, you were billed as an unskilled labourer: what gives, boy, you trying to con me?

Connolly Between last year and this I have qualified as a – –

Manager Okay so you qualified. You gotta union card?

Connolly Naturally not yet, but I've no doubt I could – –

Manager AF of L closed shop in this business. No union card, no job.

Gompers (*re-enters briefly*) That's right, that's how it goes . . . yeah . . .

Connolly I see. Would there be perhaps a chance in the editorial department?

Manager You wanna write for the paper? Go talk to Dan De Leon – Christ, I only *produce* his goddam organ, what else? – will ya do me a favour, will ya let these presses roll? Rabinovitch, I want them proof-sheets!

Exit MANAGER. CONNOLLY, *disconsolate, goes towards* DE LEON *who is at his desk, writing.*

De Leon Comrade Connolly, well, well, well, this is a surprise. Oh you have all your baggage, I see, maybe not after all so much of a surprise. I didn't imagine it would be long possible for a young man of your ambition to rusticate in Dublin, Ireland. So you have come around at last to the correct point of view. The New World, comrade, the massive industry, the teeming population, the ferment of constant social mobility – only here can mankind after centuries lay hold of his ultimate noble destiny. You will settle in New York?

Connolly I was enquiring about a job on *The Weekly People* . . . as a linotype operator, but . . .

De Leon Ah – you should see my manager about that. Frank Lyon, I think you know him – ?

Connolly Yes. Er – on the editorial department –

De Leon Well, naturally, any article you care to write upon political or economic matters will be seriously considered for publication in the newspaper. But you will first of course have applied for membership of your local branch of the SLP, and then anything you put your pen to can be checked out with the membership there before you submit it: and errors of political emphasis eliminated and corrected. I wonder what will be your local branch . . . where are you staying?

Connolly (*very cast down*) I . . . er . . . I imagine, to begin with, I won't actually be in New York. I have cousins up the Hudson River, in the town of Troy, I can stay with them.

De Leon Troy. Yes indeed, we have a flourishing branch in Troy. Let me know how you get on there – I'm sure that in a year or two we shall be hearing your name quite frequently in the reports of our party activities . . .

Connolly (*almost with violence*) Comrade De Leon, I do think I am capable, you know, of being very useful to you on this newspaper!

De Leon Comrade Connolly, we need men who have thoroughly mastered the essential idea of the identity of America, and the leading place this country holds in the future of world socialism. You can get that in Troy quite as well as anywhere else.

Connolly But when I was here last year –

De Leon You lectured for me very competently upon conditions in Ireland. Yes. And it was certainly of advantage for us to show the American-Irish that an unskilled Dublin labourer could be as keenly imbued as any night-school graduate with the elements of scientific socialism. But now you are settled here for good, as you tell me, the task before you is – –

Connolly Can I scotch once and for all this unskilled labourer business. I have been a professional political organiser since eighteen hundred and ninety-six, and –

De Leon Didn't I hear you say something about linotype-operating? Are we not a little inconsistent?

Connolly Comrade De Leon, is not your manager maybe not a little inconsistent? He told me I would need a union card from the AF of L.

De Leon Correct.

Connolly You recognise the AF of L? But in the meantime your own trade union – –

De Leon The Associated Trade and Labor Alliance. Yes.

Connolly You tell me it is not recognised in your own publishing house, Comrade De Leon!

De Leon Are we to close down because Brother Gompers blacks our product? Is our analytical voice throughout the land to be muffled because an enthusiastic young man from a pre-industrial economy prefers impracticable idealism to the hard struggle of political tactic? Enough of this foolishness, my good friend: go to Troy: learn your business.

CONNOLLY *makes as though to go.*

Oh comrade, just one moment. The Irish Socialist Republican Party has collapsed in disorder, has it not, despite all your professional organising since eighteen ninety-six?

Connolly There were reasons for that collapse. We have no more than the very beginnings of a revolutionary proletariat – we – –

De Leon You were requested to resign after a premature attempt to enter local electoral politics. I suspect you have a tendency to be premature in many matters. The secretary of the Troy Branch of the Socialist Labor Party, Comrade Passano, is a very careful man and very precise as to his theory. When you get to know him I suggest you follow his example as accurately as you can. Good morning, comrade. Glad to have met you again.

Exit DE LEON.

SCENE 4

The stage fills with children running backwards and forwards with parcels of linen products – an urgent chorus of 'Collars and cuffs, dollars and cents, cents and dollars, cuffs and collars, call it Troy, call it Arrow, call it Arrow, call it shirt . . .'

Connolly Troy. My cousins are glad to see me: they go so far as find a house for me to rent so my wife and my six children can come over from Ireland just as soon as I'm settled. So how do I get settled? I told them I would be working for De Leon's paper, and I'm not. I need an opening for a man with no recognisable skill: but a certain facility at putting people's backs up . . . door-to-door commission work, the all-American answer . . . the Metropolitan Life Insurance Company: here they are.

Enter insurance company MANAGER.

I want a job.

Manager Experience?

Connolly No. I was for a while a class of a pedlar in Dublin . . .

Manager No experience. So what? You're a human being. What better experience can you have? So here's a list of our customers between Tenth Street and Twenty-fifth, they pay twenty cents a week for accident/disability/funeral insurance: and it's up to you to collect it. You get seven cents for every dollar you pull in. If you want to increase your commission, you increase your list of customers. How you do it is your business. But if they don't pay, you don't get paid: get it? Okay.

Connolly Well, here I am on Eleventh Street: I suppose these are all my customers.

Manager So right away get into it. Disintegrate the competition. Get your percentage off the ground.

Connolly It's not very promising. Who are all these wee children tearing back and forwards with parcels of linen? Is there a first communion, or what – ?

Manager Company runners for the Arrow shirt factory. It's a company town this. Call it Troy, call it Arrow, call it Arrow, call it shirt –

Connolly Call it shirt, call it sweatshop . . .

Manager Call it what? It's good business. Why friend, there's hardly a human being in this town over the age of five unemployed. It's the other side of Main Street you get the bad influence.

Connolly Eh?

Manager An outfit of socialists in a boarded-up store front. Beats me the cops haven't raided the joint. Keep a tight hold on your bankroll if you find yourself in that area. Okay, friend, get to it. . . .

Exit.

Connolly So the boarded-up store front was the first place I went.

I was known to the SLP here. My reputation a little bent,
I discovered, by my being Irish. Dan De Leon, it appeared,
Had conveyed a general aroma that all born catholics were men
to be feared:
And the work in the party that they gave me was in accordance
somewhat slow.
Quite a contrast with the speed at which my two feet had to go
In frantic search for the daily dollars for the Metropolitan Life
And my own meagre seven per cent for myself and my house and
my wife . . .
My list is long and I am not strong
And I cannot but think there is something very wrong
When twenty cents a week to ensure a poor man his grave
Cuts the heart out of his body even while he is still alive.

So let's have a look at it. Number three five three eight Fifteenth Street, here we are, overflowing dustbins on the steps of the porch, overflowing children in and out of the dustbins, a dog, goddammit – get out of it – ow! Ah you wouldn't ever think I'd ever left Dublin. Oh these staircases. Knock knock. He's not on my list: but I'll give him a try. Good morning, sir, I represent the Metropolitan Life – I wonder if I could induce you to buy some insurance . . .

Customer And I wonder if I could induce you, Comrade Connolly, to take some of these copies of *The Weekly People* on your rounds?

Connolly If I'd known it was you, comrade, I wouldn't have bothered you. If you want any insurance, sure you can get it from me at the party offices. In fact I do sell the newspaper to half-a-dozen of my customers: if I need more I'll let you know.

Customer Tell me, the insurance business: is good these days: or slow?

Connolly Slow.

Customer I think slower than the production at the shirt factory, yes? Did you hear, they have this speed-up?

Connolly Heavy?

Customer Is two hundredweight extra work for every operative: no wage increase. There is talk even of a strike. Now here is a question of interest for both of us. I am a member of the AF of L shirt-makers' local. Have to be, is all there is! Is either now strike or lockout, I don't know which. What now will be done by our Socialist Labor Party?

Connolly Did you talk to Passano about it?

Customer Ach, Passano. All he says is: 'What for the hell you in an AFL union, comrade? The party has its own union.' I tell him, 'Not in Troy, not the Arrow plant, so what to do?' I tell him, 'Give me literature from the party in support of this strike, I will distribute in our local, maybe the strike or lockout will then from the start become a move towards socialism, revolution: solidarity!' He tell me nonsense.

Connolly Nonsense? What do you mean, nonsense?

Customer He tell me to demand better wages for increased production is no more than to put up prices so we are all where we were before. If the union call a strike, then I too must go on strike, but I must not trouble myself to instigate such action, no: nor yet expect the party to concern itself in any way. I ask you, Comrade Connolly, do you consider this good sense?

Connolly Dear God, this is worse than nonsense. Did he justify it?

Customer Passano? He said: is correct doctrine. He said to read weekly *The Weekly People*. I said not only do I read but I sell the damned paper. Where, I said, in all this paper do you find it is good socialism to keep the proletariat ignorant of the strength of their own struggle? *Teufelsdreck*, is a branch secretary, tells me nothing but nonsense.

Connolly We could bring it up at the branch meeting, I suppose. But Passano will – –

Customer Will fuck about with his agenda: it will never be discussed. Now I am not so good with the English, *nicht wahr*? But for you, you could do it, you could write –

Connolly I could write to the paper and have the whole thing put out in public. Why wouldn't I? I will –

Exeunt.

SCENE 5

Enter GOMPERS.

Gompers Sure a letter to the party, what harm can a man do?
United we rise, divided we fall, that's all –

If you hadn'ta wanted to splash your vest, you shouldn'ta pissed
so close to the wall!

Exit GOMPERS. *Enter* DE LEON *with a letter: and his newspaper* MANAGER.

De Leon The single-handed creation out of nothing of the foremost revolutionary party in this great country, of the only revolutionary party in
this entire hemisphere: first the master, then the disciples, then the
completely informed and corrected nucleus of activists and agitators:
and finally, the masses, in control of their own destiny. There is a flaw
in it, what's the flaw? I will tell you: the very make-up of the masses
themselves upon the moment of their arrival: they unwittingly succumb
to the anarchic laissez-faire of the American way of life, within the very
context of the socialist theory itself. Comrade Connolly has taken it upon
himself to write this letter to *The Weekly People*. He criticises the official
stance of the Socialist Labor Party upon wages, upon unionisation, upon
marriage, upon religion, upon God knows what. I have asked the secre-
tayy of the Troy branch of the party to call in and have a word about it
next time he was in New York. In the meanwhile, Frank, we will publish
this letter – without amendment. It does come from a paid-up member:
and by open controversy alone can such gross errors be corrected. Go
see if Passano's here . . . Fragmentism, economicism: this fool could
split the party just like it was split before! My God I thought we'd
cleaned that mess for good and all . . .

MANAGER *goes off and brings in* PASSANO.

Comrade Passano. Very glad you could find the time. Did Comrade
Connolly tell you he was preparing this effusion?

Passano No, comrade De Leon, he didn't . . . So what do we do with him?
Expel him?

De Leon Dear me, no: no no no. We must make a strong attempt to put him
back on the right path.

Passano Sure, sure, I do appreciate he challenges the very leadership of the
party with his – –

De Leon Not so much the leadership – the entire *structure* he calls in question!
From his experience of the potato-trade in Ireland, he comes over here
to lecture us! Of course he's out for nothing but his own personal
publicity. Do you hear how he concludes his letter? 'I hold that mine
is the correct SLP doctrine. Now will someone please tread on the tail
of my coat!'

Manager The son-of-a-bitch is flippant.

De Leon But self-assertive. Oh yes. Comrade Passano: you make sure you
keep your eye on him in your branch. The letter in the newspaper will
be taken care of in the newspaper.

Passano Yessir, Mr De Leon, thank you, sir: I'll do just that. . . .

Exit PASSANO.

De Leon Tread on the tail of his coat . . . ! Oh yes, what he asks for, he will certainly get. But upon our terms, not his.

Exeunt.

SCENE 6

Enter CONNOLLY, *some Troy* SLP MEMBERS, *some* WORKING WOMEN.

Connolly If we're not going to do anything, then nothing will be done. My opinion, it's high time we stopped confounding ourselves with theory and took a long strong look at what's happening in this town.

1st Member (*Connolly's customer from Scene 4*) I ask please for you comrades to take your noses from *The Weekly People*: we have a branch meeting in ten minutes and the agenda is about what? About speed-up, about strike? About the shirt-collar trust conspiracy that puts all Troy upon the bread-line? If not, I say why not?

2nd Member Don't yell at me. There's one helluva shellacking right on the front page from Comrade De Leon about that damnfool letter you wrote – Connolly, I'm talking to you! You out to make the name of the Troy branch stink from one end of the party to the other – or what –

Connolly Comrade, these young ladies here have *not* read *The Weekly People*: they have come to our committee-rooms to interest a united and intelligent group of political activists in *their* problem, their problem alone. Do we do them the courtesy to give them our full attention? Ladies?

Woman Worker (*with interjections and prompting from her friends*) Look, we ain't in no trade union: and we don't know about no politics. We're all from the Bluett-Peabody plant –

Connolly Subsidiary of Arrow Shirts, right?

Woman Worker We make the collars, see, starched collars: they put in this new starcher, works off a gasoline engine, starching and pressing like on a – like on a cable-railway, sorta . . .

1st Member Conveyor-belt technique: creates the redundancy of one-third of the women hand-starchers.

Woman Worker But this machine it don't work so good. So they cut piece-work rates by half, speed up the whole shop, give us overtime without the option: and any work on the machine that they say comes through spoiled – –

1st Member *Mein Gott* with that machine, is *all* of it spoiled!

Woman Worker If it's spoiled they take the cost of it out of our pay. And if any of us falls down for one minute on the job – –

1st Member The sister of my wife Truda herself for sneezing at her work is all, has dismissal given her yesterday! As I inform you, conspiracy: Bluett-Peabody, *mit* Arrow, *mit* one two three *vier fünf* six *sieben* – is nine altogether *fabriken* in Troy *zusammen kaput*!

3rd Member Okay okay, hold it, Hans, you're after leaving us all behind . . .

Woman Worker He means we've walked out – in nine factories, we've all walked out. We're on strike.

Connolly Deliberate pressure by nine companies to *force* them all out on strike – sure they know the AF of L has only a minute fraction of the Troy workforce properly organised: and they mean to break all hope of any further unionisation in this industry from now on! I suppose you have your demands worked out?

Woman Worker Sure thing, mister, we've worked 'em out! Say, take a look at this!

She hands CONNOLLY *a paper.*

Connolly I see. Very good indeed. And now you deserve and need the very fullest political support that the committed socialist movement can give you – and not only in Troy – now here, comrades, is surely something that the SLP with its press facilities can – –

Enter PASSANO *and some more* SLP MEMBERS.

Passano What the hell goes on round here? We gotta branch meeting, not a social. Will you get these broads outta here pronto? Don't you know that the meetings is exclusive to the membership?

1ST MEMBER *whispers in his ear.*

Oh . . . Oh yeah . . . Comrade Connolly . . . ? It figgers . . . Look, ladies, I guess there's some mistake, this ain't no meeting yet to discuss your dispute. Say, we'll take a report from the member that brought you in here, and when maybe we've considered it, there'll be some sort of action forthcoming, I can't say what. Sure we know where to get in touch with you, we'll let you know, okay, good-night . . . So let's have some order around here, this is a meeting!

Exeunt WOMEN, *dissatisfied.*

1st Member Now look, comrade: first things first. Important beyond all things we give help to the people in Troy.

3rd Member I think maybe there's a good case here for an immediate resolution. Sure to God those girls have spirit. If we don't stand up with 'em, they'll be left to the AF of L. . .

Passano First things first? On *my* agenda first things first is Comrade Connolly and his indiscipline – has he or has he not been attacking the party in public! If he has, he should be punished. But seems it ain't to be up to us to decide whether he has or he hasn't. I gotta communication here from Comrade De Leon, no less. He says, don't mess with it in Troy. Now it's ventilated in *The Weekly People*, the place to discuss it, what he calls the 'appropriate forum' is the national convention, to be held in six weeks.

Connolly And in the meantime – –

Passano In the meantime how far do you comrades want to debate the attitude to Comrade Connolly we should adopt at this convention?

1st Member Debate? Debate nothing! Circulate such debates among the wage-slaves of New York State in order to make them more prejudiced against us? Comrades, *Gott in Himmel*, be as cunning and as cute as the capitalists are: but *Sakrament*, do not confuse the true and only purpose of the struggle of the working class!

Loud expressions of approval, and disapproval for PASSANO.

Passano Okay okay okay – discussion on this matter adjourned *sine die*. So we leave it to the convention. Comrade Connolly – you'd better be there.

Exeunt all but CONNOLLY *(one or two clap him on the back as they leave), and* 3RD MEMBER, *who is Irish.*

Connolly There's a hell of a lot of work to be done. All those out on strike who aren't in the union need strike funds collected for them. Sure, I can do some of it on my insurance-company rounds – if it comes to that, those out on strike who aren't in the union are finding so much difficulty in paying their insurance, I guess it leaves me with all the time in the world. Collect funds, sell the newspaper – ugh, with my name mud in it – get out a few hand-duplicated leaflets of my own – Passano's a dead loss, the party-branch as a branch does nothing: but we have friends . . . most of them, as it happens from the Irish quarter . . .

3rd Member No comment . . .

Enter insurance MANAGER.

Manager Hey, Connolly, I want you! Look, feller, the assets of this office as of right now are frozen. So hand over your books, and your current takings – if any.

Connolly You mean – –

Manager I mean you're fired. In this situation, with half of Troy out of work, there just ain't no future here in the insurance business.

Connolly But who's to collect the subscriptions from now on?

Manager You deaf or sum'pn – no-one!

Connolly But some of these people have been paying you money for years . . .

Manager If they'd wanted to continue to be covered by our policies, they oughta had more sense than to be agitated into a strike! And who by? Don't tell me! I'm wise to you, Connolly! The Metropolitan Life Insurance Company tucks its shingle under its arm and takes the first train outta town!

Exit MANAGER.

Connolly There are times when I wonder whether
       The old practice of tar-and-feather
       Would not have its good uses elsewhere than the Far West . . .

> And any time now my family comes from Ireland – oh God,
> what to do for the best . . . ?

3rd Member Jim, get out of Troy as soon as you can, find work where you
can get it, feed your stomach for the fight – you've stirred up enough
of us here to carry on where you've left off.

Exeunt.

SCENE 7

Enter HAYWOOD.* MINERS *with placards* ('*Western Federation of Miners
on strike for 8-hour day*') *stand behind him. They all have pistols or rifles.*

Haywood (*sings*)

> Way out west there's a union built, and we built it strong and
> wild:
> The Western Federation of Miners, Goliath the giant's child,
> We got no truck with tenderfoot pussyfoots, if we're beaten we
> never will yield,
> In the town of Leadville Colorado for a year we have held the
> field –
> For a year and a day so take it away
> Big Bill Haywood is my name
> Revolution is my aim
> . . . So take it away . . .

You'd better get this and get it good, across the prairie into the mountains there ain't never no end to a strike but gunfire and bloodshed:
yeah they call in the yellow-leg horse-soldiers and they shoot us down
in the streets like dogs . . .

> In the town of Leadville Colorado we been striking for the eight-
> hour day
> We'll never sit down to starve to death but fight it every yard of
> the way
> Let 'em shoot us dead and harry us in to the bull-pen or the
> county jail
> I tell it to you and I tell it true our courage will never fail:
> A year and a day so take it away
> Big Bill Haywood is my name
> Revolution is my aim
> . . . So take it away . . .

> And take away too your AF of L setting slave against jealous
> slave:

* Haywood is a one-eyed man.

United miners stand or fall into many a lonely grave
In Salt Lake City, Coeur d'Alene, Telluride and Cripple Creek
When the bosses and the bulls come hunting blood they don't
    have far to seek:
A year and a day so take it away
Big Bill Haywood is my name
Revolution is my aim
. . . So take it away . . .

Ain't no doubt about it, the men of the West has the Easterners licked
for militance, endurance, revolutionary sure-fire grit: class-conscious?
We got noth'n in these mountains to live on but pit-props, and boy,
that's a diet sure will stiffen a man's neck!

A fair day's wage for a fair day's work? Trash, boy, take it away!
Abolition of the whole wage-system is the only game we play:
Abolition of the American boss-class, destruction of the power
    of gold:
And who's gonna help us grab this nation from the plutocratic
    hold?
For a year and a day so take it away
If we get no help we'll die where we stand
With gun in hand
. . . So take it away . . . !

1st Miner

From the coalfields of Illinois here comes old Mother Jones
To lend us the strength of her seventy-five-year-old bones.

Enter MOTHER JONES.

Mother Jones

Eugene Debs of the SPA
Is coming to help you, to help you today!
He's a-coming to Leadville on the high-noon train
To set this union on its feet again!

Haywood

Boys, give a welcome to Eugene Debs with your pistols at your
    hip –
If the Pinkerton finks and the company bulls hear that man shoot
    off his lip
There ain't no insurance outfit take a policy on Debs's life:
The dark dark nights of Colorado make a widow of a socialist
    wife!

2nd Miner

Here comes his train, hear the engine blow and blow –

1st Miner

What way will the sheriff and his deputy-killers sneak around and
try to go . . . ?

Sound of train arriving. DEBS *enters, and is immediately guarded by the*
MINERS *as armed labour detectives lurk in the shadows.*

1st Detective

Now lookit, boys, go careful, don't try nuth'n sudden and rough:
Bill Haywood and his gunmen radicals are out today to play it
tough –

2nd Detective

Bill Haywood and his gutless gunmen are bringing in too many
friends –

1st Detective

High time this subversive anti-American conspiracy was brought
to an end.
Socialist leaders outta the East, next time it'll be a Democrat!
We gotta find a way the shit leaks outta the brim of Bill
Haywood's hat,
Find a way the radical bastard's face is streaked with worse than
tears –
Put him away, put him away for years.

2nd Detective

Like for murder . . . who's he killed?

1st Detective

No-one yet, but he will . . .

The DETECTIVES *sneak back into the wings.*

Haywood Look, Gene, this miners' union gets nowhere because we've got no
ties with the rest of the national working class: the rest of the national
working class are stifled and bound by the swaddling clothes of Sam
Gompers. From coast to coast there are millions of men outside of the
corral of the AFL who want to organise but find no framework.

Debs I've come to Colorado specific to discuss just such a framework. For
the lack of it in ninety-four, the Pullman strike, we were drowned down.
I have a list here of thirty names, all of them in some way leaders of
radical groups.

Haywood That's it, that's what we want. Now if you, me, and Mother Jones
was to get them guys together, in secret to begin with, and then talk them
all together, and by God *hold* them together –

Mother Jones Hold a wildcat together with a coyote – landsakes – I mean,
this name, Daniel De Leon. De Leon for years already has his Thanks-
giving turkey plucked pulled and trussed: you think he'll let the rest of
you come into his kitchen and help him fire his stove? No sir.

Haywood Maybe no maybe yes. We got no choice but give him the choice.

We're either capitalists or revolutionists: and them capitalists are banded together like wolves in a bad winter. If wolves can do it, men can do it, and we're men, we ain't no sheep. So we put a bait out for De Leon and anyone of his views: we invite him to this conference to discuss ways and means of uniting the working people *on correct revolutionary principles*. For me there ain't no such word as *correct*: the only adjective I know about revolution is *successful* – but De Leon is De Leon and we got no choice but bring him in. Will you do that, Gene, get the invites out?

Debs I see it, I see it grow, the birth of freedom, the dawn of brotherhood, the beginning of mankind!

Haywood Sssh-ssh-ssh – we're overheard . . .

Exeunt.

SCENE 8

Enter DE LEON *and* SLP PARTY OFFICIALS, *and take their places for the convention.*

The hall fills. CONNOLLY *enters to take his modest seat.*

Connolly The convention is in session.
  The inevitable procession
  Of resolutions, amendments, determinations to retrench
  Passes over my unheeding head as I sit here upon this bench:

I'm very well aware they're coming along to me personally – item twenty-seven on this morning's agenda, 'Consideration of the conduct of Comrade J. Connolly, Troy branch, etcetera etcetera . . .' Enough by itself to put a man's concentration into a state of random flux: but there's another thing – my wife Lillie – she was supposed to be arriving at Ellis Island last week on the Cunard boat from Liverpool and I met the boat and she wasn't on it – sure the last I heard from Dublin was she'd been ill but was now better – I mean very ill – could she have had a relapse? Neither letter nor telegram . . . what's he talking about now . . . ?

De Leon (*who has been conducting the convention all this while*) We come to item twenty-seven.

Connolly and De Leon (*together*) Consideration of the conduct of Comrade J. Connolly, Troy branch, etcetera etcetera . . .

De Leon In view of the gravity of the political tasks before us . . .

De Leon and Connolly (*together*) It is not proposed to waste much time upon this trivial matter . . .

De Leon But –

Connolly and De Leon (*together*) More confusion than it's worth among the rank and file of the party has been caused by the controversy . . .

De Leon Let me briefly sum it up. Comrade Connolly in his letter to *The*

Weekly People April ninth, nineteen hundred and four, wrote as follows, 'The theory that a rise in prices – '

De Leon and Connolly (*together*) 'Always destroys the value of a rise in wages sounds very revolutionary, but it is not true . . .'

De Leon (*as if this is all part of the quote*) Of course, if it's not true, then the foundations of the party doctrine rest on a basic falsehood, and if the foundations of the – –

Connolly (*interrupts*) Comrade De Leon, I did not write *that*! I demand you make clear what you are quoting from my letter and what you add on yourself as a gloss!

Chairman (*seated next to* DE LEON) The interruption is out of order.

Connolly So the interruption and every other interruption I could offer was out of order. So he tore me shreds. So I think myself damn lucky to be let off at that. He sums up. Oh, I'm off: what the hell has happened to Lillie. . . . ?

De Leon We will proceed with item twenty-eight: the request from Comrade Haywood of the Western Federation of Miners that the Socialist Labor Party demonstrate in practical form the solidarity we have already expressed for his union's courageous struggle. I would emphasise at this point that the doors of this convention are now closed and that the subsequent business under discussion is highly confidential and not to be revealed to anyone outside the party.

Sensation. CONNOLLY, *about to leave, resumes his seat, amazed.*

Comrade Haywood's overt request contains an inner meaning known only heretofore to the members of your National Executive Committee. I will now disclose it. At a meeting held in Chicago at which I was present, at which Comrade Haywood was present, and at which Comrade Debs of the Socialist Party was also present – –

Sensation.

a manifesto was drawn up announcing the formation of a totally new labour organisation, provisionally entitled 'The Industrial Workers of the World'.

Renewed sensation.

Yes. Wait a moment. 'The working class and the employing class have nothing in common . . . between these two classes a struggle must go on until all the toilers come together on the political as well as on the industrial field and take and hold that which they produce by their labor through an economic organisation of the working class, without affiliation with any political party.' I am quoting from the provisional terms of the manifesto. You will wonder perhaps how I could have put my name to a document that denies the possibility of affiliation to any political party? Don't it leave the SLP, my friends, just a little bit in the cold? My friends, don't it leave the Socialist Party of America much more permanently frozen hard in the arctic blizzards of their own impotence? Moreover, this new body will not confine itself to existing unions. We intend to create out of it an entire syndicate of the dispossessed: to include beneath the panoply of its united national strength all those millions and millions of unorganised migrant labourers who at present are protected by no organisation, and who likewise are affected by no political doctrine, save the deeply-felt bitterness of their miserable exploitation! In the Industrial Workers of the World, the one party involved that possesses a precise doctrine will be the one and only party in the end to achieve the allegiance of this hitherto amorphous mass.

A Member Say, comrade, d'you mean you think there's a chance we can take over the whole damn thing!

DE LEON *smiles and stands silent.*

Ovation. Exeunt all save CONNOLLY.

GOMPERS *crosses over, as though eavesdropping.*

Gompers (*to audience*)

    Secret session, closed doors, windows locked and barred –
    Communication in the direction of Big Bill Haywood, the word is heard ... ?
    Haywood, Debs, De Leon, three men in a leaking tub:
    So what gives, these two wiseguy socialists get their scrawny backs a stiff rub
    From a Colorado maverick with four bull's hoofs and a blinded eye?
    Aint no kinda threat, no sweat –
    Such a miserable mean medicine-show alive on its legs yet?
    Ten years them Western miners had to lie themselves down and die ...
    Take it easy, Sam, relax, *rigor mortis* gets well set
    At its own speed and its own speed alone –
    Law of nature, no two men have the same damn marrow in their every bone.

Exit.

SCENE 9

Connolly 'The Industrial Workers of the World' ... ! 'The working class and the employing class have nothing in common' ... nothing! Every ship that comes in brings more and more to fill our ranks: I can smell it, I can feel it – oh let my family be amongst them ...

Enter IMMIGRATION OFFICIALS *and* PASSENGERS *arriving.*

1st Official Cunard passengers from Liverpool, this way now, let's have some order. D'ye hear me at the back there, if you don't speak no English don't try and speak at all, then we ain't in no danger of no misunderstanding – get that? No spikka da English, no spikka da nutt'n – okay? Fathers with families this side of the barrier, single men in the middle, women and kids on their own to the left. . . .

As the IMMIGRANTS *are processed,* LILLIE (*supposed to be with children*) *comes along the line.*

Lillie Connolly – Mrs James Connolly . . .
2nd Official Where from?
Lillie Dublin.
2nd Official Dublin Ireland? Okay. Anyone here for Connolly – Connolly from Dublin Ireland?
Connolly Connolly – yes – here – !
3rd Official (*keeps them apart*) Oh it's you, is it? Ain't I seen you here before?
Connolly I've been here every day this week –
3rd Official Yeah sure, I remember you – you said a wife and six kids – she got six kids, this man's wife?
2nd Official (*calls over the heads of the crowd*) Ain't your lucky day, mac, there's a woman here with five kids, but – –
Connolly No – wait a minute, let me past – *please!* Lillie! Lillie!
2nd Official Wait a moment, lady, I don't have your destination.
Lillie *Please!* I'm going to Troy –
2nd Official Troy Alabama, Troy Idaho, Troy Iowa, Troy Kansas, Troy Montana, Troy New York, Troy Ohio, Troy Pennsylvania, or Troy Vermont?
Lillie Troy New York – oh please, there's my husband –
2nd Official Then why can't you say so, d'ya wanna keep me here till Washington's Birthday? Okay, pass along – Next!
Connolly (*bursts past* OFFICIAL *and getting to her at last*) Lillie – ! Why, what's happened? Where's – where's Mona?
Lillie Oh, James, Mona's gone . . . The day before we were due to leave Dublin I sent her to her auntie's house to pick up some messages. She was left alone in the kitchen there. She thought she would surprise her auntie by making the tea for her. She put the kettle on, when it began to boil she tried to lift it. The handle was hot. She took a corner of her pinafore, to hold it with, you see: the other corner flew into the fire and caught alight. Every bit of her was burnt, every bit except her face, even inside of her, James, she was all burnt, she took twenty-four hours to die . . . you see, with the corner of her pinafore, she tried to hold the hot handle. That's why we couldn't come last week on the boat we said we'd come . . .

Exeunt PASSENGERS *and* OFFICIALS.

SCENE 10

Enter HAYWOOD, *to be suddenly hemmed in by* LABOUR DETECTIVES. *They have their guns out, he makes to draw his own pistol, but one of them is behind him and holds a gun in his back.*

1st Detective Haywood – !

2nd Detective Billy Boy, we got the drop on you, don't move, son, or you're blasted.

1st Detective You wanna know what it's about, Billy? You ever heard of a man called Steunenberg?

2nd Detective He was Governor of Idaho, he was in cahoots with all the mine-owners, he was an enemy of the union, and he's dead and you killed him.

1st Detective Killed him dead, Billy Boy, with a bomb: or if not you, personal; then Butch Cassidy and the Wild Bunch, they're on your payroll and you paid 'em: and for that you're gonna *fry*! Take him.

Haywood It's a frame-up!

They take him out.

NEWSBOYS *run in calling out headlines.*

Newsboys Fiendish conspiracy! Fiendish Conspiracy! – Big Bill Haywood charged with murder – Charles Moyer and George Pettibone accused with Haywood – Miners' Union linked with revolutionary bandits – death plot charges stun national labour leaders – 'It's a Frame-up' yells Haywood – Idaho lawmen reveal confession of co-conspirators – Haywood, Moyer and Pettibone for electric chair, D A urges . . . *etcetera etcetera. . . .*

Connolly (*hastily snatches a newspaper*) Frame-up, it must be a frame-up – of *course* it's a frame-up! The Pinkerton Detectives ran an *agent provocateur* into the union and had Steunenberg murdered themselves.

Enter SLP MEMBERS, *in excitement, and severally. All shouting:* '*Haywood is framed!*' '*Agent provocateur*', '*They're trying to break the union!*', *etcetera . . .*

1st Member (*to* CONNOLLY) There's an extraordinary general meeting of the New York State branches, comrade, tonight – Comrade De Leon in the chair – pass the word –

Connolly (*and others, pass the word*) Socialist Labor Party emergency meeting tonight – Comrade De Leon in the chair – all members without fail to attend if they can – Godsake, it's up to us to move three times as fast as they do!

A banner reading 'Free the Idaho Three' is brought in at the back. Amidst cheering and slogan-shouting DE LEON *takes his place in front of it. The meeting is all ready for him.*

De Leon Never in my entire life as a socialist organiser have I been confronted with such overt intimidation, with a provocation so bare-faced! 'Moyer and Haywood suspected of fiendish conspiracy'? There has indeed been a fiendish conspiracy: its aim has been two-fold – to break the miners' strike and to stultify at birth the Industrial Workers of the World! In token of which this evening I have invited on to the platform of the Socialist Labor Party none other than a man whom the capitalist enemies of our class fondly hoped would remain for ever excluded from these premises: comrades – Eugene Debs: of the Socialist Party of America!

Enter DEBS, *to vast applause.*

Comrade Debs and I have had our differences. In this emergency I prefer to sum them up thus – what he can do, I can't, and what I can do, he can't ... Comrade Debs, the floor is yours.

Debs Can do or can't – in this emergency, brothers, there's no question – the only thing we have to consider as what we *must* do: and must do it *now*! Okay, so the Idaho lawmen attempt to terrify the people with the threat of revolution – there may well be a revolution – I know that I for one will do all in my power to precipitate it!

Connolly (*jumps up in the midst of all the applause*) By direct action, Comrade Debs, and by *organisation*! I suggest at once that defence committees be formed from as wide a spectrum of workers' groups as is immediately practicable. Our own arrangements for printing and distribution of propaganda should be thrown open without restriction to the general effort – –

De Leon Yes. ...

Everyone is excited after CONNOLLY'*s outburst, though* DE LEON *is seen to be a little sceptical and calculating.*

Why not indeed? This party already, I am glad to say, has the machinery ready for precisely such a situation. Comrade Connolly, for example, I am quite certain would be capable of taking charge of all activities to secure the release of the Idaho Three in the area where he works ... Troy, Comrade Connolly?

Connolly In point of fact I shall no longer be living in Troy. Newark, New Jersey.

De Leon Then let me recommend to the party branch in Newark New Jersey that Comrade Connolly be appointed forthwith to this onerous task.

He comes down and shakes CONNOLLY *by the hand.*

My friend, you'll have a great deal of work to do, and so little time for unproductive speculation ... And that too applies to all of us – we have a revolutionary objective – if we fail to achieve it, the only possible alternative is the destruction of all socialism throughout the United States.

Debs On my way to this hall today I stopped off to visit the railroad men at the New York Central roundhouse. The news from Idaho had already reached them – I'm an old railroad man myself and, next to telegraph operators, we get hold of everything first – and already they had begun to sing. No, it wasn't exactly Puccini – but it meant what it said and it said what it meant.

He sings:

> If Moyer and Haywood die
> If Moyer and Haywood die
> Twenty million working-men
> Will know the reason why – !

General singing and the hall is emptied amidst immense excitement.
CONNOLLY *gathers* LILLIE *to his arms and supports her: they go out after the crowd.*

END OF ACT 1

ACT 2: Out of the Party

SCENE 1

Immigrants arriving in the USA from a ship; with the Statue of Liberty, watchful police, and skyscrapers filling the background, so that little or no sky is visible. (Backcloth 6.)

The wide open spaces of America, mountain, desert and farmland, with groups of workers with red flags confronting armed posses of sheriffs' deputies, Ku Klux Klan etc. (Backcloth 7.)

Enter GOMPERS.

Song 'If Moyer and Haywood die' etc chanted by crowd off.

Gompers (*sings*)
        If Moyer and Haywood die
        If Moyer and Haywood die
        Twenty million working men
        Will know the reason why . . .

    Moyer and Haywood, Moyer, Haywood, and Pettibone – born losers all three of 'em, born to squat on the hotseat for a trumped-up charge of murder in the boondocks of Idaho: which is where they're at right now and where to God I wish they'd stay! Yet hysteria we are now given, demagogic diarrhoea yet, to run around ourselves like hosepipes, tear the Idaho Pentitentiary brick-by-brick apart in the name of liberty . . . every loudmouth in the nation now restricts *my* liberty with the call for it! Only one purpose to be served by either hearing it or playing deaf: the quickest way to break the Industrial Workers of the World and the Miners' Federation and at the same time preserve the AF of L with its reputation unsmirched for the safeguarding of human rights . . . ?

While he has been talking, two of his AFL OFFICIALS *have come in and adopted obsequious postures.*

1st Official Haywood and Moyer and the third guy this Pettibone, the three of 'em is working men, and working men should be supported by an organisation of working men. Boss, I speak only as my two ears have heard, from our membership is all.

2nd Official Such membership, boss, is solid respectable American family men, pay their taxes, pay their mortgages, Sundays they go to church – hell they don't wanna be mixed up defending no dynamite-bombers alleged have slain a state governor!

Gompers *Ex*-state governor: in cahoots with the mine-owners: he *deserved* it: did they *do* it? Sure we all know the slogan of the IWW is 'the working

class and the employing class have nuth'n in common' – but assassination . . . ? Could be . . .

1st Official On the other hand, boss, could be, it is, as claimed, a frame-up . . .

Gompers Big Bill Haywood is an *anarchist* – he's a *socialist* – he's a *red* – he
is everything I *hate*! Do I have to stick my neck out and tell the world
that such a bum should be totally innocent of what I know in my heart
he would dearly love to do to *me*?

2nd Official So we hold off from the defence campaign, and we don't say
nuth'n – sealed lips?

Gompers You gotta better policy? So serve up a better policy. Meantime
Sam Gompers keeps his trap shut, but tight.

Enter ELIZABETH GURLEY FLYNN.

1st Official You got an appointment? Mr Gompers don't see nobody without
an appointment.

Flynn Mr Gompers will see me: I'm from the IWW. I came here to speak to
you about the Idaho trial.

Gompers It figgers . . .

Flynn Mr Gompers, we need you: the American working class in their hour
of national crisis need – –

GOMPERS *snaps his fingers at his* OFFICIALS *who retire.*

Gompers Little lady . . . sealed lips. Who am I to try to prejudice the course
of justice with reckless comment?

Flynn You think no reckless comment has already been made? Why, the
president himself –

Gompers Has delivered an opinion in his wiser moments he will regret. We
all know that Mr Roosevelt is the lackey hireling of the Wall Street
barons – now and then I read the newspapers, even *your* newspapers,
that surprise you? But in this office, *I'm* the president: non-political,
unaffiliated, the interests of the hard-working American wage-earner is
all. Which in my book is not compatible with the agitation of subversive
reds. On the other hand, I stand for justice . . .

Flynn *I* stand for justice and I'm a red, I'm not ashamed of it.

Gompers That at your age you should be so certain . . . ? Say, kid, do you
know what in these circles is the name we give the Industrial Workers
of the World? We call 'em Wobblies – if you like, Inexperienced Wobblies of the Wild – because you wobble: between the gun and the camp-
meeting, between Dodge City and Moscow Russia, between wanting to
build Jerusalem and not knowing how to stop yourselves falling down
with the walls of Jericho: hell, you're young and you're new and you're
not ashamed of nuth'n. Now look here, child, I'm old: and I guess I *am*
ashamed of it. I guess poor old Sam Gompers hates like hell to see three
good men walk head-high into Death Row, and just for a mess of
politics, there ain't nuth'n he can do for 'em, nuth'n . . . Kid, am I on the

way out – am I a has-been? Does Big Bill Haywood send me children, like my own daughters, to prove to me my course is run?... now wait a minute, there's no-one here, I sent Jake down to the printing-shop to see about some committee rosters, oh child, I'm telling you, you've twisted and twined Sam Gompers up and down your wide white thigh, for God's sake let him put his eyes on where his heart has already reached, put his eyes, put his poor old fingers – –

Flynn I'll break your poor old fingers off like a pair of used matchsticks.

Gompers You would?... She would... Goddammit, child, you don't believe I'd try a dirty thing like that? Okay, Wobbly, on your way. You done your good deed for the day.

She is about to go out, scornfully, but 2ND OFFICIAL *has entered and silently blocks her way.*

And now I'm gonna do mine. For Haywood and his associates, justice: nuth'n but justice! The AFL will call for it! Sam Gompers' word is gold, girl: no need to answer me – on your way.

She goes out, dumbfounded.

2nd Official Boss, do you mean to tell me...?

Gompers My friend, I had my hand around her pretty little butt and she wouldn't let it stay there! Brought the tears into my eyes.

2nd Official And for that you...?

A phone is heard ringing, off...

Gompers For that I took good care, Al, to let it stand hard in her fiery mind that the AF of L comes into this campaign nervous, undecided, without initiative, quite happy to let the Wobblies and the socialists make the running! That we got no kind of strategy – for the blood-beat of a prudish broad I personally would sell out all the deals I ever made with both Wall Street and the government! And with that she's gonna bring her friends into competition with us, in public? With all that they're three parts beaten before they've even entered the ring.

Enter 1ST OFFICIAL.

1st Official Hey, boss, on the telephone – Washington – it's the White House, no less!

Gompers I'll take it in here. For Teddy Roosevelt I should wear a tuxedo? In my shirt-sleeves! Gimme the phone.

He talks into telephone.

Gompers here, AF of L... Mr President!... Yeah... Yeah... Okay, Mr President, I read the message, sir, I read it good – how far is the present frenzy among labour organisations a genuine response to injustice in Idaho: or is it but a prelude to the same state of chaos like is happening in Russia? . . . Mr President, I read the newspapers, and I know very well that what's happening in Russia nineteen-hundred-zero-five is an overt and planned attempt to overthrow the Czarist tyranny. And for why do they overthrow it? Because a genuine response to injustice in Petrograd was met by the bloodstained Cossacks with a volley of shot, that's why! . . . Mr President, you have spoken – I read it in my newspaper, an exceedingly rash statement, sir, that prematurely assumed Haywood's guilt: and I am, as of right now, holding back my unions from a catastrophic public outburst that would make Petrograd look like popcorn! If I have to join with the IWW in alleging the Idaho trial to be an unprincipled frame-up, then American democracy will have found itself a *soviet* from which to publicise its grievances! Mr President, such bad news, sir, and for me just as much as for you. . . . Mr President, who said anything about 'convinced of their innocence'? A fair trial, with honest testimony, prove them guilty or not guilty according to the constitution. If the verdict goes against them, let the socialists carry the odium of having proclaimed it a frame-up: but if it turns out they *are* innocent, then government and responsible labour take credit together for preparing the simple justice that delivered them from their ordeal. Sure there's wide spectacular speeches Sam Gompers will spout out in this forthcoming campaign: but not one demand in them larger than what his own president has guaranteed . . . So we both know where we stand. I thank you, Mr President! I am so grateful you see it my way – and I'm honoured, sir, most honoured . . .

He rings off.

Now then: in the meantime. With their leaders in jail, the Western Federation of Miners is chopped off at the neck: and the cadaver is open for bids: so we bid. I want our people in charge of that self-styled wildcat union by the end of next month. If there's gotta be an election, then fix the election. If shotguns and hoodlums is in order, then indent for them as per the usual contractors – but just you make damn sure you don't let me hear you do it. The minute we get control we yank them mule-faced miners clear outta the IWW, horse, harness, axle and lynch-pins, and pull 'em back into the AF of L. Get it?

1st Official Got it.

Gompers So go to Colorado – don't stop by at no whore-houses – I want work, boy, I want it smart!

Exit 1ST OFFICIAL.

Al, you go to Idaho. Get an entree into the jail: and see what you can make of softening up Moyer. You gotta make him believe that if his buddy Bill Haywood hadn't a been so damnfool reckless in linking with all them socialists, then nobody woulda railroaded the poor sap the way they have.

2nd Official Guess that ain't no fairy-tale, boss: it's plain true.

Gompers Okay, so get with Moyer and tell him the plain truth. If he comes innocent out of court, I want him *my* man: no more a Wobbly! Get it?

2nd Official Got it.

Gompers Go.

Exit 2ND OFFICIAL.

Sings:

> My name is Samuel Gompers and the direction of my movement
> Is never where you think it goes but always at a tangent:
> Up the town the sun shines bright and down the town its
>   raining –
> Galoshes in my pocket-flap, I will not be complaining . . .

Exit with a little dance.

SCENE 2

A scene in the dark. Campfire. HOBOES. *Train noises in the distance.*

Hoboes (*sing*)

> When springtime has come
> O won't we have fun
> We'll git out of jail
> And we'll go on the bum –
> Hallelujah I'm a bum
> Hallelujah, bum again
> Hallelujah, give us a handout
> To revive us again . . .

Enter IWW ORGANISER.

IWW Organiser Howdy, friends – I'm half-frozen, travelled over the Sierra twelve hours through a blizzard, riding an open coal train from Sacramento – you got coffee? Trade you a can of beans for it.

1st Hobo Put your beans in the stewpan, pardner, take your whack of what's made of it.

IWW Organiser I got holes in my coat and patches in my pants but the only thing that keeps me warm is a little pink card in the heel of my sock . . . Am I talking to my friends?

2nd Hobo Boys, pull your cards out, show them to the man. Okay, mister, ride it easy, we're all IWW here. What's the news from Sacramento?

IWW Organiser From Sacramento the news is great. Money for the defence of Haywood and Moyer taken in by the bucketful. You look at the back of my card, you see I'm entitled to collect. You won't have a dollar, so gimme a quarter, you won't have a quarter, so gimme a dime –

Sings:

> If Moyer and Haywood die
> If Moyer and Haywood die
> There's twenty million working men
> Will know the reason why . . .

Rattle of money contributed.

IWW Organisers (*at all corners of the stage*) You won't have a dollar so gimme a quarter, you won't have a quarter, so gimme a dime. . . .

Song repeated and taken up all round in the dark and rattle of money.

Debs (*in the dark*) This Idaho trial is the greatest legal battle in American history. Already from trade unionists and members of socialist parties more than sixty thousand dollars have been collected to fight for the cause.

The songs and collections continue . . .

1st Reporter (*in the dark*) Protest parades held in every major city of the entire United States. In San Francisco the corrupt motives of the prosecution were laid bare by a phalanx of platform orators, addressing the largest crowd ever seen in the streets of the city.

2nd Reporter (*in the dark*) Fifty thousand men marched chanting through the streets of Boston Massachusetts.

1st Reporter Twenty thousand persons in double file paraded uptown from the Lower East Side of New York City. At Fortieth and Lexington they merged and continued to Grand Central Palace where John Chase, Morris Hillquit and Joshua Wanhope proclaimed Haywood's innocence and reiterated 'Frame-up!'

General Cries Frame-up: frame-up: frame-up!

Debs President Roosevelt has alleged that Bill Haywood before trial is already a guilty man! We protested in the strongest terms the illegality of the president's statement: he has now taken space in the newspapers to deny he ever said it! I say he thus stands pilloried before the American people! If he continues to attempt to deny it, I shall convict him with the proof! Nevertheless, his denial, hypocritical though it may be, is the first decisive victory for organised labour in the kidnapping battle of the class war in the United States –

Tremendous cheers. Continued singing.

De Leon (*in the dark*) Comrade Debs and the Socialist Party, myself and the Socialist Labor Party, William Haywood in his jail cell and the Western Federation of Miners he created are together against all odds, and against all odds we shall march forward! Comrades, give your money, without stint, for this noble struggle!

Cheers, more calls for money, more collecting, more singing.

Urgent Cries Watch it boys, it's the Pinkerton men – it's the Pinkerton men
and the Feds – get the hell outa here, scram, boys, the Feds is coming!

Police Voice (*with bullhorn*) I am declaring this meeting a prohibited assembly:
if the area is not cleared my peace officers have orders to break up the
crowd by force!

*Confusion; excitement; anger; scuffling. Then a violent charge by the
peace officers. Screams, casualties, and the stage is cleared. Lights come up.*

SCENE 3

Enter CONNOLLY.

Connolly Transported, exalted, to Newark New Jersey,
      On the hard wind of these new politics comes the Irishman
        Connolly –

I'm on the Press and Literature Committee of the New Jersey Socialist
Labor Party: I'm controlling and co-ordinating the Newark Working-
men's Defense Committee: with our sometime bitter rivals of the
American Socialist Party I am on a full dozen committees and sub-
committees for the propagation and extension of the Industrial Workers
of the World – I've got a contact-group set up to explore relations with
the Newark locals of the AFL! I've even got the use of the AF of L
union-halls to hold meetings, distribute literature, and present petitions
for the release of the Idaho Three.

LILLIE *has entered as he speaks, and stands at the other side, speaking
directly to the Audience without reference to Connolly.*

Lillie No work for him in Troy after the strike in the shirt-industry: his removal to Newark a most perilous speculation on the strength only that
he thought there were one or two in this town whom he knew who could
put the word out for him: all the weeks we have been here, nothing. He
has his politics, and in the meanwhile he trudges as always round the
'situations vacant'. It's no part of my game to sit in the kitchen and wait
for him. Sure I did that enough and to spare in the old days in Dublin:
we are here, in the New World, and the word they all tell me is 'hustle'.
So I did: and I did discover – for a woman with a needle and enough time
on her hands there is everything from ball gowns to dust-covers to be
taken in on a piecework contract and hemmed and stitched till my hot
eyeballs dissolve down the fold of my cheek. I say nothing about the
pay that's offered – measured in cents – but by the week's end it can
sometimes add up into dollars. You don't believe I tell him about it – he
sees the children at school and their food on the table, and that's enough
for him in his present state, as he organises the starving millions. But if

he doesn't get work soon at least one of the children will be forced to go out and get hold of it in his place. And if that happens he will never stand for it: I'll have no choice but to deceive him. Not hard: look at him now. He hasn't even noticed I'm here, let alone what I'm doing . . .

During the above speeches, CONNOLLY *has been engaged in a constant bustle of party activists and union organisers – messages, money, piles of pamphlets and newspapers etc.* LILLIE *has been similarly engaged receiving bundles of garments and lingerie, which she is arranging in piles and laying out her spools of thread etc. When she has done this to her satisfaction, she goes out with all her work.*

Connolly Will you look at me – I'm flat broke:

> No money in my pocket and where the hell can I get work?
> Try my luck as I did, before, with the insurance companies: no luck.
> Carried tiles up a ladder for a craftsman on a roof: no luck: I fell off.
> No union card, except the pink one in the heel of my left sock –
> And that one will feed no family: more like it will break my back . . .

A Party Worker (*Irish, comes up to him*) Jim, at the news-stand at the corner of Eighteenth Street – the feller there won't take our papers because he says that there's no demand. It's a lie.

Connolly It's a lie, sure, he's in fear of the police: don't I know the man, a sound commercial argument would convert him in two minutes. He wants a demand, so create a demand. Send six or eight of our friends to ask for the paper one after another on their way home from work this evening – and the moment the last one in the line has put the question you follow it up once more with the offer of your bundle. Won't he jump at it?

Party Worker In the nature of a bluff?

Connolly It's worked before: it'll work again . . .

PARTY WORKER *goes off, laughing, singing, 'Yes sir, that's my baby . . .'*

Sure the whole of American capitalism uses no other technique . . .

Sings:

> Yes sir that's my baby
> Yes sir, that's the way we
> Roll the dollars
> Roll the dollars
> Roll the dollars, roll. . . .

Sure the whole of American capitalism claims itself to be nothing but the promotion of the individial – we say enterprise – we say bluff – so why the devil not? Public library first of all. Take a look at the daily papers . . .

From a newspaper rack he selects a paper and pores over the columns.

'Wanted, skilled machinists for Singer Sewing-Machine plant.' So we go
forward to the bookshelves . . .

Library Assistant What's your pleasure, sir, can I help you?

Connolly I fancy, ma'am, I'd get enormous pleasure from a technical discourse
upon sewing-machine manufacture. You wouldn't, I suppose, have – –

Library Assistant Indeed we have, sir, here it is. In connection with the Singer
Company I guess? That sure is an invention put New Jersey on the map!

Connolly (*with book*) So let's hope that James Connolly finds his geographical
position as decisively determined . . . Yes . . . Yes . . . It's not impossible . . . We say enterprise . . . We say bluff . . .

*He wanders about, reading over to himself little splurges of technical
jargon, and memorising things on his fingers' ends.*

Yet I know from the start it'll never come off
If they take me for a tile-hanger who got scared at one steep roof!

He thinks for a moment, then starts rapidly to change his appearance.

Gotta go there like I look like I know everything that I do not know:
Razzmatazz, go get it, boy, go get up and go!

*He puts himself into a loud checked jacket, clip-on bow-tie, flat straw hat
etc., and caps the effect with a cigar.*

I never smoked in my life. Should I chew it? What the hell . . .

He retires as Singer's MANAGER *and* SECRETARY *enter.*

Manager You're late, doll, don't apologise, an apology's a sign of weakness,
got your pad, got your pencil, take a letter.
'For attention Mr Blumenkrantz, Chickabiddy Camisole Company,
Seventh Avenue, New York. Hi!'

Secretary Hi?

Manager Sure – hi – why not? Ikey Blumenkrantz is an old buddy of mine, do
you want I should alienate the guy before I break him in two? So write
it down –
'Hi! Ikey I am sore at you. But plenty. Complaints through your lawyer
against alleged treddle-defects in the seven Singer machines model forty-
three dispatched to your plant as per enclosed schedule are herewith
repudiated. Now listen, Ikey, get this good – '

CONNOLLY *sets his hat at a sharp angle; puffs, with nausea, on his cigar;
squares his shoulders; and strides forward.*

Connolly Mr Schmidtkopf? Please don't rise! I won't take thirty seconds of
your valuable time. Now, sir, I understand you have a vacancy in this
plant for a qualified machinist – ?

Manager Say, have you an appointment?

Connolly Sir, a man with an appointment is a man with time to waste: and I well know that Singer Sewing Machines got no time for wasters! They tell me, sir, your clients have trouble with the treddle-connections of your model forty-three?

Manager They tell you – who tells you? Why, goddammit, that's a trade secret!

Connolly (*aside to audience*) If you want to keep secrets, don't dictate in a high-pitched bellow. Lesson Number One for political subversives . . .
(*To* MANAGER) Now this here, sir, I take it, is your model forty-three?
He approaches a sewing-machine mounted for display. Aside to audience:
If it isn't, I'm done. But thank goodness it has a number plate on it. Lesson Number Two: under conditions of expanding industrial economy, the capitalist adversary has as yet felt no need to conceal his intentions. Read, mark, learn, and *don't* do likewise. Bear in mind what happened to Haywood – tough and rough but a foredoomed loudmouth.

He has turned the machine over and is activating the moving parts.

(*To* MANAGER) Yes indeed, Mr Schmidtkopf, there's a definite indication that the left-hand treddle-bearing is inclined to run sticky. Have you checked the possibility that the bore-gauge of this casting is a millimetre too narrow?

(*Aside to audience*) Lesson Number Three: never forget your adversary is quite as much a blind eedjit as you yourself would have been in the same situation. He hadn't checked the bore-gauge.

(*To* SECRETARY) Now if you, my dear, will hold the female component of the double-activating screw-manifold, I'll take the other end and ease it through, so, till we've worked it clear of the bed-trunnion. Bully for you. Can I trouble you, Mr Schmidtkopf, to get a good grip on the treddle itself so it don't slide out of its housing, I apply a small file to the metal-work at the joint. . . . Bully. One millimetre. No more. . . . There we are, that should do it. Right y'are, then how does she ride? . . . Oh bully bully hot dog, Mr Schmidtkopf! You can write Mr Blumenkrantz this minute, sir, tell him call his lawyers off, tell him cash on delivery rush his male components express back here to Newark, you shave off them one millimetre circumference with your power-lathe, return them to New York the same day carriage-paid: and Mr Schmidtkopf, you both are saved one helluva lotta grief!

Manager Why, say, boy, that's not bad! Why, hell, not bad at all! Angelina, re-write that letter just like the man said. Say, I don't know what your name is, who the hell cares what your name is – you understand sewing-machines: that's all that concerns me!

Connolly Am I hired?

Manager Goddammit, man, of course you're hired!

Exeunt MANAGER *and* SECRETARY.

Connolly Lesson Number Four: sharp practice by itself will avail you nothing unless it's backed by a solid foundation of theory . . . Likewise without practice, the best theory in the world droops and dies before it's blossomed. No danger of that these days with the Socialist Labor Party – no sir, in Newark no longer dare they call us an impracticable talking-shop – upon the streets, among the people, like an avalanche – we have *moved*!

SCENE 4

The stage fills with people, all greeting each other in different languages – Italian, German, Russian, etc. A lot of red flags and one large banner saying 'Freedom for the Idaho Three' and 'Freedom of Speech in Newark'. The 'Internationale' is sung, in several different languages. ELIZABETH GURLEY FLYNN *and the Irish* PARTY WORKER *join* CONNOLLY.

Party Worker There's already twenty thousand Italians in Cutler Street.

Flynn I've got the Irish crowd contained three blocks back down Seventh Avenue. I should think at least eight thousand.

Connolly I'd have hoped there'd be more Germans. What's happened to the Germans?

Party Worker Don't you know their committee insisted they should march in step to a brass band? I think they're still forming fours on the recreation field with a serjeant-major, but don't worry – they've all turned out!

Connolly I'll bet the Italian Socialist Federation never thought when they began this protest that every bloody nationality in Newark would be joining them in such numbers – Lizzie, begod, it's a roman triumph we have here and no error!

Flynn And none but yourself is responsible for it, Mr Connolly.

Party Worker Wouldn't you call it a class of a disgrace, though, the Italians had to begin it? How come that they have got their own socialist group and we the Irish are left nowhere?

Connolly You might well say how come. What's done once can be done once more: and we'll do it!

He indicates a PINKERTON MAN, *to one side of the stage.*

Pinkerton Man (*scribbles in notebook*) 'To the Pinkerton Detective Agency – Operator's Report Number Q seventy-six. So far no violence. Good-humoured assembly of unprecedented crowds none the less contains trouble-making potential assessed at grade sixteen on regular agency scale. No weapons overtly carried. Flags: red.' For some reason the word's just come down from head office: no repeat no provocation in Newark . . .

He crosses over to another vantage point, passing an AF OF L OFFICIAL *as he does so.*

AF of L Official Pinkerton man, huh? I wish to God this Haywood guy was acquitted or hanged or sump'n. All manner of Micks and Wops running in and out of my AF of L local every day with their damn leaflets – there's nuth'n I can do to stop 'em since the word came down from head office – accord all repeat all facilities to associated groups in Haywood campaign – d'you suppose that Sam Gompers has gone completely loco?

Intensified cheering and music.

Connolly It's the Germans, they've arrived! Okay, we start the speeches.

He mounts the rostrum. He speaks first in German, then Italian. He does not know these tongues well, but has been carefully coached and pleases the crowd immensely with his humorous acceptance of his own poor pronunciation.

Willkommen die Kameraden der Vereinigung der Sozialisten Deutschlands an dieser historischen Gedenkfeier! Die Sozial Demokratische Partei Deutschlands, der nachfolger von Marx und Engels, ist der wegweiser Stern heutiger Sozialismus Europas. Langemöge sie leben!

Amici, fratelli, salutiamo il vostro corraggio e solidarti e il indomito volunta contra il represso di liberte delle parole. Siete un essempio e isperatoro a ogni lavoratoro in Newark e esperiamo da oggi che ogni lavoratoro in Newark serrà egualmente un isperatori a tutta gli stati uniti!

Comrades, fellow-workers, citizens of Newark: the Italian Socialist Federation last month in commemoration of the Paris Commune of eighteen hundred and seventy-one carried the red flag through these streets. With brutality that flag was confiscated by the Newark police. An outrage and a violation of the civil rights of American citizens to express without hindrance their legitimate political views. We want that flag back. The commissioner of police has told us repeatedly we're not going to get it back. Very well: so we've made some more!

Great cheering and waving of red flags.

Last year, in Russia, not in one city, but throughout the entire heart of that rotten yet malignant Empire, the example of the people of the Paris Commune was followed yet again. I have the privilege of introducing to you today an active participant in those tremendous events – for her own safety, she has no name – we will call her Comrade B., from the

Petrograd Workers' Soviet – she was arrested, she was exiled, she escaped – and here she is!

A RUSSIAN REVOLUTIONARY *appears on the rostrum to great cheering.*

Russian Revolutionary Father Gapon, the good priest, who at that time no-one knew was also a police spy, said to the poor people: 'Come, I will lead you to the Czar – the Czar is your little father, he will hear your cry and give you bread and deliver you from your affliction.' So thousands of them marched to the gates of the Czar's palace. The soldiers stepped forward, they brought their rifles to their shoulders, and – as a loving father disciplines his thoughtless children – they shot those people down. So after that it was nothing but the general strike – every factory in Russia was made desolate, closed and empty; it was the mutiny – the whole Black Sea Fleet was set at derision by the fury of the sailors of the ironclad 'Potemkin' – even the dreaded Cossacks for a time were without power to intimidate, to trample down the aroused and vengeful people... Yet here I am: a refugee. Not for ever: indeed not. But when our work is to be done again, and I go back to take part in it, we must have thoroughly understood the reasons for what went wrong. First: we were too spontaneous. Second: the industrial workers received little or no support from the broad mass of the rural peasantry. Third: and most important: there was no fully-informed cohesive party of the revolution to seize and hold the political leadership. It is from now on to be our task to correct these grave mistakes. I recommend you, American workers, to take heed of our disappointment, to relate the lessons of our struggle to your particular situation. Above all, remember this: the failure of a revolution is the springboard of the next success! Long live the heroic martyrs of the year of nineteen hundred and five! Long live the determined workers of the United States of America! Long live the Soviet Socialist Revolution in Russia, in America, and throughout the entire world!

During the cheers at the end of this speech the RUSSIAN *nervously pours herself out a drink of water – straight into* CONNOLLY'*s hat.*

Connolly (*among laughter*) I hope it won't shrink. It's the only one I have! Miss Elizabeth Gurley Flynn, who needs no introduction in Newark.

Flynn (*on the rostrum*) Paris, Russia – and now Idaho – we're on the go, we can't be stopped! The bosses know that their days of unquestioned power are now numbered. The Industrial Workers of the World is an aurora borealis that hangs blood-red in the sky above them – and in their terror they try anything to make the decent family people who support their local police turn and run like squealing piglets into the warm protective sty of the 'democratic process'. I suppose there's no-one in this place requires to be told the difference between a hog and a human being – –

Mother Jones (*interrupts from the back*) No lookit, Lizzie, honey, you got no call to go running down good healthy hogs! 'Cos I raised hogs and I raised human children, and I tell you in some respects them hogs has got the edge on us!

Flynn Brothers and sisters the oldest and the toughest fighter in the whole American labour movement! – Mother Jones, from the Illinois coalfields, from the Western Federation of Miners, from the Industrial Workers of the World!

Mother Jones (*mounts rostrum amidst cheers*) Midwinter in the mountains when every pond and creek is frozen, and there's four-legged critters everywhere can get nary a drop to drink, what does your hog do then? He ain't no slouch at finding out just where that water's got to – and nothing, brothers and sisters, *nothing* will hold him back from quenching his thirst. He sets his four sharp hooves splayed-out on the shining ice, and he bends his big strong head, and he bashes with that old snout of his, bang bang bang till the ice is cracked and broken and shivered into a thousand fragments! And that's what we're aiming to do, and it's what we *can* do, and it's what we *will* do, brothers and sisters, right now, bang bang bang, till Haywood Moyer and Pettibone is busted out of the Penitentiary and Old Man Grabitall and all his dirty dollars is busted out of the seat of government in Idaho and Colorado and Nevada and Montana and Washington DC! Say, gimme a flag there – yeah, we got this revolution – so let's get it upon the road!

She starts singing; everyone joins in and exeunt.

If the boss gets in the way we're gonna roll it over him
We're gonna roll it over him, we're gonna roll it over him
If the boss gets in the way we're gonna roll it over him
We're gonna roll the Union on . . .

etcetera etcetera . . .

SCENE 5

Enter DE LEON *and an* SLP PARTY OFFICIAL, *looking through letters.*

1st Party Official Queries, comrade De Leon, queries, forever queries –

De Leon From every branch in the country it seems –

1st Party Official What is exactly our relation with the Socialist Party? What is exactly our correct attitude to the IWW? How far can we go in association with the AFL? Is there not a danger of too diverse a collaborationism? Is it proper for our members to speak on the same platform as –

De Leon I thought on such points I had made myself perfectly clear?

1st Party Official Of course you have, comrade – but –

De Leon You know how to answer all these, do you not? Hello, what's this one?

1st Party Official Newark New Jersey . . . Branch secretary passes on a recommendation that the Newark Italian Socialist Federation be affiliated with the Socialist Labor Party.

De Leon En bloc? Certainly not!

1st Party Official It would mean a considerable and very welcome increase in our membership –

De Leon I've no doubt. And that's why. That's exactly why, comrade. Do you not appreciate the credentials of Italian socialism? Three-quarters anarchist: and the remaining one-fourth mafioso. Newark. Dear me, Newark . . . Comrade, I will unreservedly hand over to you five cents if the name of James Connolly is not somewhere in that letter.

1st Party Official You win. The whole thing seems to be his idea. He says, on account the Italians showed such spirit in their Paris Commune festival –

De Leon Ha! The Irish faction-fighter smelling blood on the end of his old shillelagh, wouldn't you guess it? And of course, as we well know, the Irish predilection for secret societies is even worse than the Italian. Are you familiar with the history of an occult cabal called the Irish Republican Brotherhood? Its 'secret melodramatic conspiratorial methods' – I quote Karl Marx – which have ended universally and inevitably in failure? Its invariable penetration by the informer and the police-agent? Its consistent vulnerability to the influence of the Catholic Church? Its – I won't go on. The answer is definitely 'no'.

1st Party Official Comrade, I don't know how you're going to take this: but he says – he says if we are prepared to accept the Italians, then maybe in due course we will also accept his *Irish* Socialist Federation –

De Leon His *what*! Oh my God. He has in fact formed such a body? In Newark?

1st Party Official It has been formed. And not only in Newark. He mentions New York, Boston, Buffalo, Baltimore . . . I don't think we issued any precise directive against it?

De Leon We did not. And we're not going to. I like to believe I have a *flexible* approach. But heaven knows, this must be stopped. How to do it . . . ? I know . . . Where's Comrade Zimmerman?

1st Party Official Zimmerman!

Enter 2ND PARTY OFFICIAL, *out of breath.*

Comrade De Leon . . .

2nd Party Official (*to* DE LEON) Yes, comrade?

De Leon Zimmerman, I want a member from a district well away from the metropolitan area of activities, who belongs to a non-English-speaking minority which is not known to possess any ethnic socialist grouping of its own: and who is able to write legibly and coherently upon the danger of centrifugal racial tendencies within the movement. Give me a name.

2nd Party Official Comrade Stromqvist, Arizona. He's a Swede. I guess he fills

all the requirements. He is in New York this week. Do you want me to – –
De Leon Request him to drop in and have a word with me: yes. He is to prepare a short paper for inclusion in *The Weekly People*. We will see if it is
replied to by any individual from Newark New Jersey: and if it is: we go
in for the kill.

Exeunt.

SCENE 6

Enter GOMPERS, GRABITALL *and* BOSSES.

Grabitall (*sings*)

> All around this great nation in fury they call
> For red revolution to be our downfall –

Chorus Revolution revolution revolution – take heed
> Revolution feeds fat on the food of our greed!

1st Boss (*sings*)

> We try to do good and make wealth and make growth
> But red revolution will swallow them both!

Chorus Revolution revolution revolution – take heed
> Revolution feeds fat on the food of our greed!

2nd Boss (*sings*)

> We've all gotta gather we've all gotta cling
> Each one to each other to beat off this thing.

Chorus Revolution revolution revolution – take heed
> Revolution feeds fat on the food of our greed!

3rd Boss (*sings*)

> Sam Gompers, Sam Gompers – we thought you our friend:
> Will you let revolution get us all in the end?

Gompers (*sings*)

> Revolution revolution I ain't Jesus Christ
> To bring out no miracle to save you your life!

Grabitall Wait a minute, now, that sentiment is detrimental to the cordial
atmosphere that should prevail in this pan-American industrial manage-
ment-labour good neighbour-relationship gathering! Mr Gompers,
withdraw, please, your impertinent remark!

Gompers I come today to Newark because somebody writes to me that
Singer Sewing-Machines Incorporated is hosting the gathering: and I
find the prosperous city of Newark New Jersey struck flat in its own
streets like a crazy man with a cut-throat razor!

2nd Boss And what the hell else? Are you too dumb to realise just what
happened here last weekend! The red flag flown openly the full length
of Seventh Avenue, flown openly and unhindered – not one Newark
peace-officer so much as pulled out his night-stick! Moreover, it says
here –

He is reading from a newspaper: all the others except GOMPERS *have newspapers open as well.*

– that a communist anarchist from Russia was allowed to freely advocate open mutiny in the armed forces!

Gompers Can I just ask you one little non-incriminating totally innocent question? Is your Singer Sewing-Machine Company a unionised plant or not?

2nd Boss Goddammit, that's not germane – !

3rd Boss Don't evade it: we got no time to play games: you damn fool, this is an emergency!

1st Boss Just answer the man, goddammit. Just explain to him the ingredients of your own stupid stewpot.

2nd Boss Lookit here, over my dead body will Singer Sewing-Machines become unionised!

Gompers And so you wonder why the hell I choose to question your credentials. You make me sick to my gut.

1st Boss It ain't only Newark – these Wobbly demonstrations are held over the length and breadth of the continent!

Bosses (*read out from newspapers*) Chicago – Philadelphia – Seattle – Cleveland – Detroit – New York City –

Gompers You think I don't know it? And you think I don't know why?
(*To* 1ST BOSS) Mr Senator: when you were elected to the legislature of this great republic, did you or did you not swear to be a friend to labour: and did you or did you not receive the sincere endorsement of the AF of L in that election?

3rd Boss Don't evade it!

2nd Boss Just answer the man, goddammit!

1st Boss Yeah.

Gompers Without our endorsement, do you reckon you coulda won?

1st Boss No.

Gompers And since the day you obtained office, upon what particular issue have you swung your political weight in favour of labour and against the Wall Street trusts? . . . Don't answer. We know the answer. The answer is not one! Not one lousy stinking Congressional motion – ! Any wonder that the wild-wood radicals, the Wobblies, the egalitarianising fanatic socialists have made such appalling gains!

Grabitall Say, I been reading the newspaper: the Newark newspaper: *your* sheet, Mr Chairman of the Singer Sewing-Machine Incorporated. You said, over your dead body would subversive combinations get a foothold in this plant? You said it maybe with the intention of talking kinda *tough*? So how come I see here that a Singer employee was in the middle of that socialistic *kaffeeklatch* last weekend on Seventh Avenue?

2nd Boss What, that's a goddam lie – I never – no – say, gimme that newspaper! My God! Where's my manager! Schmidtkopf! Hey, Schmidt-kopf, goddammit: get your feet inside this office!

Enter Singer MANAGER.

Schmidtkopf – *WHO IS CONNOLLY?* James Connolly, Singer machinist – will you look at it, man, page five, column three – will you look at it and then tell me – WHO THE HELL HIRED THAT HOOD-LUM HERE!

1st Boss Wait a minute, what's that noise?

3rd Boss Why, it's right outside your entrance, there's a man making a speech to the morning shift as they come off duty!

1st Boss He has a banner –

3rd Boss Can anyone read it – ?

Gompers Socialist Labor Party – Industrial Workers of the World –

CONNOLLY *has appeared in a far corner of the theatre with his banner, addressing the workers.*

Connolly There is no law in this country that forbids a working man to organise himself with his fellows into a legitimate labour union –

Bosses Schmidtkopf – !

Manager That's *him*!

Bosses Him – *who*?

Manager James Connolly!

Bosses and Grabitall James Connolly . . . !

Grabitall Gentlemen, I think the moral of this is clear to all. By the beginning of next year, nineteen hundred and seven, men, women and kids in this country'll be glad to get *any* work, any work at all for any rate under any conditions – *I* seen it coming, Brother Gompers, so should you. Slump, my friend, will mean there's a few mouths around here won't talk so goddam uppity. Get it?

Gompers Got it. And get this. The working class don't make no slump. And when slump comes, the working class is gonna fight against it, hard. Remember – *my* membership could be *that* man's membership tomorrow lunchtime – and if it is, I weep no tears.

American democracy, my entire life, goes down the drain . . .
For the ruin of that democracy let Sam Gompers sustain no blame . . .

He goes out, one or two of the BOSSES *trying to catch him up and talk to him, almost pleadingly. Exeunt all.*

SCENE 7

Enter LILLIE *with a bundle of clothes. She is heavy with child.*

Lillie *I* know: but *he* does not know yet

> The word already has gone out
> He's lost his job for what he did
> With his word and banner at the factory gate.
> And I myself am almost brought to bed
> With his seventh child, much sooner than I thought.
> Nora!

Enter NORA.

Do you suppose, child, you will be able to take over my piece-work, and go to school – at least in the mornings – and also make sure that your father gets his food and your brother and sisters get theirs, and that they all go to sleep at the right time of night, and above all that he doesn't discover how much work you are doing when his back's turned?

Nora I don't see why not, Mammy. He spends half his time in New York now, fixing up his arrangements with the IWW – whenever they don't need him at Singers in fact, he's needed three times over at the Wobbly headquarters.

Lillie Whenever they don't need him at Singers will be *every* day from now on: and its best you should know it at once. So even when the baby's born and I'm able to be about again, we are still going to need your two hands: do you understand that? It's a heavy responsibility for one so young. Can you deal with it?

Nora So many of the girls in my school already deal with it: and besides aren't they always telling me the Irish are good for nothing but work!

Lillie   Nothing but work and the breeding of children
>   Till the ache of the one of 'em's given way to the pain
>   Of the other: and the time has arrived once again:
>   So they've sent for my husband, they have sent for the doctor . . .
>   While I lie down and fight by myself in my bedroom alone:
>   Let them come, let them run . . .

She goes out, followed by NORA *in a panic, dropping clothes everywhere. A pause. Enter* SUPERVISOR.

Supervisor (*knocks*) Hello there – Jim Connolly – anyone at home – ?

Re-enter NORA.

Nora Oh Doctor, is that you – thank heavens you got the message – oh.

Supervisor Say, I'm not no doctor – you expecting him, what's wrong? Look, I guess it's a bad time, honey, if somebody's sick in the house – but I gotta talk to your father, it's only for a moment –

Enter CONNOLLY.

Connolly Nora, where are you? I came as fast as I could! Has the doctor been sent for? Where's your mother – is she in bed?

Nora She's upstairs and everything's ready, and Ina ran round for the doctor:

we had everything laid out the way we were told to and I don't think we forgot anything – oh.

Connolly (*follows her look and realises* SUPERVISOR *is standing there*) Oh. Not just now: I can't deal with it just now.

Supervisor I won't be one moment but I gotta put it to you straight just what Schmidtkopf told me –

Nora Here's the doctor now!

She lets the DOCTOR *in.*

Connolly Thank God. Dr Rosen, she's gone into labour, now I think everything's ready. I'm not without experience –

Doctor Hot water?

Nora In the kitchen, Doctor –

Doctor Towels, napkins, clean sheets –

Nora They're all on the fender in front of the kitchen stove –

Doctor Fine, that's just fine – you got a grand little nurse on the premises, that's one thing, Mr Connolly –

Exit at opposite side.

Connolly What on earth is all this clutter? You should have had the whole house tidy for an occasion like this . . . Never mind, never mind, dear: I'll sort it away myself . . . Dear me, I had no idea I had this many shirts and collars . . .

Supervisor I guess I'd better go and come back in –

Connolly In the morning?

Supervisor – in an hour or two – it *is* urgent.

Connolly I'm *not* having you round here in the next two hours, that's flat. Tell me what you came to tell and for Godsake get it over with!

Supervisor Okay: so when Schmidtkopf came and told me he was putting you in my machine-shop, I told him after one day that sure as hell your qualifications were as phoney as a bald hairdresser. I clamped my teeth and *accepted* you, just the same I had to do for two-thirds of all the others. But when they asked me last month to put forward a good man's name for a replacement for Joe Lambrini, goddammit, I gave 'em yours!

Connolly You did? That was very generous –

Supervisor I tell you they are making shit-pies out of Schmidtkopf – permitting, indeed condoning red revolutionary anarchism to be preached at their very gates, so where the hell does that leave *me*!

Doctor (*briefly reappears*) Mr Connolly – the hot water –

Connolly (*to* SUPERVISOR) Just a moment –

Nora It's all right, I've already got it –

Connolly (*sudden panic*) Nora, come back here – you are not to touch that kettle!

But she has already carried it past him. He turns back to the SUPERVISOR.

I defy either you or Schmidtkopf to prove I have done more than recommend a few workers to consider joining a labour union –

Supervisor So lookit, Jim, I worked for Singers for twenty-five years, my wife
for the past five years is sick, crippled with the arthritis, we got one
grown-up daughter has lived in an institution since eighteen hundred
and ninety-five on account as you know she has got this disability . . .
Jim, if I lose my place in Singers, what in hell am I gonna do?

Connolly If Singers was a union shop these questions would never arise.

Supervisor I ain't got nuth'n against the unions – I want only to keep my job.

Connolly (*after a moment's thought*) Okay: for you: I will quit.

Supervisor But – but where will you go?

Connolly I have a class of a possibility of a political job in New York – an
organiser for the IWW.

Supervisor They would *pay* you for that?

CONNOLLY *shrugs.*

Crazy, goddam crazy – oh hell, I've gotta tell you, I feel very bad about
this – here you take this –

He offers money.

No, don't you look at it. In your pocket. I insist. And keep your goddam
mouth shut. And if anyone in the plant asks me should he join with a
union, I will tell him yes he should, and to tell everyone else that's
exactly what they should all do – *all* of them, goddammit!

Connolly Oh shut up and get out and let me wait for the baby!

The SUPERVISOR *looks as if he would say something else, but thinks better
of it, shakes* CONNOLLY *by the hand, and exits.*

CONNOLLY *waits in silence. A rush of feet. Enter* NORA.

Nora Daddy daddy daddy – !

Enter DOCTOR.

Doctor Mr Connolly, congratulations. A little girl, sir, in very good shape,
and Mrs Connolly as well, sir, fine spirits, excellent shape . . .! I've given
her a sedative, you are not to go upstairs for another two hours at least.

Exit. CONNOLLY *starts rummaging for something.*

Nora Daddy, what are you looking for?

Connolly The manuscript of the history of Irish Labour I was writing – I
thought maybe for an hour or two, if you wouldn't mind helping me –
there's a chapter I'd like to hear you read over to me for correction.

Nora It's in the other room.

Connolly Then we go to the other room! And for heaven's sake leave your
friends to do their own sewing for once!

He gives her a big hug and exeunt.

SCENE 8

Enter ELIZABETH GURLEY FLYNN, *the* IRISH PARTY WORKER *from Scene 5, and a crowd of Irish-Americans (including a* PUBLICAN *and an* OLD FENIAN*). A banner in green, reading 'Irish Socialist Federation (New York) – "Faugh-a-Ballach" ', is unfurled at the back. Irish music, dancing, conviviality.*

Flynn To every group of immigrants who arrive on these shores there needs to be made available their own socialist club, where, through a course of comprehensive political education, they can eventually find their way into the mainstream of the Socialist Labor Party.

Party Worker (*sings*)
>Now all our people can learn at last
>Home Rule is not the cure for the nation
>But a sound republican line laid down
>By the Irish Socialist Federation.

Enter CONNOLLY *and leads the chorus.*

Connolly (*sings with the crowd*)
>Giddy-i-ay from the USA
>Giddy-i-ay we'll send it homeward
>Giddy-i-ay we'll bear in mind
>The future of our native land!

Flynn (*sings*)
>Or else we know they will all too soon
>Fall prey to Tammany graft and corruption:
>The political boss, the commercial boss
>Outvie one another in exploitation.

Connolly and others (*sing*)
>Giddy-i-ay the New York Irish
>Giddy-i-ay are fleeced and cheated
>Giddy-i-ay in the sacred name
>Of Freedom for our Native Land!

Connolly We have a programme of lectures and discussions – the leaflets are available over there – I intend when funds are sufficient to start our own newspaper – No political group, however modest its intention, can ever do anything without some sort of news-sheet – and our intention is *not* modest. Nothing less than the complete liberation of Ireland and the establishment therein of a socialist republic! I am already in contact with a number of old colleagues of the movement back in Dublin – ideally our newspaper should be a transatlantic publication: but as to that we shall have to see. I thought we might call it *The Harp.* Any opinions?

Publican (*who has not really been listening until this moment*) And by the same token, more power to you, boy! Say, feller, I don't know your name – Connaughton, O'Conroy – ?

Connolly Connolly.

Publican So put it there, Connolly: you're a little guy, but you're a man! *The Harp*! Yeah – swell – 'The Harp that once through Tara's halls . . .' Say, you tell me you need funds? I'm Slattery. Shaun Slattery from Sally-noggin, Sallynoggin County Dublin: and of Slattery's Irish Bar, one hundred and seventy-nine East Eleventh Street, New York! I'm over here forty years – and I made it and I made it good! You want freedom for the ould country? Shaun Slattery will stake you out!

He ladles money out of his pockets and thrusts it into CONNOLLY'*s hands.*

For a newspaper, you need capital, you need investors, you need advertisers – and in this city you need protection! No better man than Slattery! – Chief ward-boss for the Democrats five blocks around East Eleventh Street – ask any man down Second Avenue: where stands Slattery? And he'll answer: 'If Slattery is not on his knees in the confessional: then look for the bould Shaun among the wheel-and-deal of City Hall!'

Connolly I wonder, Mr Slattery, did you altogether hear my programme?

Publican Is it socialism? Sure aren't all the Irish socialists, when it comes to denouncing th'brutal tyranny of th'crown of Britain? But these two things I have no time for: that's atheism and protestants. The day we get Home Rule and a Dublin parliament of our own, we'll drive the pack of 'em into the sea like St Patrick with the snakes!

Connolly (*to* PARTY WORKER) Jack, get rid of him.

Publican Wh – what – ?

Connolly Trying to buy *me* with your wheeling-dealing dollars – get out of here, you parasite, before I forget meself!

A Guest Mr Connolly, it's not wise to be having trouble with Mr Slattery . . .

Publican (*on his way out*) We'll not forget this, Connolly! You'll be marked for it, I'm tellin' you! I know men in this town who are *killers*: they're in my pocket!

The PARTY WORKER *expels him. The* OLD FENIAN *takes* CONNOLLY *aside.*

Old Fenian He means the police.

Connolly I don't care if he means the state governor and the president all rolled up into one!

Old Fenian Sure he has New York's Finest bought-and-sold, there's no doubt. But I don't think you'll be hearing from them. Sure I know the man well. Sixty-seven indeed he did come over here, 'tis true, but whereas some of us were accredited rebels in the insurrection of that year, there was more than a suspicion your man Slattery was an *informer*: he knows that I know it: I don't think you'll have trouble. Oh he keeps very quiet where the Brotherhood is in question. Did you know, Mr Connolly, that the

Irish Republican Brotherhood, or the Fenians, as it was then, had close
ties with the Revolutionary Socialist International that began in Europe
in forty-eight?

Connolly I had heard it, sir, yes. My uncle was involved in the business of
sixty-seven. MacBride was the name he adopted.

Old Fenian I know it well: we checked it out. We're very interested in your
programme. I wonder if I could take a moment, while our friends are at
the revels, to put down a few feelers to judge what yourself would be
thinking of ours?

Connolly I am not thinking of anything beyond public organisation for a
defined political goal. Conspiracy is not my angle.

Old Fenian There's no denying that in the underground side of the business
we do have to rub up against a few you'd find abhorrent. One day, don't
you know, you too may be in search of a very similar class of 'parasite'.
If you need a man to put you on to them, don't you be looking any
further than me. I have a feeling, don't you know, that 'one day' could
be quite soon. . . . Good luck to you, so: I'll take occasion to purchase a
pile of your literature . . .

DE LEON *has come quietly up to them, having bought one or two of the
pamphlets.*

De Leon Comrade Connolly – no – don't disturb yourself. I was just passing
through and I thought I should drop in to congratulate you on your
achievement – on being elected, I mean, by the New Jersey SLP, to the
National Executive Committee of the party. A product of your hercu-
lean efforts in the Haywood-Moyer defence campaign? And this, I
suppose –

Holds up one of the pamphlets.

– a product of your energetic pen? 'Socialism and Religion – the known
and the unknowable' . . . unknowable indeed . . . I met a certain in-
fluential local Democrat on his way out: he seemed annoyed?

Connolly He was.

De Leon Good. Might it not have been better had you avoided involving his
emotions in either direction? I never find him on the threshold of any
of *my* meetings, Comrade Connolly . . . Oh by the way, here is an advance
copy of tomorrow's *Weekly People*. You might care to take a look at it?

Exit.

Flynn What did he give you that for?

Connolly There must be something in it of a *correctional* nature . . . by God
there is! Stromqvist, from Arizona. Writes a letter denouncing the whole
idea of socialist federations within ethnic communities. We must
answer it.

Party Worker How?

Connolly With a firm argument. It is impossible for poor immigrants to relinquish all at once their foreign roots in favour of a strange abstract doctrine. Make it clear to the silly man that it's time he had some humanity.

Party Worker De Leon won't like it.

Flynn I sometimes get the idea we all came here in the first place to drive De Leon into the looney-bin.

Connolly Lizzie, I do believe he really believes that. At all points I seem to find myself attacking his centralisation of power: and yet God knows, I do stand fast, very fast indeed, for a well-organised disciplined party. Sure, what could I not have done with one, had I had it in Dublin? At all events I intend to keep quiet as a mouse on the National Executive Committee. No, I'll not give them a fingerhold to raise one single objection to me. . . .

Exeunt.

SCENE 9

A scene in the dark. VOICES OF NEWSBOYS.

1st Voice Big Bill Haywood acquitted! Jury find no evidence for labour leader's involvement in Idaho conspiracy!

2nd Voice Jury verdict in Idaho pins guilt for frame-up on Pinkerton Detective Agency!

HAYWOOD *appears in spotlight, as just released, amidst cheers.* MOYER *and* PETTIBONE *beside him.*

1st Voice Brother Haywood, have you a few words for the Socialist Party newspaper, *Appeal to Reason*?

2nd Voice Comrade, the Socialist Labor Party's *Weekly People* would be glad of an interview!

3rd Voice *The American Federationist*, house organ of the AF of L, wants to ask a few questions . . .

Haywood I'm out and I'm proven innocent and I'm back in circulation: they tried to break the Miners' Union and they tried to break the Wobblies, but instead we broke *them* – and brothers, the class war goes on from this regardless! Unabated!

3rd Voice Bill, is it true that Charlie Moyer and yourself are no longer such good friends?

Haywood I don't want to say nothing against my old pardner Charlie Moyer. I hold my views as I always did and you all know what they are. About his views, you should ask him.

3rd Voice Say, Charlie, is it true that a majority of the Western Miners aim to pull out of the IWW and they're asking for your leadership?

Moyer My opinion the time has come to return to a moderate and practicable basis of day-to-day trade union business and to quit playing cowboys-and-injuns with the livelihoods of working men.

HAYWOOD *and* MOYER *move ostentatiously apart.*

2nd Voice We haven't heard from Comrade Pettibone –
1st Voice Brother Pettibone, what's your angle?
Pettibone It was all a mistake. I was never in no radical plot: I was never no more than a sympathiser with the union. I got sick inside of jail. I got myself real sick. Guess I wanna go home and just talk no more about it . . .

He goes out.

Haywood Through national working-class solidarity alone we stand here free tonight: I appeal to the whole movement throughout America not to break that solidarity!
Moyer No, we gotta see somehow this kinda thing never happens again: we gotta keep our heads clear, we gotta . . .

HAYWOOD *stalks away and out in disgust.* GOMPERS *is revealed coming up to* MOYER *and putting an arm round his shoulder.*

Gompers We gotta get them Western Miners re-organised now on a totally new system of the best thing for the most members at this one point of time. Charlie: you got no option – in the AF of L, or nowhere!
Moyer In the AF of L. . . .

GOMPERS *takes him out, protective and paternal.*

Haywood (*calls from the shadows*) The class war goes on regardless: regardless and unabated!

Lights up, stage empty.

SCENE 10

Enter CONNOLLY.

Connolly Oh yes, I have risen up, I am now tall, I am a marvellous man; I am elected, no less, to the National Executive Committee of the Socialist Labor Party – and I'm supposed to have turned docile. Oh I've said nothing yet – at least not much – at least just a few headings jotted down as to what's wrong with the entire party and why Dan De Leon with his arrogant exclusivism leads us all into the wilderness . . . ! I began, very modestly, at my first major meeting of the National Executive Committee, by asking my fellow-delegates what exactly they conceived to be the overall role of the newspaper . . .

Enter DE LEON, *separate from* CONNOLLY, *at another corner. The two address the audience alternately, without overt reference to one another.*

De Leon As it happens I was not present at this particular meeting. I had a prior engagement – –

Connolly Lounging on the beach at Miami, it was rumoured – –

De Leon Addressing a university seminar at Yale upon international economic trends.

Connolly At all events, I had discovered that a hard-working party group – the New York executive sub-committee, to be precise – had had notice of their resolutions published as of right in *The Weekly People*. Now, it so happened, in this case, that one particular resolution had for some reason caused De Leon a certain amount of annoyance.

De Leon The resolution of the sub-committee had completely misrepresented the position of the party on the matter of the supply of funds to overseas socialist groups! In the newspaper such an indiscretion would be taken all over the world as evidence that my policy had radically changed! 'For some reason' indeed – it was an issue of the utmost importance – I made it clear that the sub-committee from now on had no right to insert its half-baked notions into the official party organ.

Connolly I wanted it made clear that the role of these sub-committees could only come to its necessary fruition within the party if they were allowed full scope to express their activities in the newspaper. So I put down a motion. I knew De Leon's creatures would of course all be against me, and that if the motion had been worded: 'The National Executive Committee considers that the sub-committee has the right to insert official matter in the *People*' then automatically it would be rejected and nothing more would be said. No: I needed to make certain that even if it were rejected, it could only be rejected after a very full and wide discussion. Dammit, it was more than time that *somebody* discussed the central oligarchy of the party and the . . . the dictatorship that they imposed! So I played it crafty – –

De Leon The classic technique of the professional wrecker! Sowing confusion and disunity with deliberate ambiguous tricks!

Connolly I worded my motion thus: 'This committee considers that the National Executive Committee *and* its sub-committee have the right to insert official matter in *The People*'. D'you get it? The National Executive Committee, the NEC, that's *us* – we already had the right: it was only the sub-committee had had their right taken away. I made it an issue it was *both* committees or nothing. They couldn't reject the right of the sub-committee without rejecting the right of the NEC as well – the only way they could get out of it was by proposing amendments: and if they'd done that, they'd have given me just exactly what I wanted: a full and wide discussion of the whole business of central control! But d'ye know, they didn't do it! The bloody eedjits couldn't see one single implication of – –

De Leon Please take note all this went on when I myself was not present – addressing a university seminar at Yale upon – –

Connolly The bloody eedjits could see nothing but that James Connolly had put a motion down. The word was out that any nonsense emanating from the man Connolly was automatically to be opposed. Without an iota of reasoned argument they voted against me *en bloc*: just like that! And the result is –

De Leon The result is that the National Executive Committee – *my* committee – the policy-making body of the foremost revolutionary force in the entire western hemisphere – has been manipulated into denying itself access to its own newspaper!

Exit.

Connolly So what in the devil's name are they going to do next? Would they honourably admit they had made a mistake: go back over the whole question? How could they? Because if they did, they would have to grant me the full and wide discussion I had intended in the first place. So I expected some small deviousness. I was prepared for it. I wrote out statements . . . In my wildest dreams I never thought that they would refuse to accept my statements, that the columns of· the newspaper would be closed to me absolutely, that an irregular meeting of the NEC would be held when I was not present – deliberately so held . . . and that all I could do against them was to wearily write out copy after copy of my personal deposition and circulate it by hand to individual party-members . . . three-quarters of them never even bothered to acknowledge it. Oh what's the use . . .

Exit.

SCENE 11

Enter DE LEON *and Socialist Labor Party* OFFICIALS.

De Leon (*as they take their seats*) Comrades, if you please, just take it easy, one and all . . . As you know, I was not at the NEC meeting when this ridiculous Connolly motion was put forward and misunderstood. I have only the minutes of the meeting to go on: but it seems to me quite incredible that a caucus of intelligent socialists could take a vote on they know not what.

1st Official The fact remains, Comrade De Leon, we have gotten ourselves entangled into a position of unresolved deadlock. If we – –

De Leon If we allow ourselves to get rattled we will only make it worse. Comrade Zimmerman, you've always been a pretty cool customer, I guess. What did *you* think you were voting against? Speak carefully. Take your time.

2nd Official (*as though repeating lines learnt by rote*) I believed, Comrade De Leon, that the motion had reference alone to the . . .

De Leon To the . . . ?

2nd Official To the sub-committee, and nothing else.

De Leon Hah. And it was only when you – ?

2nd Official It was only when I saw the minutes several days later that I knew there had been a – –

De Leon So if your well-trained analytical memory is contradicted by the minutes, then in all probability, the minutes are incorrect. Comrade Secretary?

Secretary I don't know . . . I could swear, comrade, I got it right . . . According to my typescript . . .

De Leon We know what's on your typescript. But what about your original pencilled notes?

Secretary I don't have them any more. I threw them away, I guess . . .

De Leon I guess therefore we assume that the motion referred only to the sub-committee, that the mention of both committees got into the minutes in error: and that the minutes will accordingly be amended to comply with the – with the collective memory of those present.

3rd Official Comrade, may I point out that those present do not include Comrade Connolly himself? If he is not here when his own business is being discussed – –

De Leon Was *I* here when *my* business as editor of the newspaper was discussed at the last meeting? Comrade Connolly had every warning that his activities were to be investigated: if he has chosen to absent himself, he has done so in a petulant and non-co-operative spirit: he must therefore take the consequences! Amend the minutes.

Secretary (*does so*) 'Motion before the meeting: "This committee considers that the NEC sub-committee has the right to insert official matter in *The People*." Motion rejected.' Is that right?

De Leon Of course one can see how easily the mistake arose. 'The NEC sub-committee' . . . a smudge on our good friend's notebook led him to transcribe it as 'the NEC *and its* sub-committee' . . . well, we're all of us fallible. Be more vigilant in future, please. Next business?

Secretary A letter from Comrade Connolly, offering his resignation from the National Executive Committee.

De Leon I see. Comrade Zimmerman?

2nd Official (*as though prompted*) May I move a resolution that this committee reject Comrade Connolly's resignation until he has first appeared in person before us to receive censure for his provocative conduct: and if it is decided that this committee would be better off without him, he be expelled herefrom with ignominy.

1st Official I second that.

3rd Official And I oppose it! Comrade Connolly has been the object of an unscrupulous and vindictive personal campaign – –

De Leon Comrade, these individualist petty-bourgeois outbursts are scarcely compatible with our revolutionary task! How can you say 'personal'

when you consider the social background of an Irishman of this type?
At what college was he educated?

3rd Official I don't know the sort of colleges are available in Ireland . . .

De Leon Well, *I* do. Clerical seminaries: and the best of them Jesuit! Oh my own family lived in just such a society – we were Sephardic Jews, if you please, in Spanish America – we knew all about the Jesuits, pursuing their secret mission till the whole world has been subverted to the grand design of the church of Rome! If James Connolly is not an undercover Jesuit, the only other thing he could be is a complete and blundering idiot. I have read too much of his literature to believe that: far too much . . . I call the meeting to order. Votes? . . . The resolution is carried by a substantial majority. Thank you, comrades: good-night.

He gets up and goes. The others follow.

SCENE 12

Enter GOMPERS *and* GRABITALL. *An* AFL OFFICIAL *in the background.*

Grabitall I thought you told me the AF of L had taken over the Western Miners!

Gompers Work in progress . . . procedural hold-ups . . . maybe next year all the deals will be finalised . . . how can I tell?

Grabitall There is a *strike*!

Gompers Sure there's a strike. In this business, mister, there's nuth'n but goddam strikes . . .

Grabitall At Goldfield, Nevada: the Federation of Western Miners in cahoots with the IWW – I thought you told me – –

Gompers You think you can break that strike?

Grabitall The state militia has been sent in! We have martial law proclaimed all over the – –

Gompers So maybe then you'll break it: so maybe then the Western Miners and the IWW will speed up their split: so maybe procedural hang-ups will be liquidised before next year. Mister, you just relax. Sam Gompers knows his onions.

Grabitall What instructions have been given your AFL locals in the area of Goldfield?

Gompers To pass the pickets, what else? Are you satisfied?

Grabitall I am not! I'd have you know that the mining company is bankrupt!

Gompers That's your problem. Glad to have met you.

He turns abruptly away. Baffled, GRABITALL *goes out.*

Official In Goldfield *we* got problems. Our carpenters in the mines have cut up rough about the militia. They don't want to pass the pickets: there's been words heard like 'betrayal'.

Gompers In my outfit! Such delusions! My integrity was never better.

Enter 2ND OFFICIAL *and a* PEACE-OFFICER.

2nd Official Hey, boss, there's a pig here, come to *arrest* you! What'll we do?

Gompers Arrest? Okay, I'm a martyr. Tell me the charge.

Peace-Officer Contempt of court. Your newspaper *The American Federationist* defamed the Stove and Range Company of St Louis Missouri in connection with a strike. You was injuncted by the court to refrain from interference. You defied the injunction. You're awarded six months inside.

Gompers (*holds out hands for manacles*) Didn't I tell you my integrity was never better? Lead the way.

Exeunt.

SCENE 13

Enter CONNOLLY.

Connolly I need not explain I did not in person present myself to De Leon's committee to be censured, expelled with ignominy! Instead I did succeed in securing myself a paid appointment – Building Section (New York) Organiser of the Industrial Workers of the World! And I brought the family there to live, in a deplorable Bronx apartment, and the Irish Socialist Federation has its headquarters just round the corner . . . it's as though I have been reborn into a whole new phase of American life . . . !

Sings and dances.

> With De Leon and his party I am finished and done:
> For all of four years I played his tune
> On a broken-backed fiddle with the strings all gone –
> And I danced like a dervish in a dumb dark room
> With a carpet on the wall and cork on the floor
> And wood across the window and a nailed-up door!

And now thank God I've busted out of it: I am my own man at last, can activate and organise in full liberty to my heart's content: and, merciful hour, they pay me *money* for it!

> Poor old Dan, determined man,
> The only bloody socialist in God's own land!
> And when in the end revolution comes
> He'll be there in his kitchen just a pile of old bones.
> The people will march and the bones will stir—
> But who will hear them knocking on the floor?
>
> The statue of liberty will loose her hair
> And toss her crown into the air,

Unbuckle her gown and let it fall
And jump into the harbour like a great white whale!
Who is it will swim astride her limbs
But those whom dead old Dan condemns?

Free in the air and free in the water
Watch us sport with liberty's daughter –
Sport and swim, good-bye to him –
His fiddle is broke but trumpet-and-drum,
The jews'-harp, the spoons and the cute banjo
Will rattle up a tune and away we go . . .
Tum ta-ta ra-rah – tum-tum . . . !

Exit, dancing, and waving an IWW banner, followed by a surge of Wobbly demonstrators in great excitement.

END OF ACT 2

ACT 3: Forward to the Revolution . . . ?

Immigrants arriving in the USA from a ship; with the Statue of Liberty, watchful police, and skyscrapers filling the background, so that little or on sky is visible (Backcloth 6.)

The wide open spaces of America, mountain, desert and farmland, with groups of workers with red flags confronting armed posses of sheriffs' deputies, Ku Klux Klan etc. (Backcloth 7.)

A breadline of UNEMPLOYED *with a placard: '1907 – Slump Hits USA – Five Million Out of Work!'*

At the other side, CONNOLLY *and* LILLIE *– he in bed, she sitting with a candle, sewing. Atmosphere of intense cold.*

Unemployed (*sing*)
> I don't want your millions, mister:
> I don't want your diamond ring.
> All I want is the right to live, mister:
> Give me my job back again.

Connolly (*unable to sleep, stirs, sits up*) Five million. So cold, cold. Freeze to death on the streets at night. They told me at the Pennsylvania Station that a train came in from Baltimore with three hoboes frozen fast to the rods under the coaches, with crowbars they had to break their arms and legs from the iron. One of them with the small pink card in the heel of his sock. He'd have come to see me if he'd lived. Could be that he'd come to New York for no other purpose but to come to see me. District organiser, Industrial Workers of the World – what in hell could I have done for him?

Lillie James, why don't you roll over and go back to sleep – you have to be down at Hoboken tomorrow morning for that open-air meeting.

Connolly Twelve thousand waterside workers will be voting to enter the IWW en bloc. It could be the biggest thing for us since – –

Lillie Half-past six by torchlight, in the cold wind of the waterfront – James, you could get pneumonia: do, please, have some sleep first!

Connolly The American Federation of Labor put out the bids for 'em, but no, their leaders said 'it's the new union or nothing!' We must have that mass membership – it could be the one thing to save us in New York . . . Lillie, what the devil are you doing, girl! Leave your sewing till tomorrow or you'll make yourself ill.

Lillie I've only got another twenty of these bodices to finish – I'll come to bed then, I promise – but, James, it's a rush job and Mr Shapiro insisted that – –

Connolly You don't have to do it! I am paid by the union, Lillie, you do not have to make a slave of yourself in this way.

Lillie Last week you were paid. But next week? You can guarantee it? Shapiro can guarantee it. He's a man of his word.

Connolly How can he be, he's a damn slave-driver: he makes you into the slave of a slave: for me and the children you have to – –

Lillie James: you have your job and it's the only job you want to do. So please let me do mine: and then the children can be fed. Nora already earned six dollars this week in that dressmaking house: if I can bring in four, with your eighteen that makes – –

Connolly Does it make enough to pay the plumber to fix the frozen pipe, will you tell me?

Lillie Will you pass me the red cotton? Now turn over and go to sleep.

Unemployed (*sing*)

> We worked to build this country, mister
> While you enjoyed a life of ease:
> You've stolen all that we built, mister:
> Now our children starve and freeze.

Connolly (*checks through his notebooks*) Building and Construction Workers' Section, local ninety-five. Good. Steel-erectors . . . bronze-workers . . . carpenters . . . good. Brooklyn local number fourteen. Not so good. Plasterers in difficulty with the AF of L. There's a new local for their craft-workers on the site of the warehouse project. They made trouble on the job. Donovan told me the AF of L sent delegates down to the site . . .

INTERLUDE 1. *Enter* FOREMAN *and* BUILDING WORKERS: *to them an* AF OF L OFFICIAL. HOODLUMS *enter behind.*

AF of L Official You the foreman here? You got non-union labour on this site, that correct?

Foreman This ain't no closed shop, mister – –

AF of L Official From now on as far as the plasterers is concerned that's exactly what it is, mac – which of you guys holds a union card? Show! Okay . . . okay . . . Who are you, you ain't got nuth'n, stand aside . . . What the hell's this?

1st Worker That's what they call the little pink card, friend – IWW –

AF of L Official Since when was the IWW a Plasterers' Union?

1st Worker It's a Construction Union, fair and square – we pay our dues, we –

AF of L Official You swallow up the employment of skilled men like it was oatmeal porridge, you damned Wobbly! Construction Union my ass – crowd of conniving scabs. Here we are, boys, he's a Wobbly – get him off!

HOODLUMS *beat up* 1ST WORKER *and throw him out.*

You, without a card: you have the choice to follow him or apply for probationary membership of the Plasterers' Union, AF of L. Which?

2nd Worker I'll apply.

AF of L Official There's a fee for examination of your skill of three dollars.

> 2ND WORKER *hands it over.* AF OF L OFFICIAL *gives one dollar to* FOREMAN.

> From now on, that's the arrangement, get it? Sorry for the trouble, but as you see the AF of L members refuse outright to work with Wobblies. Remember that, next man you hire – okay?

> *Exeunt. (Throughout these sequences,* CONNOLLY *and* LILLIE *remain.)*

Connolly Only way we can break the stranglehold of the AF of L is to recruit and recruit new members from all over. The IWW Propaganda League has nothing but that for its object, but in this city – so vast, so contorted an ice-bound labyrinth – how in the name of God to get hold of the men? We do not even have any premises for our meeting . . .

> INTERLUDE 2. *Re-enter* AF *of* L OFFICIAL, *with his* HOODLUMS. *They prevent* WORKERS *from passing into an IWW meeting.*

AF of L Official The vote taken by this local of an AF of L Union for provision of premises for the IWW was overruled on account of irregularity, get it? If you aint got no hall of your own for your meetings, that's your funeral. Move! For anarchists and red subversives we got no provision in our rule-book – Sam Gompers is a loyal American.

> *Enter* GOMPERS.

Gompers To keep the American Federation of Labor, in this time of depression, uncontaminated by those who seek only to destroy the entire fabric of our democracy, is a task of the first importance. The IWW is deliberately encouraging an uncontrolled flood of unskilled revolutionary immigrants to pour into this country to lay hands on the prosperity American workers have amassed through generations of patient toil. They gotta be stopped – be stopped right now.

> *Exit, with* AF OF L OFFICIAL *and* HOODLUMS.

Connolly Unskilled revolutionary immigrants . . . ha . . .! Are the Irish revolutionary . . .? Oh rebels, aye aye, no doubt about that, and when we come in to this country: against Britain; against imperialism every man of us is a Dan O'Connell: and so enchanted with our own verbiage we drift in a dream of whiskey through the portals of Tammany Hall.

> INTERLUDE 3.

Irish Immigrant (*sings*)

> I'm a decent boy just landed from the town of Ballyfad,
> I want a situation and I want it very bad:
> I have seen employment advertised, 'It's just the thing,' says I –
> But the dirty spalpeen ended with 'No Irish need apply.'

'Whoo' says I, 'That's an insult but to get the place I'll try';
So I went to see the blackguard with his 'No Irish need apply'.
Some do think it a misfortune to be christened Pat or Dan
But to me it is an honour to be born an Irishman . . .

Enter Irish-American PUBLICAN.

Publican (*greets* IMMIGRANTS) Shaun Slattery of Slattery's Irish Bar, East Eleventh Street is your man for every wrinkle to get around the likes of that. Come in with you, boys, and drink your fill, sure Slattery pays every round, 'tis on the house for the sake of your arrival in the land of liberty. Now I'll tell you what it is, boys, next year is the election-year, and the Democrat Party needs all hands to turn out and bring in again in triumph the good ould cause – do you tell me you don't know what our candidate has promised? The word must be bloody slow then getting back to the Ring of Kerry! Have ye never heard of the congressional resolution demanding be all means short of war that the King of England packs his bags and quits Ireland on the double? Sure 'tis only for the backing of the Democratic lobby here that the Home Rulers in Westminster have it going for them at all at all . . . Now there's five dollars a man from the hand of Slattery if the Republican meeting at Cooper Union tomorrow night should be accidentally cut to ribbons be an unacknowledged element inserted in amongst the crowd – sure the police have all been squared . . . And let me tell you, boys, any man here having trouble with his accommodations or his taxes or his eventual American citizenship has only to put the word out and the bould Slattery will come running . . . There you are then, and you after thinking there was no good for you at all in the streets of New York . . . And when the Cardinal Archbishop of Armagh pays his visit here at the end of next week, wouldn't we all be keen to render him the full honours of our new country . . . ?

The IMMIGRANT *crowd accept his munificence with due respect and gratitude.*

INTERLUDE 4. *Enter the* CARDINAL, *as though for a press conference, managed by the* PUBLICAN. ELIZABETH GURLEY FLYNN *is among the crowd.*

Cardinal My visit to America of course is primarily a spiritual mission: the faith of the Irish is justly celebrated throughout America as the backbone of the Catholic Church – but I agreed to meet the press today in the expectation that perhaps a few more worldly matters might be of interest to some Americans . . . yes?

A Reporter (*from the back*) Your Eminence, do you consider that Congress should put pressure on Great Britain to introduce Home Rule for Ireland?

Cardinal The Irish National Home Rule Party seeks the fullest Irish autonomy consistent with the unity of the British Empire and I am unequivocal in lending my support to that – ah – most justified aspiration . . . yes?

Reporter Your Eminence, would you consider that, given Home Rule, there would be scope for American business to invest in Irish industry?

Cardinal Irish industry already is a flourishing child – but she will need the most sympathetic help if she is to be reared to that status fully commensurate with – ah – maturity . . . yes?

Flynn (*also from the back*) I wonder would His Eminence care to comment on how Home Rule might mend the condition of the working class in Dublin, where the housing is notorious as by far the worst in Europe and where –

Cardinal Ah, now as to housing – Mr Slattery, what newspaper does this lady represent?

Flynn *The Harp* – official organ of the Irish Socialist Federation!

Connolly Oh Lizzie, well done, Lizzie, but she didn't get too far with it – oh dear . . .

Publican Begod, that's the atheistical rag that lowdown louser of a Connolly edits up hill and down dale! Let the stewards at the back there control the disturbance now! Aye aye have her out of it!

ELIZABETH GURLEY FLYNN *is thrown out.*

Cardinal Let me say about socialism – this importation from the continent of Europe – that it denies the existence of God, the immortality of the soul, the right of private ownership, the rightful existence of our present social organisation, and the independence of the church as a society complete in itself and founded by God.

Publican True for you, Your Eminence – didn't Father Sherman S.J. make an echo of your very voice when he told us last month that the socialists are nothing else than hell's lowest vomit? And didn't the Bishop of – –

Cardinal I am not here however to interfere in any way with the American political process . . .

Exeunt CARDINAL *and* PUBLICAN.

Connolly God in Heaven! What wonder that the immigrants from the bog and mountain are such material for scabs and blacklegs, the foul lies they have been choked with before even they reach these shores!

He strides about in agitation. Abruptly changes the subject:

Lillie – I never asked you what you thought of the motto we have posted on the front page of *The Harp*? 'In things essential, unity: in things doubtful, diversity: in all things, charity'?

Lillie For a man that's been slung out of the American Socialist Labor Party and was forced to resign from his own party back in Dublin, I'd say that your conception of charity was a little large, James. Yet you still write every week to O'Brien in Dublin: and that old wretch De Leon of the SLP has a great deal of influence in the IWW.

Connolly He helped found it: so why wouldn't he. But as for O'Brien – the boys in Dublin have their own new party now, the Socialist Party of Ireland, and whatever my old hurt, I have no choice but keep in touch with them . . . Lord, I wish I was there now!

Lillie Not even in Dublin was it ever so cold as this. Only five more to finish now . . . and then we must go to bed.

Connolly Aye aye, we have *The Harp* – and most of my foolish pamphlets have a decent circulation – you know I actually earned money from my *Socialism Made Easy* – in Australia moreover! If I can only find time to finish my *Labour in Irish History* – Lillie, if I do that, I will have published a *book*! And to whom else should I dedicate it but you?

Lillie   In Scotland he began, in Ireland carried it on,
In huge America can we together yet reach
The wrecked ship stranded on the golden beach
And make it swim?
I don't know: but I do know that for him
There is no other voyage, therefore my part
In it is marked inevitably on his chart.

James, it's ridiculous to pretend there are no successes for the movement in New York. The garment workers' strike – twenty thousand women all on the streets at once: if that was not the principle of One Big Union, what was it? And our own daughter in it – did she make you proud?

INTERLUDE 5. *Enter* GARMENT WORKERS *including* NORA *with a placard* '*Recognise Garment Union Now! Ban Sweatshop Labor!*'

Garment Workers (*sing*)
There once was a Union maid, she never was afraid
Of goons and ginks and company finks and the deputy sheriffs that made the raid –
She went to the union-hall when a meeting it was called
And when the company boys came round she always stood her ground:
Oh you can't scare me I'm sticking to the Union
I'm sticking to the Union till the day I die!

Connolly Russians, filled with the spirit of the revolution of nineteen hundred and five, Poles, Jewish, Italian, Irish girls – all of 'em –

Garment Workers We raise our right hands and swear, 'If I turn traitor to the cause I now pledge, may this hand wither from the arm I now raise!'

Nora   Nora, James Connolly's daughter, at the age of sixteen
Knows all of her father's life and understands what it should mean
To be begotten by a man who will turn the whole world upside-down.

Exeunt. Enter an IWW OFFICIAL.

IWW Official Jim – where's Jim Connolly – look, Jim, you've to go to

Yonkers! There's trouble at the tramway company – say, they've all come out on strike except the electricians in the AF of L craft union, and none of the others is organised worth one cent. The AF of L have instructed their members to pass the picket-line. The strike committee's solid if we can back their action they'll join the IWW en masse – will you come?

Connolly My God, will I not! Lizzie Flynn can go to Hoboken in my place – just wait till I get my trousers on – Lillie, for God's sake, go to bed!

Lillie But what about you?

He runs out without answering, with the IWW OFFICIAL. *Exit* LILLIE.

SCENE 2

Enter STRIKERS *with a placard: 'Yonkers Tramway Strike: Fair Wage and Eight Hour Day for all Crews Now!'*

Tramway Strikers (*sing*)

It is we who plowed the prairies; built the cities where they trade
Dug the mines and built the workshops; endless miles of railroad laid.
Now we stand outcast and starving mid the wonders that we made
But the union makes us strong! Solidarity for ever
For the Union makes us strong!

Enter AF OF L OFFICIAL.

AF of L Official What the hell gives with you guys, why you ain't even *got* a union – now listen, the Teamsters' Union AF of L will give you backing in your grievance: but first you gotta come off strike and pull these pickets: there's good union men in the electricians are withheld by you from work!

Strikers Union men? Scabs!

The scabs crawl in and the scabs crawl out
They crawl in under and all about . . . (*etcetera*)

Trouble as SCABS *try to pass picket.* POLICE *break it up. Enter* CONNOLLY.

Connolly Now wait a minute – the IWW undertakes to back this action: but the problem of scabs? There's regular blacklegs, right, brought in to do your work: but they can't do it unless the electricians are providing the power for the trolley-cars, right? So you start with the electricians. Go picket them on their own doorsteps, in the streets where they live and shame them into supporting you. You do that, you won't need to run in trouble with the police. Don't listen to this Judas – he wants nothing better than to sell you out. You have a grievance has gone unsettled for twelve months – you said strike, so then strike, and don't let yourselves be diverted. But watch out for provocation –

AF of L Official I don't know no provocation more likely to lead to trouble than these bums of goddam Wobblies – anarchists, syndicalists, non-negotiators, revolutionists!

(The STRIKERS *jeer him.) A* HOODLUM *enters.* AF OF L OFFICIAL *takes him aside.*

Provocation? They can have it! Where the hell's my man – oh there you are. This morning you're no union employee, you're a scab: so go and scab like you was born to it.

The HOODLUM *pulls a gun and runs in towards the picket.*

Hoodlum I'm demanding police protection to afford me the right to work!
Connolly Stand clear of that man, boys, he's a –

But the HOODLUM *has already tangled with a* STRIKER*: in the fight the gun goes off and the* HOODLUM *falls.* POLICE *are whistled up by the* AF OF L OFFICIAL.

AF of L Official I'm a witness of this, officer: he was shot dead by a dirty Wobbly – case of unprovoked homicide!

The STRIKER *is arrested and taken off. The others are shocked rigid.*

Police Officer As of right now I declare this picket in violation of the state law governing public assembly. Break it up or you're all accessories to the homicide – d'you hear me – break it up! Don't speak to me, you, Connolly, or I'll gun you down right now! You got no mandate with these men.
AF of L Official Membership cards of the Teamsters Union may be obtained from my office on payment of the usual fee. Do what the man says, boys, break it up, these fool Wobblies have ruined everything. But listen, you leave it with me – maybe tomorrow with your bosses I can fix you a fair deal . . .

Exeunt, except CONNOLLY.

Connolly All they ever need to do is to mention revolution and then prove that it means murder. That poor fellow's defence must be seen to at once. And after that, the waterside workers . . .

SCENE 3

Enter ELIZABETH GURLEY FLYNN.

Flynn Jim, I don't know that the waterside workers can get into the outfit at all – De Leon is opposing it at the highest level.
Connolly He's out of his mind, the old idiot, twelve thousand of them, one quarter of all the longshoremen that work in Brooklyn, Manhattan, Hoboken – it's ridiculous – and De Leon lays claim to have done more than any single socialist to build the IWW? Tell me why?

Flynn I don't know why . . .
Connolly We'll put a stop to it – now.

Exeunt.

SCENE 4

Enter DE LEON *and a Socialist Labor Party* OFFICIAL.

De Leon Totally unrealistic padding out of the membership rolls of the IWW
by means of these mass-admissions of . . . of what are they? Italians?
SLP Official Italians and Irish –
De Leon Italian and Irish catholics: and why? Look at the name of the
organiser who sponsors them! *James Connolly*, who else? Not one of
them by any stretch of the imagination can be regarded as even the
potential possessor of any sort of socialist doctrine! He aims to swamp
the organisation with these reactionary ethnic elements for the sole
purpose of ensuring that the Socialist Labor Party is permanently out-
voted upon the IWW policy-making committees! Aha, we discover the
real reason behind the Connolly gang's promotion of these dubious
IWW propaganda leagues he has so assiduously been fostering. Hoho,
we discover the occult plot to emasculate the nation-wide movement
for which the Socialist Labor Party has heretofore been the sole source of
political doctrine! We'll put a stop to this – now! When is the next
meeting of the general executive board of the IWW?
SLP Official First week of January, Comrade De Leon – in Chicago.
De Leon Have them hold it in New York! Have it convened as a special
emergency tribunal – –
SLP Official There'll be trouble about that. I mean, travelling expenses for
delegates.
De Leon Expenses, what expenses? I am prepared at the drop of a hat to
travel to Chicago – and back the next day – if thus I can bring with me
the essential members of the board! Go get me reservations on the railroad at once – while you're doing it I'll send a wire to forewarn them of
the emergency.

Exeunt.

SCENE 5

Enter CONNOLLY, *shivering with cold, and* ELIZABETH GURLEY FLYNN *is
selling his papers in cold, snowy weather.*

Connolly So he wants to create crisis, does he, with his special meeting in
New York? Does he not know we have already such a crisis of unemployment and poverty in this city that his sectarian feuds when he brings
them here will be pelted from off the pavements? Okay, so it's a crisis.

Lizzie; go tell the committee members that in view of the urgency of the industrial situation here, any meetings of internal import must be got rid of as rapidly as possible – so why the hell wait till January – let's have De Leon's meeting on December the twenty-third and get it over with before christmas. Hurry. I'm not well.

FLYNN *hastens out.*

I've been five years in America, ye'd have thought I could have warned myself a winter's night in New York is by no means the same thing as the same thing in Dublin – like a damnfool I sell newspapers for three hours outside the Cooper Union. Nora – where are you, dear, will you – will you get me my cup o' tea?

Enter NORA *who finds him collapsing.*

Nora Daddy, you must come to bed, you can't go out again to a meeting tonight.

Connolly No, not tonight, but the twenty-third – I'll be fine by the twenty-third – I must have the documents on the waterside workers – will you bring them to the bedroom –

Nora I'm quite sure at the moment that's not at all a good idea –

She helps him off.

SCENE 6

Enter IWW DELEGATES *for meeting.* ELIZABETH GURLEY FLYNN *is one of them.*

Chairman Fellow workers: we are here at Daniel De Leon's insistence to discuss the affiliation of the waterside workers – goddammit, didn't he say it was a matter of extreme urgency? So where is he? Where the hell is he? If it comes to that, where's Connolly?

1st Delegate All the way from Chicago two days before christmas and there ain't nobody here who knows anything about why this meeting was convened?

Flynn Now wait a minute, Jim Connolly's sick. He's left all the documents with me to handle it for him. On account of it being right on top of the christmas holiday he wants the whole thing finalised, if we can, with the least delay.

2nd Delegate Shouldn't we wait for De Leon?

3rd Delegate Wait hell for De Leon! It's De Leon made all the racket about dragging us all down here – if he don't turn up, that's *his* funeral. Let's get on with it, we got a quorum.

Chairman You've all read Jim Connolly's recommendation. Any objections?

1st Delegate To the incorporation of twelve thousand new proletarians into the outfit? Objections hell! Pass it through and for God's sake, don't waste no more time!

2nd Delegate Say look here, this meeting was called by De Leon. He must have his reasons. We can't just agree to – –

Flynn Why not? He's not here?

Enter DE LEON.

De Leon Comrade Chairman, my apologies: being under the impression that this meeting was scheduled for January the twelfth – –

Chairman Didn't you get the documentation that was sent to you in Chicago? On representations from certain New York delegates the date was changed –

De Leon At the last minute and I received the notification almost too late. Moreover my train from Chicago was held up by snow. You have not yet taken a vote?

2nd Delegate (*smiles and shakes his head reassuringly at* DE LEON)

De Leon Before we do take a vote, may I request that all those persons present who are not members of the IWW Executive Committee be excluded from our deliberations?

Chairman Elizabeth Flynn was presenting – –

De Leon Comrade Flynn is not a member of this committee, I believe.

Chairman In the enforced absence of Comrade Connolly, who fell sick – –

De Leon And very nearly in the enforced absence of Comrade De Leon? Well? Does the lady intend – –

Flynn The lady as requested is on her way out. I'll be in the lobby if you change your minds.

Exit.

De Leon This project for the affiliation of the waterside workers is by no means what it seems. It is a brainchild of James Connolly. *James Connolly*, unskilled labourer, who five years ago tried to pass himself off to me as a qualified linotype operator, who four years ago nearly demoralised the Socialist Labor Party in the city of Troy, who less than two years ago was instrumental in sabotaging the entire working relationship between the SLP Executive and their own newspaper *The Weekly People* – *James Connolly* whose past record in Irish political circles has been shown to consist entirely of faction, subversion, and the internal destruction of the very party he claims to have founded in Dublin – *James Connolly* who has been proved to be not only an agent of the Jesuit Order – how many of you realise the close contact he had with Cardinal Logue during his recent visit to New York: at every meeting that rapacious prelate attended, the man Connolly was there in the front row! – but also we now know that he is an active agent of the New York police and continually gives information to – –

1st Delegate Look, mister, I tried to hold out till you came to the end of a sentence: but with your sentences – hell. I'll be back in thirty seconds.

De Leon Back? Back from where? Where are you going?

1st Delegate If you gotta go, you gotta go. There's only two places where that can be said of, and one of 'em's the morgue . . .

Exit 1ST DELEGATE

De Leon Where was I? Oh yes. Jesuits. Police. Now the Jesuit Order, as maybe you did not realise, was founded in the sixteenth century by Ignatius Loyola in order to – –

3rd Delegate We really must suspend business while one of our members has left the room.

De Leon Why?

3rd Delegate I was addressing the chair.

Chairman Comrade De Leon, if you don't mind, let's keep it on ice till he gets back.

De Leon But I have a great deal more to say, a very great deal more . . .

Chairman Yeah, that's just it . . .

Ominous silence till 1ST DELEGATE *returns.*

1st Delegate I just been talking to the guys outside!

De Leon You had no business to do that!

1st Delegate Every goddam business! Come on boys, Elizabeth, come on in. Dan De Leon's gonna prove his allegations right now before a wide-open forum of the entire organisation – !

FLYNN *and other IWW Members come in angrily. Fury and turmoil.*

Chairman I am about to make a ruling! I am within my rights as chairman: you will not controvert it! Until Comrade Connolly is in a state of health to reply to these accusations, the business of this meeting has gotta be held over. The National Annual Convention of the IWW will be held in Chicago within a matter of months – why don't you put all your gripes on a *small* piece o' paper, Comrade De Leon, and then see what they look like there? In the meantime, this meeting is adjourned. Merry Christmas.

De Leon Comrade Chairman, I insist. Comrade Chairman, I protest – –

Chairman The meeting is adjourned.

Exeunt all save DE LEON *and* 2ND DELEGATE.

2nd Delegate Dan, are you out of your mind? You gone and put the back up every man and woman in this room the way you handled this.

De Leon You are a member of the Socialist Labor Party. I had counted on your support.

2nd Delegate Yeah, you had it, before you came in the goddam room. After that, like, it didn't strike me, you were putting over an *ideology* . . .

Exeunt.

SCENE 7

The IWW CONVENTION *of 1908. A big banner announcing this.* DELEGATES
*enter, confusedly, amid a babel of slogans, snatches of song, voices all
round the theatre (and from loudspeakers).* CONNOLLY *is conspicuous,
handing out leaflets.*

1st Voice

To Chicago in the mid-months of nineteen-hundred-o-eight –

2nd Voice

Make or break, revolution now, revolution tomorrow too late –

3rd Voice

Revolution through preparation, agitation, education, my ass –

4th Voice

Revolution through nuth'n but the surge of the swell of the mass
Of the rage of the deprived proletariat – we are here:
America walk in fear!

General Voices

Walk in dread, walk in fear,

Walk in terror of the present time

That men turned round and said no longer, 'Buddy can you
spare a dime?'

But, 'Buddy can we spare your goddam life!'

3rd Voice

Lemme tell you from now on there ain't nobody safe!

2nd Voice The Western Federation of Miners was broken away from us by the
treachery of the AF of L –

4th Voice The Socialist Party of America does nuth'n but play lousy electoral
politics with the organisation, our men is starving in the streets of
Pittsburgh, starving, and all they can do for us is promise us paradise
for the sake of a lousy vote to run Gene Debs for President.

3rd Voice The Socialist Labor Party don't want no kinda action except all
according to the rules and regulations of two-three kraut textbooks Dan
De Leon keeps in his hip pocket –

1st Voice (*sings*)

Hallelujah I'm a bum –

General Voices (*sing*)

With nuth'n to lose –

Do we do what we're told

Or do what we choose?

Do we lie down and fight

Or rise up and die

Hallelujah we got here

And we're all going sky-high . . . !

Connolly From all corners of the world, and the English language sits in their
mouths like a hot coal in a pan of water – with their blankets and their

dixie-cans and their backs bent and their feet twisted from hanging on like spider-monkeys from the bogies of the freight-cars. The working class and the employing class have nothing in common – and these men here today have so crowded in with such rage into their convention that I cannot believe they can ever get out of it without throwing away almost everything brought them together in the first place. They begin by throwing away the very framework of their procedure – –

Chairman Order, fellow workers, order – we gotta have order here; we gotta make ourselves heard, dammit! It has been moved – it has been moved that the minutes of last year's Convention be read in accordance with – –

Voices No minutes, no minutes, no minutes! Can that bullshit, man, get on with it, get on with what we come for!

Chairman Okay okay, so we bow to the will of the meeting. We got one crucial business that I know and you all know has gotta be settled today and that is – –

Voices Get the politicians out of it – spring ourselves clear of the goddam intellectuals – crack the eggheads outa the outfit – we're proletarians here or nuth'n – Industrial *Workers* of the World so let's have some workers' action – ! *Etcetera . . .*

Chairman Just ain't no good going on, boys, without we do it *orderly*! Minutes or no minutes, we just gotta have a motion down—so who's gonna propose it?

Enter DE LEON. *Boos. A few cheers.*

De Leon Comrade Chairman –

3rd Voice Will ya can that *comrade* bullshit! We're one hundred per cent Americans here and we don't want no fucking European faggot-talk: 'fellow-worker' is the word we use, Dan, and you shape it up our way or you ship out, professor!

De Leon Am I going to be heard or not?

Chairman Willya lissen what the man says! He's gotta right to be heard like you've all gotta right to be heard – you've elected me here to ensure that you get that right! Okay. We keep it reasonable or this chair as of now by me is vacated . . . Dan De Leon of the Socialist Labor Party has the floor.

De Leon *James Connolly* – of the New York Building and Construction Workers' local – I have demanded the dismissal of that man Connolly from his post! I am appalled he is still here with his sectarian Irish propaganda in his hand! I have consistently and unequivocally published evidence of his treachery to the movement and I demand before any other business is concluded that this convention examine his so-called credentials and take action thereupon.

Elizabeth Flynn Can we have please a statement of the credentials of Professor De Leon?

De Leon I am not a professor! In the context of this convention I am a . . . I am a . . . Comrade Chairman, if my credentials over the past twenty years in the socialist movement are not recollected the length and breadth of this great nation, there seems little I can do at this late stage to refresh your memory . . .

Voices Answer, answer – !

De Leon I am a member of the IWW by virtue of my status as –

3rd Voice As a company director!

De Leon That is absolutely untrue! I am the managing editor of a socialist newspaper – –

4th Voice He's the only one he can trust down there to keep his fingers outa the till!

De Leon Which is and always has been conducted upon principles of – –

Flynn Which union do your printers belong to?

De Leon I myself am a member of a labour-organisation – –

3rd Voice You yourself refused to join the IWW printers' local!

De Leon That was only because – –

Connolly Because you were already a member of quite another local – the store and office workers, were you not, which does not happen to be affiliated to this organisation? It's a technical legalistic non-intellectual issue. A ruling from the chair, please, yes or no?

Chairman Ain't no doubt about it: he shows up his card of membership of an IWW union or he quits this hall pronto.

De Leon I am here ex officio as an elected representative of the Socialist Labor Party –

Chairman Which for sure ain't no trade union.

De Leon Which was recognised at the founding convention of nineteen hundred and five as part and parcel of the structure of the Industrial Workers of the World –

Voices This is nineteen oh eight, not nineteen oh five – get wise, man. What happened in nineteen oh five is dead and deep down under – we ain't bound by none of last year's structure, tear it out – ! (*etcetera . . .*)

De Leon I'm within my rights to demand a vote.

Chairman I question that. But you can have one. Representatives of political parties have an ex-officio place at the IWW Convention. Those in favour? . . . Those agin? . . . Two-thirds agin. One-third in favour. Sorry, friend, just ain't your day. Come back again next year with your little pink card in the heel of your sock and show it to the man at the door.

Connolly Before he goes, my own position. I'd be obliged for a vote on that. If people really believe I acquired this card of membership under false pretences as a detective, or a priest, I am more than content to take the majority decision and surrender it, here and now.

Chairman Okay, we'll make it regular. Vote of confidence, here and now, upon the credentials of Jim Connolly. Those in favour that he's on the level?

. . . Those who think that he's a rat and should be druv back into his hole? . . . Okay, justice triumphs. Keep your seat, Jim, guess you've earned it, you're one of us, boy . . . We get to business.

A short pause as DE LEON *ostentatiously leaves the body of the hall (but remains where he can observe the ensuing business) amid boos and a few cheers.*

In the preamble to our constitution we have the sentence that pronounces the necessity for economic as well as political action to achieve our ends. There's a motion put down to delete the word 'political'. Proposer? Big Bill Haywood.

Haywood (*amid a storm of cheering*) Just so long as we can keep ourselves together as an organisation of industrial workers, with the power to strike, the power to picket, the power to sabotage inside the plant, we are capable at a moment's notice of pulling out every man that shovels coal and greases wheels from San Francisco to New York: and the whole bad edifice of Wall Street finance-capital both knows that power and trembles at it! But let the political parties – whether capitalist or so-called socialist – get their hands on our united strength, they will strip us off like onions, skin by skin, to enable them the better to trade vote against vote and so slip into their seats in state and national legislature and fix themselves a good career! Get rid of that damnfool preamble and make use of your huge energies to totally bankrupt the plutocracy! 'Cos there ain't no other way but that, and that's it and I'm finished . . .

Chairman Hold it, now, order! Didn't I tell you, I will have order! So let's hear the opposer.

2ND DELEGATE *from Scene 6 rises to oppose.*

Opposer So if only the union's big enough, it can grind America to a halt . . . so we starve . . . so what then? There still ain't no way we can actually *run* the goddam country! I quote Karl Marx: 'The proletariat will use its political supremacy to wrest, by degrees, all capital from the bourgeoisie, to centralise all instruments of production in the hands of the State – i.e.: of the proletariat organised as the ruling class – and to increase the total of productive forces as rapidly as possible!' Yeah, you threw out Dan De Leon, but I tell you, without De Leon and the nationwide party newspaper he edited for this movement, the expression of our struggle would be utterly denied to us!

Chairman Those in favour of deleting the word *political* from the preamble of our constitution? . . . Those against? . . . Motion carried. The word's deleted: and that's it.

De Leon

From now on the IWW has not one chance on God's earth
To beget the revolution and bring it forth to triumphant birth.

He stalks out and through the DELEGATES. *A moment of dead silence. Exeunt.*

SCENE 8

The presidential election campaign of 1908, Balloons, posters, tickertape, etcetera.

Enter REPORTERS. *They speak rapidly to the audience while all the election razzmatazz goes on behind.*

1st Reporter Come on come on come on roll up roll up and leave aside these chicken-shit minority preoccupations. The people of America nineteen-hundred-and-eight under God are about to elect their new President! Endorsed by the outgoing incumbent Teddy Roosevelt, for the Republicans runs William Taft! The year of depression and slump is finally lifting, the Republican Party stands revealed as the precursor of ever-increasing prosperity for more and more Americans!

2nd Reporter For the Democrats William Jennings Bryan repeats his clarion call 'You shall not crucify mankind upon a cross of gold!' and brands the obstructive financial practices of the cartels and monopoly trusts.

1st Reporter The obstructive financial practices of the cartels and monopoly trusts have no more ardent antagonist than the remarkable third candidate – Eugene Debs of the Socialist Party of America. In the election of nineteen hundred and four Debs ran a campaign in opposition to the big parties that brought him nearly half-a-million votes: this time he intends to more than double that figure. We have seen the repudiation of political action by the IWW in Chicago. Will we now see the justification by the SPA of the very stance so many of its trade unionist members have already renounced? For there's no doubt that in their thousands the individual Wobblies flock to the Debs bandwagon and urge him forward to the polls!

2nd Reporter This is the greatest, most spectacular national campaign ever launched in the name of socialism – with a locomotive and a sleeping-car, hired at the unprecedented and almost unattainable cost of twenty thousand dollars, Eugene Debs has left Chicago on the first leg of his coast-to-coast, whistle-stop tour, the scarlet flag of his amazing doctrine flying proudly from the pilot and the smoke-stack of his aptly-named 'Red Special'!

Enter GOMPERS.

Gompers If Debs gets one million votes, then the Democrat-Republican two-party system will be thrown into the melting-pot and maybe next time round in nineteen twelve we're gonna see but one candidate running for capitalism and one candidate run for socialism, and the entire delicate balance between organised labour – *my* organised labour – and the representatives of big business will be thrown into the melting-pot. The

American working man is *not* a socialist – he is an unfulfilled capitalist – and to save for him his hopes and dreams I add my voice – 'Stop Debs!'

Enter GRABITALL *and* BOSSES.

Grabitall and Bosses
>Stop Debs!
>Vote for Taft, vote for Bryan
>Vote for *either*, vote for *or* –
Gompers Hell no, not Taft, vote Bryan and sweep the floor!
Grabitall and Bosses
>Just so we all know
>Devil Debs is shown the door!
>Stop Debs!
Gompers (*sings*)
>All the bums called Eugene in nineteen-eight
>You'd better get movin or you're gonna be late
>If the old locomotive don't run outa steam
>You're gonna drive slap-bang through the American dream!
Grabitall and Bosses (*sing*)
>Eugene Debs, he's mounted to the cabin
>Eugene Debs with his orders in his hand
>Eugene Debs with his German ideology
>On the great Red Special to the promised land!

DEBS *and his election team, as though conveyed on the train, pass round and over the stage, waving red flags.*

Enter CONNOLLY.

Connolly In this election I helped Debs. Not on the Red Special but on my own appropriate speaking tour in what they call the Pope's backyard – the Irish communities of the East Coast, hoeing hard at the potato-rows of the traditional Democrat vote. Socialism . . . ? Well, they *listened*. But to Debs they did more than listen. Why they hailed that man like John the Baptist . . .

Debs The capitalists who rule America understand one language and one language only – the language of power! Give me one million votes and already we begin to hold that power in our own hands! The Socialist Party aims to compel Congress to put an end to court injunctions against strikes and lawful picketing: to enact laws affirming the statutory eight-hour day: and to enforce liability and safety regulations upon every industry in the USA! With that for a beginning the working class has the road open for its own industrial triumph, through the unions, to destroy the evil monster of finance-capital exploitation! The Red Special runs west – Des Moines, Muscatine, Corning, from Iowa into Nebraska: Omaha . . .

Gompers (*sings*)
>Pour on the water, shovel on the coal
>Put God's own country under alien control
>He's comin for your dollars and he's comin for your wife
>And he's comin for *you* for the rest of your life!

Grabitall and Bosses (*sing*)
>Eugene Debs, he's mounted to the cabin
>Eugene Debs with his orders in his hand
>Eugene Debs, with his German ideology
>On the great Red Special to the promised land!

Connolly Whether or no the depression, as claimed by the Republicans, was in fact easing up, the IWW proved unable to pay me even my starvation stipend of eighteen dollars a week. From the SPA in the full flush of its election fever I could earn enough speaking-fees to keep my family alive for a wee while longer. Moreover the party have given me nation-wide facilities for the distribution of *The Harp*.

Debs Denver, Colorado: Leadville, Colorado: Santa Barbara, California . . . Did I hear someone say that a vote for socialism is a vote thrown away? That's right, friend, that's right: don't vote for freedom – you might not get it. Vote for slavery – you have a cinch on that. Ye gods, but these are pregnant days! San Diego, Los Angeles, Spokane, Billings Montana – the heartland of the Wobbly country . . .

Gompers (*sings*)
>Toot on the whistle and ring on the bell
>There ain't no heaven and there ain't no hell
>He's gonna drag you down and level you out
>And your hard-earned wages goin up the spout!

Grabitall and Bosses (*sing*)
>Eugene Debs, he's mounted to the cabin
>Eugene Debs with his orders in his hand
>Eugene Debs with his German ideology
>On the great Red Special to the promised land!

Connolly The Socialist Party of America includes all, expels none: but Debs as their candidate talks sound industrial unionism in every city where he speaks. I can do no better than stay with him.

Debs St Paul Minnesota, Duluth, Chicago, Toledo, Rochester, New York City . . .

1st Reporter The greatest political meeting ever held in this city! If, as Roosevelt says, the adherents of this doctrine are undesirable citizens, an enormous number are going to have to be deported before this nation regains its health.

Debs Philadelphia, Camden, Newark, Pittsburgh, Harpers Ferry . . . The work begun here by John Brown is now carried on by the Socialist Party of America. We today are the true, the only, abolitionists of slavery!

And so back to Chicago, with my voice so weak with speaking I can scarcely be heard . . .

Gompers (*sings*)

> Oh it's beans and bacon for every man
> And a two-dollar charge when you go to the can
> If you can't pay your way, boy, don't you mind –
> There's a train full of bullshit on the socialist line!

Grabitall and Bosses (*sing*)

> Eugene Debs, he's mounted to the cabin
> Eugene Debs, with his orders in his hand
> Eugene Debs with his German ideology
> On the great Red Special to the promised land . . .

1st Reporter And the result? William Taft becomes President.

Gompers Yeah: with the Republicans I can maybe do a deal . . .

1st Reporter William Jennings Bryan has been heavily defeated.

Gompers Sure, Bryan was just a crazy man – a small-town, shyster lawyer with crank notions about currency. That guy wouldn't know the difference between an affiliated craft union and a goddam temperance guild. Good riddance . . .

1st Reporter And Eugene Debs – ?

Gompers His million votes – ?

Grabitall and Bosses His power of opinion to lobby Congress into ruinous legislation – ?

1st Reporter Less than half-a-million votes – hardly better than he did in nineteen oh four . . .

Debs The campaign is ended. But the loyal support given me in every part of the country expressed the true spirit of socialist comradeship, which is the making of our movement and which will sustain it through every ordeal until it is finally triumphant.

Connolly Of course the effect of the ballot is limited by the degree of democratic supervision which can be exercised over the actual boxes. For instance in Terre Haute where Debs himself voted –

Debs Not one vote for the socialists was registered in that precinct. Am I supposed to believe in a moment of amnesia I cast my name for William Taft?

Exeunt all save CONNOLLY. GRABITALL *and* BOSSES *go out in a posture of mock innocence and giggling at* DEBS'*s disclosure . . .*

SCENE 9

Connolly After the defeat, the discussion of the reason therefor.

> Reordering of the battalions for the next battle in the long long war.

He withdraws.

Enter DEBS.

Debs   Health broken, spirit for the time being diminished,
I walk gloomily aside while recrimination rolls over and fro –

Enter HILLQUIT, HAYWOOD *and other* SPA MEMBERS *to take their seats in committee –* HILLQUIT *in chair,* HAYWOOD *and* 1ST MEMBER *on left,* 2ND *and* 3RD MEMBERS *on right.*

I am sure you guys will know
Where to find me if you want me the moment you're finished.

DEBS *sits down well away from them with a bottle.*

Hillquit Why didn't the working-class vote match up to the mass support given Comrade Debs on his tour, hey? I'll tell you why, plain as the nose on your faces, because the American worker has either gone crazy lone ranging with the non-political Wobblies, or else he sticks with Sam Gompers of the AF of L – and Gompers backed Bryan, who promised a whole load of phoney reform. Add to that, with the slump, three-quarters of the proletarian vote had left home in the depression to look for work somewheres else, so their names were on no voting register.

1st Member Gene Debs talked fine about revolution and industrial unionism: but there was more than Gene Debs to the campaign and the people knew it. Yeah, a working-class party? What the hell does a man think when he sees the potential socialist president of the USA backed by a crowd of college professors, society sob-sisters, and old-style baptist evangelists?

Haywood I'll tell you what he thinks – he thinks, 'With those guys in the White House, what chance has a regular two-fisted immigrant Yid like Karl Marx even to get his toecaps past the guard at the gate!'

3rd Member I don't wanna hear nuth'n, ever again, about Karl Marx and his two fists! If I wanted any saints I'd prefer to turn catholic and buy 'em up wholesale!

2nd Member Immigrant – yeah, you said it!

3rd Member It's the yellow peril on the west coast that chaws 'em up the worst. Why, there's Chinamen and Japs by the million coming in to San Francisco any day of the week. Get that herd to join a union, let alone a political party? Goddam lunacy to let them in, and it's high time our voice was heard on it!

Haywood You ever worked with Japs?

3rd Member I know enough about them, and their rate of propagation, yeah and the number of wives and concubines they're allowed to have back home! Do you know, an oriental, on one little saucer of rice per day, will – –

Haywood I said, you ever worked with Japs? I have: in the mining camps: and I can tell you, in a no-holds-barred labour struggle there ain't no better fighter in the world!

1st Member If I'm told the Jap will carry the socialist banner in a place where the white man fails, then all hail to the Jap – let him carry it for me!

2nd Member And let you carry the can, comrade, for every vote you're gonna lose! Oh, Sam Gompers knows his onions – as a matter of pragmatic tactics, we simply don't dare to alienate that guy's membership – four-square white Americans and the only possible bedrock for a socialist campaign!

Uproar. Right and left bellow incoherently and shake their fists at each other.

Hillquit Comrades, for God's sake! We're all falling apart. Okay, so it's time to offer up some sort of compromise. We gotta get rid of these right-wing fool arguments about saucers of rice and the oriental birth-rate – that's not socialism – nothing less than Ku-klux-klannery, and the sooner we forget it was ever spoken, the better. On the other hand . . .

Debs (*lurches to his feet, and speaking to the audience*) On the other hand . . . ?

Hillquit There's no doubt the race question *is* a sore point. We already have enough problems with the negro in the south . . . Hey, how about this – 'The Socialist Party of America favors all legislative measures tending to prevent the immigration of' – wait for it – 'strike-breakers and con-tract-laborers brought about by the employing classes for the purpose of weakening the determination of American workers'? You get the tactic – lay the blame on the boss class: and emphasise the inability of these backward ethnic elements to understand trade union principles.

Haywood My God, but I just told you – –

Debs (*lurches into the meeting*) Unsocialistic, reactionary, outrageous . . . The revolutionary character of our party must be preserved in its integrity at all cost . . .

He lurches out again.

Hillquit We take a vote on it? In favour? Against? Motion tied. Casting vote from the chair – in favour. Motion passed. Okay, so what next? Question of attitude toward trade unions. The IWW has been so all-fired hostile to the AF of L, I guess we've got no option but to take stock, and that fast.

2nd Member We don't want to go so far as to *repudiate* the Wobblies.

3rd Member We don't want to go so far as to repudiate *anybody*! Least of all Sam Gompers – as a matter of tactical pragmatism. But Gompers ain't no socialist, and we can't just endorse his outfit, outa hand. Not just yet.

Haywood Sonofabitch! You mean that in due time you believe you *can* endorse it!

2nd Member Now wait a minute, he didn't say – –

Haywood I heard what he said!

Hillquit If we don't repudiate Gompers and we don't repudiate the Wobblies, it means in effect we decide to take no position on the trade union question. Maybe that's just exactly the position that we should take. So why don't we ease up on this theoretical controversy and bad blood, hey? Get some regular all-American propaganda put over. We've got newspapers and lecture-tours and ginger-group organisers set and ready to go all over the country. Say, there's thousands more read our papers than dared to put the vote in for us: we gotta get hold of those guys through the medium of the printed word and just boost 'em to the polls next time round, what do you say? Slow and systematic education of the working class, *education* – so let's get on with it! Gene, we've finished.

Debs Yeah, I heard. We have already catered far too much to the AF of L – a halt will have to be called. So for God's sake, boys, just you call it . . .

Exit.

Haywood

From now on the SPA has not one chance on God's earth
To beget the revolution and bring it forth to triumphant birth.

Exit, followed by all except 3RD MEMBER.

3rd Member Okay, so where are all these party workers we got feeding their face on our goddam payroll? Hey, you there – Comrade Connolly –
Enter CONNOLLY.
Here's your newspapers – get 'em sold, willya, quick, and then go to Philadelphia – there's a lecture-date fixed up for you – go tell 'em the good news about 'Workers of the World Unite' – you can draw your expenses from my secretary before the banks close. Hey, after Philadelphia, how about Tucson Arizona, an'a whole load o' dates way up toward Montana – boy, in this outfit you sure get to go places!

Exit, leaving CONNOLLY *with a great pile of papers.*

SCENE 10

Enter LILLIE.

Lillie (*addresses the audience without reference to* CONNOLLY)

While he goes to Arizona there's a public holiday in New York.
Would you believe my daughter Nora and the young people with
her at work
Are actually made able to take me on a holiday picnic, a trip by
boat
Up the Hudson River, a whole day to do nothing in a green park
Except rest and enjoy ourselves and do nothing from morning
till dark . . .
And some of this she pays for and some of it *I* pay for and none
of it comes from him –

Because at last from his regular wage we can cover all that we
need in the home
And what's over is extra – we can spend it however we like:
Do you know it's the first holiday I've ever had in the whole of
my life . . . ?

Exit LILLIE.

Connolly Twenty-one dollars per week, three more than I got from the
Wobblies, that's it –
Plus travelling expenses, commission from sales of papers, not a
bit
Good complaining that the work is a repetitive drag
So long as I can kid myself that in the end, deep down in the
bottom of the bag
I can grope for and find and haul out into the sunlight glare
The true jewel of revolution, like Venus from the ocean,
Long-legged, wild-eyed, red-gold-haired bare
Terror to the closed mind, the closed-down forehead, the envious
shoulders that stoop
The shadow of capitalist rule over the length of this working
world . . . small hope,
I know that; all the smaller for the decisions that have just been
made.
Yet here I am, the wheels turn round, the pistons plunge and
slide
Day in, day out, the locomotive blows for the climbing of one
more grade –
So much paper, so many acres of print:
But how much power in all these words so fabulously spent
And sent about, perhaps read, perhaps not read,
But understood?
No good
To talk about it: act.
This literature is a fact.

The titles of it alone would fill a graveyard – *The Appeal to Reason, The
Worker, The Socialist Weekly Bulletin, The Socialist Party Official
Bulletin, The Socialist, The Social Democratic Herald, The Workers' Call,*
pamphlets moreover – *The Socialist Campaign Book, Capitalist Union or
Labor Unions, which? Party Politics and the Trade Unions, The Attack on
the Trade Unions, Shall the Unions go into Politics?* – translations more-
over of the publications of the permitted immigrant federations:
Bohemian, Finnish, Italian, Polish, Scandinavian, South Slavic, Lettish,
Hungarian – add to this all my own stuff – *The Harp, Erin's Hope* – oh
my God, Erin's hope . . .

Out of Ireland, what hope? Out of Ireland where is the horn
That will tear the heavens asunder and proclaim that at last is
   born
In Belfast or in Dublin the achieved fulfilment of our mortal need?
Seven years in this great wilderness where nothing will breed
But dry bones,
Thorns and broken stone . . .

Larkin (*voice off*) I had a mission in Belfast! To create a trade union among perhaps the most backward industrial people in the whole of western Europe – the carters and coal-fillers and dock labourers of the swarming sectarian slums.

Connolly (*suddenly roused from his gloom*) James Larkin – I'd never met him – he came over from Liverpool after I had left for America – could it be that this man – ?

Larkin (*voice off*) I created that union, and I brought them on strike: for the first time for over a century protestant and catholic were united in defence of their rights as human beings! No, we were not going to be beasts any longer – we were to rouse the working classes out of their slough of despond and with the microbe of discontent in our blood to lift ourselves up on to the peak of Mount Optimism!

Still orating, he strides in, but a good distance from CONNOLLY, *rather as though he is descried in a vision.*

And the result, the entrenched leaders of the bureaucratic craft union, from their headquarters in Britain, struck with terror lest our revolt should develop into revolution, dragged me back out of the struggle and demanded I should repudiate the very militancy I had set aflame. For such runagates, I will defy them! We will begin our *own* union – the Irish Transport Workers – for the unskilled casual wage-slaves, whatever their religion, in Belfast, Dublin, Cork, and every corner of the land! An independent Irish union for an independent Irish nation – One Big Union One Big Strike – and let the cross-channel labour fakers go to hell where they belong!

Connolly Why does it have to be him in Belfast and not me . . . ?

Larkin James Connolly, why does it have to be me in Belfast and not you? Come home, man, you are *required* here!

Exit LARKIN.

SCENE 11

Connolly Oh sure, if my old comrades in the Socialist Party of Ireland could break into the bank on College Green when the cashier was not looking and get hold of the passage-money, and send it – within a week I'd be on my way . . .

Enter LILLIE.

Lillie How many letters have you sent to O'Brien in Dublin to find out what he can do for you?

Connolly Would you have me count the wild geese in their migration to the tide-filled sloblands?

Lillie How many answers have you had?

Connolly I am waiting for but *one* answer – I have told him if I get it, future generations of little Connollys will rise up and call him blessed ...

Lillie   In Scotland he began, in Ireland carried it on –
    In America it had seemed I could make for him his secure home:
    From America if the wild women of revolution in his mind
    Call him forth and he must go, I will not stay behind –
    To turn the whole world upside-down
    Is a task for no fixed citizen of an enclosed and guarded town ...

Letter appears, as though by magic – a sort of deus-ex-machina *episode.*

Connolly and Lillie (*breathlessly, together*) It's the letter – and it says – ?
Voice of the Letter
    James Larkin is in prison on a trumped-up charge
    We must have Connolly, till Larkin is at large
    All Ireland quakes and shudders, revolution is at hand
    James Connolly, come home to your own proper land!
    Your fare will be paid, your position assured
    At last your Irish comrades send authentic urgent word:
    Don't look back, leave your wife to follow after –
    The whole new world of socialism breaks to birth across the
      water!

Connolly If I do not at once at last go home once more
    This huge America will kill my heart
    And nail my worn-out body to the floor –
    In nineteen-hundred-ten, July,
    I wave my children and my wife good-bye
    Aloft aboard the boat to cross the sea –
    So soon, so soon you follow after me. ....

Exeunt severally.

SCENE 12

Enter GRABITALL – *wearing round his stars-and-stripes top hat a mass of red, white, and blue ribbons like a mane falling on to his shoulders.*

Grabitall Mr Gompers – !

Enter GOMPERS.

Gompers Mr President, Mr Senator, Mr Congressman, sir – oh, Mr Inter-locutor, please sir, call me Sam!

Grabitall Sam, boy – call me Uncle! Well, hell, goldarn it, Sam, what are we gonna do about this Panama Canal?

Gompers Build it, Uncle, build it good.

Grabitall On an eight-hour day at a guaranteed minimum wage? Boy, you push too far!

Gompers In that climate, for the white labour, just ain't no alternative, Uncle.

Grabitall In that climate, if the white labour don't sweat twice as hard as the greasers, then nobody, nohow's gonna do any work at all. Unlimited hours, Sam, and the wage rates raise proportional.

Gompers No! No, sir, Uncle, there just ain't no deal forthcoming.

Grabitall Say, hell, Sam, now look at it this way – hey! Say, what d'you say, Sam, we're gonna *do* with that damn canal?

Gompers Why, Uncle, ship the navy through it – the United States Navy, ocean-to-ocean, in control of the entire hemisphere!

Grabitall And do we have the navy, boy, to control the entire hemisphere?

Gompers Uncle, we must build it, we must build it goddam good!

Grabitall On a guaranteed eight-hour day in every government-contract shipyard!

Gompers Uncle: it's a deal . . . ! Hot dog – copper-bottomed – for the con-struction of the canal you can lay down your own terms – !

Grabitall And by nineteen fourteen the keels of our new ships will be breasting every tideline from Buenos Aires to El Salvador –

He sings:

> So soon in every Dago port our cruisers drop their anchor
> To set on land with bag in hand the modest Yankee banker –

Enter BOSSES.

Bosses (*sing*)
> He will not come with sword and gun nor buccaneering forces:
> We keep those hid till every bid lies on the floor of auction.

Grabitall and Bosses (*sing*)
> Bananas in the jungle and tobacco on the plain
> And copper in the mountains bursting out at every vein
> The oil that gushes upward will come down again like rain
> For the NEW CONQUISTADORS!

GOMPERS *is marshalling a line of* WORKERS, *whom he dresses in a long stars-and-stripes cloth: the head of the line clutches the waist of* GRABITALL, *thus forming a Chinese-style dancing dragon, which begins to perambulate the theatre in time to the music.*

All (*sing*)

> Glory, glory hallelujah
> Dollar bills will live for ever
> Every man a Rockefeller
> With the NEW CONQUISTADORS!

Grabitall (*sings*)

> I stuck my finger up a Dago's hole
> And the Dago said 'God bless my soul –
> Revolu – Revolu – Revolu – Revolution.'

Bosses (*sing*)

> Oh Diego, what a curious word you use:
> For the revolution you will get is the one that we will choose –
> Your colonels and your justices from us will take their pay
> And twice the money they receive they'll give back every day.
> Oh Diego, you know we cannot lose:
> For there never was a dollar yet you ever did refuse!

MARINES *march across with rifles and flags.*

Marines (*sing*)

> And if any should find reason to doubt us or mistrust
> Remember in due season how much the Spaniards lost
> At Manila and Havana in eighteen ninety eight
> When the old imperial Europe heard the thunder at the gate!

Gompers and Grabitall (*sing*)

> When Capital and Labour are at last identified
> In the gathering of profit from the world both far and wide
> The power of our great nation will be felt on every side
> Through the NEW CONQUISTADORS!

All (*sing*)

> Glory glory Hallelujah
> Here we come to take you over
> Bow your heads and follow after
> The NEW CONQUISTADORS . . . !

Exeunt.

END OF PART FOUR

Part Five: The Great Lockout 1910-1914

Act One: 'Donnybrook Fair'. James Connolly returns to Ireland and its furious political and trade union confusions. He meets James Larkin, who sends him to Belfast to organise the new Irish Transport Workers' Union. He has ideological clashes with William Walker of the Northern Ireland labour movement.

List of characters:
> JAMES CONNOLLY
> LILLIE CONNOLLY
> NORA CONNOLLY (their daughter)
> Their other children
>
> JAMES LARKIN
> WILLIAM O'BRIEN
> WILLIAM WALKER
> Miss GALWAY
>
> OFFICIAL of the Seamen's and Firemen's Union
> BRITISH TRADE-UNION LEADER
>
> 2 DOCKERS
> SHOP ASSISTANT
> FAT WOMAN of BERMONDSEY
> CLERK
> OFFICE MESSENGER
> 4 MILL GIRLS
> Middle-class and working-class SUFFRAGETTES
>
> GRABITALL
> 3 EMPLOYERS
> POLICE OFFICER
> PRISON WARDER
>
> CATHOLIC PRIEST
> PROTESTANT MINISTER
>
> ASQUITH
> LLOYD GEORGE
> REDMOND
> CARSON
> CHURCHILL
> BONAR LAW
> Old EARL
> DUKE

3 CIVIL SERVANTS
Member of IRISH REPUBLICAN BROTHERHOOD
SPOKESMEN for: Nationalism, Ancient Order of Hibernians, Sinn Fein,
Gaelic League, Orange Order, Southern Ascendancy unionism, Northern
Protestant trade unionism

NARRATOR

workers, strikers, police, citizens, Ulster Volunteers, peers of the realm
shop assistants, bandsmen, etc.

Act Two: 'Keir Hardie's Promise'. James Connolly continues his work in Ireland for the labour movement. The Irish Labour Party is founded. The Dublin Employers' Federation is founded. The 'Great Lockout' is imposed: Larkin, aided by Connolly, responds with a general strike.

List of characters:
JAMES CONNOLLY
JAMES LARKIN
DELIA LARKIN (his sister)
COUNTESS MARKIEVICZ
WILLIAM O'BRIEN
DALY
FRANCIS SHEEHY SKEFFINGTON
WINIFRED CARNEY
TRAM DRIVER
ALUMINIUM WORKER
STRIKE PICKET
NEWSBOY

WILLIAM WALKER

KEIR HARDIE

CITIZEN of WEXFORD
CITIZEN of DUBLIN
GIRL

EAMONN CEANNT
PADRAIC PEARSE
SEAN MacDERMOTT

ARTHUR GRIFFITH

GRABITALL
3 EMPLOYERS
2 BISHOPS
LORD MAYOR of Dublin
POLICE SUPERINTENDENT
POLICE OFFICER
POLICE CONSTABLE
PRISON WARDER
SCAB NEWSBOY
DRUNK

HARLOT
3 TRAMCAR PASSENGERS
3 HECKLERS

PROTESTANT MINISTER

CARSON
BONAR LAW

CIVIL SERVANT

NARRATOR

workers, citizens, police, strikers, sectarian mobs, trade-union officials, etc.

Act Three: 'Once More Go Down to Hell'. James Connolly sees the Dublin General Strike collapse when the British trade-union leadership fails to respond to the demands of its rank and file that the Irish workers be given positive support. The Irish Citizen Army is formed. The Irish National Volunteers are formed. The climate of violence intensifies.

List of characters:
> JAMES CONNOLLY
> LILLIE CONNOLLY
>
> JAMES LARKIN
> COUNTESS MARKIEVICZ
> WILLIAM O'BRIEN
> Captain WHITE
>
> At the Albert Hall rally:
> Ben Tillett
> George Lansbury
> Cunningham-Graham
> Bernard Shaw
> Sylvia Pankhurst
> George Russell
> William Haywood
>
> 3 British TRADE-UNION LEADERS
> 2 Delegates at TUC General Meeting
>
> Striker's WIFE
> Working-class SUFFRAGETTE
> MOURNER
>
> MATT TALBOT
>
> ARTHUR GRIFFITH
>
> GRABITALL
> 3 EMPLOYERS
> BISHOP
> JUDGE
> TIM HEALY
> POLICE CONSTABLE
>
> ASQUITH
> REDMOND

CIVIL SERVANT

ULSTER VOLUNTEER
NATIONAL VOLUNTEER

NARRATOR

bandsmen, Gaelic Leaguers, workers, strikers, strikers' families, mob, scabs, Citizen Army Volunteers, police, TUC delegates, etc.

Part Five: 1910-1914

ACT 1: 'Donnybrook Fair'

A bird's-eye view of Dublin around its bay, with the Georgian buildings rearing up amongst the slums. The whole guarded by redcoat soldiers and police. (Backcloth 3.)

The little streets of working-class Belfast, opposed gable ends painted respectively with protestant and catholic slogans. The sky filled with a shipyard crane, factory chimneys, and a giant Red Hand of Ulster. (Backcloth 8.)

Enter CONNOLLY. *Throughout Part Five there is a* NARRATOR – *whose entries and exits are not indicated in the text.*

Connolly In America through one final year
        I launched myself upon a tour
        For Eugene Debs urging support
        On countless platforms south and north.
        My wife and children stayed alone
        In New York City: if they groan –
        Complain that I should be away
        So much so far – all I can say
        Is that at last from the socialists
        I get enough between my fists
        To keep supplied their daily need –
        They do not nibble now – they *feed*:
        They do not window-shop – they *buy* –
        What did I see
        West of Ohio in a jewelry store
        But would you believe this watch – ?
        Pure gold – I can afford it, can restore
        At last the treasure which my wife
        Put out at pawn to save my life
        In Dublin, eighteen ninety-six:

LILLIE *and* CHILDREN *have joined him.*

        Lillie, my love, we are not rich
        But at last, I have enough put by
        To get myself to Ireland where I live or die . . .
        If I do not at once at last go home once more
        This huge America will kill my heart
        And nail my worn-out body to the floor.

Narrator In nineteen hundred ten, July,
He waves his children and his wife goodbye
Aloft aboard the boat to cross the sea –

Connolly So soon so soon you follow after me . . .

Exeunt LILLIE *and* CHILDREN.

Meantime, what turbulence must I prepare to meet
When on the Irish side once more I set my heaving feet?

Narrator Hurley and blare
Of your Donnybrook Fair
Where every politic whore will hire
His slogans out to any fool
To pay for at the going rate –

A whole range of political SPOKESMEN *enter, each shouting his wares like mountebanks at a fair. They wear labels of their titles, on their breasts. The* NARRATOR *wanders among them in the crowd, heckling them at intervals. A member of the Irish Republican Brotherhood lurks with hidden face.*

Nationalist Home Rule and a Dublin parliament under the protection of the English Liberals!

Narrator What about foreign policy?

Nationalist Under the protection of the English Liberals – we'd have little to do at home if we were to worry about that!

Ancient Order of Hibernians Catholic supremacy within the framework of Home Rule!

Narrator What about the Northern protestants?

Ancient Order of Hibernians Are they not well enough able to look after their own up there? Why else do we exist but only to stand up to them – Joey Devlin in Belfast has the Knights and the Sodalities and the Hibernians all well organised – sure we have no fear of a heretic minority!

Sinn Fein Ireland independent is Ireland free. Economic self-sufficiency and a king of our own!

Narrator Which king?

Sinn Fein Why him that reigns, who else? He's a German, not an Englishman, so there's nothing wrong with him at all provided he wears two crowns and the second one put on in Tara.

Gaelic League (*speaks in Irish*) Ireland independent is Ireland free! Ireland with her own language is a nation once again!

Orangeman No surrender! Preserve the Union! Preserve the protestant tradition!

Narrator What about the Northern catholics?

Orangeman Let them declare their loyalty! Under the protection of ourselves, under the protection of the English Tories.

Southern Ascendancy Unionist The ordinary simple people would be perfectly content if they were not being *stirred up*. Everyone in this place is involved in *stirring things up*: I do wish that the lot of you would take yourselves off and allow me and my agent to collect our ground-rents without disturbance. Where are the police?

Northern Protestant Trade Unionist No surrender! Preserve the Union! Preserve the protestant tradition! Preserve the historic connection between loyal northern Labour and the industrially-advanced society of the imperial motherland without which the struggle against international capitalism becomes a snare and a delusion.

Narrator What about the British unions?

Northern Protestant Trade Unionist Are they not well enough able to look after their own strength? Why else do we exist but only to draw strength from them?

Narrator What about catholic employment in the shipyards and the mills?

Northern Protestant Trade Unionist Let them declare their loyalty or away to hell outa this –

Orangeman To Connacht or to hell!

Northern Protestant Trade Unionist and Orangeman No surrender: kick the Pope!

Narrator The going rate today is faster than it ever was

> There is no doubt Home Rule
> Will come to pass
> There is no doubt
> The great debate
> As always at the Fair
> Means broken bones
> And sticks and stones
> And sometimes guns,
> Between each other and every man:
> But first they all do what they can
> To make sure one man's bones at least
> By all are broken all at once –
> Provoked and goaded on by every swearing beating priest –
> See how the driven scapegoat runs – !

Enter LARKIN, *hounded through the* CROWD *by everyone.*

Larkin One Big Union One Big Strike – !
Orangeman Republican!
Northern Protestant Trade Unionist Fenian!
Nationalist Socialist!
Ancient Order of Hibernians Atheist!
Sinn Fein Agent of British commercial competition!
Gaelic League Purveyor of foreign materialist doctrine!
Southern Ascendancy Unionist Hooligan, ruffian, layabout, thug!

They all beat him to the ground. A POLICE CONSTABLE *comes and drags him out of it, dispersing the* CROWD.

Connolly Who is it?
Narrator Who else would it be but Larkin? See they have put him in gaol.
Connolly Who have? For what reason?

Enter BRITISH TRADE-UNION LEADER.

British TU Leader For a perfectly sufficient reason, brother. Jiggery-pokery with legitimate trade-union funds.
Connolly You mean he embezzled them?
British TU Leader I wouldn't go so far. But it was all highly irregular: and all of a piece with his unscrupulous attempt to demolish the well-tried structure of the unions in your country. Why, you'd never believe it: but the bugger's formed a new one, completely disconnected from the British TUC – and reeking, bloody reeking of syndicalist republicanism. I've had the most dreadful complaints from Belfast of the games he's been playing up there. There's one thing we won't stand for, brother, and that's meddling with religious differences. To recruit unskilled catholics into a separatist dockers' and transport workers' association is tantamount – I speak deliberate – to the incitement of civil strife: and Brother Walker bears me out.

Enter WALKER.

Walker For the development of social services, there is no doubt that Belfast is the most progressive community in this island: directly attributable to the constitutional link of both employer and employed with their British opposite numbers. With whom does a catholic upstart like Larkin expect he can link?

> Why who else but those dark men with their hidden faces
> Who through the crowd in this and all like places
> Imply the secret presence of the oath-bound Brotherhood
> Unending in our midst. See there he goes, there's one –

IRB *man slips through the* CROWD *and makes his escape.*

> Here he has been –
> Here he will come again:
> Arrest him, finish him, lock him up for ever . . . !
> The man who can do that will be this nation's saviour.

The CROWD *disappears.* CONNOLLY *is left alone looking around him.*

SCENE 2

Connolly In America through letters I was led to believe
That the socialist movement in Ireland had at last come alive –

> The prowl and leap of Larkin like a lion,
> The precise endurance of O'Brien,
> Combined inside this jungle to ensure
> The hunting path that leads the working class to power
> At last drives forward, vigorous as a spear:
> Direct effect, we go, from here to there –

But not at all – nothing – odd socks all over the laundry: O'Brien, where is he – ?

Enter O'BRIEN.

O'Brien Jim –! At last –! Thank God you are here – I couldn't find you in all this crowd – did you have a good journey?

Connolly *The Harp* . . . what has happened to *The Harp*? There's every newspaper in the country on sale in this place except ours – when I had it transferred from Chicago to Dublin last year and you told me that Larkin was going to have the management of it, I naturally looked forward to . . . for God's sake, man, what's happened? It hasn't collapsed?

O'Brien Temporarily suspended: four legal actions for libel, no less, impending against it. Jasus, I had no idea: your man's not an *editor* – he's a waterfront brawler with a mouth like a machine gun . . .

Connolly So what's to be done then? I have a family to bring over from the United States, have you forgotten? Did you tell me that the Socialist Party of Ireland could pay me as an organizer?

O'Brien Now, Jim, there may have been a hint dropped a month or two ago, Jim, but as things stand at present – –

Connolly But as things stand at present I find myself a tour of lectures on the Theory of Socialism and earn myself a few fees. . .? Scotland, maybe Liverpool, up and down a bit in this country . . . There must be at the end of it a precise defined goal. On the one hand the Socialist Party of Ireland: on the other Jim Larkin's new Transport Workers' Union. And across the two of them we put a cross-bar – a genuine, national, working-class Labour Party for the first time in history belonging to the trade unions, supported by socialist theorists. You have talked with Jim Larkin about it, I hope?

O'Brien Oh I have. It is in progress.

Connolly I had best go into the prison and have a word with him before all else.

Exeunt.

SCENE 3

Enter ASQUITH *and* LLOYD GEORGE. LLOYD GEORGE *stands up to make a speech* – ASQUITH *is endeavouring to calm him down, with little success.*

Narrator Mr Asquith is Prime Minister

> Mr Lloyd George is his thorn:
> Mr George holds liberal gentility
> In well-merited Celtic scorn.

Lloyd George At the very next colliery to the one I have been visiting, just a few years ago three hundred people lost their lives in a deluge of fire. And yet, when the Prime Minister and I knock at the door of the great landlords of Britain and say to them: 'Here, you know these poor fellows who have been digging up coal royalties for you at the risk of their lives – they are old, they are broken, they can earn no more – won't you give them something towards keeping them out of the workhouse?' – they scowl at us: and we say, 'Only a ha'penny, just a copper' and they say: 'You thieves!' I am determined in this Budget to find money for the old age pensions – if the landlords will not support us, then land must be taxed: if the coal-owners will not support us, then the coal-mines must be taxed: and if the House of Lords will not permit the Budget to go through, then the constitutional prerogative of the House of Lords must be challenged – under the threat, if need be, of creation of Liberal peers by His Majesty in numbers sufficient to overwhelm the Tory vote!

Enter MIDDLE-CLASS SUFFRAGETTE *and interrupts him.*

Middle-Class Suffragette What about the women's vote? When are you going to bring in a bill for female suffrage?

Lloyd George Oh dear . . . not again . . . will you escort the lady out, please, as courteously as possible . . .

A POLICE CONSTABLE *removes the* SUFFRAGETTE.

I was talking about creation of Liberal peers by His Majesty. Now, the Prime Minister Mr Asquith –

Asquith (*at last gets a word in*) The Prime Minister Mr Asquith is not afraid to go to the country upon this issue!

Narrator For the second time in one short year.

> But Mr Asquith is in fear
> The mandate that he will receive
> Will be so narrow as to leave
> None but the Irishmen alone
> Between his party and complete defeat.

Enter REDMOND.

Redmond

> We will not undertake to vote
> For this new Liberal government unless we get
> Immediate promise of a Home Rule Bill.

Asquith Mr Redmond: didn't I tell you, you shall have it? And you will!

Enter an OLD EARL.

Old Earl The Conservative Unionist Party in both Commons and Lords
Takes urgent note of those malignant words.
The inherited power of England will not yield
Until our corpses in the last deep ditch pollute the bloody field.

Exeunt

SCENE 4

Enter LARKIN *in prison.*

Larkin In the gaol of Mountjoy
The lion is held at bay
In the gaol of Mountjoy
They do not even try
To cut the tongue or clip the claw
Or strap a muzzle round my open jaw.
They do not really know, you see,
Whether or not to be afraid of me –
They let me roar and listen for the echo
And note it down and count its volume so . . .

CONNOLLY *is brought in to see him by a* WARDER.

You'll be wanting to know, brother, what the devil I got up to with your
newspaper: you'll be wanting to know what the devil I got up to with the
union finances of Cork – and truth to tell, I can't tell you: I'm in here and
I want out . . .! One objective: we drive right on: the Transport Workers'
Union of Ireland to be built up strong, regardless! Belfast is the bugger.
Would you go there? The problem is sectarianism. Our new union has
been damned as a totally papist set-up – for the simple reason, of course,
that in fact it is totally Irish. Give a dog a bad name and he will answer to
it all his life. I want an organiser in Belfast who will be known as a pure-
blood socialist with no religious affiliations.

Connolly Could you pay me?

Larkin Pay . . .? Problems . . .

Connolly There always are . . .

Larkin But in a few months' time, well, maybe . . . Meanwhile, could you
establish your reputation down here as an uncompromising spokesman
for the Socialist Party of Ireland? Cork. If you went to Cork and spread
socialism in the streets of croaking Cork – man, they'd drive you out of
town with a crozier and a red-hot candlestick! The Orangemen are not
clever: but they do read the newspapers. If the church should curse you:
then you must have cursed the church. For Belfast, no better man!

Warder Time's up.

He moves to lead CONNOLLY *away.*

Larkin And remember – get me outa here –!

He turns to go back in. On his way he addresses the audience:

> So now the revered Jim Connolly has come back into the land.
> We have a man now to coil the cable, make fast the knot, gather the
> slack into his careful hand:
> It is curious that in prison I should be afraid of getting out lest I
> find myself *confined* . . .

Exit.

Connolly It is curious that this giant whom from America I came to seek
> This thunderbolt I heard through roof and rafter tear and break
> This Finn MacCool hurling his basalt causeway down the strand
> Should make me, from his prison, feel captured and *confined*,
> Cross as two sticks, old before my time,
> Pedantic, tiresome, a damned nuisance in my own home.
> I said I'd get him out. If I said it, it must be done.

Exeunt.

SCENE 5

Narrator In Cork they are prepared for him. At the Cobh of Cork honest
> trade
> Hardens its heart for the fear that they have of the mild-mannered
> man with the power to persuade.
> Activities are set afoot. Certain hints are conveyed . . .

Enter EMPLOYERS (*Corkmen*).

1st Employer Sure, the fellow is after speaking last night and the night before in
Cork: I had my foreman go to the meeting to hear what kind of nonsense–

2nd Employer Was it socialism, councillor?

1st Employer First, a trade union: and second a political party: and thirdly
withdrawal of labour! There was not a few had drink taken and they
cheered him to the echo.

2nd Employer Councillor, it has to be stopped!

3rd Employer It has to be stopped *now*! Do you see this advertisement? The
town hall of Queenstown, no less, has been rented to this gang of envious
gougers.

1st Employer I have a contract, a government contract, at a fixed bloody
price, so I do, for the twice-weekly washing of the white duds of the
sailors at the naval station here. If my wages are forced up I make a loss
on that contract. It's only for the Royal Navy I'm in business here at
all . . . So I put it very forcibly to the council, d'you see, and I've good
hope I have it fixed that the town hall will be restricted.

2nd Employer I put the word out to Father Benedict to have it conveyed in various quarters that not a pub, not a billiard hall, will prove itself available.

3rd Employer A meeting in the street could be even more provocative . . .

He beckons to a group of SHOP ASSISTANTS.

If you people want to keep your jobs in my emporium, you'd do well to occupy yourselves on your afternoon-off attending any meeting that I see fit to suggest to you. You know the way it goes. Councillor Healy will lead off, it's up to you to back him up. I want to hear the right noises. 'Taking away the people's faith for a bowl of protestant soup' . . . 'Breaking the bonds of the Irish family by attacks on the vows of marriage' – Miss Fallon, Mrs Mooney, I think that should suit you –

Assistants Very well, Mr Hennessy . . .

General ribaldry.

CONNOLLY *and* O'BRIEN *arrive with a red banner reading 'Socialist Party of Ireland'.* O'BRIEN *has an armful of pamphlets.* CONNOLLY *mounts a rostrum.*

Connolly The Socialist Party of Ireland has set up a branch in Cork. If enough people interested, should be possible to establish one in Queenstown here as well. My colleague has literature. Our immediate campaign: number one, to secure the release of Jim Larkin. My colleague has the literature, a form for the petition. Moreover, we are leading an agitation for the provision of free school meals. Will I talk about that? School nowadays, at last, for the poorest, is free. The Liberal Education Act: reform: the bould Lloyd George. But dinner at the school has still to be paid for. A small head gains no knowledge if the belly is in dispute with it as to which will be filled first –

1st Employer A question.

Connolly Sir?

1st Employer Did you write a book?

Connolly Several pamphlets – there is a book –

1st Employer Did you write a book that the Jesuits murdered the Pope?

A murmur of consternation in the CROWD. CONNOLLY *becomes aware that a* PRIEST *at the back is leading some people in saying the rosary.*

Connolly Oh . . . Ho ho . . . ah. The expected appeal to prejudice. Very well. No I didn't. What I did write was a reply to a certain Jesuit, Father Kane, who had accused socialists of wanting to make laws in contradiction to the laws of God and the church. I pointed out that his own order had frequently involved itself in political intrigue which was taken at the time as being in contradiction to the policy of the Pope: and I gave proper historical instances of this – names, dates, and places. My colleague has a copy, if you want to see what it says. Shall we get back to free school meals?

A Shop Assistant What about free love?

Connolly If that's a proposition, madam, it would be better for all parties if you first got in touch with my wife. . . ?

To O'BRIEN

Watch it, William, it's getting awkward – gather up those papers, look after the small change . . .

The CROWD *starts making an ugly noise.*

Crowd Up the Hibernians, the Mollie Maguires, they're atheists, soupers, drive 'em out of town . . . *etcetera.*

3rd Employer Look here, my good man, the decent people of this town want neither ye nor your doctrine. Let you take yourselves out of here or I'll not answer for what may happen.

A POLICE OFFICER *comes up to* CONNOLLY.

Police Officer Now, Mr Connolly, we advised you not to speak here – you can see how right we were. Will you please take note of Mr Hennessy?

2nd Employer Come on, boys, drive 'em out!

Violence. CONNOLLY *and* O'BRIEN *are chased out.* CONNOLLY *loses his hat.*

Connolly (*as he goes*) We'll be back!

1st Employer Thank you, Inspector.

Police Officer Thank you, Councillor.

2nd Employer Thank you, Father Benedict: Mr Hennessy, thank you!

3rd Employer (*to his* STAFF) Well, now, Mrs Mooney – and what does it feel like to go into combat as a little soldier of Christ the King . . .?

1st Employer Ha! What about free love . . .?

Exeunt, with noisy self-congratulation. SOUTHERN ASCENDANCY UNIONIST *passes by.*

Southern Ascendancy Unionist This is the sort of thing, you see, that will be going on all the time once the Liberals give Home Rule. Perfectly incapable of managing their own affairs unless directed at all points by Father This and Brother That . . .

Connolly (*re-enters, picks up his hat*) They broke my hat . . .

Exit.

SCENE 6

Enter CARSON *and his cat.*

Narrator Sir Edward Carson had a cat
        It sat upon the fender
        And every time it saw a rat
        It shouted 'No Surrender!'

Carson Wee pussy pussy pussy drink a dish of milk
        From the hand of the black lawyer
        Clothed all in black silk.
        There's one, pussy, catch one, catch one, cat –!
        Lloyd George destroys the constitution just like that:
        Plays with it, moiders it, murders it, swallows it down
        For the sake of the half-baked vote of every ignorant loose clown –
        Pensions for pitmen, for poxed prostitutes a free cure –
        While the imperial protestant union bangs itself to bits like an
            unhinged boghouse door!
There's only the one place left where all things hang together –

Enter 1ST EMPLOYER (*Ulsterman*).

1st Employer Sir Edward Carson, it is an honour and a privilege for us to offer you the chairmanship of the Ulster Unionist Council.

Carson A council is good to start with: before we are finished, sir, we may yet find ourselves calling ourselves a provisional government.

1st Employer But that would be rebellion . . .?

Carson The defeat of legalised treason can never be called rebellion. Can you deny Home Rule is treason? Don't worry, sir, your great estates, your mills are all secure, your shipyards, your engineering workshops – what are you building?

1st Employer Range-finders for the navy to be installed in their new dreadnought.

Carson Last month, in Germany, new dreadnoughts – they built two.
        Dear sir, they can't hang you.
        You hold them in the hollow of your hand:
        O'ersway the ocean wave and regulate the land.
        'England Expects . . .' But Ulster will command.

Exeunt.

SCENE 7

Enter CONNOLLY.

Narrator Another thing, it would seem, that Ulster will command, is the continued control from Britain, of the trade-union movement throughout all thirty-two counties of Ireland . . .

Connolly Because the centre of gravity of our industrial population is the loyalist two-thirds of Belfast. William Walker goes to Galway and by thirty-two votes to twenty-nine holds the Irish Trades Union Congress to his own entrenched policy that there should be no separate Irish Labour Party established by Irish trade-unions only.

Enter WALKER – *ignoring* CONNOLLY, *he addresses the* AUDIENCE.

Walker An Irish Labour Party, separatist and socialist, is a contradiction in terms.

Connolly Does he deny the national identity of the Irish people, which for seven hundred years has been maintained at the cost of an unending line of martyrdom?

Walker That's irrelevant. The *class* identity of the Irish working people is totally indivisible from the class identity of those in Britain: and only in Britain does there exist a political structure with the strength to achieve for us our hard-won workers' rights! If we let go the hand of Britain and the British Labour Party, we have cut ourselves off from the civilised modern world. We are workers, we are craftsmen, we are twentieth-century technicians – if we listen to these nationalists, we will be nothing but barefoot peasants, aye, and riddled with false religion.

Exit.

Connolly Thirty-two to twenty-nine is a very small majority. If I had but the plinth to spring from I could change that in one year. Yet here I am in Belfast, kicked about like a coathanger in search of a hook, I joined a local branch of Larkin's Transport Workers' Union, simultaneous with the establishment of a branch of the Socialist Party of Ireland. But seven members only at my first union meeting: are we really further forward than when I left for America? The stupidest thing I did was to go to that country – and the next most stupid thing was ever to come back home . . . Consolation: certain steps. A conference in Dublin appoints a national executive committee for the Socialist Party of Ireland. They decide of course *not* to give me a paid job . . . Larkin at last is released out of gaol: but *I* can't take much credit. I have my family, out of America. The Falls Road. We sit in lodgings at the top of the Falls Road and we can't imagine how much longer we are going to be able to pay the rent . . .

SCENE 8

LARKIN, *released from prison, enters among a crowd of cheering* SUP-PORTERS, *with torches and placards* (*which read 'Welcome Home, Jim!'* *Etc.*)

Larkin Out of gaol and on the prowl
Larkin comes and Larkin goes

On the prowl and out of gaol
Loudmouth Larkin bursts with urgent news –

His SUPPORTERS *go out, leaving him alone with* CONNOLLY.

The seamen and the firemen of the merchant navy at Southampton have
declared a general strike: and the seamen and firemen at Goole and Hull
have joined in with them already. Liverpool and London next: the Clyde,
the Bristol Channel, the Firth of Forth, the Liffey, the Lagan – they want
everything. From a minimum wage to improved living conditions in the
focsles of the ships – !

Narrator Units of the British army have been moved into the valleys of the
South Wales coalfield in response to demands from the owners of the
collieries where the pitmen have been on strike for months. Pitmen on
strike, seamen on strike, everyone asks: 'Who next . . . ?'

Larkin There's a sympathetic strike of the labourers in the English docks to
support the striking seamen. We have got to have it here. We must show
the British unions that our separatism in Ireland is in no way prejudicial
to our class solidarity.

Connolly Will the National Union of Dock Labourers respond to their call?

Larkin They won't if they think its *my* call. I want suggestions for this city.

Connolly In effect here in Belfast there are two ports, not one. Cross channel
and deep sea. Cross channel work is regular day by day according to a
timetable. Therefore, the employment, as always with regular work, is for
protestants. The deep sea dockers are catholic, casual, disorganised. The
protestants are all involved in the National Dock Labourers –

Larkin A union controlled from Britain . . . yes?

Connolly So we concentrate on the catholics – but only to begin with. I do
think it can be done.

Larkin So do it. You're official organiser for the Transport Workers' Union
from now on. Here's two weeks' pay in advance. By the way: we have a
newspaper.

Connolly Not *The Harp* . . . ?

Larkin We can't call it that. But I can promise you it will be as defamatory as
ever. *The Irish Worker*: sixteen thousand I am having printed this month.
You'll write your articles for it of course.

Exit LARKIN.

Connolly With a circulation of sixteen thousand I'd write articles for the Book
of Kells . . . !

SCENE 9

Connolly I set up my new office
In a street by the docks:
Hardly there half a day
When at the door – who is it knocks?

SEAMEN'S UNION OFFICIAL *knocks and enters rudely.*

Seamen's Union Official Hey you, what the hell are you on?

Connolly I know you? Seamen's and Firemen's Union. How are you? Connolly: Irish Transport. The minute I had time I was coming around to look you up.

Seamen's Union Official There was a man into me this morning from the National Union of Dock Labourers.

Connolly Aye?

Seamen's Union Official He told me you had been putting out round the docks you were recruiting for the seamen's union – *my* union – well?

Connolly Rubbish.

Seamen's Union Official Do you tell me I was misinformed . . . ? Deliberately, do you think? Trying to smear you, do you think, with the accusation of poaching?

Connolly I hope not.

Seamen's Union Official It could be . . . You see, your people and my people are in a similar position here. We're both as anaemic as hell. The National Dock Labourers have bugger-all to do with us – why, we're not even affiliated to the Belfast Trades Council. We're supposed to be on strike: but the ferry boats to Scotland are still being run on a skeleton service with non-union crews: and they are loaded and unloaded without a bloody word said by the National Dock Labourers. I was arguing all morning with your bloody man beyond: and all he could talk about was the Fenian poacher sent up here by Jim Larkin – he meant you. We've got to have a picket on the ferry boat dock-gate!

Connolly We'll go down to the dock and we'll put it to the men.

SCENE 10

They walk round the stage. Enter a number of DOCKERS, *heaving at loads.*

Seamen's Union Official Hey, this is the deep sea dock – I said the cross channel dock-gate . . .

Connolly I know. We start here. Hullo there, Clarke: you know me. Connolly, transport workers.

1st Docker It's the Orange union loads up the cross channel boats. Why not go talk to them?

Connolly Suppose we were to put a picket on the cross channel docks, and at the same time state *our* claim for better pay, shorter hours, and a safe speed upon the job: don't you think then the protestant lads would be driven to take their cue? They'd demand their own demands: and their leaders would have to follow. If they didn't, they'd be out –

2nd Docker That like of leader is never out, never – it's all fixed in the Orange Lodge –

Connolly By their book, we fix ours in the Ancient Order of Hibernians, and travelling barefoot to the back door of the Bishop of Down and Conor.

1st Docker D'you aim to lead this on to a sympathetic strike?

Connolly For a strike – if we have to – but not exactly sympathetic: for *ourselves*, as I have said.

1st Docker Where's the funds? A strike without strike pay?

2nd Docker Man, we're well aware of the state of your kitty.

Connolly If funds are needed we have no choice but to see they come in. I am seven years in America: and I understand the bally-hoo – razzmatazz – the great parade . . . !

Narrator In the streets of Belfast one and all will come
>At the bang of a banner and the flap and the rattle of a drum:
>But until James Connolly showed them the way
>Never in the one same street and all on the one same day . . .
>The non-sectarian labour band plays its music and holds out its hand
>For love and for money and for power against those lords
>Who themselves having no religion, determine that all words
>Of dogma and divinity in the town of Belfast
>Mean two things to two men, and that both of the men at last
>Break out blood between their utterance of the destiny of the soul . . .

Connolly Today we play the requiem for colonial divide-and-rule . . . !

The NON-SECTARIAN LABOUR BAND *enters – its name carried on a red banner – its members a ragged collection of people playing on a range of improvised instruments. They march around the auditorium, led by* CONNOLLY, *and supported by* WORKERS *with collecting-boxes.*

Connolly (*after the parade*)
>The Trades Council now invites –
>And none dare ask them, why so late? –
>The Seamen and the Firemen's Union
>To come in and affiliate.

Narrator Four and sixpence in one week
>And the next week five bob
>Strike-pay paid to every docker
>Who walked off the job.

Connolly Not much indeed, but were they working
>Fifteen bob per week
>Is all that they could earn
>With every sinew in their back.

1st Docker
>Crack, crack, the back gives way –
>No mercy in the docker's speed of work –
>Y're Hercules can ye last it beyond the third successive day.

Strikers We want a rise in pay
We want recognition
We want contracted rights
For union negotiation!

Narrator The owners of the short cross channel ships
Declare a settlement with their seamen.

Seamen's Union Official
We'll not accept till we hear Connolly say
The dockers too are satisfied and may
Without dishonour call off their own strike.

2ND *and* 3RD EMPLOYERS (*Ulstermen*) *have entered.*

Narrator Ship owners tell the port employers some truth they do not like
To hear . . .

2nd Employer (*twists the arm of* 3RD EMPLOYER)
The ships must sail, the cargo and the gear
Must urgently be loaded. Let you not fear
To offer to your gangs a compromise.

3rd Employer
James Connolly is hard: but his crafty narrow eyes
Insinuate a man who knows when he can win no more.
No thunderbolt, no Larkin: a fixer who can listen to two words
with one sharp ear . . .

3rd Employer (*confronts* CONNOLLY) Perhaps the time has come to spread
proposals on the floor. Ninepence a day extra for one hundred tons.

Connolly One and six.

3rd Employer Tenpence.

Connolly One and two.

3rd Employer Call it a shilling?

Connolly Done. Provided . . .

3rd Employer Provided what?

Connolly Full recognition for the Transport Workers' Union.

3rd Employer Not acceptable.

Connolly All off.

3rd Employer Informal recognition of a negotiating committee.

Connolly We have that already, not acceptable, all off.

3rd Employer We can't concede further.

2nd Employer (*in* 3RD EMPLOYER'S *ear, twisting his arm again*) No option. You
must. Would you have all the Irish trade go through Newry, Dublin,
Waterford? Cork?

3rd Employer (*to* CONNOLLY) Full recognition.

Connolly Done!

To STRIKERS:

It's not a victory. A compromise: Belfast still remains the lowest-paying port in the United Kingdom: but the work will be so much less and the pay for every man increases three shillings a week.

Exeunt all except EMPLOYERS.

3rd Employer He never would ha' done it if it hadn't ha' been for that unnatural perverted non-sectarian band . . . ! Reverend, am I right?

Enter a PROTESTANT MINISTER.

Protestant Minister It amounts to indifferentism, devoid of morals, anarchy . . .
2nd Employer Let's put it to a good man that digs with the other foot . . . Father, wouldn't you say it smells of apostacy? Father, am I right?

Enter a CATHOLIC PRIEST.

Catholic Priest It amounts to indifferentism, devoid of morals, anarchy . . .

Exeunt.

SCENE 11

Enter a POLICE OFFICER.

Police Officer Anarchy, anarchy, anarchy in the slums of London . . . ! Where is the Home Secretary? Mr Churchill – Mr Churchill . . . ! You must call out the soldiers!

Enter CHURCHILL.

Churchill Impractical. They are in South Wales.
Police Officer It's a house, sir, in Sidney Street, it's been invaded by armed Russians, anarchists, nihilists – they have opened fire upon the police . . . !
Churchill Without doubt to co-ordinate the seething tide of unrest that would overwhelm the entire powerhouse of our national industry.
Police Officer There is always the Brigade of Guards –
Churchill Ha! Yes! Let them proceed, formidably accoutred, and invest with fire and sword this den of sombre virulence – with machine guns, if need be. Wait a moment, I myself will assume command of the assault.

He goes out with the POLICE OFFICER. *Shots are heard, off. Enter* 1ST CIVIL SERVANT.

1st Civil Servant Oh dear, oh dear, why cannot he leave the direction of the military to the military themselves? The Port of London dockers are all out again on strike: and we thought we had it settled: and as for this report about the fat woman of Bermondsey –
Narrator She walked through the streets with her hair thrown back in tangles and her great mottled arms uplifted to the sky – from one factory to another, where the women of South London all sweated at their machines . . .

The FAT WOMAN OF BERMONDSEY *enters at the head of a crowd of* WOMEN.

Fat Woman (*storms across the stage*) All out! All out! We're all going out on strike! All the women in the world is going out on fucking strike. Strike for your flaming rights, girls, its too hot for fucking work . . . !

As they pass they knock 1ST CIVIL SERVANT *off his feet.*

Narrator There is nothing the Home Secretary or anyone else can do. Wage increases to a total of seven thousand pounds per annum have had to be conceded: and the National Federation of Women Workers has augmented its membership by no less than four thousand.

Enter 2ND CIVIL SERVANT *in a great hurry. He meets* MIDDLE-CLASS *and* WORKING-CLASS SUFFRAGETTES, *and they knock him over.*

Suffragettes Votes for Women!
1st Civil Servant Get 'em off, get 'em out of here!

POLICE *enter and chase the* SUFFRAGETTES, *ineffectively, but the stage is cleared.*

2nd Civil Servant The Foreign Office. An urgent message. Where is Mr Churchill?

More shots heard, off. 1ST CIVIL SERVANT *shrugs helplessly. Enter* 3RD CIVIL SERVANT.

3rd Civil Servant The War Office. Mr Churchill . . . ? My God, we need those soldiers! We need them in camp at once!
1st Civil Servant Whatever is the matter?
2nd Civil Servant North Africa. You know the Italians have been extending themselves into Libya?
1st Civil Servants A threat to the integrity of the Suez Canal.
2nd Civil Servant Not only the Italians – –
3rd Civil Servant The Germans are at it now! The Kaiser has sent a gunboat to the coast of Morocco!

Enter LLOYD GEORGE.

Lloyd George Gentlemen, contain yourselves. The intensity of immediate emergency is reduced. I have a dispatch to the Foreign Secretary from the Wilhelmstrasse in Berlin. The German government had decided in the interests of world peace – –

Enter CHURCHILL.

Churchill (*holds a rifle*) Democracy prevails! The anarchists have perished!
Lloyd George The German government has decided, in the interests of world peace, that the gunboat which was sent to North Africa shall be recalled.
Churchill (*disappointed*) Oh . . .

Exit CHURCHILL.

Lloyd George (*gives a document to* 2ND CIVIL SERVANT) Now this dispatch is not to be published until your minister gives you leave . . . Because I want to speak very particularly today to those workers –

He makes a speech down front:

– to those workers whose employment is directly concerned with the security and the supply of our national armed forces. You will all have read in the newspapers of the grave developments in North Africa. *I* do not believe that the German emperor will be mad enough to provoke a world war: but I *do* believe that if *he* believes Great Britain is unprepared to resist his outrageous, his piratical adventures, then the jackboot of the conscript Prussian will be stamping out the goose-step among the peaceful little terraces of Wapping and of Bootle, of Greenock, Pontypridd – yes, and Stoke Poges! Could Nelson's men have won Trafalgar if British workers had deprived them of their bread, meat, and gunpowder in the hour of their greatest need? Once again, as in those days, the Royal Navy has been mobilised. The nation stands in imminent peril. For the sake of your noble heritage as free citizens of Great Britain, I appeal to you: go back to work! And I promise you, if you do, all your grievances will be attended to. You know my reputation: for the British worker, first and foremost; but a live worker, not a dead one: a free citizen, not a slave!

Narrator And for the time it seemed the state was saved . . .

Exeunt.

SCENE 12

Enter LARKIN *to a rostrum at one side, to address a crowd of* WORKERS.

Larkin (*to* AUDIENCE *before he speaks to the* CROWD) Life all around appears to stagnate, everything miserable, depressing – I must get them to realize there is such great hope for the future – something worth working for, if only the workers will rouse themselves . . . To plead with them –

To the CROWD:

Cast your eyes upward to the stars instead of grovelling in the slime of your own degradation: think of your manhood: your love for your little ones: your race instinct as Irishmen –

Aside to AUDIENCE *as he is greeted with sullen apathy:*

All these appeals seem to fall upon deaf ears . . .

Enter at the other side GRABITALL (*as* MURPHY – *he plays this role throughout Part Five*) *and* 1ST, 2ND *and* 3RD EMPLOYERS (*Dubliners*).

Grabitall Oh no they do not . . .

Larkin (*still to* AUDIENCE *but turning his words gradually to* CROWD) You whose lives flow on like a placid stream cannot appreciate the temperament of those who like myself, go down amongst the exploited in the field, factory, workshop, and aboard the great argosies that convey the products of field workers from one area to another. We who are born with the microbe of discontent in our blood must of necessity live the strenuous life, one day down in the depths of despondency, and the next day lifted up on the peak of Mount Optimism . . . !

Exit LARKIN *followed by his hearers.*

Grabitall Throughout the island every industry is either on strike or has been on strike or is about to go on strike!

1st Employer O'Grady!

Enter a CLERK.

Will you please bring in the coffee and biscuits?

2nd Employer Mr Murphy, I have a list.

Grabitall The Transport Workers' Union is collecting recruits among the rag, tag and bobtail of disorganised unskilled labourers from one end of the country to the other.

1st Employer Just one moment: Houlihan!

Enter an OFFICE MESSENGER.

Will you clear this waste paper?

OFFICE MESSENGER *takes the basket out. The* CLERK *is passing round coffee cups*, etc.

2nd Employer Mr Murphy, I have a list.

Grabitall (*with newspaper*) I would call your attention to the tone of voice with which your man Larkin thinks fit to edit his newspaper. He refers here to a candidate whom I in my own newspaper –

Employers *The Irish Independent* – a most reliable journal!

Grabitall – am endorsing for a seat on the Dublin Corporation. 'Here is a creature whose only prayer is a blasphemous and obscene oath, a creature who is a byword and reproach to all decent men, whose career has been one debauch of drunkenness, vice, and sin; whose very name breathes pestilence, standing as the champion of religion and nationality . . .'

3rd Employer Sure the only thing to do with a rag of such a class is to fling it on the rubbish heap – where *is* the rubbish heap . . . ?

Grabitall Houlihan, what have you done with that basket – ? Houlihan, make haste!

1st Employer O'Grady, I said coffee – this pot contains tea!

2nd Employer Mr Murphy, I have a list.

Clerk There's no coffee. There's been none delivered to the shops this past week. If it's not the dock strike, it's the rail strike, if it's not the rail strike, it's the sailors.

3rd Employer Biscuits.

Clerk Oh no, there's none o' them. The biscuit factory's been out since the beginning of last month.

Exit CLERK.

Grabitall Socialism, syndicalism, the sympathetic strike . . . Have you heard of those gurriers they call the 'Wobblies' in America? If Larkin has not got his malignant ideas from them – then from where has he got them!

2nd Employer But please, Mr Murphy, just listen to my list. Newsboys, clothing workers, golf caddies, tanners, maltsters, dock workers, dairy workers, tramwaymen, railwaymen – what can they all have in common?

Grabitall No more and no less than we have in common. Except that the man Larkin has organised them all together: and we, their employers, still believe ourselves to be competitors.

> Therefore, gentlemen, may I suggest
> That we ourselves unite – put to the test
> Our own ability and will to organise
> Ourselves in our defence. We prize
> Our individual advantages above all else:
> But to continue in the face of *this* –

He waves the coffee pot.

> And *this* –

He kicks the crumpled-up newpsaper.

> Is to prove false
> To every principle of our class and caste.
> The day for private gain from other's grief is gone and past.

If all of us could agree that none of us would employ anyone who had ever made any arrangement with Larkin – ?

They look dubious.

Or would you prefer that all free national trade should be swallowed up by socialist thieves? We call ourselves to begin with *The Employers' Federation of Dublin* and we put out a manifesto. Our object is the mutual protection of all employers of labour, and the promotion of freedom of contract between employers and employees. We open an indemnity fund. The strategy is obvious. Our exact *tactics* we need not clarify, merely note that they are subject to mutual agreement and further discussion: and sign our names. McCafferty, pen and ink!

No-one responds.

Where is he? McCafferty! O'Grady! Dammit – Houlihan! Is there nobody in this office?

LARKIN *re-enters still orating at the far side. The* CLERK *and the* OFFICE MESSENGER *are seen amongst those listening to him.*

Narrator Jim Larkin has them gathered up
        Jim Larkin has them caught
        Larkin at the servants' door
        Proves the truth of what is taught –

Larkin Who is it speaks of defeat?
        I tell you a cause like ours
        Is greater than defeat can know –
        It is the power of powers!
        As surely as the earth rolls round
        As surely as the glorious sun
        Brings the great world moon-wave
        Must our cause be won . . . !

Grabitall Gentlemen, in a matter of months, Home Rule will be granted us. Gentlemen, observe and hear the new ruler of your home!

He indicates LARKIN, *who goes out with his listeners amidst great cheers.*

SCENE 13

Enter REDMOND.

Redmond Murphy . . . Psst – Murphy . . . ! The crucial debate in the House of Lords on the Parliament Bill is about to take place. If the government are successful, then the House of Lords will have voted – in a constitutional, peacable, and entirely twentieth-century fashion – for the immediate limitation of their own archaic powers: which will mean that the government at once will stand pledged for the introduction of Home Rule. Mr Asquith is confident that the bill will be passed in the Lords. If so, he wants we, the Irish, to take the matter as quietly as he takes it himself. Can we not, just for once, man, leave all the hysteria to the English beyond . . ?

Enter OLD EARL *and* DUKE.

Duke If we can win but one hundred and twenty-three votes, then the bill will be rejected. I have letters of assurance from one hundred and twenty.

Old Earl Not enough.

Duke Six of them, dammit, have sent me doctors' notes.

Old Earl We need at least another nine . . .
        From moated castle towers and battlemented halls
        Go dig them, jerk them, delve them out –
        Uncover crumbling mouldering ancient noble limbs
        From moss-encrusted dank ancestral tombs,

> Robe them in scarlet, crown their worm-chewed skulls
> And haul them in their hearses to the vote!

A procession of LORDS – *actors in robes and coronets carrying each a pair of dummies in robes and coronets to treble their numbers – totters past into the vote. The* DUKE *and the* OLD EARL *bring up the end. Enter* ASQUITH.

Asquith His Majesty has given his word that if this bill is not passed, he will abide by my advice and turn into peers of the realm so many soap manufacturers and Liberal Birmingham ironmongers that never again never will the House of Lords be dominated by the landed aristocracy. He doesn't want to do it. I don't want him to have to do it. It would totally upset the equilibrium of the class structure, and the effect upon trade would be highly inflammatory . . .

Narrator (*suddenly*) The bill is passed! Those in favour: one hundred and thirty-one. Those against it: one hundred and fourteen.

The LORDS *pour out again and over the stage, screaming with passion such words as 'Judas! Rat! Traitor!' The* DUKE *and the* OLD EARL *remain on stage as everyone else goes out.*

Old Earl Where is Carson?

Duke Belfast.

Old Earl Send him at once a telegram. He must do what comes next.

Enter CARSON.

Carson What comes next is easy to say:
        Already the work is under way . . .

Narrator Draw back the curtain and reveal
        The Ulster Volunteers at drill.

Enter ULSTER VOLUNTEERS *with an orange flag and sashes drilling to the tune of* 'The Sash My Father Wore'. *They carry broomsticks like rifles.*

Carson Legal, irreproachable, magisterially authorised . . .

Enter 1ST EMPLOYER (*Ulsterman*) *in magistrate's gown.*

1st Employer (*reads from a legal scroll*)
        Lest the liberty of our citizens by disloyalty be surprised
        It is given to the Justices of the Peace to permit protective drill:
        Communal exercise without weapons and the marching of men
          in line.

Narrator A new leader for the Conservatives:
        The presbyterian Bonar Law.

Enter BONAR LAW *and joins the* DUKE *and* OLD EARL.

Bonar Law
        Savage tooth and bloodstained claw

> According to the way that nature lives
> Will mark our policy from this out.
> We lost the game because we were polite.
> The Liberals have no right –

Narrator No right to do what . . . ?

Carson He finished what he meant to say. It is enough.

Exeunt.

SCENE 14

Enter CONNOLLY.

Narrator D'you ever wonder how much of all their words are pure bluff?

Connolly Sure in the last resort they will never fight and kill:

> Their homes are too comfortable, their coffers are too full.
> The only ones who dare to struggle in blood till their eyelids
>   close
> Are those who are so poor that, poor men, they have nothing to
>   lose.
> Poor men, forbye poor women . . .
> In the Belfast mills they weave the linen –

A group of MILL GIRLS *enter and stand as though working at their machines.* 1ST EMPLOYER (*Ulsterman*) *walks up and down inspecting their work. At intervals he gestures as though operating a crank that increases the speed of the machinery, and the women have to work faster.*

Narrator In the mills below the Belfast hills

> The heat of the steam to preserve the thread
> Will drench your body and stifle your head,
> Where the protestant girls have a shop on their own
> And the heaviest toil is for papists alone,
> And the cry of the harried master is for always 'Faster faster –
> More work for no more pay
> No more idleness this day . . . !'
> Strand by strip the thread will snap:
> They all come out – they've had enough!

The MILL GIRLS *stop work and hurry across shouting for 'Mr Connolly – where's Mr Connolly . . . ?' He is surrounded by a throng of angry* WOMEN, *all talking in a furious jumble . . .*

Mill Girls We're all out . . . We've no funds . . . We're not going back . . . How would you like it, mister, if you were threatened with the sack for just pinning up your hair . . . ? Two minutes at the toilet and she's gone from the job for ever . . . That bald-headed bugger found three peppermint sweeties in Moira McCann's shawl, he fired 'em out of window – any more o'that, says he, you're on the street for good, ye fenian get, and can ye tell me a better place for a bitch of your habits . . . ? It's not for only sweeties he's after rummaging her shawl . . . D'ye know what he says to me when all I did was to warble three staves of a bit of a jig . . . ? Ye got money for our men, mister, when the docks was called out, what will you do for us . . . ? Or are the women to be driven like cows to the field while the men prop up the walls of the bars drinking stout like fresh milk . . . ?

Connolly Nora – ! Where's my daughter? Ah, there you are –

Enter NORA.

Nora – you'd best stay with me – I'll never deal with them all on my own.

Nora But they're not in your union – ?

Connolly As far as I can discover they're in nobody's union – (*stems the tide*) –Nora! Pencil: paper. First of all: I take the point that you have all walked out in a body and that the Linen Workers' Union as organised by Miss Galway will have nothing to do with it?

1st Mill Girl Nothing to do with it? That bloody bitch, mister, will have nothing to do with *us* whether we walk out or stay in!

Connolly Aye . . . ? Now you're sure of that? Tell me, was it ever put to you that the union was there for you?

1st Mill Girl It was not. And when a few of us put the question to *her*, was the union open for everyone? – the prods in the making-up shop said 'fuck-off if you know what's good for you!'

Connolly Right. Write it down.

Nora All of it?

Connolly Oh yes . . . we shall need it, all. Now, your main complaint. Wages?

2nd Mill Girl We want more.

3rd Mill Girl Who doesn't?

4th Mill Girl But that's not it.

All the Women (*together*) It's the rules, mister, the new rules. They have them posted on every floor. Forbidden adjusting of the hair: forbidden adjusting of the dress: forbidden unauthorised temporary absence from the job: forbidden unauthorised conversation irrelevant to the job: forbidden unauthorised laughter: forbidden unauthorised singing – forbidden forbidden forbidden . . .

Connolly Forbidden unauthorised existence, irrelevant to the job? Now listen: I am happy to take as many of you as want to into the Transport Workers' Union, and to back you in this strike to the best of our power: as a result of the dock strike, we've no funds – you know that? So all we can give you is our name, for what it's worth. I wonder what way I could persuade Miss Mary Galway that she ought to give you yours?

Mill Girls You needna bother, we'll do without it, we don't bloody want it –

Connolly Ah but she does have funds . . .

Enter MISS GALWAY.

Miss Galway Mr Connolly, you should know the unofficial action of these women is gravely resented by the members of my union. Employment has been jeopardised by a frivolous and hysterical outburst . . . I am on my way now to see the employers and to put to them our point of view.

Connolly You'll excuse me: but representing the women who walked out, I think I have a right to get to them first.

1ST EMPLOYER, *on the far side of the stage, struggling to meet* MISS GALWAY, *is foiled by the crowd of* WOMEN.

1st Employer Ah – there you are – Miss Galway . . . !

Connolly Just one moment, sir –

1st Employer (*turns his back on* CONNOLLY) I don't know who *you* are . . . Where is she? Where's Miss Galway? How dare you obstruct me! Connolly, I say Connolly, will you please remove these females!

Connolly I thought you didn't know who I was . . .

CONNOLLY *motions to the* WOMEN *to get out of the way, and they move round to stand behind him as he confronts* 1ST EMPLOYER.

1st Employer Your demands.

Connolly Six shilling rate for an eight-hour day.

1st Employer Not acceptable.

Connolly And the abolition of the new rules.

1st Employer Not only not acceptable but out of the question. Ridiculous. And don't think I don't know just how you are situated. I see her – over there: it's quite all right, Miss Galway: I can see you – over there! I am very well aware that the whole of the trades council is on *her* side, not yours.

He turns away.

Connolly
> Bring out the non-sectarian band
> And once again hold out your hand
> For love and for money and for power for the working class.

The BAND *begins to assemble, as before.*

Enter CATHOLIC PRIEST, *as the music starts, and* CONNOLLY, *as before leads the parade.*

1st Employer (*as the parade ends*)
> The band, the band, the non-sectarian band!
> The devil's trump at the churchyard gate the very hour of the holy mass:
> I wonder, Father, can you stand it? For a fact it makes me sick
> And myself as black a protestant as ever beat drum with a stick . . .

The PRIEST *gets up to preach. The* MILL GIRLS *form his congregation.*

Priest My dear children, this James Connolly, in Queenstown in the county of Cork, uttered slander against the Pope! He was driven out of Queenstown by the anger of the people. Shame indeed upon Belfast if you do not so serve him here.

Exit PRIEST.

1st Mill Girl We can't go against the priest.

2nd Mill Girl And what right has the priest to go against his own people?

3rd Mill Girl From the collection with the band we've got two bob a week strike pay. Because the bosses have bought the church they needn't think they've bought us. We hold out.

1st Mill Girl Ah, you wouldn't keep a dog on two bob a week . . . !

Connolly The beginning of a split: the front will be broken.

        What more can I say to them I have not already spoken?

        Nora, can you think of no argument that would work?

Nora   Why wouldn't we tell them of the time in New York

        When all the women of every nation throughout the city were on strike

        For the Garment Workers' Union, and the bosses were so confident

        That in religion and in race and in language they were all so different

        They could never get together: yet they did and they held out –

Connolly Tell it to them, so tell it to them, your turn, get up and spout . . .

Nora I can't – !

She turns to speak to the WOMEN *with her back turned to* AUDIENCE.

Narrator Her mouth, she said, was very dry,

        She stammered as she spoke

        She knew what she wanted to say

        It came out as a kind of croak:

        But in the end she got through with it and brought it to an end:

        She said she felt that they felt that like her father she was their friend –

        And her father said –

Connolly Well done: it worked. They are determined to carry on.

To 1ST EMPLOYER.

        They are determined, sir, to carry on.

        Once more, will you accept the proposition they have laid down?

1st Employer Wages within certain limits I am prepared to negotiate.

Connolly The question of the rule book . . .

1st Employer Out of hand: rejected: flat.

Connolly For an eight-hour day a six-shilling rate.
1st Employer No time-limit on the day. Measure it in weight.
Connolly Seventy tons output, for as long as it will take.
1st Employer Ninety.
Connolly Not acceptable.
1st Employer Split the difference. Eighty-five.
Connolly Too high. Split it my way: seventy-five.
1st Employer Eighty.
Connolly I'll recommend it. We must take what we can get.

> *To* WOMEN.

> For an eighty-ton day a six-bob rate.
> Not good but not bad. The difference has been split.
> Now: we all know that it was not wages but the rule book that
> brought you out.
> Having gained your wages maybe you will also have gained the
> will
> To defeat the rule book where it matters, earning your pay within
> the mill . . . ?

He goes out.

The WOMEN *stand to their machines again. They begin to work.*

Narrator Forbidden unauthorised singing . . .
Mill Girls (*whisper together conspiratorially*) What are we to sing then . . . ?
'The Croppy Boy . . . ?' Oh God what a misery . . . !
Mill Girls 'Alexander's Rag-time Band' . . . ? 'It's a Long Way to Tipper-
ary' . . . ? There's only one song would fit this. But we don't start with
that one. Teresa, you've the best voice, you start with whatever you want:
and we'll all fill in with what comes after . . . !

As they work 1ST EMPLOYER *comes along to inspect them. One of the* MILL
GIRLS *starts singing – a song of her own choice.*

1st Employer You – you there – singing – I'd ha' thought after six weeks on
the street you'd ha' damn well learned your lesson! All right then –
singing – *out!*
All Women Together (*sings defiantly*)
> Cheer up, Connolly, your name is everywhere
> You left Old Baldy sitting in his chair
> Crying for mercy: mercy wasn't there
> Cheer up, Connolly, your name is everywhere . . . !

Baffled, 1ST EMPLOYER *throws his rule book on the ground and storms out.*
The WOMEN *cheer, and then exeunt.*

Narrator Mysteriously the book of rules was gone, forgotten, lost . . .
No reason to believe that production decreased.

CONNOLLY *tears up the rule book. Enter to meet him,* WALKER *and* MISS GALWAY.

William Walker on behalf of the trade-union establishment
On behalf of Miss Galway, gave vent to his complaint.

Walker We would ask you, Brother Connolly, to confine yourself to the class of workers you were sent here to represent.

Connolly I was sent here to represent those who were not represented . . .

He takes his notebook from NORA.

'That bloody bitch, mister, will have nothing to do with us . . .'
Miss Galway Now wait one moment –
Connolly Excuse me. 'The prods in the making-up shop said "fuck-off if you know what's good for you" . . .' Excuse me. It's not my language.

Exit MISS GALWAY.

Of course, we all know that if the Transport Union becomes large enough in Belfast, it will not be possible for Brother Walker to obtain his majority at the Irish Trades Union Congress next year . . .
Walker The international socialist champion, we are intrigued to discover,
Has run the keel of his world-wide purpose on the mud of a
sectarian river . . .
Connolly Internationalism, by your book, is a branch of imperialism. Your loyalty to British labour is no more than the servility of a stray cat beneath the table rubbing ankles to get cream. But there's nothing for you but skim milk . . . Why, the best paid, the best organised of all the workers in Ireland –
Walker Whom I represent!
Connolly None the less receive less money than they would if they worked in Britain.

Exit WALKER.

It's quite obvious from what's happened, Nora, that these women in the mills enjoy nothing more than a bit of music! Wouldn't you think this a good chance to take a leaf from the book of our friends in the Gaelic League and connect the music with the struggle in a more direct and pertinent fashion? I've arranged a series of socials, for them to learn the traditional dances: and I'd be glad if you could help me get some sort of small ceilidh going so they can show off their new footwork! How about this then?

He fetches a fiddle and plays a traditional Irish tune.

The MILL GIRLS *enter, happily: but they begin dancing the tango to music that drowns* CONNOLLY's *performance. He sits there unable to continue. The* MILL GIRLS *notice his dejected attitude, stop dancing, and gather round him humorously.*

Mill Girls (*sing*)

> Cheer up, Connolly, your name is everywhere
> You left Old Baldy sitting in his chair
> Crying for mercy: mercy wasn't there
> Cheer up, Connolly, your name is everywhere . . . !

Connolly (*puts up his fiddle*) Ah, well, you win. If we count up our victories, we must also cut our losses. It's no doubt a political error to force concessions from the employers and culture upon the workers in one and the same week . . .

The tango continues, and exeunt, singing a ragtime song.

END OF ACT 1

ACT 2: 'Keir Hardie's Promise'

SCENE 1

A bird's-eye view of Dublin around its bay, with the Georgian buildings rearing up amongst the slums. The whole guarded by redcoat soldiers and police. (Backcloth 3.) The little streets of working-class Belfast, opposed gable ends painted respectively with protestant and catholic slogans. The sky filled with a shipyard crane, factory chimneys, and a giant Red Hand of Ulster. (Backcloth 8.)

Enter GRIFFITH

Griffith The pseudo internationalism of the syndicalist labour movement is nothing more nor less than a branch of imperialism, and the man Larkin himself is an agent of Threadneedle Street.

Narrator Arthur Griffith of Sinn Fein –

Griffith – believes in Irish manufacturers employing Irish labour to produce Irish commodities to be sold on the world market totally unrestricted by British tariff and restraint of trade, for the particular profit of the Irish investor and the general prosperity of the nation at large. The iron foundry in Wexford has been for many years a classic example of independent Irish enterprise, of a type I would wish extended to every similar provincial township of equivalent dimension. That this industry at this time should be brought to a standstill by the activities of Larkin and the Transport Workers' Union has therefore a pointed and sinister significance.

Narrator Many foundrymen have been persuaded to become members of the union by the success of a local dock strike.

Griffith And therefore to repudiate the common interest which they hold with their employers as national minded Irishmen in resistance to the imperial business cartels. Sinn Fein therefore welcomes the action of the Wexford iron masters in dismissing from their service all those men who have joined with Larkin.

Enter EAMONN CEANNT, PADRAIC PEARSE, SEAN MACDERMOTT.

Ceannt (*in Irish*) My God!

Narrator Eamonn Ceannt . . .

Pearse (*in Irish*) Gracious heaven!

Narrator Padraic Pearse . . .

MacDermott (*in Irish*) Dear goodness, is the man gone mad?

Narrator Sean MacDermott . . .

Griffith I am very sorry to hear that my distinguished fellow nationalists and supporters of my movement should take exception to my few small words of analytical condemnation, but – –

Pearse Have you no words then to condemn the Wexford employers? Is there one law for them and another for their servants?

Griffith What is happening in Wexford is the banding together of one section
of the Gaelic race to extort advantage from the remainder. I regard it as
national treason!

Ceannt, Pearse, MacDermott Banding together . . . extortion . . . national
treason indeed . . .

Exeunt CEANNT, PEARSE, MACDERMOTT

Narrator It cannot be denied
    The Employers' Federation
    Is a section of the nation,
    And it *has* securely tied
    All its members in a band
    To enforce its grand demand
    On every workshop in the land . . .

Enter GRABITALL *and* EMPLOYERS (*Dubliners*).

Grabitall I intended to begin
    With the city of Dublin –

1st Employer
    But a number were faint hearted
    And insisted that we started –

2nd Employer
    With but one small coat to trail
    On a far more modest scale –

3rd Employer
    For fear that we should fail.

Grabitall Oh timid foolish feebleness
    To prejudice our whole success!
    The foundrymen are all locked out:
    I warned you now without a doubt
    The dockers of the port
    Will strike in their support.
    Have any of you thought
    Of what is next to be done?

3rd Employer
    The police have been brought in!

2nd Employer
    There are riots in Wexford town!

POLICE *and* WORKERS *rush struggling across. One of the* WORKERS, *savagely
batonned by the* POLICE, *is left on the stage when the others run out.*

Narrator And a worker is struck down
    And he dies. There he lies
    With the flies in his eyes . . .

2nd Employer

This was not wise.

GRABITALL *and the* EMPLOYERS *withdraw to the sidelines.* DALY *enters and looks in horror at the dead man.*

Narrator Brother Daly of the Transport Union
Makes a quick ad hoc decision.
All our history will be changed
By what he has arranged
In a frantic little flurry
While his friends go off to bury
The remains of Martin Leary . . .

WORKERS *straggle back in and pick up the body. While they are doing this,* DALY *makes an announcement.*

Daly If law and order in Wexford obeys no law, we have to make it for ourselves. I'm taking the names of volunteers for a workers' defence force, a workers' *police* force – if *they* carry batons, *we* carry pick-handles, I want strong registered union men only, who can hold themselves with discipline and obey the instructions of those who are set over them. Those who are set over them will be elected to that office – the election to be supervised by delegates of the union . . .

He is about to follow the funeral out, when POLICE *enter and silently arrest him.*

Narrator James Connolly comes at once from Ulster –
Not a man could travel faster.
He takes control: he will enrol –

Enter CONNOLLY *at great speed. He jumps up on the stage and calls around him a number of well-dressed people.*

Connolly – – the modest middle classes with all due speed
To counteract the bosses and their greed.
Shopkeepers, journalists, teachers, lawyers, doctors, priests –
d'ye not realise
The town and trade of Wexford falls to bits before your eyes!
Did the Employers' Federation invite you into the room
The day they decided to choose your home
For their first demonstration of the art of confrontation
And bloody murder in the market place?
Did they even have the grace
To send a small polite note
To inform you that civil war was about to break out?
Did you know that this would happen the last time you cast
your vote?
Mr Murphy represents you in parliament? Or not?

A Citizen Neither does Mr Larkin.

Connolly Mr Larkin, in the union, represents five thousand people. And that union in Wexford provoked nobody, attacked nobody, locked out nobody. We didn't even call a strike. The dockers' action in our support was spontaneous. I have been sent here to settle it. I have certain proposals. Gentlemen, I require your help. So great has been the fury of the Employers' Federation against Jim Larkin that they have felt themselves in some danger of appearing to be deranged. The more moderate members of the group therefore have fallen over backwards to explain that they are not absolutely opposed to trade unions, as such. It is merely the Transport Workers they refuse to accept. I'm glad to say this disclaimer has been committed to print: and I will take it at face value. I suggest that all those workmen who joined the ITWU, and have accordingly been sacked, should resign therefrom directly and re-apply for admission into the *Foundrymen's* Union –

A Citizen I didn't know there was one?

Connolly Into the Foundrymen's Union – which I am happy to inaugurate, in Wexford, this morning . . .

A short pause while the penny drops. The CITIZENS *laugh.*

Connolly (*laughing*) You see, the weakness of these people is that for all their ruthless arrogance, they claim respect for the law – it is the ground of their own choosing: I am well prepared to meet them on it. Gentlemen, you must agree, playing around with legal fictions is much better than street fighting? And from the point of view of your property, a great deal less destructive . . . ? Now: if you would be so good as to act as intermediaries with the Employers' Federation – they won't negotiate with me – and persuade them to recognise the Foundrymen's Union: I will undertake to recommend to the dockers an immediate return to work.

He is clapped and congratulated by the CITIZENS, *who go out.*

Grabitall Not satisfactory. We began it all too soon.

Connolly Not satisfactory. In Dublin they will try again.

Exeunt.

SCENE 2

Narrator In South Wales one million miners are on strike.
　　　　　Wages fall. Profits and unemployment both alike
　　　　　Are rising to the sky. Gold or paper put
　　　　　To usury abroad will cut
　　　　　The porridge from the spoon, the bacon from the rind,
　　　　　The soft bread from the crust for those who find
　　　　　No place to eat but in their own small home.

Paris, Berlin, New York and Petrograd and Rome
Stretch out the croupiers' hooks to rake colonial shekels in:
The green baize table-top is wearing very thin . . .
The bargemen are on strike in London river:
Nineteen thousand blacklegs loot from them their labour.
Imprisoned women calling for the vote
Refuse to eat, so down each tender throat
The tubes of food are thrust until they choke:
It has been said (and there are many men
Whose secret loins turn over at the hope it might be done)
Such harpies should be stripped as naked as they were born
Their bodies splahed with green and yellow paint
From tit to cunt
To show them who they were
And force them ask themselves how could they dare
Aspire . . . !

Enter CONNOLLY.

Connolly Truly the whole world is already turning over:
Truly the time has come to find out what we most desire . . .

SHEEHY SKEFFINGTON *enters, orating to a derisive group of street-corner* LAYABOUTS. *He has a placard reading 'Labour demands Female Suffrage'.*

Sheehy Skeffington Manliness, virility, masculinity, the courage of the noble warrior – oh indeed we all pride ourselves on possession of such qualities! How many of us in these days, I wonder, pause to ask how these attributes are advanced by the torture of helpless women?

1st Heckler What about the torture of helpless bloody men?

2nd Heckler Hey, mister, what'd you do if a bloody great German sodger asked your sister for the vote?

3rd Heckler Pull his pants down and examine him to see would he fill her ballot-box for her – !

1st Heckler Pull his pants down and examine him – come on, lads, let's have 'em off!

They make an attack on SHEEHY SKEFFINGTON. CONNOLLY *runs to his rescue.* POLICE CONSTABLES *intervene.*

Police Constable (*to* SHEEHY SKEFFINGTON) All right now, Mr Skeffington, you'd better come along with us.

Connolly You're arresting him? You've no right – –

Police Constable Just you keep out of it – we're bringing you in for your own protection – liability to give occasion for a breach of the peace.

Sheehy Skeffington (*clings on to the corner of the stage*) One final word, before I conclude . . . The entire misconception of the male-dominated society is based, I have maintained, upon the – –

The POLICE *are unable to loosen his hold. They look round and see that the* LAYABOUTS *have dispersed. They stand back and reconsider.*

Police Constable Alright now, alright . . . Just behave yourself in the future . . .

Exeunt POLICE CONSTABLES.

Sheehy Skeffington (*readjusts his damaged trousers*) You were saying the time has come to find out what you most desire. You are quite right, James, I do believe that the Socialist Party of Ireland requires a radical re-appraisal. Shall we have an exchange of views . . . ?

Narrator
> Francis Sheehy Skeffington,
> Socialist, pacifist, and tireless champion
> Of the rights of women in a world that has not even got so far
> As understanding the rights of man . . .

Connolly *I* want, to begin with, an independent Irish Labour Party. To represent and to be subsidised by the Irish trade unions.

Sheehy Skeffington Twelve months ago we failed to persuade them of this.

Connolly So this year we must do it better. We will start by calling a conference of all the small left-wing groups that exist throughout the country. The Socialist Party of Ireland will put it to them, fair and square – are we all in agreement? If we are, we can go together to the Trade Union Congress and lobby them to some purpose.

Sheehy Skeffington
> Sound, James, very sound:
> We will first have laid our ground
> With the good radical hardened core
> And upon it set in plumb-line order
> The altogether more
> Conservative trade-union structure –
> I hope they won't think it a bore
> When I as usual insist
> Upon –

Enter WINIFRED CARNEY *with a placard reading: 'Women Workers' Union demands Equality'.*

Winifred Carney
> Skeffy, I was told there had been an arrest!
> Yet here he is as free as air
> His trousers all in ribbons and his–

Sheehy Skeffington
> His bare behind declaring that he dare
> Say what he wants and all he wants as long as he wants
> In the Dublin street! James, I was saying I am going to insist
> At the trade-union congress as an absolute *must* –

Winifred Carney That the trade unions being male-dominated, any Labour Party they are likely to produce will not in itself make any difference to the rights of women.

Connolly It goes without saying, Miss Carney, that complete equality between the sexes must of course be in the programme.

Winifred Carney No it doesn't, Mr Connolly. They'll all think you mean no more than to give women the vote.

Connolly Isn't that what you want?

Winifred Carney To begin with, yes it is; but have you thought what would happen if all the women were to use their vote as instructed by their husbands? Support for our labour policies is small enough as it is – it would actually be decreased by that sort of reform.

Connolly Women will most certainly vote as instructed by their husbands, unless we can make it clear that *social* as well as *political* equality is what we demand.

Winifred Carney And it *is* what you demand?

Connolly Oh yes.

Winifred Carney Provided, Mr Connolly, it is also understood that social equality involves not only equal pay, but a recognition that working women require certain facilities. For example: temporary absence from work with full pay when they are having a baby – child-care for working mothers to be paid for by the employers –

Sheehy Skeffington I know that patience is a virtue reserved *by* men *for* women: but we are getting here into some very long-term issues. I mean, the women workers' section of the Transport Workers' Union has only just been set up, and it may well be you don't want to hear about – –

Connolly Don't apologise – *Long-term issue* is a defeatist word for a *principle*: and to establish principles is our sole purpose – or should be – in setting out a party programme. We all agree that capitalism means masters and slaves. The majority of women are, therefore, the slaves of slaves. If they are not to be liberated, then slavery will continue: and it will still be very much slavery even though we call it socialism. Your principle is agreed, and it is stated: with these others – now what have I done with my list – ?

Winifred Carney I typed up some extra copies in the office last night.

She produces a paper and reads:

'An industrial commonwealth based on the common ownership of the land and the instruments of production, distribution, and exchange. Proportional representation, universal suffrage, complete political and social equality between the sexes' – I'm adding that in now–'And immediate opposition to the proposed Home Rule Act as being entirely inadequate, particularly in view of the suggested partition to exclude protestant Ulster.'

Narrator With the exception of one British-dominated socialist group from Belfast, a united programme is drawn up and is taken to – –

Connolly Clonmel . . .
> Where the trade unions impatiently wait
> To hear what we propose and to decide on it with their vote.

On behalf of the Belfast branch of the ITWU, I put forward the motion that this congress, from every subscribing member, at the rate of one shilling a year, will maintain and support a political party. To offer candidates for election upon every public body from local councils to the House of Commons. Which means Westminster today, but tomorrow it will be in Dublin. Once Home Rule comes in, every Irish political party that at present has its eyes on London will be completely re-orientated, and will find itself automatically representing, in Ireland, one particular class or faction of Irish society. The largest of these classes is the organised working class. We are entirely without political voice. It is the business of this congress to make sure that we get that voice.

WALKER has entered and is standing at the far corner of the stage.

Walker Irish trade unions upon their own in their own home
> As a mere matter of statistics can have no voice but the voice of Rome!
> Oh, the Pope he will pronounce, and every man will bow his head:
> I tell you, in the end
> Each decision of this damned new party will be seen to depend
> On whether hell, heaven, or purgatory is your destination when you are all dead . . . !

Exit WALKER.

Narrator Votes. Forty-nine in favour. Eighteen against. The resolution is successful. The expected opposition from the delegates from Belfast was defeated – –

Enter LARKIN.

Larkin Thanks to Connolly!
Narrator By the delegates from Belfast . . .

Exeunt SHEEHY SKEFFINGTON and WINIFRED CARNEY.

SCENE 3

Narrator
> From resolution into action:
> Local government election.

CONNOLLY and LARKIN stand on rostra at opposite sides of the stage, with small CROWDS around them.

Connolly James Connolly stands in Belfast.

Larkin James Larkin stands in Dublin.

Connolly Mr Lloyd George, for whom I hold no brief –

Larkin – has so far succumbed to the pressures on the cabinet from the British Labour Party –

Connolly – with whom the Liberals unwillingly are compelled into coalition –

Larkin – that he has had to force through parliament his National Health Insurance –

Connolly A great part of this essential reform must now be administered by the local authorities –

Larkin – and if the health of the working classes is to be left to the tender mercies of the publicans, crawthumpers, shylocks, scrooges and assorted gombeen gutter rats whom the traditional political parties thrust up from the sewers to solicit your votes –

Connolly – then you can all rest assured that the fruit of Lloyd George's harvest will be let rot upon the tree! Vote Labour for social justice!

Larkin Vote Labour to turn reformism into genuine revolution!

Connolly Vote Labour for the ultimate re-conquest of Ireland!

Hecklers (*at* CONNOLLY'*s corner*) Re-conquest of Ireland is a Fenian conspiracy! Home Rule is Rome Rule! Up the Orange Order! Up the UVF! King Billy and the Boyne! Kick the Pope! No social reform if it comes from the Lundy Liberals! *etcetera* . . .

Narrator For Connolly in the Belfast docks
       The voice of Carson spoke no hope.
       For Larkin every Dublin dosshouse turned
       Its dragon-teeth of drab rebellion out to vote –

Tremendous cheers from LARKIN'*s hearers.*

Larkin My victory was terrific.
       My defeat was automatic.

A CIVIL SERVANT *enters with an official document.*

Civil Servant (*reads*) Mr Larkin, being a convicted felon, though apparently elected by an overwhelming majority, is legally prohibited from assuming his seat.

Exit CIVIL SERVANT.

Larkin Jim Larkin is the people's choice
       The muffling of the people's voice
       Just puts him back to where he was before:
       With the trade union, of the trade union, for the trade union,
       In the forefront of the rank-and-file that fight the people's war . . . !

Exit LARKIN *with his* SUPPORTERS.

SCENE 4

Connolly (*alone on stage*)

If a Fenian thinks an Orangeman is a hooligan sectarian,
What does an Orangeman think of a Fenian
When his children out of school on a picnic in fine weather
Are attacked by the keys of Peter swung like flails from the papal
banner . . . ?

A cluster of screaming CHILDREN *are chased across the stage by a mob of catholic* ADULTS, *dressed up in Hibernian regalia, one of them using the papal banner as a weapon. Shouts from the mob of – 'Let's have ye out of here, ye wee protestant whoor – Wee Joe Devlin'll tear out your heart – get the hell out of this field, it's a catholic field, ye heretic young scum . . .' etcetera.*

I ask every man in Ulster, what loyalty is due to a church
That is not alone content to leave its people in the lurch
But works in the name of the Lord to augment the trouble and
harm
Heaped upon them by their masters? Catholic and prod
Both over-ruled together by the chartered accountants' God . . .

The same catholic MOB *come screaming back again, chased by* ADULT ORANGEMEN, *in their regalia, with banners, yelling slogans. The Orangemen, having cleared the field, stand for a moment, take breath, remove their regalia, and line up as though working heavily on a production line.*

Narrator (*sings*)

In the port of Larne near Belfast town
They manufacture aluminium:
The religious men of the port of Larne
Have nothing to do with the Pope's dominion.

Workers (*sing*)

Giddy-i-ay we work very hard
Giddy-i-ay it's a seven-day week with
Giddy-i-ay tiddle-iddle-oo
The protestant workers of Larne.

Narrator (*sings*)

The religious men of the port of Larne
Rightly regard it as a dreadful hardship
That they must work on the sabbath-day
Instead of attending a place of worship.

Connolly (*sings*)

Giddy-i-ay but God doesn't mind
Giddy-i-ay He is not abandoned
Giddy-i-ay tiddle-iddle-oo
The employers all go to church.

Workers (*sing*)

> Seven days a week twelve hours a day
> They make us work at the aluminium
> What can you find for your leisure time
> But drink yourself into oblivion?
> Giddy-i-ay you would not think
> Giddy-i-ay we could ever pull out of it
> Giddy-i-ay tiddle-iddle-oo
> But Connolly brought us the word –

Connolly and Workers STRIKE!!

A Worker (*sings*)

> For the first time ever for seventeen years
> I went to church with my wife and children:
> The minister's eye was round and wild
> In surprise at the size of his congregation . . .

The PROTESTANT MINISTER *climbs on to the rostrum and surveys the* WORKERS *grouped before him, their heads bent devoutly in prayer.*

Minister (*sings*)

> Giddy-i-ay what have we here?
> The Church is filled with idle strikers!
> Giddy-i-ay tiddle-iddle-oo
> You must all go back to work!

Narrator And in the end that's what they did:

> James Connolly was born a papist – and it could not be hid.

CONNOLLY *goes out and the* WORKERS *recommence their labour.*

Workers (*sing*)

> We did not know what we should do
> With Connolly gone we were quite forsaken
> But Sir Edward Carson took his place
> And undertook to save our bacon.

Enter CARSON *with a large document.*

Carson (*sings*)

> Giddy-i-ay I have here a paper
> Giddy-i-ay will ye put your name to it
> Giddy-i-ay tiddle-iddle-oo
> The Ulster Covenant Oath!

Workers (*reassume their Orange regalia and line up formally as they sing.*)

> We swear by the Lord and the battle of the Boyne
> By old King Billy and the siege of Derry
> That we'd die in the ditch before we'd strike
> Our flag to any but an English Tory!
> Giddy-i-ay is that quite right . . . ?

Carson (*sings*)

> Giddy-i-ay you are left no choice in it
> Giddy-i-ay tiddle-iddle-oo
> All the rest have been bought by the Pope!

Repeat after me: 'Never under any circumstances will we submit to Home Rule. In the event of a Home Rule parliament being forced upon us we solemnly and mutually pledge ourselves to resist its authority. In sure confidence that God will defend the right, we have here subscribed our names. God save the king!'

> One Law One Land One Throne . . .

Enter BONAR LAW.

Bonar Law

> If England drive you forth
> You shall not fall alone . . .

As Leader of the Conservative and Unionist Party I give you this message: that though the brunt of the battle be yours, there will not be wanting help from across the Channel . . .

Exeunt to the tune of 'The Sash My Father Wore'. Orange flags waved with panache.

SCENE 5

Liberty Hall in the midst of the Dublin dockland, the river on one side, the Custom House on the other. (Backcloth No. 9.)

Enter LARKIN, DELIA LARKIN *and a number of* ITWU OFFICIALS, *all very busy with documents – a great mess of papers on* LARKIN'S *table.*

Larkin Will you get to hell out of it, man, with that bloody ledger. Can't ye see I have enough papers on the ould desk as it is? What's this here?

Delia That's the proofsheets for the leading article for next week's *Irish Worker* – and this here's the supplementary feature from the Women Workers' Union.

Larkin Sure I went over that yoke the last day, Delia – cannot a man's own sister remember what he's after telling her twenty-four hours since!

Delia Didn't you tell me after tea that you wanted it back, ye had something to add to it – a poem or something, you said . . . So add it and don't be asking me any more damnfool questions.

She goes out.

COUNTESS MARKIEVICZ *comes in and sits down at the end of the table.*

Countess

> So much confusion in the room
> So little time

So much great haste
So many words and so much waste
I don't propose to keep you, Jim,
More than a moment – I have begun
To write down what I think should now be done
To set the union of woodworking men
Into some frame and order once again.

Now first, if you don't mind – we must look at –

She tries to show LARKIN *a set of documents. He is, however, constantly distracted by* OFFICIALS *shoving papers in front of him and taking others away.* O'BRIEN *and* WINIFRED CARNEY *are very busy amongst these.*

Narrator Countess Markievicz, great lady of the family of Gore-Booth
        Turns her back upon her heritage of ascendancy rule
        In and out the crowded passages of Liberty Hall
        With long white hands and voice so calm and cool
        Instinctively she attempts to bring reasoned control
        To the Larkin rage
        And the ink-smudged page
        And the bank account that seems to be always in the red:
        Poor lady: he has not heard one word of what she said ...

Larkin Wait a minute now, what's this? Now who in God's name put this on me desk!

O'Brien I did.

Larkin And when didja?

O'Brien At two-thirty o'clock on Tuesday precisely.

Larkin Look, William, for God's sake, I have asked you this before – I'm to have these damn things read to me or I can never know what they are. I've a notion for some time we should look out for bigger premises.

O'Brien But, Chief, we have only just moved into these –

Larkin A rat-hole of a flea-bed of a bug-ridden commercial hotel! Liberty Hall, how-are-ye ... ? I want to scrap that leading article. Winifred, have you got your notebook? Because now we have these figures in we're to make a big boost of them, all over page one and page two and page three. The membership of this union in two years has gone up from four thousand at the beginning of nineteen eleven to over fourteen thousand today. Work that out as an approximate average of one hundred per week who take out the subscriptions. And that – be it well noted – is permanent annual membership only – if we add in all the casuals who come in for a week or a month and then for one reason or another forget about it or drop out, we have a current human turnover in all parts of the country of something in the order of twenty-five thousand. Let alone me sister Delia with the Irish women workers has got at least a thousand there –

Countess Winifred, you can take these figures of the United Woodworkers' affiliations as being checked, final and accurate with no approximation . . .

Larkin – and the Wexford men from the iron foundries run at somewhere between five hundred and nine hundred – and Jim Connolly in the North has his own figures for the textile workers. I've heard no word from Connolly for going on now a fortnight – he's not sick, d'ye suppose?

O'Brien There's a letter in this morning. Which is why I brought the ledger in. He's in a state of mind about the contributions for the National Insurance Act –

Larkin He's in a state about something every minute of the day –

Enter CONNOLLY, *hot and angry.*

Connolly I have absolutely no notion what's been happening to the funds I am supposed to administer and account for in Belfast.

Larkin What are you doing here?

Connolly I came to look for a ledger. I've been writing every day for the past month about these returns. I suppose somebody's been noting somewhere a list of figures in some book? William, are you aware of the condition of my account?

O'Brien There's about two-thirds of it down here.

Connolly In that ledger?

O'Brien In this.

Connolly Then where's the rest? Don't ye realise, Jim Larkin, I have the man from the ministry on me doorstep this minute? If we don't give him satisfaction, they will prosecute: they'll do it tomorrow!

Larkin You're not telling me they've frightened *you* with a threat of prosecution!

Connolly Do you believe a trade union should be an illegal organisation?

Larkin If William Martin Murphy has his way that's exactly what we'd be.

Connolly But he hasn't, and we're not . . .

He has been shuffling through the ledger and assorted documents.

I thought so, Brother Larkin, you've been shifting the bloody money outa one column into the other to pay arrears on God knows what.

Larkin Are you accusing me of financial chicanery?

Connolly I'm accusing you of nothing. I'm just turning out your papers, man, till I get hold of what I need! Good heavens, what have we here!

Larkin I was looking for that – that's the second verse of my poem – give that here, I have to – –

Connolly You don't propose to publish this?

Larkin Why wouldn't I? It's a good laugh.

Connolly (*reads*)

> With money to pay the rent
> Which Lloyd George has kindly lent
> Happy sick hundred –

And though they are badly crushed
Into the pub they rushed
Later with faces flushed
Homeward they went . . . ?

Larkin Jasus, man, it's only a joke . . .

Connolly Do you actually dare boast you have been distributing the sickness benefit for purposes otherwise than what was intended?

Countess Is there a better definition of sickness than chronic unemployment in a Parnell Street tenement?

Connolly I am sure there isn't, Madame Markievicz, but it's not covered by the act. And my organisation is sufficiently tenuous to need every ledge of legality we can conceivably put a toecap on.

Larkin (*scribbles on a scrap of card*) Your organisation in Belfast is too small.

Connolly If it hadn't been for me picking up where you broke down there'd be no organisation in Belfast at all! And anyway, all these figures you are making such a brag over – 'enormous inconceivable growth in the power of Labour . . . ' I don't believe three-quarters of them are of real value whatever. Devoid absolutely of political education, with no understanding of the meaning of socialism, the minute the hard times come – and I can tell you they are coming *tomorrow* – they will drop from us like tea-leaves outa the bottom of the pot! And who do I blame for it? Jim Larkin, I must say this – –

Larkin (*gives him the card*) I think you need this one.

Connolly The back of a bloody score-card for a game of housey-housey . . . !

O'Brien It'll have to be transcribed.

Larkin Don't despise the housey-housey – we made twenty-five quid last Saturday for the union contingency fund –

Connolly Are you sure that these figures are an accurate statement?

O'Brien They have what I might call a broad approximate sweep. Chief, I simply don't believe this two hundred and fifty quid.

Larkin Too much of a round figure?

O'Brien It looks bloody suspicious.

Connolly Look here, write it down: two hundred and forty-nine pound six shilling and eightpence ha'penny.

O'Brien What's the ha'penny for?

Connolly Postage.

Countess (*has sorted out and entered up a whole sheaf of documents*) There you are, all complete, you can put it straight in the file as it stands. Why don't we all go back to my house and have a really decent supper for once. Come along. . . .

Exeunt.

SCENE 6

Enter GRABITALL *between two* BISHOPS.

Grabitall

By knowing when to sell and when to buy
When to combine and when to destroy
I have enlarged myself into my present size.
Down any street in Dublin shoot your eyes:
Much, if not all, of what you see
In that august perspective belongs to me.
There is a tram, by electric current fed,
The hand of Murphy drew it from its shed:
There is a ragged man sells papers on the curb,
Printed by Murphy, filled with Murphy's word:
There is a huge hotel where men and women,
White-tied, bare-shouldered, champagne and diamonds gleaming,
In wine and waltz defeat their immortal souls:
Murphy supplies the bed, the liquor, and the lascivious bath . . .

1st Bishop

God writes each name upon His judgement rolls . . .

Grabitall

Murphy at holy mass will deprecate God's wrath.

2nd Bishop

The conduct of the guests in an hotel
Is matter surely for their own free will.

Grabitall

Like Adam in the garden before he fell:
For virtue quite as much as vice is charged upon my bill.

Bishops And no-one's forced to send himself to hell.

1st Bishop

The profits William Martin Murphy makes . . .

2nd Bishop

Are spent of course upon good works.

Grabitall

St Vincent de Paul, the blind, the deaf and dumb,
Receive their benefits from beneath my thumb.
And when a generous prelate drinks his port
I like to think his warm hierarchical thought
Includes the name of Murphy . . .

1st Bishop

We must remember that the master has the right
Of ownership; his place of work: his property. He may direct
Unchallenged, in all love, the policy
Of his own enterprise. The man who works for him is likewise
free . . .

2nd Bishop
> To work no longer . . . if he does not wish.
> But let him not
> Brigade himself together for this purpose and extend
> His individual voice into a common shout:
> Such a proceeding can have but one end . . .

1st Bishop There is no class of persons in the entire civilised world less capable of determining the course of industry than the lower orders of the city of Dublin. The tenement houses they inhabit –

Grabitall Infest –

1st Bishop Are notoriously the worst in Europe.

2nd Bishop The death rate per annum is twenty-seven point six per cent. Why, the plague and cholera of Calcutta kill no more than twenty-seven per cent, and in Moscow, where – as we all know – the government is arbitrary and the church is both schismatic and corrupt, the comparable percentage is as low as twenty-six.

1st Bishop Twenty thousand entire families in the tenements of Dublin have but one room for all their needs.

2nd Bishop Five thousand families are compelled to make do with two rooms.

1st Bishop The infant mortality in nineteen hundred and ten was a hundred and forty-two per thousand.

2nd Bishop And as for the actual safety of the buildings, leaving aside for the moment their convenience and salubrity, fifteen hundred out of five thousand have been condemned by the proper authority: and yet they still stand.

1st Bishop Those of them that do not fall.

Narrator Two have collapsed already, during the year, and seven people died . . .

Grabitall The mitigation of all this misery is to be found in the ministrations of the priesthood and the undoubted devotion of the people to their ancient faith.

1st Bishop Yet that devotion has been challenged . . .

2nd Bishop Socialism secularism syndicalism humanism modernism –

1st Bishop Marxism!

Grabitall To coin a phrase – Larkinism . . .

2nd Bishop I understand, Mr Murphy, that the Employers' Federation has at last found so much unity you can at last challenge Larkinism on its own ground?

The EMPLOYERS *enter and stand beside* GRABITALL. *One of them gives him a document, a report which he studies with satisfaction.*

Grabitall We start with my own newspaper. We have no time to waste . . .
> This people must be purged before the Home Rule Bill
> Puts us and all our future at the mercy of our own free will.
> We will begin upon Friday – pay-day . . .

1st Bishop You might prefer to think of it as the day of the blessed passion of the Son of God . . .

Exeunt.

SCENE 7

Narrator (*sings*)

On the Friday Mr Murphy ordered
All those who worked for the *Independent*
To quit the union or the job:
Such were the terms of his commandment.

On the Monday Murphy ordered
Two score and more of his obstinate servants
To take their cards and be paid off
And to leave the shop without disturbance.

On the Tuesday none of Mr Murphy's papers
Were displayed on sale in street nor suburb:
To inquire for a copy of the *Independent*
Was to meet dead silence or a furious hubbub . . .

Enter a NEWSBOY *and a* CITIZEN.

Newsboy *Independent*? I don't keep it.

Citizen But you do. I bought one yesterday.

Newsboy And yesterday there was forty fellers had jobs in the despatch department. Today they're on the streets. Ye can whistle for your damn paper.

The CITIZEN *walks away and is met by a* SCAB NEWSBOY.

Scab Newsboy (*furtively*) *Independent* . . . ? *Evening Herald*? Buy your independent newspapers from an independent purveyor, no truck with the unions here, sorr: Mr Murphy has determined to control his own arrangements – here you are, sorr, under your coat – don't let them fellers see it . . .

As the CITIZEN *walks away he is accosted by a* PICKET.

Picket Hey, you; where didja get that paper . . . !

Citizen I purchased it in a normal fashion from the person that was selling them –

His paper is snatched from him and torn up.

Picket (*whistles through his fingers*) Hey – Johnny – get the lads up Dawson Street, he has the scabs there flogging his papers – look sharp or they'll be away from ye – !

A chase – the PICKETS *flush out the* SCAB NEWSBOY *and make off with his stock. Exeunt.*

SCENE 8

Narrator (*sings*)
> On the Tuesday Mr Murphy ordered
> That all those men in the tramway service
> Who had joined the union should be paid off
> And leave the depot without disturbance.

> On the Friday Larkin recommended –

Enter LARKIN *with a group of* UNION OFFICIALS *at one side.*

Larkin No strike just yet – !
Narrator (*sings*)
> In the tramway service:
> Let the work proceed all quiet and normal
> No threat no noise and no disturbance.

> On the Saturday Mr Murphy wondered –

Enter GRABITALL *and* EMPLOYERS *at the other side.*

Grabitall
> Now what the devil is Larkin up to . . . ?
Narrator (*sings*)
> The tramcars rolled all fully loaded
> From stop to stop without disruption.

Grabitall He's decided to lie low, has he? No reason why *we* should. A letter sent off to every employee: demand he reply at once by return of post with the most rigorous pledge to refuse to obey any call for a strike that Larkin should put out. Failure to reply means instant dismissal. Type it in the form of a proforma: all they have to do is put their name at the bottom.

Exit 1ST EMPLOYER.

Narrator (*sings*)
> On the Saturday Brother Larkin mustered
> A secret meeting of the tramway workmen:
> He said to prepare for immediate action –
Larkin (*joined by more workers*)
> The word when it comes will have no forewarning.

LARKIN'*s confidants hurry away. Re-enter* 1ST EMPLOYER *to* GRABITALL.

Grabitall Report on the response to my ultimatum – yes?
1st Employer Out of seven hundred and fifty, one hundred and fifty either don't reply or reply unprintable. Of the remaining six hundred, I would estimate four hundred and fifty can be relied on to stay loyal.

Grabitall As indeed they should. I have taken pains to recruit dog, devil, thief and saint into my company over the past few months . . .

Enter a DRUNK *in a tramway conductor's uniform, with a* HARLOT.

Drunk (*sings*)
> I tell ye Mary Madigan ye sure would never know
> The rags and tatthers on me back I wore but a week ago . . .

Harlot (*sings*)
> But now as we shtagger in and out the boozers and the bars
> In his royal tramway uniform like a fighting son of Mars
> Ye would never think that such a man will ever forgo his pride
> In serving Misther Murphy where the town's commuters ride . . .

Drunk (*sings*)
> *Anymorefaresplease!* – as I shout it, in me loyal heart I know
> That to virtuous Misther Murphy all I have in the world I owe . . .

To Larkin I owe nuthn . . . He's done nuthn for me . . . Nuthn . . .

Exeunt DRUNK *and* HARLOT.

Enter the LORD MAYOR *in robes and chain. He is seen by* 2ND EMPLOYER *who attracts* GRABITALL's *attention.*

2nd Employer The Lord Mayor of Dublin . . .

Lord Mayor Mr Murphy.

Grabitall My Lord Mayor.

Lord Mayor Mr Murphy, this week is the week of the Dublin horse show.

Grabitall A commercial and social event of international importance.

Lord Mayor A transport strike at such a time would be unthinkable. I beg you, sir, to use your best influences to avoid – –

Grabitall I have no better influence than this pile of letters in my hand. And if this fails, I expect you, sir, to make use of your own best influences with the authorities in Dublin Castle.

Lord Mayor Do you mean the police?

Grabitall I mean the military, if need be.

Lord Mayor I thought you were a Home Ruler.

Grabitall I am indeed. With our own parliament the national coercive force would be in our own control. As it is, we depend on Whitehall. Larkin, I would remind you, is not a Home Ruler. He is a republican and a socialist.

Lord Mayor Mr Murphy, the civil power must not be seen to take sides in a purely industrial dispute – at any rate till the rights of the matter are correctly adjudged . . . Mr Murphy, sir, what *are* you doing!

Grabitall Picking your pocket . . . Whose is this watch?

Lord Mayor Mine!

Grabitall Yours. You have a right to it. And if I tried such a trick in the street you would call a policeman. That's all.

He gives the LORD MAYOR *his watch back and goes out with the* EMPLOYERS.

SCENE 9

Narrator (*sings*)
>On the Tuesday Brother Larkin issued
>A call for a

Larkin STRIKE!!

Narrator (*sings*)
>At ten in the morning
>The trams all stopped, the drivers left them
>The conductors went home without forewarning.
>
>On every set of rails in Dublin
>A silent tramcar stood like a statue
>From the windows projected the heads of the passengers
>Calling and crying in the hope of rescue . . .

A group representing several PASSENGERS, *with a* DRIVER *in front of them have trotted in like a moving tram. They stop suddenly and the* DRIVER *walks briskly away.*

1st Passenger But I promised Lady Kilpesant most faithfully I would be there to see her nephew the Colonel put Harbinger over the jumps . . . !

2nd Passenger If I'd known this was going to happen I'd have ordered out the barouche.

3rd Passenger Not a cab or a side-car to be seen in Pembroke Road! I had arranged to meet Count Tannenberg at the RDS at ten fifteen. It really looks to me as though we must *walk* to Ballsbridge.

1st Passenger One wonders, does one not, why the troops are not called out?

The PASSENGERS *hobble away in disgust, calling frantically for cabs.*

Enter GRABITALL.

Grabitall Unfortunate the small proportion of men determined to go on strike should have comprised the greater part of the actual crews of the vehicles . . .

The Tram Driver (*looking back from over near Larkin*) Unfortunate me granny – 'twas all planned with the precision of the building of the Brooklyn bridge! Begod if ever Jim Larkin comes to terms with the social order, 'tis himself should have the management of the tramways of this town!

Grabitall I am replacing them as soon as possible by those servants who are still loyal.

Enter a POLICE OFFICER.

Police Officer Mr Murphy, please tell your men who are still upon the job that it is not possible to use a tramcar as though it were a war chariot!

Goddammit, sir, it's made of glass! Outside Trinity College this moment there's a crowd of thousands blocking the road. We cannot allow the cars to be driven through at full speed!

Grabitall Why not? They are *my* cars.

Police Officer Mr Murphy, you have no right to foment riot in this town . . . ! What the devil are you doing, sir!

Grabitall Picking your pocket . . .

Police Officer By God, sir, give that back!

Grabitall D'you know what you've just done? You've laid your hands on me with violence. If this had taken place in public there might well have been a riot. And who would have fomented it? That's all . . .

He gives the POLICE OFFICER *his watch back.*

In the interests of law and order I am prepared to withdraw my skeleton service. Withdraw everything . . . By all means . . . Not a tram upon the street: and therefore no riot . . .

Exeunt GRABITALL *and* POLICE OFFICER.

SCENE 10

Narrator (*sings*)
On the Wednesday Larkin organised
At the Custom House an enormous meeting:
It was not the first: every night of the strike
There were thousands who crowded to hear him speaking . . .

LARKIN *gets up on the rostrum and the* CROWD *gathers round.* O'BRIEN *is beside him.*

Larkin I promise you that living or dead they will never break me: and if dead I will be a greater force against them than alive! My advice to you is: if one of our class fall, then two of the others must fall for that one. By the living God, if they want war they can have it! There is no surrender in this fight. No surrender – no cars tomorrow – I will put it that no car can ever run on the streets of Dublin till the tramway men have got their terms. Sir Edward Carson has discovered that the men of Ulster – for Tory purposes – have a right and a duty to take up arms and prepare themselves. Sir Edward Carson is not in prison. Sir Edward Carson is already disposing the posts and the patronage of a provisional government. If William Martin Murphy continues to defy us, we will take our rebel pattern from the rebels of Ulster! The working men of Dublin are the people of Dublin, the property of this city belongs to every one of you. O'Connell Street, where Mr Murphy lays claim to a huge hotel – how many of you here can afford the price of his cabbage and bacon . . . ? – that hotel is in your street, and I think it is high time we put to good use

the property for which we pay. On Sunday, whatever happens, at half
past one in the afternoon, we will hold our next big meeting, in the middle
of O'Connell Street: and we will hold it in front of the Imperial Hotel,
William Murphy's hotel. Let every man in Dublin see that every man in
Dublin is the master of his own town . . . !

Great applause. The meeting disperses. LARKIN *comes down with* O'BRIEN.

How was that?

O'Brien Dangerous.

Larkin Did I pitch it a wee bit ambiguous, do you think?

O'Brien Ambiguous . . . ? Not exactly. Why wouldn't we wait till they had
got themselves some weapons before we talked to them about taking
them?

Larkin How could they ever take them, unless there was first talk about it?

O'Brien Very well: but I said – dangerous . . .

Larkin A logical continuation of what Daly did in Wexford. A workers'
defence force – a workers' police force –

O'Brien That meeting in O'Connell Street will never be permitted.

Larkin William: it will be *held*.

POLICE *enter suddenly and arrest* LARKIN.

Larkin (*as he is taken away*) Send a wire to Belfast – get Connolly down here!

Exeunt.

SCENE 11

Narrator (*sings*)
> On the Thursday Dublin Castle ordered
> The release on bail of Brother Larkin:
> Bound over in hope of his good behaviour . . .
> But his Sunday meeting was forbidden.

Enter LARKIN, *with* O'BRIEN *and* CONNOLLY *and a crowd of* SUPPORTERS.

Larkin (*waves a paper*) I have here the proclamation which categorically
prohibits the assembly of the Dublin people! With your permission – I
am going to burn this proclamation! I am a rebel and the son of a rebel.
I recognise no law but the law of the people.

He sets the paper alight.

Connolly The meeting referred to in the words of the proclamation is supposed
to be held in a place of the name of Sackville Street . . . I take Sackville
Street to be some class of precinct provided for the use of the king of
England whenever he has a mood to put his feet in another man's
country . . . So don't anybody go down Sackville Street. If you do, you

might get lifted. On the other hand, there can be no objection to any well-disposed person taking a short stroll down *O'Connell* Street – if only to discover whether there is a meeting being held there or not . . . Sackville Street very well may belong to the king: O'Connell Street belongs to *you*!
He sees POLICE *coming forward.*

Jim: I think it's time that you deftly disappeared . . .

LARKIN *slips away: but* CONNOLLY *is arrested.*

Exeunt.

SCENE 12

Narrator (*sings*)
>On the Saturday Dublin Castle ordered
>James Connolly to gaol for a three-months' sentence:
>No-one could tell where the devil was Larkin,
>And the town ran wild with riot and disturbance.

POLICE *with their batons rush across the stage and all round the hall, fighting with* CROWDS OF PEOPLE *armed with sticks, bottles, etc.*

>On the Saturday in the poorest quarters
>Of Dublin city the enraged policemen
>In fear and fury swung their truncheons
>Struck Byrne to the ground and murdered Nolan.

The POLICE *make a very strong attack on the* CROWD, *and clear them out for a time. One man is dragged out unconscious by his friends, and another lies on the stage, dead. The* POLICE *stand around, exhausted, waiting for the next development. A* POLICE OFFICER *reports to his* SUPERINTENDENT.

Police Officer My men, sir, are beaten to their knees. They are exhausted.
Superintendent They must stand to their duty.
Police Officer But the numbers that are against us –
Superintendent Numbers are nothing. You have discipline, you have control. In a mob there is neither. The only thing to prevent us being utterly overwhelmed is to make it quite clear that we are *not* going to go home.

He points to the dead body.

Who's this?
Police Officer I don't know, sir. After the last charge. He appears to be dead. Shall we carry him away?
Superintendent Leave him. We can spare no men for it. We are going to be compelled to withdraw from this street. Take your cordon up, as instructed, at the next corner but one. If you have the chance to take advantage of any breathing-space there, you can issue the men with a small ration of spirits.

Police Officer I have done so.

Superintendent Do it again.

Police Officer My God, can't we have soldiers. . .?

Superintendent You know perfectly well that's a *political* decision.

As the POLICE *are being withdrawn to their new position they are attacked by another* CROWD – *mostly women: and respond with another baton-charge. The* SUPERINTENDENT, *at a distance, addresses the* AUDIENCE.

So furious was the rain of bottles and bricks that the place seemed more like the haunt of howling demons than a street within a few yards of a christian cathedral. The shameful filthy expressions shouted at the tops of women's voices formed a very painful feature of the melancholy exhibition.

Exeunt.

SCENE 13

A quiet group of WORKERS *come to take up the dead body. One of them is a* GIRL.

Girl (*sings*)

> James Nolan was a quiet young man
> I would be his wife, he said,
> When he'd earned sufficient money
> To buy me a big brass bed.
>
> They tried to make him swear
> When he went to take his pay
> That he'd never join the union
> Until his dying day.
>
> They told him this on Monday
> But he would not sign his name;
> On Saturday his dying day
> Had broken into his brain.

The body is taken away. Enter O'BRIEN.

O'Brien The other poor fellow, James Byrne, in the hospital: dead. More trouble over these, there'll be the funerals, riots. O'Connell Street – riots. What on earth am I to do? Connolly inside: Jim Larkin disappeared – all his words left on the air. 'Get your guns. Copy Carson. Trust the leadership . . . ' Whose leadership? O'Brien? Leader of what? Every drunk, every beggar, every prostitute in Dublin . . . ? Entire proper procedure of a trade union gone by the board. Pass the word, for Godsake

    – there will be a *union* meeting in the recreation ground at Croydon Park. Members only. O'Connell Street – forget about it! Jim Larkin – if he's anywhere – will be with us in Croydon Park!

Enter LARKIN (*disguised as an old whiskered clergyman*) *with the* COUNTESS.

Larkin Jim Larkin – if he's anywhere – will be nowhere but O'Connell Street.

O'Brien What kind of silly joke d'you imagine that you're – my God: you're not serious!

Countess Of course he is, why wouldn't he be? He said he would be there. If he can't travel with his own face he must put on someone else's. Watch out – it's falling off . . .

She hurriedly adjusts the disguise.

O'Brien He'd be far better off without it. He can't walk down O'Connell Street dressed up like Father Christmas!

Countess He's not going to walk down O'Connell Street. He will travel in my carriage. He is an aged invalid clergyman on a visit to the archbishop and he's stopping at the Imperial Hotel. He has only thirty seconds to be seen on the pavement at all. But it has to be correct. Jim, do try and walk with a bit more of a *hunch*. And *don't* look out of the corner of your eye at the public all the time. You are *not* expecting their applause – they are *not* supposed to give it!

O'Brien If there's any one place guarded in the whole of Dublin this Sunday it'll be Murphy's hotel. Oh God, just look at the pair of you – giggling and nudging! Jim Larkin, I have a responsibility toward the future of this union and the labour movement in general –

Larkin So have I – to such an extent that neither Murphy nor the police would ever dream I'd be eedjit enough to pull a silly stunt the like o' this . . . !

Countess Now we don't want to be late, do we, grandfather . . . ? Come along, come along.

She leads LARKIN *out.*

O'Brien I repeat – the transport union will be meeting in Croydon Park. . . .
Exit.

SCENE 14

Narrator (*sings*)
        On the Sunday in the city centre
        The crowds were large but all disordered:
        No speeches, bands, nor great processions –
        The police held back round the back street corners . . .

The SUPERINTENDENT *and the* POLICE OFFICER *stand to one side, overlooking the scene. Groups of people assemble aimlessly.*

Superintendent And that's where they are to stay unless anything happens . . .

Police Officer My opinion, nothing's going to bloody well happen.

Superintendent . . . Because their appearance this morning is a perfect disgrace. Bruises, bandages, swaying about on their feet . . . Foul language . . .

Police Officer They had a very hard night.

Superintendent If they'd just keep their minds on the job for two minutes there's no reason at all why they should have a hard day. All they have to do is to make absolutely certain that Larkin does not get here. You have a man that knows him by sight at every intersection? Good. So we wait: keep it aimless; keep it vague; the crowd will get bored. They'll go home to their dinners, if they've not already had them. A crowd without a focus – –

Police Officer Excuse me sir – outside the Post Office!

Superintendent Yes! There is a focus! A small nucleus of men. It could be a diversion. How many have you got there?

Police Officer Sergeant Butler and a small detail at the back of the Imperial: Inspector McCaig and his men at the side door of the Post Office.

Superintendent Alert them. Hello, what's happening?

Police Officer The nucleus –

Superintendent The focus –

Police Officer It's beginning to shift –

Superintendent Is Larkin there, Goddammit – ?

Police Officer Don't see him –

Superintendent Every squad in every side street draw their batons, move slowly in. Any man who isn't fit for it, send him to the rear.

Police Officer Isn't fit for what, sir?

Superintendent Idiot. If we have to move in, we shall move like a steam hammer. Everyone in Sackville Street must be considered a public enemy and as though armed with an offensive weapon.

Police Officer But there's women and children, they're after coming out of church –

Superintendent This street has been *proclaimed* by an officer of the king!

Police Officer Should we not leave a corner open for the people to disperse?

Superintendent Not at all – if they get away, they will form themselves up again – don't you see, a way out will provide them with a *focus*!

Crowd It's Larkin!

LARKIN *has appeared on a balcony, to the rear of where the* SUPERINTENDENT *and the officer have been watching. They wheel round.*

Superintendent Take the name of the man responsible for permitting him to get up there!

Larkin (*having removed his disguise immediately on appearance*) I am here today in accordance with my promise to address you in O'Connell Street, and I will not leave until arrested . . .

A POLICE CONSTABLE *appears behind him on the balcony and takes him in.*

Superintendent All your men – from all four quarters – NOW!!

The POLICE OFFICER *blows his whistle.* POLICE *rush in and beat and beat the people until the stage is clear, except for one or two injured, who drag themselves away.*

SCENE 15

Narrator Sunday was called Bloody Sunday
      It was not the first nor would it prove to be the last
      In Irish and in English history.
      Why get angry over old blood, shed and gone and past?
      And the men and women from whom it flew will nearly all of
        them today be dead . . .
      No great claim to fame or cause to remember their name
      Except that in nineteen thirteen they were hit over the head
      When they did not expect it and it was not deserved.
      Nor can it be said public order was preserved.

Enter SUPERINTENDENT.

Superintendent Mr Murphy could not be blamed, he was not even there.

Enter POLICE OFFICER.

Police Officer The policemen could not be blamed, poor fellows, they were so tired.

Enter COUNTESS *and* LARKIN *in prison.*

Countess And sure Jim Larkin was not to blame, all he did was appear
      According to his promise –
Larkin When touched upon the shoulder I immediately retired.

Enter CONNOLLY.

Connolly It is just that there was this great field full of folk
      And all of a sudden they were aware
      That all of their lives they had been lined up for war:
      And all of a sudden, on Sunday, it had come.
Narrator The priest had left the church and his dinner had gone into the pan.
Larkin It was already decided for all of them which side they were on.
Connolly That is what they understood between the running of the feet and
      the truncheons falling down . . .

Exeunt all except CONNOLLY.

SCENE 16

CONNOLLY, *on stage, is pacing up and down in frustrated rage.*

Connolly Myself in Mountjoy gaol
Shout out these words to no avail
When they're hit on the head
There is nothing need be *said* –
Just to *do* and to *do* and to *do* – all *I* can do
Is beat upon my cell door for the screw –

He knocks violently.

I was told by the governor that newspapers could be sent in: nothing has come in. I get no news, no visitors, are they all arrested – where are they . . . ?

Enter a WARDER.

I am going to go on hunger strike.

Warder God, you don't want to do that . . . Look, you do have a visitor. The celebrated Mr Keir Hardie from England.

Enter KEIR HARDIE.

Keir Hardie This won't do.

Connolly Who's to stop it? I'm inside. Larkin's inside. O'Brien's an old woman. I have heard the most terrible stories – –

Keir Hardie
Your police went through the houses of the poor people of the town
And they broke bones and they smashed furniture and they tore the curtains down –

Connolly And the holy pictures from the wall they put their foot on on the floor –

Keir Hardie
The viceroy, the parliament, will do nothing –

Connolly It is not their war.
Murphy has the police to himself and he will rule!

Keir Hardie
We need common-sense in this business: we need someone to take control.

Connolly We need *Labour* to take control! If we are all locked up, then from over the water.

Keir Hardie
We have so tricky a turbulence of our own to look after . . .
The coal miners, the railwaymen, the dockers, these last few years
They have had all these strikes, first one and then the other:

> Each union in its turn set aside and isolated,
> Its demands partly granted and partly evaded
> Leaving behind every time in its turn the same resentment
> Till now there is nothing for it but to attempt one great
> sustainment –

*The three of them together have arranged what they call the triple alliance:
the leadership is appalled at it, but the rank and file have forced it on to
them – if they all clench the fist at their respective employers at the same
time, d'ye see, they will be taking on the whole establishment . . .*

Connolly Aye, the government!

Keir Hardie
> The ruling class!

Connolly Win all or lose all:
> By this stroke we rise or fall?

Keir Hardie
> Dublin, in such context, is a squashed fly on a pane of glass.
> Obscures the vision, diverts attention, has nothing to do
> With anything that goes on in the inside of the room. I wonder
> that you
> Are so eternally bent
> At all costs to keep your union so damned independent.
> For here you are, out of it, set aside, self-isolated:
> Your people are beaten, your leadership checkmated.
> Will you tell me is there anything we can do for you except talk?

Connolly Look here: it must be recognised in Britain that this fury
> Was forced upon us not alone by Murphy
> But as the first thrown stone in a raging hail
> That comes this winter down upon you all!

Keir Hardie
> They told me outside you could do with a daily paper . . .
> And one of your patriot friends asked me to bring in this Gaelic
> grammar . . .

Connolly What did the Kaiser tell to the emperor
> Of Austria last week? He said that general war
> Must cover Europe, now, within the year!
> And this here is part of it. The brokers of the gold all run in fear
> Through every frontier. Fear of each other, fear of us,
> Fear of the people. For fear cut off the thickest heads and those
> most near
> And those most new.
> The men of our new union are still few
> And therefore weak
> And therefore we receive the testing stroke.
> Your triple British alliance must enlarge itself to four –

Ireland comes in: but upon the level floor
Of equal status, independent, our own men,
Subordinate to none.
Go home and see if this cannot be done.

Keir Hardie

I will do it. And I promise. If I can . . .

Exeunt.

END OF ACT TWO

ACT 3: 'Once More Go Down to Hell'

Liberty Hall in the midst of the Dublin dockland, the river on one side, the Custom House on the other. (*Backcloth 9.*)

Enter CONNOLLY.

Connolly

For a week in Mountjoy prison I went without food.
It did some good.
I was released.
Seven long drear days of human corporal waste –
Though with a grammar of the Irish language I could try
To feed my head and renovate my racial memory.
Like that of everyone else displaced
And starved and pruned and grafted: till the words that grew
Green branches from my father's lips now seem to me and you
Crude and absurd, unwieldy to be learned, impossible to speak:
You need something in your throat like an eagle's beak
To scream these phrases out . . .
I am too occupied and old to rediscover myself a Gael:
My word must yet be English. If it fail

It is the shape of thought behind it by which we are all deceived . . . The shape of thought of a racial memory is not necessarily contradicted by internationalism. All these deep romantic yearnings have a most practical use. For instance: the Gaelic leaguer can realize that capitalism did more in one century to destroy the tongue of the Gael than the sword of the Saxon did in six. The apostle of self-reliance amongst Irishmen and Irishwomen can find no more earnest exponents of self-reliance than those who expound it as the creed of labour: the earnest advocates of co-operation can find the workers stating their ideals as a co-operative socialist commonwealth. The earnest teacher of christian morality can see how in the co-operative commonwealth alone will true morality be possible: the fervent patriot can learn that his hopes of an Ireland reborn to national life are better stated and can be better and more completely realised in the labour movement for the re-conquest of Ireland. A matter of interest . . . to take note: after the savagery of Bloody Sunday, just how many of all these groups are prepared to support the Transport Union . . . ?

Enter the COUNTESS.

Countess Larkin is out as well . . . !
Connolly Again? They gave him bail . . .!

Countess Reluctant to be rid of him and relieved.

Connolly I would scarcely have believed –

Countess Ah, the magistrate who sentenced both of you held far too many shares in Murphy's company. Once this became know, not even the Lord Lieutenant could pretend that justice was blind . . . Larkin is at my house. You too – come along . . .

Exeunt.

SCENE 2

Enter 2ND EMPLOYER.

2nd Employer Of course I hold shares. I've a perfect right to hold shares. No-one has ever made a law to prevent magistrates holding shares. My individual contribution to the framework of democracy . . .

He is joined by a CIVIL SERVANT.

Therefore, when this gentleman from the Whitehall Board of Trade comes to see me as a means, I understand, of sounding out the opinion of the Dublin men of business with a view to the arbitration of the industrial dispute: I can only declare to him: You have no mandate here, sir. As a man of business, not a magistrate, I must inform you that my business is no business of yours.

Civil Servant I beg to differ. Twenty-five thousand work people are locked out by their employers. Four hundred and four employers. The dockers have come out on a sympathetic strike against what they call 'tainted cargoes' – altogether in Dublin: and in Belfast at least those members of them who were organised by Connolly. There is a general demand for similar strikes in Britain. I believe the port of Liverpool is almost entirely closed by unofficial strike action. Can you tell me this is not an economic civil war? Can you tell me this is not the concern of an elected government?

GRABITALL *enters and stands behind* 2ND EMPLOYER.

2nd Employer It is only the concern of government because the government decides to make it so. A Conservative government would very probably think different – as indeed would a parcel of Liberals, if they were not bound hand and foot to Keir Hardie and his Labour Party.

Civil Servant Also bound hand and foot to Mr Redmond and the Irish nationalists – or so it is alleged . . .

Grabitall Or so it was fondly hoped . . . !

Civil Servant My duty in Dublin is to establish a judicial enquiry. Mr Murphy, it is so provided by democratic act of parliament. Sir Edward Carson has defied parliament. Will you follow his pattern?

Enter REDMOND, *lurking in a corner behind* GRABITALL.

Redmond Psst – Murphy . . ! I say, Murphy . . .

Grabitall Mr Redmond?

Redmond No defiance of parliament, Murphy – absolutely the wrong thing . . . !

Grabitall (*turns back to* CIVIL SERVANT *as* REDMOND *slips away*) Very well, sir: to your enquiry, when it assembles, I will submit.

Exit the CIVIL SERVANT.

2nd Employer We want the sharpest barrister in the land to prepare a brief for us. Who do you think?

Grabitall Timothy Healy.

2nd Employer The militant catholic champion who exposed and destroyed the corruption of Parnell . . .

Grabitall Get him.

Exeunt.

SCENE 3

Enter CONNOLLY *and* LARKIN.

Connolly While we wait for the enquiry, twenty-five thousand are living like mice out of the seams of their pockets. I spoke to Keir Hardie – he went home, what happened?

Larkin While we wait for the British Labour Party and the British TUC twenty-five thousand could be dying like rats on the doorstep of the pawnshop. I am over to England to stir up their leadership and show myself to the rank and file who have come out in support of us.

Exit CONNOLLY.

Narrator Larkin goes to England with one word in his mouth –

Larkin I am out for revolution – what do I care!

Narrator And he shouts it in the north and he shouts it in the south –

Larkin They can do no more than kill me, there are thousands more to come after.

Narrator And the wind of revolution blows out of his tousled hair

Through the treetops and the chimney-tops and across the
coal-black water:

The men who once when they were young

Hewed the black coal and fed the engines so strong

Sit now like coal-black ravens and croak upon the bough –

Enter British TRADE-UNION LEADERS.

TU Leaders

No no, no no, Jim Larkin, no revolution now . . .

1st TU Leader Fact of the matter is, we're in a grave situation here –

2nd TU Leader This so-called triple alliance is threatening in one great outburst of irresponsible syndicalism –

3rd TU Leader To destroy the work of decades.

Larkin Your rank and file are demanding –

1st TU Leader Far too much.

Larkin Are demanding that your brothers over in Ireland –

1st TU Leader Look, brother, if you're a brother, why aren't you affiliated?

Larkin We must have a sympathetic strike in this country! Already your people have begun to –

TU Leaders Aye, they have.

3rd TU Leader Disciplinary action is already underway to reduce this regrettable spate of unofficial strikes.

1st TU Leader We urge all concerned to patiently await the results of the judicial enquiry –

TU Leaders (*sing*)

> For every action we will bring
> Reaction in our turn
> We pour on water where the fire
> Looks like it wants to burn.
> Labour's burning labour's burning
> Fetch the engines, fetch the engines
> Fire fire, fire fire
> Pour on water, pour on water . . . *etcetera.*

1st TU Leader In the meantime –

Exit 1ST TU LEADER.

2nd TU Leader A nationwide charitable effort is being urgently set afoot and consignments of food for the needy folk of Dublin are being urgently loaded at Liverpool.

Exit 2ND TU LEADER.

3rd TU Leader We sincerely trust the dockworkers will recognize the class nature of these shipments and reconsider their unofficial strike sufficiently to load the vessels.

A Liverpool Docker (*at a distance*) You make our strike official, whack, and we'll load the vessels twenty-four hours a day!

3rd TU Leader Oh do please be patient for the results of the official enquiry . . .

Exeunt (*except* LARKIN).

SCENE 4

Narrator With delight in his eye and despair in his mind
Jim Larkin returns –

Larkin (*enthusiastic*)
> There are ships on the sea!
> Full of food for the people, black puddings and beef,
> Sacks of oatmeal and flour and boxes of tea!
> Come and feed, come and feed at the Liberty Hall –
> There is coal there is candle-light
> And good food for you all. . . !

Enter CONNOLLY *and the* COUNTESS *unloading great bales and boxes,* WORKERS *methodically passing them from hand to hand across the stage.* LARKIN *also joins in the work.*

Countess How many do you suppose we shall have to feed for how long?

Connolly I dread to tell you what I think to be the correct answer to that. Nor how many more ships will come when the cargoes of these are exhausted.

Countess Short rations, then, for everyone . . . ?

Connolly Very short. Don't stint on the perishable food to begin with, let them eat that and enjoy it and it's gone. But the stuff in the tins and boxes, keep it back – it'll be needed. Open each tin, d'ye see, as deliberately as I explore every paragraph of this brief I must prepare for our case at the tribunal . . .

The supplies are all moved and stacked at the back somewhere. The COUNTESS *and* WORKERS *go out.* LARKIN *and* CONNOLLY *sit down together at one side and get out papers.*

SCENE 5

Enter a JUDGE *in his wig and robes, as chairman of the enquiry. Opposite* CONNOLLY *and* LARKIN, GRABITALL *and* EMPLOYERS *take their seats, with* HEALY *in lawyer's gown to represent them.*

Connolly (*to* AUDIENCE) Larkin presents the case that I have presented to Larkin. The ultimate tribunal to which we appeal is not of course this court, but the verdict of the class to which we belong.

Judge (*taps for silence*) For the employers – Mr Healy . . . ?

Healy (*steps forward to plead*) For the past five years there have been more strikes than there have ever been since Dublin was a capital.

Connolly (*interrupts*) Practically every responsible man in Dublin today admits that the social conditions of Dublin are a disgrace to civilisation!

Larkin (*who was not quite ready before, now takes over from Connolly*) Have these two sets of facts no relation one to another?

Healy The Irish Transport Union can not be trusted to keep its contracts.

Larkin The majority of shipping firms in Dublin are still in operation, with the perfect confidence in the faith of this union – I instance in particular the City of Dublin Steam Packet Company which continues to run its regular services –

Healy Until Mr Larkin of a sudden determines to call a sympathetic strike . . . ?

Larkin Or unless Mr Murphy takes it into his head to prevail upon the directors to call a sympathetic lockout!

The JUDGE *calls* LARKIN *to order with his gavel.* LARKIN, *who has allowed himself to stand up against* HEALY, *now sits down with an apologetic gesture.*

Healy Mr George Jacob, of Jacob's Biscuits.

3rd EMPLOYER *takes the stand.*

Your experience, Mr Jacob, of the sympathetic strike?

3rd Employer At the end of August it came to my notice that some of my people were refusing to handle certain flour, obtained under contract from a firm which apparently had incurred the displeasure of Mr Larkin – I don't know why. It emerged that a large proportion of the persons in my employ had covertly become members of the Transport Workers' Union.

Healy Had you forbidden this?

3rd Employer Not at all. But I was made aware that recruiting for the union had been prosecuted within my factory by means of threats and intimidation: of course I had no option but to put a stop to that.

Larkin (*as Healy sits down*) In fact you closed your business down because your workers would not agree to repudiate the union? You even then saw no likelihood that they could have joined it of their own free will?

3rd Employer I cannot understand why they should have found it necessary. I regard Jacob's biscuit factory as a model institution. I give steady employment to upwards of three thousand of Dublin's workers of both sexes. It is impossible not to be impressed by the cheerful atmosphere that everywhere prevails. All give their services with that alert activity which is the best testimony to a willing disposition. On the top of the building the whole of the flat roof has been covered with shingle to convert it into a 'lung' for this great working hive. Here the girls come during their dinner-hour, play games, read, or otherwise recreate themselves. If they should be of an aesthetic turn of mind, they may watch the changing light on the Wicklow hills, note the effect of the golden western sunlight on the dancing waters of the harbour, or look into the brooding city and admire the picturesque . . .

Larkin You don't pretend to carry on your business as a philanthropist? Well, sir? . . . Well?

Judge I think, Mr Jacob, you must answer the question: though the tone of it, Mr Larkin, leaves much to be desired.

3rd Employer You cannot carry on any business at all if you are not to make money. The more successful your business, the more you can do for your workers.

Larkin What *do* you do for your workers? I don't mean the aesthetic roof garden. Wages, Mr Jacob. Wages. How much?

3rd Employer The wages of course vary . . . But . . .

Larkin Your carpenters. How much?

3rd Employer Carpenters . . . ? Er, we haven't very many . . . Er . . .

Larkin Mr Jacob: how much?

3rd Employer Off the cuff, I don't know, but –

Larkin Don't know how much you pay? Don't *care* how much you pay! And here you are asking for the protection of this court. Let's try another one. If you don't know the exact figures, you are surely aware of your differential scale? The weekly wage of your master-carpenter as compared, say, with the master-bakers? Expressed as a proportion?

3rd Employer I cannot answer that.

Judge I don't see why not.

3rd Employer It is confidential information. It could give aid and comfort to my competitors in the biscuit trade –

Larkin Rubbish. The man's ashamed. He's ashamed of himself, he's ashamed of his position. The conditions of work at his factory are damnable slavery. You ask him direct questions, he refuses to answer. It is people like these are causing all the disorder. He won't recognise trade unions and here he is now refusing point-blank to recognize this tribunal. Oh it's no use wasting time with him . . . !

He sits down. 3RD EMPLOYER *retires.*

Healy Mr Murphy?

GRABITALL *takes the stand.*

Mr Murphy yourself and Mr Larkin are generally believed to be the prime antagonists in this unfortunate conflict.

Grabitall I have never before today had the pleasure of meeting Mr Larkin. And never – until the present year – have I, in all my long experience as an employer, had any difficulties whatsoever with any of my employees. I regard myself, in fact, as having been singled out for an unscrupulous, sustained, and vindictive attack for ulterior political motives.

Judge Suppositional . . . ?

Grabitall I would say not. Mr Larkin is desirous of establishing what he calls a co-operative commonwealth. He cannot do this while private enterprise continues as the principal form of industrial transaction. I am a private employer on a very large scale. So therefore Mr Larkin finds it necessary to offer threats to my business – and indeed to my life – in the columns of his newspaper, and by means of the activities of the trade union in his control.

Larkin (*on his feet again as Healy sits*) Threats?

Grabitall I have already stated publicly that a certain article in your paper was an incitement to murder – and so it was.

Larkin Your own newspapers, I think, are not entirely free of threats?

Grabitall Self-defence, Mr Larkin.

Larkin Who, in fact, has been killed?

Grabitall Killed?

Larkin James Nolan. James Byrne. Struck down by the police. For whom were the police acting?

Grabitall For the general good order of the city of Dublin – I hope . . .

Larkin Or the general good order of the profits of the house of Murphy? Did you ever see myself or any other official of the Transport Workers' Union going about your premises and intimidating your men?

Grabitall Not yourself, certainly. You are generally in a safe place.

Larkin You generally see that I am put there, Mr Murphy. I have here a letter from a decent Dublin working man who used to work for Mr Murphy –

Grabitall Very well . . .

Healy (*jumps up*) I object.

Judge Objection sustained.

Larkin Mr Murphy does not object. I don't see why Mr Healy should.

Judge The document has not been proved.

Larkin Oh well, if that's it. Time and money for the lawyers . . .

Healy I am only a humble wage slave . . .

Larkin We're not all getting paid a hundred guineas for attending here.

Healy I am obliged to you for that suggestion indeed. My instructing solicitor will look into it at once.

1st Employer (*aside*) Perhaps Mr Larkin's union could better your lot . . .

Sniggering from the EMPLOYERS' *side of court.*

Larkin At least one industry in this country – the lawyers and the politicians – we could do very well without. I only came over here from Liverpool because I'd heard Mr Healy had decided to live in London . . .

LARKIN *and* CONNOLLY *enjoy their joke.* GRABITALL *leaves the stand and sits down.* LARKIN *addresses the court.*

Gentlemen: the employers of Dublin have taken to themselves to deny the right of the human being to associate with his fellow. Why, the very law of nature is mutual co-operation. Man must be associated with his fellows. Heaven knows the employers themselves are associated with each other. And having thereby let it be understood that they are to control the means of life in this city, then the responsibility for this city rests upon *them*! Twenty-one thousand people multiplied by five – over one hundred thousand people huddled together in the putrid slums of Dublin – and these appalling statistics are part of the very case that Mr Healy himself has put forward to this court! We are determined that this shall no longer go on: we are determined that the system shall stop: we are determined that Christ shall not be crucified in Dublin by these men! It is true that I believe in a co-operative commonwealth. Which is, I admit, a very long way ahead. The present system can yet be worked in a proper reasonable way, conducive to both sides, and I have suggested machinery that may be put into operation: recognition of the Transport Union for a start. Well, what about it? If the employers want peace, we are prepared to meet them: but if they want war: then war they will have! I have a witness: here he is.

Enter 2ND BRITISH TRADE-UNION LEADER. *He takes the stand and opens his briefcase in a fussy way.*

2nd British TU Leader As a representative of the Trades Union Congress of Great Britain, I am sent here to point out that the Dublin employers will not be allowed to destroy the Transport Union as long as the British Trades Union Movement exists.

HEALY *signifies he does not wish to ask questions.* 2ND BRITISH TU LEADER *gathers up his papers and leaves.*

Connolly (*aside to* AUDIENCE)
>Bold words are brave black smoke
>From a hillside fire swept high and hot
>By one wind, by the next wind blown right out.

Judge The enquiry concludes. Findings: we have no power to impose these upon either party, please note . . .

He takes off his wig.

But: on the one hand: no community can exist if resort to the sympathetic strike becomes the general policy of trade unions. On the other hand: the document repudiating the union, which the workmen were expected to sign, imposed on the signatories conditions which are contrary to individual liberty, and which no workman or body of workmen could reasonably be expected to accept. Gentlemen, do your best, please, to mitigate intransigence . . .

The court rises. The JUDGE *leaves. The two sides confront each other.*

Connolly We are perfectly happy to refrain from making use of the sympathetic strike – except where an employer rejects conciliation. But the union must be recognised!

Grabitall Never: until Larkin has been removed from the head of it!

Connolly And the strikers must not be victimised!

Healy The masters will not yield upon that. They must preserve their liberty to dismiss whom they think fit. Either an employer runs his business: or he does not.

GRABITALL, EMPLOYERS *and* HEALY *go out on one side.*

Connolly So we are left with the conclusion that the position is unchanged . . .

SCENE 6

Connolly We can't have this. Bring out the band!
Parade the streets, hold out your hand
For love and for money for the right to organise –

The BAND *assembles as before. It is the same as the Belfast band, but has a banner inscribed 'Irish Transport Workers' Union: Dublin'. The* BAND *parades with* CONNOLLY *just as in Belfast, and behind it follow a number of* COLLECTORS *with cash boxes calling out in Irish: 'Money to support the families of the strikers!'*

Narrator The Gaelic League has opened out its eyes,
Old poetry of potent ancestors is put away:
The Gael must eat before he talks today . . .
While Arthur Griffith, patriot of Sinn Fein,
For self-sufficient Ireland, holds his own
Himself alone, adds his own diagnosis
To his dependent nation's mortal crisis . . .

GRIFFITH *has entered and looks with disgust on the* GAELIC LEAGUERS *with their collecting boxes. When* CONNOLLY *and the* BAND *have gone out he addresses the* AUDIENCE.

Griffith Workless fathers, mourning mothers, hungry children, broken homes . . . The homes of families got together by years of saving are broken up and denuded of their inhabitants. Why, the wives of the men whom Larkin has led out on strike are begging upon the streets . . .

A STRIKER'S WIFE *comes up to ask him for money.*

Narrator He offers them relief . . . ?
Griffith (*not giving money*)
Put Irish gold through an Irish beggar into the hand of an Irish thief
Is self sufficiency gone mad . . . !
Nothing in my pocket they could not have had
By way of rightful earning from their rightful employer:
If ever Arthur Griffith becomes the ruler of this state
The like of Larkin will find his liberty
Within the hinge of a prison gate!
It is no wonder the British viceroy prefers to let him go free:
Sure well can he see
How this socialist from England brings his conquering ships of food
To ruin the Irish nation and choke the throat of the people's trade . . .

Exit GRIFFITH.

Narrator But he is not free: he's out on bail;
When his breathing space is over he goes back into gaol.

LARKIN, who has been following the BAND, is confronted by a POLICE CONSTABLE with a summons.

Larkin (*Avoids the summons*) Not yet! I have still to struggle with the Labour Party of Great Britain – and they are about as useful to us as mummies in the museum – !

He dodges across the hall and shouts out his message

I have appealed and I appeal again to the railwaymen's union in Britain – the north-western route to Ireland via Liverpool and Holyhead has got to be blacked – !

Enter 2ND BRITISH TU LEADER.

2nd TU Leader You damned fool, how can we, we've got agreements, we've got contracts –
Larkin To hell with contracts!!
2nd TU Leader That's it then: that does it.

He ostentatiously turns his back on LARKIN who is forthwith arrested and chained into a corner.

Enter CONNOLLY with LILLIE and the COUNTESS.

2nd TU Leader If we've told him once, we've told him till we're blue in the face: he will not be supported till he negotiates with Murphy!

Exit 2ND TU LEADER.

Lillie James, what's to be done for the children – does nobody care for the children?
Connolly Of course we care for the children, Lillie, that's what it's all about.
Lillie They are not in a position to make a political judgement: and yet they are the first of the hostages to suffer. And Murphy is aware of this – and he calculates it, James.
Countess (*brings in a WORKING-CLASS SUFFRAGETTE*) The women's suffrage movement of England has come up with an idea.
Working-class Suffragette The women's suffrage movement inside the British trade union movement has answered the call of British and Irish workers. If the children of the Dublin strikers can be brought across to England we can put them into good homes until the emergency is over.
Connolly Serious reservations at the practical strategic value of accepting this form of relief. Oh it clears the English conscience at very little cost, and makes it even easier for the Labour Party and the TUC to avoid any other action.
Larkin (*shouts from his prison*) Jim! You are too scrupulous! If we are seen to

reject a humanitarian proposal, we will appear to be making use of these children as hostages!

Lillie Exactly the same as Murphy.

Connolly (*to* COUNTESS) Can we feed the children, clothe them, can we administer it ourselves? A straight exact answer: pounds shillings and pence.

Countess I have gone into it very thoroughly. No, we are not capable.

Connolly Then let them go to England, if the parents actually want it. But not too much publicity. There is something very wrong with the very notion of this scheme . . .

During the above dialogue they have been busy getting out foodstuffs and preparing the soup-kitchen. Soup and bread are now distributed to a line of poor HUNGRY PEOPLE.

Countess Soup for all at Liberty Hall!

Soup Queue (*sings*)

> It's a long way down to the soup line
> It's a long way to go
> It's a long way down to the soup line
> And the soup is thin I know –
> Goodbye Mr Murphy,
> And the rest of the bosses too
> It's a long, long time along the soup line
> But the union pulls through . . . !

SCENE 7

While the SOUP LINE *is shuffling along,* MATT TALBOT *appears on the fringe of it. He does not join it. He wears a ragged coat over his naked breast and has a holy medal round his neck.*

Matt Talbot

> I creep in quietly: not well known
> In the wicked streets of this hungry town.
> I make my daily prayers to God the Father, God the Son
> And His blessed Virgin Mother my only heavenly perfect queen.
> They say they are on strike, my fellow men:
> Their grievances are just, I don't complain.
> I will not forsake them in their hour of trouble –
> I creep in quietly to the chapel
> And meditate upon the savage drunken private crime
> Of my past life, far worse than all the public trouble of this time
> And all the noise that public men give out
> To hide from God their own internal blot . . .

Exit MATT TALBOT. *The* SOUP LINE *has now all been served and* CONNOLLY, LILLIE *and the* COUNTESS *are carrying away the pans, etc.*

BISHOP *and* GRABITALL *enter at one side.*

Grabitall (*to Bishop*) Socialism, atheism, and the destruction of religion . . . !

Bishop (*makes a speech from the rostrum*) Those women who will agree to this diabolical intrusion into the rights and responsibilities of the religious Irish home can no longer be held worthy of the name of catholic mothers. Do they so forget their duty as to send away their children to be cared for in a strange land without security of any kind that those, to whom the poor children are to be handed over, are catholics – or indeed are persons of any religion at all?

The WORKING-CLASS SUFFRAGETTE *enters with a group of* CHILDREN, *ticketed round their necks for the journey to England. She is suddenly assailed by an angry* MOB, *who try to snatch the* CHILDREN *from her.*

Working-class Suffragette (*to Bishop*) I assure you, vicar, that every effort is being made to place the children as far as possible in the homes of roman catholics –

Mob (*knock her about*) Protestant proselytiser, jezebel, pagan, perverter, abortionist, prostitute!

Working-class Suffragette (*all her* CHILDREN *taken from her*) It is really impossible for a well-disposed English person with an enlightened social conscience to make any sort of headway in so bigoted a community . . . !

Exit SUFFRAGETTE. MATT TALBOT *has re-entered, and has been a horrified witness of the mob attack.*

Matt Talbot

        I creep out quietly from the holy place
        This tumult strikes me like a fist against my pale and sweating
            face:
        In palm and foot the nails are driven in
        Inside my side the javelin-thrust of sin.
        If there had been no strike
        No mother could permit her heart to tear
        Itself in two between her love and fear.
        Her fear and love: her love and love.
        O holy Virgin up above,
        My queen, if I had stayed at work when those who worked
            with me
        Came out on strike, would we now see
        Apostacy disguised as charitable light
        Blaze from the broached cask like burning brandy . . . ?
        Would I be right
        In going back to work alone to break this tainted strike?

I am not handy
To decide such things. I will creep in again
And in and round myself alone
Enfold the burden and atone
For each cleft heart in this divided town.

He takes off his jacket and wraps heavy chains round his body: then goes out.

CONNOLLY *comes back in with the* COUNTESS *and* LILLIE.

Connolly A successful attempt to divide the workers by deliberate sectarianism – but we leave it alone – in the long run, not important.

The SOUP LINE *is beginning to form up again.*

If the church is concerned for the welfare of the Irish family, let them take their own measures. For the time at least the kitchen in Liberty Hall will be closed. No, no – you will be fed: but not here. We cannot manage it. You must go to the archbishop.

The SOUP LINE *slowly drifts across and stands under the rostrum, where the* BISHOP *has been standing with his hands clasped and his eyes on Heaven.*

Bishop (*suddenly aware of all the people*) I have no facilities for feeding all these people – Mr Murphy – all these people – they appear to have no food to eat!

Grabitall I don't suppose they have.

Bishop But what do you propose to do about it?

Grabitall Your grace, for several weeks, Mr Larkin and Mr Connolly have been dealing with the matter.

Bishop But you yourself informed me they were inculcating atheism! You stand there and admit to me it has been going on for several weeks! Mr Murphy: I am *shocked*!

He comes down from his rostrum and speaks to the AUDIENCE *from the front of the stage.*

We appeal to all charitable and catholic organisations to do their utmost at once to relieve this dreadful suffering . . . !

He repeats his appeal several times, moving about the hall. There is dead silence: and he goes out, shaking his head in great sorrow.

Connolly (*after a slight pause*) The church of Christ has failed the test: the brotherhood of man must carry on. We resume the distribution of food at Liberty Hall!

Countess Soup for all at Liberty Hall!

The SOUP LINE *reassembles, joyfully singing their song again – 'It's a long way down to the soup line', etc.*

SCENE 8

While the soup is being served out, the JUDGE *appears at one side.*

Judge James Larkin!

A POLICE CONSTABLE *brings* LARKIN *across to be sentenced.*

James Larkin, for seditious utterance, you are condemned to be imprisoned for a term of seven months.

The JUDGE *goes out.* LARKIN *is led out through the angry* CROWD, *who abuse the* POLICE *and cheer him up with a variety of shouts. The* POLICE *have some difficulty in getting* LARKIN *through the people: and have to draw their batons to make way. At length they succeed in pulling him away to prison. When he is gone the* CROWD *surge aimlessly.* CONNOLLY *jumps up on the rostrum.*

Connolly Will we give in?

Crowd No surrender!

Connolly The Labour leaders in Britain would prefer us to give in and they may withhold the food ships if we do not give in.

Crowd No surrender!

Connolly The employers and their agents are evicting the families of strikers who are unable to pay their rent.

Crowd No surrender! Pay no rent! Let no trade unionist pay his rent!

Connolly Larkin is in prison at the behest of a Liberal government. The only way to get him out is to ruin that same government. There are bye-elections forthcoming in England at this moment. We must make sure whoever wins them, whether Labour or Conservative, the Liberals will lose. Appeal by telegraph to British workers to vote always against the Liberals.

Crowd No surrender! no surrender! no surrender . . . !!

O'BRIEN *comes in and distributes placards saying 'No Surrender' to some of the* CROWD *who walk around as a picket, chanting behind the next dialogue.*

GRABITALL *has sat himself down at a table to one side, and is watching the scenes grimly. Enter* EMPLOYERS *to him.*

1st Employer If the majority of the Liberals is weakened any further, Home Rule may not take place!

2nd Employer My business is collapsing, my markets are being taken over by the British and by foreigners!

3rd Employer Mr Murphy – we must make terms.

Enter CIVIL SERVANT

Civil Servant Mr Murphy, the government begs that you will attempt to make terms.

Enter BISHOP.

Bishop The souls of the people are in imminent deadly peril. Mr Murphy: you must make terms!

Grabitall No.

The BISHOP *and* CIVIL SERVANT *go out. The* EMPLOYERS *are following, when* GRABITALL *calls them back.*

Gentlemen – are we not in a federation: bound together with a sworn bond? Now I have been studying the figures of unemployment for the industrial areas of the English north west. If we guarantee protection, we can get labourers by the hundred – by the thousand, indeed. They must be brought over here in large bodies: and if necessary they must be armed.

1st Employer Have you checked it with the police?

Grabitall The police will not prevent it. If there is any sort of conflict it will give them a pretext to get their own back on the strike pickets. They've been abused by them long enough. And so, by God, have I!

Exit GRABITALL *and* EMPLOYERS.

SCENE 9

CONNOLLY *suddenly claps his hands and imposes silence on the* PICKET.

Connolly To bring scabs in like an army requires an army to receive them. Have you heard of the mass picket? Like they do it in America – I wasn't an organiser for the Industrial Workers of the World for nothing – they have *technique*, and we can use it here! Not three or four men with old placards at the dock gates – but a thousand – ready and willing to defend their right to their own work and their right to combine in that defence against all enemies. And these enemies that come now – like myself thirty years ago in the red coat of the famine queen – are those poor devils that should be our friends, had they only been told of it, and organised, and led. If the TUC has not listened to what Larkin had to say, the responsibility for their deed will lie upon them for generations. They have their own strike now forced onto them over there across the water – if they'd only had the wit to pay heed to what I told Keir Hardie, the cormorant control of capital in the entire United Kingdom could burst open like a frog's belly . . . But that's not what we're here for today: we are here to picket these docks. Any man who is a member of the union with two legs is expected to take part. The essential about this is that *everyone* takes part. I have no reason to believe that anyone will evade it. I have no reason to give out any meal-tickets to those who do . . .

More PEOPLE *have joined the picket as he speaks.*

He walks along the rank of the mass picket, sending off WOMEN *and* OLD MEN, *etc., till there is no-one left but a tough group of* MEN.

MATT TALBOT *comes up to him.*

Matt Talbot It goes against my conscience, Mr Connolly, to be involved in coercion.

Connolly You're a member of the union?

Matt Talbot Sir, I am indeed. My name is Matt Talbot.

Connolly Does it go against your conscience to have Murphy put your comrades into the workhouse for ever?

Matt Talbot So that their souls are in a state of grace, it matters little where they die.

Connolly If you think that, I wonder you'd be involved with us at all.

Matt Talbot I'd do no good presuming to stand apart from my fellows. I render unto Caesar the things that are his.

Connolly By Caesar, you mean Murphy?

Matt Talbot No sir: I mean you.

Connolly (*disconcerted*) Oh . . . Very well. But stay at home. Don't try to mix in.

Matt Talbot In the house of my Father, Mr Connolly, I'll stay there.

Connolly They give you breakfast in there . . . ? Not on your life. Here, take your meal-ticket, and get out of it.

He gives TALBOT *a ticket, but the latter tears it up, hands the pieces back, and goes out.*

Enter 2ND BRITISH TU LEADER.

2nd TU Leader Brother Connolly, the mass picket is an indiscriminate brutal weapon.

Connolly So they say. That's why we're using it.

2nd TU Leader Will you close down every company that makes use of the port of Dublin?

Connolly Tight as the skin of a drum.

2nd TU Leader But there must be some alternative.

Connolly Aye there is! Official full support by the unions in Britain. Aye and Ulster. The cross channel harbours at Derry and Belfast are wide open to Murphy's goods. If you stop those gaps we will not have to do it here.

2nd TU Leader Is this you talking, or Larkin . . . ?

Connolly You know where Larkin is.

2nd TU Leader (*takes* CONNOLLY *out of earshot of the* PICKET) If he could be persuaded to stay where he is – I don't mean in prison – no: I mean out – I mean . . . Just, *out* . . .

Connolly And a reasonable replacement at the head of this union, of the name, say – James Connolly . . . ? Who could be persuaded to persuade the union to re-affiliate where it belongs – with the British TUC . . . I daresay we could do a deal . . . Our price is the support of British labour for republicanism!

2ND BRITISH TU LEADER *reacts in outrage and stamps off.*

O'Brien (*suddenly*) Watch it, there's the scabs coming out of the docks *now*!

Connolly Get out of it, William, your bad leg will never –

A force of SCABS *in a wedge-formation, headed and supported by* POLICE, *comes rushing at the* PICKET. *There is violent fighting with fists, placard poles, etc. feet., Suddenly one of the* SCABS *fires a pistol. The* PICKET *scatters, and the* SCABS *get through. One of the* STRIKERS *lies on the ground, wounded in the leg and screaming curses.*

Hospital – quick!

O'Brien My God, who'd ha' thought they'd put *guns* into their hands?

Connolly If we can take pattern from the Yanks, so can Murphy. Come back here, men, come back here – we have got to keep it together!

But his MEN *have dispersed. The* WOUNDED MAN *has been carried away.*

SCENE 10

Connolly If the leaders over in Britain will not listen, we must try again the rank-and-file . . . !

He speaks out to the AUDIENCE.

We want all traffic stopped throughout Britain from the firm of Guinness, from the firm of Jacob, from every other firm that is making use of scab labour. Particularly, the railwaymen, from the railwaymen we are asking an immediate spontaneous response . . . !

Shouts (*from British voices all over the auditorium*) Liverpool! Holyhead! Swansea! Bristol! Heysham! Manchester! Birmingham! Nottingham! Crewe! Derby! Sheffield! Newcastle! Leeds! London!

Narrator Done! And the trains were stopped

> The steam blew off
> The fires went out
> The trucks of freight were shunted all about
> In sheds and sidings up and down the route,
> Consignments were let lie, all manifests were forgot,
> And empty ships at anchor dragged in every west-coast port.

Connolly And this also applies to freight in transit designated to the vessels of the City of Dublin Steam Packet Company, which I now declare blacked!

O'Brien Wait a moment – Jim Larkin had an agreement with that company –

Connolly It's all in or all out – I am declaring them blacked!

Narrator Done!

Connolly And now to London, to the Albert Hall . . . !

Exit O'BRIEN.

SCENE 11

Narrator Where in that great rotunda, one and all
Against the Liberal government are convened –
All those on whom the Liberals thought they leaned:
The intellectuals, and the rank and file
Of British labour, with the secret smile
Of dangerous women striving for their right –
All joined together in one cause to cut
The trembling tightrope under Asquith's foot.

Enter ASQUITH *and stands by the* NARRATOR *at the side. The stage fills with* SPEAKERS *at the Albert Hall meeting, behind them a red banner reads 'Albert Hall rally in support of Dublin Strikers – Release Jim Larkin!'*

Asquith What is this creature dragged to light of day,
This ancient brooding worm long stowed away
In half-forgotten holes of history . . . ?
Irish rebellion, Celtic anarchy, ancestral dreams of blood and treachery,
Coil upon poisoned coil implacably unfolds,
The petals of the rose
Of English liberty are rotten at the root,
And freeborn English citizens, infected to the death,
Cry 'Let Jim Larkin, let Jim Larkin out . . . !'

Cries (*from those on stage and off it, in rhythm*) Larkin out! Larkin out! Larkin out! Larkin out of prison!

Asquith (*to* NARRATOR) Individuals and organisations represented at this meeting?

Narrator (*as he names each name, the* PERSON *referred to steps forward and says 'Let Larkin out of prison!' and then steps back again*) Ben Tillett, the dockers' leader, altogether out of harmony with the regular TUC . . .

Asquith And with everybody else.

Narrator George Lansbury, member of the Labour Party, editor of *The Daily Herald* forever denouncing the government's social policy as insufficiently radical . . .

Asquith Baa baa baa . . .

Narrator Cunningham-Graham, distinguished socialist author from Scotland.

Asquith I read his short stories: the rest of him's not necessary.

Narrator Bernard Shaw, didactic dramatist, essayist, critic, theoretical Fabian . . .

Asquith And unconscionable nuisance.

Narrator Miss Sylvia Pankhurst, suffragette.

Asquith Her mother, I believe, is in prison, is she not?

Narrator She has been – not at present. It was hoped that Sylvia had moved away from the women militants – but if she's moved in the direction of social revolution and an Irish republic –

Asquith We have very little to gain from her domestic differences, yes.

Narrator George Russell.

Asquith Who's he?

Narrator A mystical poet from Dublin.

Asquith The more mystical the better. If only *all* the Irish could concentrate upon leprechauns . . .

Narrator From America, William Haywood of the Industrial Workers of the World.

Asquith I want an inquiry at once instituted into the Immigration Office at Southampton.

Narrator And finally, James Connolly.

Asquith With whom, I was told, it was thought they could do a deal?

Narrator I think by someone who heard him lecture in Cleckheaton or somewhere, and said he stammered and his manner was both diffident and gentlemanly.

Asquith Ah, but since then he has been to America? He is the boot-hill cowboy partner of Brother Haywood, is he not?

Connolly I will briefly quote the words of the manifesto that we issued to introduce our new policy of the mass-picket, so terrifying to certain people of a certain status in the labour movement . . . 'Fellow-workers, the employers are determined to starve you into submission: and, if you resist, to club you, gaol you, and kill you. We defy them. If they think they can carry on their industries without you, we will – in the words of the Orangemen from Ulster – take steps to prevent it. Be men now or be for ever slaves!'

Haywood Come on now, brothers and sisters, I want you to sing along with me and with all your comrades across the ocean the words and music that are putting the workers in control of the United States – !

He sings and they all join in, with handclapping, etc.

> If the boss gets in the way we're gonna roll it over him
> We're gonna roll it over him, we're gonna roll it over him
> If the boss gets in the way, we're gonna roll it over him,
> We're gonna roll the union on . . .'
> > *etcetera, etcetera . . .*

Exeunt, leaving ASQUITH *alone.*

Asquith If Connolly was a grasshopper
And Larkin a dragon
This grasshopper is now a locust

> And climbs up over us in a ten mile cloud.
> Before they all come down on us
> And consume us green leaf and sprout
> There is but one thing we can do:
> Let the old damned dragon out!

Exit.

SCENE 12

Enter LARKIN *surrounded by cheering* PARTISANS. *He meets* CONNOLLY *who shakes his hand enthusiastically.*

Larkin   Out of gaol and on the prowl
Loudmouth Larkin sings his song!
Narrator On the prowl and out of gaol
Does Larkin think that someone's crowned him king . . . ?
Larkin   The steam packet blacked!
Repudiate my solemn act . . . ?
Jim Connolly, what the hell's been going on!
What word had you from me to do this thing?
You've thrown the whole contrivance out of true –
The scabs in Dublin now have firearms, thanks to you – !
Connolly All right: your turn has come: I must give ground:
The floor is yours.
So do you make your play, my brother,
Make sure you win your own applause.
To the British trade union congress convey your fiery cross.
You have so much more now behind you than the last time that
    you tried . . .

Exit LARKIN.

    As usual I will finish off what you condescended to begin . . .
The creeping tide of scabs runs in and in:
Unless we keep them out we cannot win.
Guns in their hands, police on either side.
From the Wobblies, and from Wexford, I now know how to
    provide
The means to deal with these – after all these years I find
Such courage amongst us all at last
As will fulfil my made-up mind –
I am going to talk sedition. The next time we are out on a march, I want
to be accompanied by four battalions of trained men with their corporals
and sergeants. Why should we not train our people the same way that
they do in Ulster?

The WORKERS *who had greeted* LARKIN *now disperse.*

Narrator Draw back the curtain and reveal

The Citizen Army at their drill.

Left right left right and straight into the fight –

The WORKERS *re-appear, marching in formation, with hurley sticks as weapons,* CAPTAIN WHITE *at their head, drilling them.*

They are led by Captain White.

Captain White

Regular army, retired, a Boer War DSO,

My father a famous general, a unionist, how could he know

That the pig-ugly brutality in Dublin would so distract,

Conturb my honour as a gentleman, I can do nothing but thus act

In accordance with my honour, defending those who have been attacked?

So with all good will, my military skill

For Mr Connolly's disposal is carried over the hill

And his brave beaten ragged regiment

Is moulded and emboldened through the precise dance of the soldier's drill

– We march and wheel and turn:

And what we learn

Without delay

We put to use the very next day . . .

Stand to it, men, stand easy – there's another load of blacklegs going to burst on us any moment . . . while we're waiting, don't get nervous – one two three: sing!

A group of POLICE *have entered and are regarding the* CITIZEN ARMY *from a little distance with menace.*

Citizen Army (*sings*)

O the Dublin Peelers went out one night

On duty and patrolling O

They met a goat upon the road

And took him for being a-strolling O

With bay'nets fixed they sallied forth

And caught him by the wizen O

And then swore out a mighty oath

They'd send him off to prison O , . .

Captain White (*suddenly*) Company, form guard! Present hurleys! Here they come.

As a gang of SCABS, *guarded by* POLICE, *rush in on them, they receive them in a well-disciplined formation: and after fierce fighting, repel them. The* POLICE, *in fear, prevent one of the* SCABS *shooting his pistol. After the fight, the* CITIZEN ARMY *gives a cheer, falls in and doubles off with* CONNOLLY *and* CAPTAIN WHITE.

SCENE 13

Enter BRITISH TU LEADERS. *A red banner behind them reading 'TUC Annual Conference'.*

TU Leaders (*sing*)
>In the Albert Hall they were telling us all
>How we ought to perform our job
>And making sure that we'd heed the call
>Of the irresponsible mob;
>Break down, give in, call the country out
>On a national boycott strike,
>For the prize of a bottle of Guinness's stout
>Race a mile on a one-wheeled bike.
>Oh don't tie your boots up
>Don't wear braces
>Don't put an 'at on your 'ead
>Catch your 'andle-bars in the passing cars
>And fill your pedals with lead.
>While Big Jim Larkin
>Dirty ol' milkman
>Rummages the wife in bed –
>Who's so stupid
>Who's so stupid
>Who's so stupid – ?
>NOT ME . . .

1st TU Leader You might think it, but fact remains that Larkin's coming to this congress pretty damn sure he can get what he wants.

2nd TU Leader What the bloody hell does he want?

3rd TU Leader One big union one big strike . . . So that that chap can rule the roost in Dublin, he wants building sites and jam factories and wash-hand-stand assembly workshops closed down from Kent to Cleethorpes. It's fair ridiculous: I won't stand for it.

2nd TU Leader We've enough trouble and all, with this call coming in that the triple alliance declare a full-scale general strike in the autumn of 1914.

3rd TU Leader That ought to be avoided. We've got time to sort that out.

1st TU Leader We won't have if we mess with Larkin.

2nd TU Leader If we don't mess with Larkin, we've got trouble with our own folk. He's supported, he's got friends.

1st TU Leader Then it's our job to turn 'em off him. If we can but do that his membership in bloody Dublin'll fall away from him like – like –

2nd TU Leader Tea leaves. But you know, though, I've heard him speak – he works on the emotions . . .

1st TU Leader His own emotions, brother, are not always under control . . .

He sings:

> For a man who's prepared to blow his top
> At the slightest word of scorn
> And upon each shoulder carries a chip
> As big as a rhino's horn,
> We need not heed to spare his feelings
> Or run from his angry frown –
> Let Big Jim Larkin
> Dirty ol' milkman
> Muddy-up his own milk churn –

TU Leaders (*sing*)

> Oh strong boot laces
> Buttoned-up braces
> Clap the ol' tile on tight;
> With strict procedure give 'im a seizure
> Natter and niggle all night.
> Stuff 'is gullet
> With an 'alf-plucked pullet
> And cut the string of 'is kite –
> Where will he float to –
> Where will he float to –
> Where will he float to – ?
> 'OO CARES ... ?'

They take their seats on the platform of the conference as the DELEGATES *enter.* LARKIN *and* CONNOLLY *are accommodated in the body of the hall at the back.*

SCENE 14

1st TU Leader (*takes his seat as chairman*) Right, we're all convened: I imagine we have a quorum. First item on the agenda is – er, brother, what's the first item on the agenda – ?

2nd TU Leader Ah now, the first item on the agenda, ah yes ...

Some dubious shuffling and passing back and forwards of papers on the platform, whispering.

1st Delegate (*from the body of the hall*) We all know what we're met here for and we all know what we're to do! We have Brothers Larkin and Connolly over here from Dublin to put an extremely urgent plea – for Godsake let's leave the bureaucracy aside till we've settled for some definite action!

Noisy manifestations in support of the DELEGATE.

1st TU Leader Nay nay, this won't do . . . Brother, you're out of order . . . Your executive committee is exceedingly sensible of the situation of Brother Larkin and the business that brings him: but we must state clearly as a matter of regular form that the Irish Transport Union is not of a status commensurate with full membership of this congress: and we feel it would scarcely be prudent to establish a precedent.

More hostile manifestations. Mumble mumble among platform party.

However, in view of the obvious feeling from the floor, we will dispense with the normal introductory resolutions and get straight on with the first item. Mr Secretary?

3rd TU Leader Your executive committee have received a letter dated November the twenty-third from the North German Federation of Associated Labour Unions. At their annual conference held in Hamburg, November tenth, it was unanimously resolved that a formal presentation should be made by their joint membership to the Trades Union Congress of Great Britain, in order to mark the heartfelt desire for peace between the working classes of the German Empire and those of Great Britain. The presentation takes the form of a gold medallion on a chain bearing an embossed design of clapsed hands against a background of – of various industrial artefacts, like a hammer, and a sickle, and such . . . And a motto. It's in German. I am informed that when translated it reads: 'Workers of the world unite: you have nothing to lose but your chains!' It's a very handsome article . . .

2nd Delegate (*from the body of the hall*) Brother Chairman, I've kept silent: but I'm damned if I'll cram back the truth intae my wame for one minute longer! Abundantly clear – of deliberate intent – the decision has been made, that we're all gaun tae talk the most unholy load o'rubbish – I mean, who the hell cares if the bluidy chain is handsome – for if this platform is permitted to lose ony mair time ye're gaun tae lose Big Jim Larkin! God dammit the puir man canna wait on your courtesy for week after week!

More manifestations. 1ST TU LEADER *knocks furiously for order.*

1st TU Leader Order, brothers, order! Look, the meeting must come to order! Thank you . . . Right. In response to the intimations of the delegate from Glasgow and the overall popular feeling from the floor, I move that consideration of the North German gold medal be deferred to a later hour. Now then, the important question of this prolonged dispute in Dublin.

To 2ND TU LEADER.

Are you right, Brother . . . ? Right: I'll pass it over to you.

2nd TU Leader We have, as you all know, been paying very close attention ever since the month of August to the overall development of the situation over there. I myself have actually travelled, at some expense, to hold cordial discussions with our Irish opposite numbers and also with representatives of the separatist Transport Workers' Union. Brother Larkin, it must be said, has made great blunders from the very inception of the tramway strike last August. In my opinion, his tactics – –

Larkin (*bursts in among the platform*) Mr Chairman – and human beings . . . Look here – I'm not concerned whether you'll let me go on or not! I can deal with all or any of you at any place you like to name! But if you are not going to give me an opportunity of replying to the foul lying statements which are made of me and my union, it's no more than what I'd expect from a good many of those present. Oh yes, you talked big about persuading the employers to undertake negotiations – but this is not a game of beggar-my-neighbour, this is a game of *war*: and I know the men we have to deal with over there. Negotiations me ould granny! All they want to do is to *drag out* the negotiations – pretend to be having them but bloody well *not* have them – in order to gain time to starve my people out, and intimidate them out, and lock them up in Mountjoy! But I know that the rank and file of British trade unionists will support, as they have supported, the Dublin men in their battle! And I am all the more sure of it by the demonstrations I have heard today from the floor of this meeting. – Comrades, I appeal – –

3rd TU Leader (interrupts, as LARKIN'*s rapport with audience becomes clear*) I would ask the Dublin delegates to bear in mind the British delegates have got to get a word in quite as much as you have.

LARKIN *sits down in angry disgust.* CONNOLLY *rises and comes to the platform.*

Connolly Mr Chairman, there has been far too much recrimination upon both sides. Can we not, please, have an end to it? Negotiations with the employers were rendered impossible. They had set themselves out quite deliberately to break the union. The conditions over there are the conditions that exist when there is no trade union at all. Are we to be told here that the joint efforts of the trade unionists in Great Britain and Ireland can only succeed in getting us the terms that could be got – and have been got, often – by every individual in industrial societies before trade unionism was invented?

Larkin (*bursting out again*) All we want you to do is to take away your scabs –

He indicates 2ND TU LEADER

Yes your delegated missionary scabs you have had over there pretending to initiate some class of compromise with Murphy! Because he will *never* compromise: and if he won't, we can't: and if we can't, then we've no choice but to call on you to help us *win* . . . !

Signs of support for LARKIN *in the congress have died away upon his use of the word 'scabs': and now he tries to speak on against a crescendo of hostility.*

1st Delegate (*advances from the body of the hall*) Now wait a moment, wait a moment, wait a moment, Brother Larkin. My God you've got no right to make use of a word like *scabs* – you're talking about the respected and constitutional representative of one of the greatest British unions – very well, I disagreed with a great deal of what the executive has been up to upon this issue, and I damn well did my best to get you and Jim Connolly a fair hearing here today: didn't I, brothers – didn't I? But you've got to bear in mind, brother, that the British Trades Union Congress is the foremost and most progressive organisation of its kind in the whole world, and we don't take well to insults! Our chaps went over to Dublin in all good faith to help sort out your mess: and if there's nowt you can do in return but to kick us in the teeth – then be damned to you and that's that!

1st TU Leader For God's sake, you stupid Irish, *negotiate* with Murphy and leave the rest to us! Don't you think we don't know what we are doing in our own areas?

Larkin By God I thank God I'm not responsible for your intelligence!

He and CONNOLLY *storm out of the meeting, which disperses amid virtuous murmurs.*

SCENE 15

LARKIN *and* CONNOLLY *re-enter the emptied stage.*

Connolly They grunt and shout against us and they yell
    Like wolves and badgers of the dark wild wood – –
Larkin No, rabbits, lurking in their safe protective hole.
Connolly We Irish workers must once more go down to hell –
    We eat no bread of common sacrifice and brotherhood
    But choke our tongues with dust of black betrayal.
    Dublin, defeated, now is left alone.
Larkin Can we continue all upon our own?
Connolly The red flag of the peoples of the world
    Has no room in it for a single patch of green . . . ?

They meet a funeral procession with a coffin bearing white lilies. The MOURNERS *are of the* CITIZEN ARMY, *with their hurleys.*

Connolly Who was this who died?
    How comes it the Citizen Army follows her coffin to the grave?

A Mourner
    She was shot by a scab
    She was too brave

She ran in front of all the crowd
Cried out aloud
'You shall not work in Murphy's yard today!'
The bugger's gun was out
Her friends all ran away
He put the bullet in her breast and fled.
I held her in my arms and there she bled.
Her name was Alice Brady, she was sixteen years of age.
Walking out, but not engaged.
She joined the union because she had been taught
The workers of the world had promised us all support.

Connolly The first one who will run
Against a loaded gun
Will find she has no friends
Till she has been eternally shot down . . .

He and LARKIN *follow the cortège off and out.*

SCENE 16

Enter ASQUITH.

Asquith There are movements in this country coming to a head of which recent
events have been a very small foreshadowing . . .

Somehow my Liberal policies seem to have brought
More ruthless enemies than if I sought
Deliberately to impose my iron will
Like Prussian Wilhelm or that bloody fool
King Charles the First – what happened to *his* neck –
Marching, tramping, shouting, singing at my back
Carson's cruel bigots, boots and clubs of wood
Demand their right to regulate the word of God –

Enter ULSTER VOLUNTEER *with orange flag, singing.*

Ulster Volunteer (*sings*)
Tis old but it is beautiful, and the colours they are fine:
It was worn at Derry, Aughrim, Enniskillen and the Boyne –
My father wore it when a youth in the grand old days of yore
And on the Twelfth I'll proudly wear the sash my father wore . . . !

Asquith The echo now in stubborn Dublin town
Proclaims the *national* volunteers will not lie down
And see Home Rule defeated by the force
Of Tory-fed resistance from the North:
I have made decrees prohibiting the import
Of weapons into Ireland: but what good?
If they want guns, they'll get them, they've all gone mad!

In avoiding the ULSTER VOLUNTEER *he is confronted by a* NATIONAL
VOLUNTEER *with a green flag, singing.*

National Volunteer (*sings*)

> We are the boys of Wexford
> Who fought with heart and hand
> To burst in twain the galling chain
> And free our native land . . . !

Ulster Volunteer No surrender – preserve the union!

National Volunteer No surrender – preserve the constitution, protect Home
Rule!

Asquith Slogan and flag, song and subversive cheers

> From each opposed parade of volunteers
> Unionist, nationalist, eyeballs and ears
> Are filled and flummoxed by the deafening roar –
> Each way I turn I find them more and more –
> The leaders of the English labour power,
> Though they have ousted Larkin, now appear
> Forced up by their rank and file, to tower
> Upon me like a huge volcano, Krakatoa –
> Vesuvius – they rumble out their threat –

BRITISH TU LEADERS *with a red flag advance on him, singing.*

British TU Leaders (*sing*)

> The workers' flag is deepest red
> It shrouded oft our martyred dead:
> And ere our limbs grew stiff and cold
> Their life blood dyed its very fold.
> Then raise the scarlet banner high
> Within its shade we'll live and die,
> Though cowards flinch and traitors sneer
> We'll keep the red flag flying here . . . !
> Three strikes in one –
> Coal-miners, dockers, railwaymen!
> If you will not provide a living wage
> The whole of Britain feels the gathered rage
> Of all our members. Come September not one ton
> Of coal will be dug out, no ships unloaded, not one train will run!

Asquith It is not even certain that Jim Larkin has been beaten:

> Oh his people have had no food –
> But I fear once they have eaten
> There will yet again be no measure to their furious mood –
> Oh where shall I go where shall I go where shall I go to hide . . . ?

*He dodges from place to place. The orange and green flag-bearers, jousting
with their banners, continually obstruct him. Each time he avoids them,
the red flag is reared in front of him.*

Can no-one tell me as I breathless run,
What has become of all those moderate men
Those silent liberal millions in the middle, upon whom
All government must lay its only hope to stem
Extremist violence – you voted for me, did you not – ?
Stand up stand up, be counted: or we'll *all* be driven out . . . !

The BRITISH TU LEADERS *chase him: he runs out of the hall and they follow*
The NATIONALIST *and* ULSTER VOLUNTEERS *crouch at each corner of the*
stage with apprehension as LARKIN *and the remaining strength of the*
company line up under their own red flag to sing.

Larkin (*sings*)

Oh the strike has gone on and the lockout has gone on
While the whole of the city stood still:
If we don't go back to work we will never work again
We must sign Mr Murphy's little bill.

Chorus (*sings*)

So long has been the fight and dark was the night
The sunrise comes up slow
Every time that we begin to be thinking we can win
Once again back again we must go.

Larkin (*sings:* CHORUS *between each verse.*)

We must sign his little bill for to promise that we will
Never stay with the union any more
But the minute he has gained the writing of our name
We will tear it up and throw it on the floor.

We must sign his little bill but we all know very well
That the union is ours till we die:
The time will yet arrive they will find how we've survived
We will stand and we will stare them in the eye.

We will stare them in the eye with our power in our hand
And Larkin and Connolly too –
The union will live and the strength that it will give
Will be power in the future for you.

Chorus (*sings*)

Oh long is still the fight and dark is the night
But surely the sun will appear
Every time that you begin to believe you cannot win . . .

Last line spoken.

REMEMBER HOW WE TAUGHT YOU TO ENDURE.

END OF PART FIVE

Part Six: World war and the Rising 1914 – 1916

Prologue: 'King Conaire and the Prohibitions'. In ancient times good King Conaire saved the country from its enemies by fighting them against all odds: even though the circumstances of the battle were contrary to the prohibitions prescribed by his Druids.

List of characters:
> **KING CONAIRE**
> **His MOTHER**
> **3 DRUIDS**
> **3 GUARDS**
> **GIRLS**
> **PIRATES**
> **RAGGED WOMAN**
> **BIRDS**

Act One: 'Clouds of War'. James Connolly confronts the aftermath of the great lockout in Dublin. The Irish constitutional crisis brings fears of civil war, combining with the threat of a general strike in Britain. International imperial rivalries simultaneously intensify.

List of characters:
> **JAMES CONNOLLY**
> **NORA (his daughter)**
>
> **JAMES LARKIN**
> **COUNTESS MARKIEVICZ**
> **SHEEHY SKEFFINGTON**
> **Captain WHITE**
> **SEAN O'CASEY**
> **3 MEMBERS of the Irish Citizen Army**
>
> **TOM CLARKE**
> **4 NATIONAL VOLUNTEERS**
>
> **LENIN**
> **3 BRITISH TRADE-UNION LEADERS**
> **Working-class SUFFRAGETTE**
>
> **WAR DEMON**
> **2 SUBSIDIARY DEMONS**
> **GRABITALL**
> **ARMY OFFICER**
> **POLICE OFFICER**

GERMAN ARMS MERCHANT
GENERAL WILSON
DUKE
DUCHESS
OLD EARL
ASQUITH
CHURCHILL
BONAR LAW
CARSON
REDMOND
JOE DEVLIN

Asquith's SECRETARY
Devlin's HENCHMAN
2 LADIES

GAVRIL PRINCIP
BUTLER
CLERGYMAN

OPPRESSED NATIONS
CONTROLLING NATIONS
NEUTRAL NATIONS

soldiers, workers, National Volunteers, Citizen Army Volunteers, Fianna
boys and girls, etc.

Act Two: 'World War to Civil War'. James Connolly sees international socialism collapse in the face of the outbreak of the world war. Resolute in his opposition to imperialism in all its forms, he seeks desperately for allies – in particular from among the members of the Irish Republican Brotherhood within the National Volunteers.

List of characters:
JAMES CONNOLLY
LILLIE CONNOLLY

JAMES LARKIN
DELIA LARKIN (his sister)
COUNTESS MARKIEVICZ
WINIFRED CARNEY
WILLIAM O'BRIEN
SHEEHY SKEFFINGTON
3 OFFICIALS of the Irish Transport Workers' Union
SEAN O'CASEY
OFFICER of the Irish Citizen Army

LENIN
LIEBKNECHT
KEIR HARDIE
ROSA LUXEMBURG
JOHN MacLEAN
JEAN JAURÈS

2 GERMAN SOCIAL DEMOCRATS
2 FRENCH SOCIALISTS
2 BRITISH TRADE-UNION LEADERS

Belfast **SHIPYARD WORKER**

PADRAIC PEARSE
SEAN MacDERMOTT
TOM CLARKE
JOSEPH PLUNKETT
Northern member of the Irish Republican Brotherhood
2 Dublin members of the Irish Republican Brotherhood
EOIN MacNEILL

WAR DEMON
GRABITALL

3 EMPLOYERS
General WILSON
ADMIRAL
German GENERAL

ASQUITH
Mrs ASQUITH
KAISER WILHELM II
LLOYD GEORGE
BONAR LAW
CARSON
REDMOND
Middle-class SUFFRAGETTE
PRIEST

BIRD
9 SHAPES

subsidiary demons, National Volunteers, Citizen Army men, British Army recruits, leaders of the Irish Republican Brotherhood, delegates to the Zimmerwald Conference, etc.

Act Three: 'The Rising'. James Connolly brings the Irish Citizen Army into the Rising of Easter 1916: and thereby becomes the first working-class leader to enter the world conflict in the cause of Socialism. He is compelled to surrender to superior force: and is shot to death.

List of characters:

JAMES CONNOLLY
LILLIE CONNOLLY
NORA (their daughter)

COUNTESS MARKIEVICZ
WINIFRED CARNEY
WILLIAM O'BRIEN
SHEEHY SKEFFINGTON
3 OFFICIALS of the Irish Transport Workers' Union
CITIZEN ARMY VOLUNTEER

LENIN
LIEBKNECHT
JOHN MacLEAN

BRITISH TRADE-UNION LEADER

DOCKER

PADRAIC PEARSE
SEAN MacDERMOTT
DE VALERA
LIAM MELLOWS
NATIONAL VOLUNTEER
3 MESSENGERS

EOIN MacNEILL

GRABITALL
BRITISH GENERAL
GERMAN GENERAL
ADMIRAL
General WILSON
BOWEN-COLTHURST
BRITISH SUBALTERN
POLICE OFFICER
POLICE CONSTABLE

ASQUITH
KAISER WILHELM II
LLOYD GEORGE

JAMES STEPHENS
NEWSBOY

leaders of the Irish Republican Brotherhood, Citizen Army Volunteers, National Volunteers, race-goers, slum-women, rumours, looters, British soldiers, German soldiers, etc.

Part Six: World war and the Rising: 1914 – 1916

PROLOGUE: '*King Conaire and the Prohibitions*'

An idealised view of the Irish countryside in legendary times, lakes, mountains, huts of turf surrounded by palisades, cattle and drover, hunters chasing the deer, etc. A red-haired woman in a chariot dominates the foreground – she wears an embroidered robe and brandishes a spear. (Backcloth 10 – the composition as whole echoes that for Backcloth 2 in Part One, Scene 10.)

This episode all takes place on a separate stage from the main action of the play. A sun and moon hang from the flies over the acting area, if this is convenient.

GUARDS *with visored helmets hiding their faces enter with* CONAIRE'S MOTHER. *She wears white with gold and silver ornaments. They fix manacles on her wrists and chain her to a framework which encloses her on three sides as though she is in some sort of dungeon. They leave her here.*

Conaire's Mother
   I was shut tight in a small dark room
   The doors were locked and barred
   Into this room no man might come
   Though he struggled so long and hard.
   For air and light one window was left void
   Just large enough to enter in one small and frightened bird.

A small BIRD *flutters in to her prison and flies around and around, gradually getting nearer to her. He disappears in a clap of thunder and is replaced by a man-sized* BIRD, *who raises himself up on the framework, opening his wings over her. His plumage is mostly red, with flashes of green and gold.*

Bird Grow, bird, grow: and teach her how to know
   The love and liberty they will not let her have.
   The child born from your imprisoned body, child, shall save
   The whole land from destruction, from the wave
   Of small dark cruelty that has already shut you up in here
   And will next year
   Close down
   On all of Ireland from the Antrim Glen
   To Shannon Mouth
   And the long green rock-nailed fingers of the furthest south . . .

He throws off his bird-skin and is revealed as a red man with streaks of green and gold down his body. He covers her. The sun and moon swoop together like two pendulums to a clatter of bodhrans and a screaming of bird-cries. Then they swing apart again: and he steps back from her.

> There: it is done
> And in one breath:
> The rest of it is you yourself alone.

He disappears, abruptly. Several smaller BIRDS, *again to the sound of the bodhrans, gather in and around her, hiding her from sight. When they disperse again, the prison and the* MOTHER *have disappeared. A* BABY BOY, *wrapped up, lies where they have been.*

The BIRD *re-enters, again as a Bird. He picks up the* BABY *in his claws and flies away with it – if flying should be practicable.*

Bird (*as he goes*)

> The child being born, the mother dead and gone,
> The bird comes back to take his little son
> And leave him where he can be nursed
> And fostered till he grows into a man.

To the music of flutes, enter three DRUIDS *in black and white robes. They crouch down together.*

1st Druid

> Wait and wait how many murderous years
> For him to grow and come again
> And when he comes he is our rightful king –

2nd Druid

> And when he comes, by the way that he appears
> We shall know who he is –

3rd Druid

> A naked boy
> All wet, walking from Dublin Bay
> Towards Tara.

Druids Brothers: I think this is the very day.

They all stand up at once and cast their hands into the air, releasing a waft of smoke from incense sticks which they have lit. Bells ring. CONAIRE *enters, as described by* 3RD DRUID *– he carries a sling in his hand.*

Conaire Hunting birds between the tide

> Upon the sea-side –
> Didn't they turn into men and jump out on the wave and all of them
>   cried –

A crowd of BIRDS *fly in and round, casting off their bird-skins.*

Birds You are the brother of the birds: you must therefore kill no bird!

CONAIRE *drops his sling. The* BIRDS *cluster round him and then immediately disperse.*

Conaire I was afraid.

> No-one has ever told me who or what I am.

I know my name is Conaire.

The DRUIDS *advance portentously towards him. They hold* (1ST) *a crown,* (2ND) *a golden robe,* (3RD) *a sword and a cup.*

1st Druid
> This is no game.
> Chosen king by divination
> Involves art-magic, prohibition,
> If your reign over this distracted nation
> Shall be both prosperous and good.
> Mark him with blood.

3RD DRUID *puts his hand in the cup, brings it out covered with blood, and smears* CONAIRE'S *face. They all three invest him with the crown, robe and sword.*

1st Druid
> Rule wisely, child, and never be betrayed –
> One – into staying away from Tara for more than eight nights.

2nd Druid Two – into presuming to adjudicate personally a dispute between two of your subjects.

3rd Druid Three – into permitting a woman to come in behind you under your roof after nightfall.

1st Druid That's all.

Each prohibition is marked by a clang of a heavy bell. At the end of the ceremony, there is a very loud clangour of bells, a thunder-clap, and the sun and the moon change places. CONAIRE *stands rigid for a moment: then sits down in his regalia and makes himself comfortable.*

Conaire Why?

Clangour again – the sun and moon sway about disjointedly: the DRUIDS *stagger back as though thoroughly disconcerted.*

1st Druid (*after a pause*)
> No need to explain.
> We have seen it all in a dream.

2nd Druid
> Obey.

3rd Druid
> Ask no question.

Druids Rule the land by divine direction.

Conaire (*gets up and saunters about*)
> These *are* wise men: they must know far more than me.
> I cannot challenge them yet. But we shall see.

He resumes his seat. A group of GIRLS *pass across, scattering flowers and ears of corn. They are dressed mostly in flowers.*

Girls (*sing*)

> Prosperity with green and golden hand
> Year after year walks through King Conaire's land.

Three GUARDS *rush in one after the other shouting.*

1st Guard

> Feud!

2nd Guard

> Greed!

3rd Guard

> Murder!

1st Guard

> Warfare!

2nd Guard

> Fear!

3rd Guard

> The wisdom of the King is now required
> To judge between two mighty quarrelling lords!

There is a confused noise of bodhrans and horns.

1st Druid

> He cannot do it himself!

2nd Druid

> He is prohibited!

Conaire If my wise men know the words
> Then let them do it for me.

The DRUIDS *get in a nervous huddle.*

3rd Druid

> We are afraid:
> This quarrel is too great.

Conaire Then I myself must go and sort it out –

Druids King: you MUST NOT!

Conaire These rules served once but never again:
> They are a stumbling-block to my good reign –
> Away with them!

He makes an imperious gesture. The DRUIDS *scatter in panic. The sun and moon begin again to oscillate.* CONAIRE *sets off at a run, followed by the* GUARDS *with banners: they hasten round the stage and perhaps the auditorium, while the noise of the music swells. Then they come back to where they began, and stop. The music drops down and becomes a simple beat of a bodhran.*

Conaire Nine nights out of Tara adjudicating a dispute:

> Two out of three prohibitions broken: and the state saved from
>   civil war...
> On our journey home we stop the night inside this house.
> Come in, and shut the door.

He makes as though he enters a house, his GUARDS *following. A* RAGGED
WOMAN, *all dressed in strips of green, with one eye closed over with a green
patch and the opposite half of her face dead white, slips in behind* CONAIRE
among the GUARDS. *Such of her body as can be seen under her rags is all
bloody.*

1st Guard

> She ought not to be here.

2nd Guard

> She is prohibited, do you want her out?

Conaire I thought we had got rid of all of that.

Ragged Woman

> My husband's throat was cut:
> My children's necks were broke:
> Myself I have been violated. King: this was work
> Of some of those at feud with whom you dealt this week.
> Will you go back
> And make revenge upon them all for me?

Conaire I have now disobeyed my prohibitions one two three
> And if I do go back all three of them are broken all over again.
> I have no choice. She comes to me a suppliant in her pain:
> Tomorrow I will do what she says.

*Dead silence. The oscillating sun and moon are withdrawn out of sight with
one clang.* 1ST DRUID *enters with a black cloth, which he casts down across
the front of the acting-area.*

1st Druid

> King Conaire's reign from now on is accursed
> Because he stepped from underneath his sacred crown
> And tried to turn the whole world upside-down.

CONAIRE *and his* GUARDS *compose themselves to sleep. The* RAGGED WOMAN
*sits beside them, with her hands over her face. Flute music and horns, with
an irregular beat of bodhrans. A group of naked* PIRATES, *with fearful masks
and headdresses, carrying weapons and red cloth on sticks suggesting
firebrands, creep in and surround them.*

That night there came upon Ireland the most terrible danger. At all times
had the country been aware of the threat of the pirates: and King Conaire
had endeavoured throughout his reign to unite the people against them:
but so prosperous they seemed to be, they had laughed at his warnings.
And now it was the pirates who had united their forces – they determined
to strike one great blow and make slaves of the people for ever. They

landed in their shiploads at the mouth of the river Dodder: they were informed by a traitor of the house where the King slept: they surrounded the building at the foot of the Dublin mountains: threw brands upon the thatch: until the whole place was one red furnace and the King and his men inside of it.

The PIRATES *whirl their brands, forming a wide flourish of red all round about the others.*

They broke out of the blazing walls –

CONAIRE *and his* GUARDS *leap up and rush out, fighting.*

And they killed all of the pirates. They themselves were all killed: it was the woman alone who escaped.

The MEN *all now lie in grotesque attitudes of death. The* RAGGED WOMAN *has stood up in the flames and fighting, very still. Now she walks out over the corpses.*

Ragged Woman
        I have two faces: and it has been said
        I was the treacherous one who brought the pirates on his head.
        He broke his prohibitions and he died.

She goes out. The DRUID, *who has been describing the scene from one side – collapses slowly as though he too dies.* CONAIRE'S MOTHER *and* GIRLS *enter. The* BIRD *enters and spreads his wings. Music of flutes and small bells.*

Mother   And in so doing he left the Irish land
            With greater life and hope than from any other hand
            At any time for half a thousand years.
1st Girl Loch Corrib in the west, Loch Dan in the Wicklow Hills
            Were only two of all the great lakes said
            To have been filled by all the childrens' tears
            Wept for young Conaire dead.
Bird   He broke his prohibitions and so prevails
            From that day on to this the pride
            Of his new spirit and the new-made need
            Never again to be afraid.
            Ho exit the great red bird ...

Exeunt.

                     END OF PROLOGUE

ACT I: 'Clouds of War'

SCENE 1

A landscape devastated by war – broken trees and buildings, wrecked vehicles, dead men and horses, etc. (Backcloth 4).

Liberty Hall in the midst of the Dublin dockland, the river on one side, the Custom House on the other (Backcloth 9).

Enter CONNOLLY *and* LARKIN.

Connolly Nineteen hundred and fourteen
And in Dublin has there been –
Must we say that we have seen –
In the great strike and the locking-out
Through all this winter we have fought –
Immeasurable defeat . . . ?

Larkin No. We can measure it.

Connolly Measure it and assess
How far the murderous frostbite upon the life of the working class
From the black and yellow withered leaf
Has worried downwards to the earthbound root?

Larkin Not to the root. Not quite . . .
The members of our Union go back to work having apparently achieved nothing.
Connolly can hardly lift his head:
For Larkin nothing left but to fall flat upon his bed –
God, in all of my life before I never felt so bloody mad:
I'm not well.

Exit LARKIN.

Connolly Here is hell.
Two men, four years they have both worked together,
Admiring, distrusting, respecting, resenting each other –
And now at the last between them hardly one word of good grace:
Good God in the whole of my life I never felt so little damned use!

He sits wearily down with his head in his hands.

Drumming. GRABITALL (*as Murphy – a role he retains all through Part 6*) *comes in with the* WAR DEMON. *The latter is a tall figure like an oriental battle-god, all covered with spikes, flags, bits of armour and weapons. He has a small drum at his waist, which he rattles with his fist or knuckles at intervals. He is attended by two* SUBSIDIARY DEMONS – *similarly attired, but of normal human stature. They have castanets or small cymbals attached to their spiked fingers.*

Grabitall

What did the Kaiser tell to the Emperor

Of Austria last week?

War Demon

He said that general war

Must cover Europe, now, within the year:

Between class, between nation, between every rival power

Discovered in their rivalry by suddenly the failure

Of all men to find wealth in the one place and the same hour!

Grabitall The starving streets of Dublin are but part of it.

I won this round but cannot win again.

The battle now must shift from the foothills to the great wide plain.

You are now called forth by me and mine

And set to work across this world unhindered –

War Demon

Who will be master, who will be man

When once this drum has thundered?

He beats his drum. Marching SOLDIERS, *carrying flags of several nations,
begin to pass and repass across the stage, and up and down the* AUDIENCE.
The DEMONS *weave in and out amongst them. The speed of the drumming
increases in a rapid crescendo. Through the* SOLDIERS *and flags bursts the
figure of* OPPRESSED NATIONS (*she is in fact the* RAGGED WOMAN *of the
Prologue but taller by several feet*).

Oppressed Nations

The cry of the oppressed nations:

Hungary, Slovakia, Poland, Bohemia,

Serbia, Ireland, India, Arabia –

All over the world like young leopards in their cage

We lick the weals upon our beaten backs and rage

Against the nails that spike our clawed feet to the floor

And chew with broken teeth upon the bars of the hard locked door:

Let us out Let us out Let us out

And we will tear

Our swallowed life from your black throat!

Through the SOLDIERS *and flags bursts the figure of* CONTROLLING NATIONS.
*An androgynous creature, very tall and gross, laden down with innumerable
furs and rich robes, all hung about with boxes and bags on chains and
jewelled belts. Hair full of chains and pins and glittering combs.*

Controlling Nations

The cry of the controlling nations:

Germany, Russia, Britain, Austria, France –

We looked for our good luck and took our chance

And took our vantage where we found it best

And crammed our bags and slammed our boxes, wrapped all of it
    too close to our chest:
Leave us alone Leave us alone Leave us alone
Leave us alone with all the wealth that we have won
Or we will break you back and bone
And pile your severed heads beneath a cairn of stone
So high that if it does not touch the sky
The only question left will be for you to ask us why
Were we content
After so huge a multitude of death
To sit down satiate and relent . . . ?

These two figures circle each other, repeating 'Let us out' and 'Leave us alone' respectively. The giant figure of the NEUTRAL NATIONS *comes in at one side – he is dressed like the cartoons of Uncle Sam: but instead of the usual long-goateed face, he has a great broad featureless moon of a head that laughs all the time.*

Neutral Nations (*sing*)

We're standin', we're standin', on the sidewalk of the world:
We're standin', we're standin', an' we damn well don't mix in!
If we wanna have it made in dollars an' trade
We gotta wait see who will win
Gotta pick an' choose, 'cos the guys who lose
Ain't gonna be worth one pin!
We're standin', we're standin' on the sidewalk lookin' around:
Keep your pistol stitched in your holster tight
Till the last trump's ready to sound . . .
Boys, it's a cinch that that ain't just yet – keep clear of it – get wise.

Enter LENIN, *unobtrusively. He has a bundle of notes in his hand. He selects a page and begins to read, but because of the noise he cannot be heard. He knocks for silence but there is no response. The meaningless dance continues: and then suddenly – after a very loud burst of discordant noise – there is silence. The movement of the soldiers and the figures does not cease: but it is now entirely dumbshow.*

Lenin (*reads rapidly and quietly, as though he is afraid the noise will start again before he has finished*) At innumerable socialist conferences, notably Stuttgart in 1907 and Basel in 1912, resolutions were passed proclaiming that no interests of the people can serve to justify wars waged for the sake of profits, the ambitions of dynasties, the power of the ruling class.

Connolly So easy to speak when you're not there and you have no power,
        So desirable to declare anything when not a soul knows who you
        are.

Lenin The revolutionist V. I. Lenin
        From the future, three years after the start of the first world war,

> In the wisdom of my accomplished hindsight
> Can find it possible, as though we had all always known it,
> Consequentially, incontrovertibly, analytically, to declare –

He selects another page in his notes.

Imperialism – the era of bank capital, the era of gigantic capitalist monopolies, the era of the development of monopoly-capitalism into state-monopoly-capitalism – has demonstrated the extraordinary strengthening of the state machine and the intensification of repressive measures against the proletariat both in the monarchical and in the freer republican countries. World history is now undoubtedly leading to the concentration of all the forces of the proletarian revolution upon the destruction of the state machine . . .

The noise suddenly interrupts him, as loud as it was when it left off. He goes out, continuing to read, soundlessly.

Connolly (*jumps up and roars*)
> We've got to get some work done!
> This union can not be run
> By sitting down like an old hen
> And giving way to moan and groan!

The DANCERS *all whirl away, the noise decreasing. Only the* WAR DEMON *remains, squatting above the stage on a convenient platform.*

Skeffy, Madame Markievicz – Jim Larkin is ill: and as usual his accounts are all over the shop. Will you please just sit down with me for thirty minutes and we'll make some sense of 'em. Oh come on, I've not got all day.

SCENE 2

Enter SHEEHY SKEFFINGTON *and* COUNTESS MARKIEVICZ.

Countess As always the capitalist newspapers are foreseeing some sort of war.
Sheehy Skeffington Whose war, for what reason?
Connolly Oh, anybody's war – opinions differ as to the area in which it will break out.
Sheehy Skeffington I don't give a damn which area: I shall conscientiously abstain.
Countess Skeffy, you're a crank: but if England is involved, remember her difficulty will be Ireland's opportunity.
Sheehy Skeffington And what's a crank but a small arm that produces revolutions?
Connolly So long as it's connected to a moving force on the one end and to a great wheel on the other . . .
> Oh there's one moving force has left *us* well in the lurch

> But in the end I do believe will so stretch out its huge reach
> That belt and wheel and disconnected cranks and all
> Will turn like whirligigs until they pull
> The rotten frame of Empire to the ground ...

Enter 2ND *and* 3RD *British* TRADE-UNION LEADERS, *harassed by a crowd of angry* WORKERS.

> Let them try to stand fast, let them fall on their nose:
> Today they must obey, where they refused to propose.

CONNOLLY, *the* COUNTESS *and* SHEEHY SKEFFINGTON *retire, to a table labelled 'Irish Transport Workers' Union', and busy themselves with papers.*

3rd TU Leader Now wait, brothers, wait –

Workers No!

2nd TU Leader No: your action is precipitate: we must beg you to hold back!

Workers (*severally*) No, we've waited long enough – the Scots coal-owners have dropped their wages – do we do what we've been promised and strike for a living wage, or what do we do? If the Scots miners strike, then all the miners strike! If the miners strike, the railwaymen are bound to go in with them! If the railwaymen, the dockers! We invoke the Triple Alliance! We invoke it from this moment!

3rd TU Leader As your delegated leaders with a mandate to use all efforts to –

Workers To secure our just demands, so get on then and secure them! Strike, general strike, strike for a living wage!

The WORKERS *shout out their slogans repetitively. The* TU LEADERS *get into a huddle. The* WAR DEMON *has come in at the back and taps his drum to add to the mounting excitement.* 1ST TU LEADER *bustles in and takes charge of the situation.*

1st TU Leader Reluctantly bowing to this manifest popular demand: we regretfully announce that since all negotiations with the Scottish coal-owners have broken down, a nationwide strike of the mine-workers' union will commence at the start of September. The door is still open.

2nd TU Leader But if it has to be shut, then the railwaymen's union will come out on strike in sympathy.

3rd TU Leader Oh aye, and the dockers too – but the door is still open ...

Workers The door has been bloody well slammed and you know it. We've said it and what we say goes from now on.

Exeunt WORKERS. TU LEADERS *sit down to make plans.*

2nd TU Leader My God, a general strike ...

3rd TU Leader There's no holding 'em, we are committed ...

1st TU Leader So we've got to look damn sure we don't make the same mistake as Jim Larkin made last winter. We'll accept help from wherever it comes and antagonise nobody –

2nd TU Leader We need volunteer workers, if only to address envelopes – I mean the sort as are not prepared to stand out with us on picket – we need foodstuffs, we need –

3rd TU Leader First and foremost we need *cash*. We've not got it. Where from ?

Enter a CLERGYMAN.

Clergyman There are charitable funds –

TU Leaders Oh no . . . Look, Vicar, this is business – not cups o' tea for old folk –

Clergyman None the less, it is necessary that the wealthy of this land be made aware of what they do. Gentlemen, I shall spare no effort to raise money for your righteous cause wherever I can – men must not die for want of justice !

Enter a WORKING-CLASS SUFFRAGETTE.

Working-class Suffragette If they're not afraid to die, then maybe they won't have to. Justice comes when it is fought for. And not only by men. The government at last has agreed to support a Suffrage Bill for women. And they've only agreed because the women of the working class at last took up the struggle. Your general strike is *our* strike: and brothers, you can count on us !

Sheehy Skeffington You see, she was a crank, a very notable crank, that young woman: and now look where she turns herself . . .

Re-enter WORKERS.

Workers (*severally*) We've fraternal meetings organized with the printers' union – the glass-blowers – the boiler-makers – there's arrangements for sympathetic pickets set up at every tramway-shed and organised market in Lancashire – Liverpool Trades Council has voted us full support – the construction shops at Swindon and Doncaster are considering joining in in sympathy with the railwaymen – there's not a building contractor in the Rhondda Valley be able to work while the Welsh miners are out – we've said it and there's no holding us !

Exeunt with enthusiasm, leaving CONNOLLY, SHEEHY SKEFFINGTON *and the* COUNTESS: *also the* WAR DEMON, *who taps his drum.*

SCENE 3

Connolly So they have said it ; and let it go.
        But what can we say now to let them know
        They've said it all a month or two too late ?

Sheehy Skeffington
        You told Keir Hardie that we in Dublin could not wait :
        And we were beaten.

Countess Now his British friends will find
    Their enemies have had time to turn their mind
    To counter-revolution –
Connolly The knacker's yard
    Of half-united labour lies wide open and unbarred
    To bloodstained claws of every scavenging bird
    That flaps its wings and screams from the Tory tree –

Enter DUKE, DUCHESS, *an* OLD EARL, *two* LADIES, *and* WILSON. *The* DUCHESS
gathers herself up to speak :

Countess Devour our offal, lady, feed fat your power and make your privilege
    free.
Duchess My railway shares will drop to nothing and my brother's coal-mines
    in Northumbria are already in a condition of ruin. Do you realise it has
    already been seriously put forward that *nationalisation* is the only cure for
    the industry! Seriously put forward, and seriously *accepted*, if you please,
    by responsible political commentators. One need not say of what colour.
    So long as the Liberals – where is the Duke – you are the legislator, you
    sit in the House of Lords, don't stand there like a totem-pole – so long as
    the Liberals – –
Duke So long, my dear, as the Liberals, in coalition with Labour, continue to
    usurp the proper government of this country, we are all on the road to
    ruin. I am well aware of it, my dear: but constitutionally we have no
    power – –
Duchess Who spoke of the constitution? The constitution is already des-
    troyed! First the reform of the Lords, and now Home Rule for Ireland.
Old Earl If Ireland is let go, then what about India? Before we know where we
    are they'll give Africa to the blacks! But Carson has sworn that Ireland is
    not to be taken from us. His people, thank God, are loyal.
Duke But there is surely no doubt the government has the majority to pass the
    bill: and once the bill becomes law then Carson's Ulstermen must submit.
    I happen to know that Churchill, for one, is fully prepared to make use of
    military force: Asquith doesn't want it, the Cabinet don't want it: but if
    Churchill decides to push them, then by God the little renegade is damn
    well going to push: and the troops will coerce Ulster!
Duchess But my cousin has lands in Ulster, my mother's brother has enormous
    interests in the shipyards of Belfast, and even my nephew Clarence holds
    three directorships in the linen business! Father, I did ask you to have a
    word with General Wilson...
Old Earl Oh – Wilson – he's a sound man – he's an Ulsterman, goddammit –
    he gets on well with the ladies. I asked *them* to put the matter to him –
    agreeably, don't you know, keep it light, keep it non-political – and I
    gather that he said —
Wilson (*comes forward – he has been whispering with the* LADIES) Conscientious
    refusal of all sound officers in every corps to take up arms against their

kith and kin . . . You see, Churchill controls only the Admiralty; the War Office, under *my* influence, is considerably more pliable. They're going to try to call it mutiny: but it won't be anything of the sort. A conscientious General Staff will offer advice to the civil government that military operations against the Ulster Volunteers would be considered to be – ill-timed . . . Lady Barbara and Lady Jane have laid some very sound groundwork at their Belgravian social functions: and they tell me that the attitude of Buckingham Palace is not to be discounted. There is, moreover, another point that, Your Grace, *you* could attend to for me? The Kaiser of Germany is quite likely to start a war: he is terrified of Russia, in alliance with France. Now we have a very solid commitment to France, as you know. The French General Staff absolutely rely upon a British Expeditionary Force into their country in event of war. Now what pressure, do you suppose, would be brought by his French allies upon Asquith, if they were to hear all of a sudden that the British Army was about to terminate its existence?

Duke I don't understand . . .

Duchess I do. What bills are due to come up in the Commons as a matter of routine during the present session?

Duke There's the usual Army Bill, if that's what you – –

Duchess Exactly. Passed every year, by tradition unopposed, or the Army gets no money. If we were to make it clear that we intended to block the bill, for the first time in modern history –

Duke But if we succeeded, it would mean the disbandment of – –

Wilson You don't seriously imagine, sir, that the Army would consent to be disbanded at the behest of a few scheming politicians?

Old Earl My God, we'd get them both ways! If they don't have an army, their foreign policy is wrecked: if they do have an Army, then it's on Tory terms or nobody's! And the very possibility of the controversy itself will put the Army into our hands!

Duchess General Wilson, you're a genius!

Old Earl The only man in the War Office who's ever been known to use his head!

Wilson In the meantime, if it is known that Asquith cannot trust his Army, then Redmond and the Irish Nationalists will be unable to trust Asquith. To split the Liberals from the Home Rulers –

Old Earl As we did with Parnell!

Duke Means the Liberals will lose the next election . . . Yes, but – –

Duchess Unless Labour can increase its vote?

Duke On the heels of a general strike? I hardly think so. But none the less –

Old Earl If there's any danger of Labour increasing its vote there will not *be* a next election! Don't you see, you dam fool: we have brought the *Army* in to politics! Why wouldn't we form in Ulster a military base for the invasion of England and put paid to the whole damned farce with the rattle of a maxim gun? Carson's people, I am sure, would be only too glad to lend a hand. Crush the catholics and Larkin's anarchists and the whole of Ireland will be theirs. Isn't that what they want? And certainly what *we* want! At last – the revolution: the real revolution – get back into our own hands all the power we ever lost since – since 1649 when they chopped off the King's head – bah – you're all afraid of it: except for me and the general here – –

Duchess And me! I'm not afraid of it!

Ladies Nor are we, nor are we –

Enter BUTLER.

Butler Excuse me, Your Grace, there is a German gentleman by appointment to Lady Barbara, he says –

1st Lady Ah, my brother's agent, to discuss our property at Baden-Baden –

Butler Or failing Lady Barbara, Lady Jane will do as well...

2nd Lady Ah, my cousin the Count will have sent him to arrange for the purchase of racehorses.

Both Ladies Will you show the gentleman here, please?

The BUTLER *brings forward the* GERMAN ARMS MERCHANT.

2nd Lady (*to* WILSON) Dear General, you had better turn your back for a few minutes...

1st Lady (*to* DUKE) Uncle, be a dear, and turn your back for a few minutes.

German Arms Merchant (*to* DUCHESS *and* LADIES) Gracious lady, gracious lady, gracious lady: a vessel with a supply of small arms has set sail from Hamburg. I have been asked to inform *you*, as Sir Edward Carson's office desires the whole thing to be conducted with discretion: and unofficial contacts are always best in these matters. But the ship's master is apprehensive. I would be grateful for confirmation that the British Navy will not intercept the cargo before it reaches Northern Ireland?

Duchess (*indicates* WILSON) I think you will find that the military executive has turned its back and closed its eyes...

Duke (*with his back to them*) So has the constitutional conservative ruling class... Dear God, what are we coming to!

Old Earl Ha!

The WAR DEMON *taps his drum.*

1st Lady (*to* GERMAN) Thank you: you needn't wait.

German Arms Merchant Thank you, gracious lady...

Exit. They all seem about to disperse, when the CLERGYMAN *enters with a group of working-class* TRIPPERS.

Duke Oh, General, don't go. I'd like you to meet our Rural Dean. I do hope your party have enjoyed their excursion, Doctor? I ordered Benson to lay on some lemonade up at the conservatory. It is rather hot this afternoon, isn't it?

Clergyman My excursion consisted of a working-men's club from one of our industrial parishes – they are perhaps most of all impressed with the palatial kennels for Your Grace's fox-hounds. The inhabitants of those, I told them, were not likely to come out on strike, nor yet to lend an ear to the rebellious blandishments of the Irish fanatics: we are so grateful to Your Grace for letting us see round the estate, and particularly for so apposite an object lesson: are we not . . . ?

The DUCAL PARTY *disperses, and so do the* TRIPPERS, *leaving the* CLERGYMAN.

SCENE 4

Enter ASQUITH.

Clergyman (*to* AUDIENCE) Are you aware that we are now in the midst of a wave of self-murder unparalleled in living memory?

Asquith (*to* AUDIENCE, *at opposite stage-corner*) Are you aware that we are now living in the midst of a wave of terrorist assassination unparalleled in human history?

War Demon (*comes down between them*) What, when – assassinations – where?

Clergyman A young woman called Catherine Firman jumped recently in front of a train – she left a letter for her friends – it said: 'All hope gone, no work, no money.'

Asquith Since Abraham Lincoln, two Presidents of the United States: an Emperor of Russia –

Clergyman Frederick George Mann drowned himself in the canal – in the band of his hat was found a pawnticket – upon it he had written: 'I am now without hope and without shelter.'

Asquith A President of the French Republic, an Empress of Austria –

Clergyman Another man, James Honeyball, only eighteen years of age, in a reservoir up on the moor – drowned – he had told his younger brother before he went out that he was 'jolly hungry': that was all. If he found food he would come back home.

Asquith A King of Italy: a King and Queen of Serbia: a King of Portugal –

Clergyman How can we pretend such tragedies as these are acceptable normal features of harmonious society?

Asquith Russian Archdukes, innumerable minor princes – is it going to happen here?

Exeunt. The WAR DEMON *beats his drum.*

SCENE 5

Connolly The class war having been diverted into a constitutional riddle-me-ree,
　　　　The Irish have no choice but to attempt to agree

> With the rules of the Tory game: and to muster to defend
> The integrity of the constitution if need be to the bitter end.

Countess Draw back the curtain and reveal
  The National Volunteers at drill!

NATIONAL VOLUNTEERS *enter with a green flag, drilling.*

Sheehy Skeffington
  Because Carson has threatened force
  The national answer is far worse
  Good God the bold brag of the so-sheltered middle class
  When the green flag braves the orange flag, sure 'tis better than a
    play –
  Do we want to get these pamphlets checked, or do we sit here all
    day...

The drill concludes, and the VOLUNTEER *leaders sit down with some documents.*

1st Volunteer Upon this invoice only one-third of the uniform tunics ordered –

2nd Volunteer (*an* IRB MAN) Arnotts have the rest in stock, but they're holding
  back on delivery till they get paid for the first lot.

1st Volunteer My God, if a Dublin merchant cannot put his trust in the People
  of Ireland for a matter of four weeks – look, now, you mention my name
  and the name of my firm and tell them if they don't want trouble with
  their wholesale consignments of Indian jute, hadn't they better –

3rd Volunteer It's a shame we have no rifles.

1st Volunteer To bring in rifles is against the law. We are not that class of an
  outfit at all. This is very dangerous talk.

3rd Volunteer Of course, you could say the bayonet, and the sword, as worn by
  officers, is in itself sufficient symbol of our chivalric defiance.

1st Volunteer When we get to the ceremony at Bodenstown, is it intended to
  say the Rosary? Sure, Wolfe Tone was a protestant...

2nd Volunteer He was an Irishman.

Connolly (*to* COUNTESS)
    Constance, about Bodenstown, and the grave of Wolfe Tone:
    You promised me a small message that we said needed done.

She gets up and walks over to the VOLUNTEERS.

Countess The Citizen Army has asked me to ask you to obtain tickets for their
  participation at Bodenstown.

3rd Volunteer The Citizen Army, Madame Markievicz, has given vent to
  opinions upon the integrity of the Volunteers, one might say, anti-
  national...

1st Volunteer I've had more than a deal of trouble with the ruffians of that
  crowd over the wages I pay out in the course of my business: and begod
  I do not forget the riots and ructions they were created for! Is it national

heroes they're after setting themselves up now? When through the whole of last winter they all but brought the nation to its knees! Tell your friends, Madame Markievicz –

3rd Volunteer Had you not best tell your friends, Madame, that we in the Volunteers are all of us agreed to put ourselves loyally under the orders of the national parliament, when established by Home Rule. Any ground for the belief the Citizen Army is prepared for such obedience? Didn't they try to defy the bishops over the religious rearing of the strikers' children – ? Aren't they Jacobins, aren't they altogether some class of a communard – ?

Enter CLARKE.

Connolly (*aside*)
  I might have foreseen the answer she would receive:
  Not yet is this nation fit to dig for liberty in Wolfe Tone's grave.

Clarke (*to* COUNTESS) Aren't they Irishmen, the Citizen Army, and damn good ones? If they want to come to Bodenstown, of course they'll come, and welcome.

Connolly (*aside*)
  Now who the devil is that?
  And would this be the start of a split?
  Straws in the wind and watch them go –
  Once the drums start beating, every which way they will blow . . .

Clarke For sixteen years, I Tom Clarke
  Lay cramped and muffled in the dark
  Stench of an English prison cell.
  Had they had the power they'd have dropped me
  Straight down into the shaft of hell.
  I was a treasonous Fenian felon,
  A Jacobin, a low-class ruffian –
  I spat in the face of parliament and Gladstone's sacred word
  I stamped beneath my heel like a foul horse-turd:
  I knew then that the only saviour
  Of the balance of my brain was my rough and rude behaviour:
  For all Irishmen therefore who are likewise rude and rough
  I offer one comment only – we have not got enough.

Countess Thank you, Mr Clarke – I'm glad that you at least recognise that Wolfe Tone stood for 'the men of no property' . . .

She leaves them and returns to the union table. The VOLUNTEERS *go out, except for* CLARKE *and* 2ND VOLUNTEER.

SCENE 6

The WAR DEMON *beats a constant quiet rhythm during this scene.*

2nd Volunteer

>Behind the face of this and that bold Volunteer
>
>A pair of hidden eyes will switch and peer
>
>Two candles through a tiny midnight hole
>
>In what you swore by day to be a solid wall . . .

Clarke There's a man came to see me in my tobacco shop this morning. Out of Germany.

2nd Volunteer Sssh . . .

Clarke Now he says that he knows that an individual in Hamburg, who is involved in shall we call it –

Enter GERMAN ARMS MERCHANT.

German Arms Merchant The umbrella trade?

Clarke Umbrellas . . . ? Good.

German Arms Merchant This agency in Hamburg has apparently received inquiries from a certain collector whose warehouse is situated not a hundred and fifty kilometres from here –

2nd Volunteer Belfast!

Clarke Sssh . . . If the Ulster Loyalists have indeed ordered rifles out of Germany, we have no time to waste. . . Thank you, my friend: we, also, want umbrellas, and we want them at a fair price. There are persons that your associate will already have been in touch with – let him keep up his contact. It is as well you should not attempt to see *me* any further . . .

Exeunt CLARKE, 2ND VOLUNTEER, *and* GERMAN, *severally.*

SCENE 7

Sheehy Skeffington

>Some conversation there, I fear,
>
>We were not able to overhear:
>
>Not for the first time. Jim, the way my brain box ticks,
>
>Our square-head friend is playing at ducks and drakes . . . ?

Connolly Let them play what they will for as long as they dare –

>I'll tell you what *I* think of this civil war scare:

Sure the whole thing is a part of a great piece of theatricals, carefully arranged between the Liberal ministry, the official Home Rule Party, and the Conservative Unionist leaders. It's my belief the exclusion of at least a portion of Ulster from the Home Rule Bill is already agreed upon between these tricky gentry: and all the rest of these defiances are but the blinding of Nationalist Ireland to the infamous character of partition – partition to which Redmond has already given his consent.

Countess And if there *is* a civil war – then the National Volunteers who thought they would be fighting against Carson to prevent among other things partition, will be fighting under the command of Redmond to support partition – *if* he supports it, which, if what you say is true – –

Connolly Will be the fact: so there will be no fighting, only apathetic acquiescence? You're quite right, of course, unless –

Countess Unless, as you say, there is a split in the Volunteers.

Connolly You are my chief link with all of their prominent organisers: it's up to you to discover who amongst them prepares what: and with whom, in such a circumstance, the Citizen Army can link up. In the meantime, what sort of shape are we in to link with anybody?

      Draw back the curtain and reveal
      The Citizen Army at its drill.

The WAR DEMON *taps his drum. The* CITIZEN ARMY *enter, raggedly marching. The* WAR DEMON *stops tapping, yawns, and stretches out as though bored and contemptuous.* CAPTAIN WHITE *conducts the drill.*

The COUNTESS *slips out.*

      God, what a shambles ...

White (*brings the men to a halt*) This is supposed to be a *drill*! If you drill, you do it with discipline! Get back into your ranks: who the deuce told you to fall out? You, that man there – I thought you told me you were a British army reservist: I don't suppose King George made a worse bargain in his life!

Connolly (*takes him aside*) Just a moment, Captain White. You do realise these men are all volunteers – they are here to prevent bullying, not to submit to it.

White I am sorry, Mr Connolly, but I too am a volunteer: and I am trying to do my best with them, but –

Sheehy Skeffington Since the failure of the strike, there seems to so many of the poor fellows no purpose left for them: it's hard to keep going with a good bearing when they're forced by their employers to pretend to repudiate the transport union in order to retain their jobs.

Connolly (*to the squad*) Now listen to me, men: all Captain White is trying to do is to get you to make a respectable show at Bodenstown. We shall be on parade next door to the National Volunteers, and we really must be at our best –

1st CA Member In these clothes, I'd not be seen dead at Bodenstown or anywhere else, short of the mendicity institution –

2nd CA Member I thought we were all together to make a gang to resist scabs: well, the scabs are alongside us at our places of work, so: and all we have is all this talk about commemorations of Wolfe Tone.

White Mr Connolly, this is hopeless. Look, do you want to drill or don't you?

O'Casey Now, please, Captain, wait a moment. Mr Connolly, please ... This is not just an issue of discipline, is it? Nor yet Bodenstown, if it comes to that. I've been talking around a bit amongst the lads and I think they'll all agree that whether we go to Bodenstown or not, the question to be answered is – why do we think we ought to go – indeed, why do we think we ought to be here at all?

Connolly This is either a mutiny, or a democratic assembly. So let's call it the latter and keep it between comrades. Jim Larkin and myself –

Enter LARKIN.

Ah, here he is. I was just about to say, Jim, that we must not only keep in being but actually *reconstitute* ourselves. For a very urgent and precise purpose.

Larkin Partition. What does it mean to you, as the disciplined force of the Labour Movement in this country? I will tell you what partition means. It will not only divide the country: but the entire working class will be cut into two halves that can never again be joined together. The trade union movement in Ulster will be completely broken away from their brothers in the southern provinces. And the bosses in Belfast and the bosses in Dublin have their tongues hanging out for that day. You can be sure that their bank balances will not be cut in two. At all costs we must prevent partition.

Connolly We are an organisation trained to arms of the Irish working class and a phenomenon in Ireland. Hitherto the workers of Ireland have fought as part of the armies led by their masters, never as masters of an army officered, trained, and inspired by men of their own class. Now we have the chance to steer our own course, to carve our own future. Neither Home Rule nor the lack of Home Rule will make us lay down our arms.

O'Casey Mr Connolly, we haven't got any.

Connolly Not yet, Mr Secretary, not yet: but with your assistance, we shall be able to have a defined constitution – and upon that we can build for anything.

Larkin Sean, would you read it out – let the lads hear what you've written.

O'Casey A few headings. One: the first and last principle of the Irish Citizen Army is the avowal that the ownership of Ireland, moral and material, is vested of right in the people of Ireland. Two: the Irish Citizen Army shall stand for the absolute unity of Irish nationhood –

Connolly Let's add to it this: we support the rights and liberties of the democracies of *all* nations.

O'Casey Three: we sink all differences of birth, property, and creed, under the common name of the Irish people. I don't know if that's going to impress any Orangemen, but I'm reared a protestant meself and it makes good sense to me. Four: the Citizen Army shall be open to all who accept the principle of equal rights and opportunities for the Irish people. What do you think of it?

Larkin Good man, Sean, that's great. As it stands, a bit too general . . . ? How about – Five: before being enrolled, every applicant for the Citizen Army must, if eligible, be a member of his trade union, such union being recognised by the Irish Trade Union Congress.

Re-enter COUNTESS *with some uniforms.*

3rd CA Member Do we understand then, that if this is put in force, we'll have a chance to be recognised and paid-for by the trades unions as a regular – like – militia . . . ?

Connolly For labour: a people's army.

Larkin For Ireland: a red army!

Connolly For the working class throughout the world a pride and an example! We have already been recognised by the Dublin Trades Council –

Countess Following upon which I propose that funds should be raised for the provision of a uniform for every member of this army. I got a few of these run up as a suggestion for the final thing – why not put them on, and see how they look?

She hands out the uniforms. The MEMBERS *put them on with a buzz of excited approval.*

O'Casey Meself, Madame Markievicz, I'm none too keen on a uniform – look, Bernard Shaw tells us that the Irish people's fight against the English state is a perambulator up against a Pickford's removal van – the only kind of battle that could give rise to is one of dodge-and-strike, strike-and-dodge – uniforms for such a business are both dangerous and ridiculous.

Larkin A man in uniform, if taken prisoner, will be protected by international convention, as a regular belligerent. If he fights in his own clothes they could murder him on the spot.

O'Casey Wouldn't they murder him on the spot whatever he wears? Revolution is called treason: and for treason you get shot.

Connolly We are what we are seen to be, whether an army or a mob. As an army we make a statement of responsible human dignity. Let the uniforms remain.

O'Casey And following upon which I have taken occasion to provide ourselves with a banner to be carried at the head of the column.

He fetches forward the Plough and the Stars. General cheers.

Countess I don't see that O'Casey's banner has much of a *republican* message for anyone – if Wolfe Tone was not a republican, then what else was he? Misconceived . . .

O'Casey Madame Markievicz, the Plough and the Stars has a very clear message for *labour*.

Connolly A message for labour is a message for an independent republic, so long as through north and south the issue of Home Rule is still used to cover the iniquities of the capitalist and landlord class. I would much rather see the Home Rule Bill defeated than see it carried with Ulster or any part of Ulster left out. There you are: that's our function. So perfect yourselves, men, in the drill that you will be given, be a pride to our nation and class. Captain– ?

White Citizen Army, Right Marker! Get-on *P'rade*! Come on, now, you're not going to let yourselves be outdone at Bodenstown by a crowd of bent-backed shopkeepers!

He drills them and they respond with interest and skill. They end by marching off, with the new banner borne at their head. The WAR DEMON *tries to break their step with out-of-time – drumming, but fails.*

Connolly We have aroused their sunken fire at last.

Larkin I wish to God I thought that march would carry to Belfast.

The way things are up there, there's no place for *proletarian* feet in common step. I think all the work we ever did in the union in that city has been chopped into kindling-splinters.

Connolly No remedy, I must go back there . . .

Sheehy Skeffington Sean O'Casey made a remark about not having any guns.

Connolly That's right.

Sheehy Skeffington

And you reassured him. You said to him 'Not yet'.

I offered myself vice-chairman of this army because I thought

Its purpose was the defence of unarmed working men

Against blacklegs and police who had truncheon and gun:

Jim, I did not mean

To resist partition with the threat of the shedding of blood.

This is a new Citizen Army, not mine: and I resign.

Connolly That's no good.

Defence against blacklegs, defence against police:

However do you suppose it was ever done without force?

Dammit, you know well we had bloody great clubs of wood –

Haven't you heard a man can *die* if you hit him over the head?

Sheehy Skeffington

I am sorry, but I must do what I believe to be right.

You know that in general you will have all my support:

But warfare – for whatever reason – I have but the one word: no.

Exit.

Connolly I was afraid he would feel he would in the end have to go:

I tell you there is a man

Would meet Attila the Hun

And flick his handkerchief under his nose.

Larkin So he goes.

So do you. Belfast. Well, it's your proper territory. What about Dublin?

Connolly I presumed you would take charge of the union here.

Larkin Oh sure take, charge, yes – with what money? *We have no money!*

Connolly What's the matter with you, man? We know well the union's broke, but we must show some confidence –

Larkin Ten minutes ago I was full of bloody confidence . . . the only place to get some money is, as ever, in America. Bill Haywood has promised that he will organise for me a speaking tour – in a matter of a few months I should be able to earn –

Connolly Haywood? He's as poor as we are. It's a fantasy. We can't afford it. Look, you have *got* to stay in Dublin. Look, I promise you, if you *do* stay: I will *not* come down from Belfast! How's that for an inducement? You run Dublin all on your own – no quarrels, no interference!

Larkin Cunning devil, aren't you – we reorganise the Citizen Army and you leave it for me all wrapped up like a present on the christmas tree – very well then, I'll stay: dammit I'll stay till things get so bad you'll be *begging* me to go to America! Look after yourself, so, among the roarers of the Falls Road . . .

Exit.

Connolly (*to* COUNTESS) Sean O'Casey made a remark about not having guns I'd be glad if you could look into that. No question but the Loyalists are about to get hold of some: if the Loyalists, then inevitably the National Volunteers – if the Volunteers, then maybe there'll be a source available for us. Sure we can't afford German prices: we must pick up from whatever has already come in.

Countess I'll find out for you what I can. Goodbye, and good luck.

Connolly Belfast . . .

Exeunt severally. WAR DEMON *manet.*

SCENE 8

War Demon
    Blood blood blood!
    In Downing Street the windows weep
    Red tears of blood down brick and plaster –
    Asquith Prime Minister within his scarlet-curtained room must
     creep
    On slippered feet from desk-load of disaster
    To dispatch-box full of doom to letters laden down
    With month-long lack of sleep
    To newspapers that smoke and curl
    And smoulder in his hand and fall
    In ashes on his ten times trodden carpet –

Enter ASQUITH.

Asquith It is not that I can't control
The warring factions in the state:
The fact is, I cannot control
One single element, friend or foe
In this whole nation I'm supposed to rule.
The very ministers in my cabinet
Do what they want with neither let
Nor hindrance ... Oh, please wait and see –
I say to them – I have a policy –
Gentlemen, please – you can depend on me ...

Enter SECRETARY.

Secretary

Prime Minister –
Asquith Oh go away!
More than enough stupidity for today,
I want to think.
I want to take a drink.

He helps himself to port.

Secretary

But Prime Minister – naval intelligence –
Asquith Tell Winston Churchill
Don't tell me –
He is in charge of what takes place at sea.
Secretary A ship loaded with rifles has just left the Kiel Canal. There seems no doubt she is under orders for some port in Northern Ireland.
War Demon

Winston Churchill all in heat
Comes in to stir the boiling pot ...

Enter CHURCHILL.

Churchill

Our first and final duty
Is imperial integrity.
Constitutional Home Rule
Takes away the blotch of tyranny
From our Irish control,
The which henceforth shall be maintained
As from a friend towards a friend –
And thereby all the more secure.
Prime Minister, we must suffer none
To reverse by force of arms that which we have begun.

Asquith Sit down, sit down, and listen please to me –
Since sixteen eighty-eight not one convulsive movement has
    disrupted – –

Secretary
We should not have interrupted
The progress of his port wine.

War Demon
Mr Churchill, what you must do, you must do upon your own!

Churchill So I see. Orders!

He dictates to the SECRETARY.

The third battle squadron with eight destroyers of the fourth flotilla to
move at once to Lamlash on the West Coast of Scotland. Two cruisers to
cross over and drop anchor in Belfast Lough. To look out for and prevent
illegal landings on the Irish coast. Copy of these orders to the Secretary
for War. I would be obliged if he would transfer regular military units
from the Curragh of Kildare to such points in the north as were agreed at
our last conference. See to it . . .

Exit SECRETARY.

Prime Minister!

War Demon
John Redmond of the Irish Party runs,
His throat-cords choking with the threat of piled-up guns . . .

Enter REDMOND.

Redmond
Winston, for God's sake, what the devil is going on!

Churchill
Ah, Redmond, the very man:
The bellowing bull of Ulster is to be taken by the horn
And thrown rumpsteak over loin across the mountains of Mourne!

Redmond A surprise for the both of you. You have left it too late. I don't know
about the Navy. The War Office has thrown in its hand!

Churchill *What!*

Redmond Gough and Paget at the Curragh, together with their officers, have
refused to obey orders to move north into Ulster. They will resign their
commissions rather than march against their kith and kin.

Churchill Not possible!

Redmond Ask Wilson, he's outside.

Churchill So have him in. Wilson!
Now this time he is really going to have to listen to what he is told.
Me to the right arm, you to the left, heave him up now, catch hold . . .

He and REDMOND *get hold of the seated* ASQUITH *by the elbows and haul him
vertical.*

> Prime Minister, General Wilson is coming in to make his report,
> You will have the goodness, Prime Minister, to give your ministers
> your support.

War Demon

> Prime Minister, your noble soldier like a jug filled with treachery
> Hovers over your neck to pour out his conspiracy . . .

Enter WILSON, *behind.*

Wilson As I warned you, sir, we're in trouble, we're in real trouble, we were
bound to be. Fifty-seven officers of the Third Cavalry have refused – –
Asquith (*bemused*) Refused . . .
Churchill and Redmond Prime Minister – *Mutiny!*
Asquith Mutiny . . .

The SECRETARY *re-enters.*

Wilson Not at all. They have all acted in the very best of faith.
Redmond Not at all. They were put up to it!
Wilson I will ask you to take that back!
Redmond I will not take it back!

REDMOND *and* WILSON *square up to one another.*

Asquith (*suddenly asserts himself*) Redmond! Wilson! What are you doing?
Stop it, the pair of you!
War Demon

> Coagulated Tory Bonar Law
> Come trample on these Liberal men of straw!

Enter BONAR LAW.

Bonar Law

> Asquith, as Leader of the Conservative opposition
> I have come to inform you that the present situation
> Admits in my opinion of but one solution.
> You must at once drop this unworkable notion
> Of the coercion of Ulster.
> The disaffection of the army is too high a price to pay.
> Defend your wretched policy, if you must, some other way!
> But if the honour of British officers like dishwater is to be slopped
>   about and spilt
> The Conservative opposition will back them to the hilt.

He goes out arm-in-arm with WILSON.

Asquith (*after a pause, formally*) In order to prevent the possibility of the
spread of mutual violence, the Army will not be moved into the Province
of Ulster. Take the Navy away too. Ask the Secretary of War to resign.

Exit SECRETARY.

Churchill and Redmond But – but – but – –

Asquith (*confidentially*) But what are we going to do about this gun-running, eh?

> Surely my dear fellows, that is simple enough.
> If General Gough
> Refuses to fight
> And General Paget
> Continues to dodge it
> Then we find Sir Edward Carson and his military might
> Without any enemy without any war
> Are going to look as foolish as a doorknob with no door.
> Redmond – where are you going?

Redmond To take counsel with my people!

Exit REDMOND.

War Demon

> Blood, blood, blood and the first of the deeds is done –

Enter SECRETARY.

Secretary

> The guns are run!
> To the port of Larne near Belfast town –
> Ulster gentry of high renown,
> Brookes and Craigs, O'Neills and Chichesters
> Have hauled them all in Rolls Royce cars
> Into every village and outlying farm
> Where the rumble of the Orange drum
> Presages surely, sir, a dreadful storm –

Churchill

> I have no choice but to resign.

Asquith No Winston, I think not.

> Upon the cloth we draw another line
> And cut accordingly a well-shaped coat –
> Where's Redmond?

Churchill

> He went out.

Asquith So fetch him back –

> REDMOND *surprises him by returning at the opposite side from that where he made his departure.*

> Ah, Redmond, the ship of state is about to tack!
> What did your people tell you?

Redmond An absolutely unanimous demand from all quarters that government at once withdraw the proclamation prohibiting the import of arms into Ireland. Twenty thousand rifles have been unloaded at Larne. One hundred and thirty thousand rifles are required in Dublin, now!

Asquith It is a mockery of the law to permit lethal weapons to be put into the hands of an *irregular* force.

Redmond Then allow me to make it *regular*. If I can promise the National Volunteers that their guns may be obtained legally, then tit-for-tat, they must permit me as chairman of the parliamentary party to nominate enough new members to their executive council to ensure that control of the use of these rifles remains firmly in the hands of the government in Dublin.

Asquith There isn't one.

Redmond But there will be: Home Rule is due to be passed in –

He catches ASQUITH *and* CHURCHILL *exchanging a meaning look.*

Wait a moment, what the devil have you two been up to?

Asquith If your tit-for-tat for legalised weapons is control of the Volunteers, my tit-for-tat for allowing it will be an amendment to the bill.

Redmond I knew it! Partition...!

Asquith You've always sworn to your people you would never accept it: now perhaps you'll have to.

War Demon

       Sir Edward Carson, orange and black,
       Keeps his rigid mind on one fierce track –

Enter CARSON.

Carson Sir Edward Carson will never accept partition. Complete union of all Ireland with Great Britain or nothing. No surrender.

Asquith Abhorrent to both of you – but there *are* certain advantages...

Churchill (*to* CARSON) Protestants in a permanent majority in your parliament...

To REDMOND:

Roman Catholics in a permanent majority in *your* parliament. .... Won't it solve so many difficulties...?

Redmond I am not supposed to even admit the possibility of partition...

Carson If it could be achieved in two minutes, yes...

Redmond But it can't. Look at the map.

Carson The Londonderry Bogside, the Falls Road of Belfast, Newry, Armagh...

Redmond Fermanagh, Tyrone . . . How the hell can I sell such a goose and partridge fruitcake to the electorate, will you answer me!

Asquith You do not have to sell it yet.
       Indeed you'd best keep it under your hat.
       Of course it will all take time –
       The population must be reassured,

> The boundary must be surveyed,
> There'll be royal commissions, referenda . . .

Redmond
> The implementation of the whole bill will be delayed!

Asquith Delay the bill
> And thereby cool
> The passions and the bloodlust and the hate –
> We wait and see
> And soon or late
> The bill will suit
> Both you and me. . .
> In the meantime go and set your snares
> To gain control of the Volunteers.

Exit REDMOND.

Carson Pshaw! No Surrender!

Exit CARSON, *and* CHURCHILL, *and* SECRETARY, *severally.*

Asquith So Redmond goes to Dublin; and he'll be messing it all about.
> Not one single puzzle in this Irish box of tricks
> That ever yet came right!
> I build, I build my little pile of bricks
> And always some damnfool will knock them down –
> O thundercloud of death
> Bring fire, bring fire, bring roaring gouts of rain!

War Demon
> Before you can take breath
> You may well wish you had those words
> Safe back inside your brain.

Exit ASQUITH.

SCENE 9

Enter 1ST SUBSIDIARY DEMON *with a pistol.*

1st Subsidiary Demon In Sarajevo here is the gun.

Enter 2ND SUBSIDIARY DEMON *leading* PRINCIP.

2nd Subsidiary Demon
> In Sarajevo here is the man.

War Demon
> Connect the two together and then wait:

The gun is put into PRINCIP'*s hand by the* DEMONS, *and he is set waiting on an eminence at one side of the stage.*

The Archduke's carriage also waits
At the station for the Archduke's train ...

The SUBSIDIARY DEMONS *sit at* PRINCIP'*s feet. The* WAR DEMON *retires.*

SCENE 10

Enter an assembly of NATIONAL VOLUNTEERS. *To them, enter* REDMOND.

Redmond I ask for no more than twenty-five men upon your executive committee, who will be my nominees and responsible to the party.

1st Volunteer I support Mr Redmond. We are badly in need of full recognition and the strongest influence in high places.

3rd Volunteer I support Mr Redmond.

4th Volunteer I support Mr Redmond.

2nd Volunteer (*IRB man*) I protest. The Volunteers are a non-party or indeed all-party patriotic organisation.

Redmond Votes? In favour of my request. . . Unanimous? Amazing. My nominees, then, I take it, are accepted upon the committee.

2nd Volunteer You have your vote, sir. And now, sir, the legalisation of the import of guns?

Redmond Ah . . . A source close to the Prime Minister has intimated that the lifting of the proclamation will be considered very very carefully in a favourable light ...

General growls of discontent, and the meeting breaks up. CLARKE *comes out of the back of the crowd and takes* 2ND VOLUNTEER *aside as the others leave the stage.*

Clarke   Asquith will cheat
As Asquith cheats ever.
We bring in our own guns
Let them stand and deliver.

I have the message from Germany. Childers has got hold of fifteen hundred rifles and –

2nd Volunteer Good God, is that all?

Clarke That's all. Would you send them back ...? He brings them into Howth on the twenty-sixth. In his yacht. We arrange a rural route march for the Dublin Volunteers. They're to be eating their sandwiches upon the end of Howth pier at twelve-thirty on the dot. Didn't I tell you, in the end, the whole business would have to be managed through the Brotherhood?

Exeunt CLARKE *and* 2ND VOLUNTEER. *The three* DEMONS *beat a rhythm.*

Princip Death to the Archduke ... I have sworn it for Serbia ... I have sworn it for my Brotherhood ... Bosnia is part of Serbia ... Sarajevo is in Bosnia ... Sarajevo in Bosnia is ruled over by the Austrians ... Death.

SCENE 11

Enter CONNOLLY *and sits down at a table.*

Connolly In Belfast I, James Connolly, my ears filled with the tramp of
      soldiers,
      Reconstruct in weary carefulness the rubble and broken boulders
      Of my union, brought down from an aspiring tower to a sprawled
      heap
      In a field . . . Great Babel of the Bible had ended in no more hopeful
      shape . . .
I do not propose to answer this invitation to speak to a gathering of
British trade-union leaders. Let them obtain their speakers from the
heads of those loyalist unions who kept the port of Belfast open when
my people were shot down by armed scabs in the streets of Dublin.

Devlin (*voice off*) Connolly – where's Jim Connolly? I want a word with that
man!

Enter DEVLIN'S HENCHMAN.

Henchman Mr Connolly, it's Wee Joe Devlin of the Belfast branch of the
Nationalist Party – he's here, sir, he wants a word.

Enter DEVLIN.

Devlin Aye, I've come here. It's a wonder you took no heed of my message to
come to *my* place to see *me*.

Henchman It's a wonder ye took no heed – when Wee Joe sends a message –

Devlin Shut your mouth, Mick, I do the talking . . . Oh we're too big, we're too
proud, we take messages from nobody? So be it. But your strike died –
and why? Don't tell me: I'm telling *you*. You had nothing to offer good
catholic folk but your godless German socialism! The holding of women
in common, that's what . . . You have attacked me on public platforms as
an advocate of partition.

Connolly Advocate be damned. Ye never advocated in your life. *Connived* at
it, that's all!

Devlin Now you listen to me – –

Connolly No. I am in my office. Here, you will hear *me*!

Devlin Partition deprives Ireland of that God-given territorial heritage which –

Connolly Partition gives you power. The only question left in London is
whether Ulster is to be nine counties or six or inbetween. Whichever they
choose in the end, it'll be hire, fire, fix and patronage for Wee Joe Devlin
in his ghetto – ambitious though you may be, it'll be more than enough to
stay your stomach. Man, I'm seven years in America – don't you think I
don't know you!

Devlin Is that a fact? Well, I know *this*! Upon the eleventh of July every pillar
box and lamp standard was plastered with this leaflet alleging that King
Billy of the Boyne was a papist in disguise!

Connolly (*as the leaflet is flapped under his nose*) You should read it; that's not what it says.

Devlin Your socialists put it up.

Connolly Of course we put it up. Politically it suited the Pope to give thanks for the victory of the Boyne, which he construed as a Dutch victory against the imperialism of France, to which he was hostile. A perfectly accurate small lesson in history. I'm surprised you should be so furious at it.

Devlin It confuses my catholic people.

Connolly You mean it informs them.

He takes the leaflet from DEVLIN *and gives it to the* HENCHMAN.

Here – you: read this – learn!

DEVLIN *snatches the leaflet back.*

> You do not dare to have him read it.
> You do not dare to believe
> That the poorest, most stupid, most superstitious man
> Has none the less a brain.
> For if you recognise that, you must also recognise
> That the day will shortly come
> When two and two do not make five.
> When your people, as you call them,
> Add them up and at last find *four*,
> Your entire Hibernian Saints' Parade
> Will for ever be kicked out at the door.

So get along with you and march with them. This morning, you're wasting my time.

Devlin I am against partition. You are against partition. Let you hold your meetings on that subject in my territory, I'll pack the hall to smash your platform and the legs of any man that has the nerve to try and stand on it.

He goes out.

Henchman Wee Joe says he'll smash your legs.

Exit. The DEMONS *beat out a sudden flourish.*

Princip Bones have been broken . . . Skin ripped and flesh burnt . . . Cripples have been made as a potter will make vases, in the prisons of the Austrian Empire . . . Death.

Henchman Mr Connolly, I'm a trade unionist and I stand for solidarity.

Connolly Splendid.

Henchman I have no truck with the church when it interferes with politics. But with Wee Joe, ye see, he's different. Didn't he organise the defence of our street off the Falls when the orange mobs were in it with their swabs of burning petrol? Didn't he expose for me the crooked fiddling that went on in the City Hall to keep my da from his proper pension? Look, when the strike was on in Dublin, me and the lads came down for some of the action – and weren't the priests making a holy show over the wee children that went to England? I said to this curate: 'What business is it of yours where the weans are being put to, seeing they don't belong to you?' Why, he ground his teeth like ratchets!

Connolly Oh he did? And because you were once rude to a priest you believe you can establish yourself my jackal at the same time as you are Wee Joe's?

Sure, that curate was a bigot.

But he thought he did his duty.

Whereas, away from home, you felt safe when you did not.

The test is, in Belfast, do you ask them can they outline

The number of *protestant* pensions diverted by Devlin's machine?

And in Dublin, the test was, to go to the bishops and say:

'Fathers, what have you done to see that these children are fed?'

Go on, get away:

Your dishonesty swells in my head!

Henchman

Wee Joe is right and you are wrong.

Too big, too proud to live here long.

Trade unionists belong

In a good catholic union controlled by their own

Where they eat the bread of God, not your foreign socialist stone ...

Exit.

Connolly As ever in the streets of this sectarian city

You are orange, you are green,

Either way you have your 'own'

To hide and slide with and pursue your need.

If not, you are worse than nothing, condemned by both –

No remedy: no pity.

For this union, so strong only three years ago –

Dear goodness, out of all this appalling waste paper can I dig one word of hope ...?

He busies himself with his documents.

SCENE 12

War Demon

In Dublin County at the Pier of Howth

They gather waiting waiting for the boat:

The boat comes in, the guns are handed out –

The sober Sunday broken with a shout –

Cheers heard, off.

> And so with high delighted mind
> Through empty lanes they make their way –
> No-one to stop them, bloodless and unbound ...

Enter VOLUNTEERS, *marching with rifles. The* WAR DEMON *beats his drum.*

2nd Volunteer (*from earlier scene: he stands at side and narrates*)
> The police indeed were so amazed
> The police had been so blind
> That the march of the rifles from Howth
> Was not stopped till we came to Clontarf
> And there at Clontarf the assistant commissioner
> Gave somebody for some reason a piece of his mind.

Enter POLICE OFFICER *and halts the column.*

Police Officer I insist that these weapons, which are illegal, must be surrendered.

Volunteer Officer (*at head of column*) At the same time, the same place as the twenty thousand rifles which were brought in last month for the Ulster Loyalist Volunteers at Larne?

All rifles are handed back down the column: and vanish. He checks to see that none are left in sight: and then turns back to POLICE OFFICER.

Weapons, did you say?... Now what weapons?... Please be so good as to permit us to continue our legal and recreative Sunday afternoon march.

Princip The whole world is under arms for the maintenance of tyranny – why should not the tyrannised possess their own protection ...?

The POLICE OFFICER *stands back, baffled. The march continues.*

2nd Volunteer (*sings*)
> So we marched on down
> Through Dublin town
> And the column grew small
> And smaller yet.
> The police spread out
> And they thronged all about
> And they called for the soldiers
> To spread the net.

As they march, members of the column shed away from the rear, till only the VOLUNTEER OFFICER *is left. He salutes the* POLICE OFFICER *and walks quietly away with* 2ND VOLUNTEER. *Meanwhile, a* CROWD OF CIVILIANS *has filled up the stage, they are jeering at the* POLICE OFFICER. *Enter, hurriedly, an* ARMY OFFICER *and* SOLDIERS.

Police Officer (*to* ARMY OFFICER) No indeed I did not send for you – your presence here is most illegal. But now that you *are* here, you can make yourselves useful – all these rifles in the outskirts of the city – a tactical search operation – don't you see, turn everything over – have your men split up with mine into small groups and go everywhere . . .

Army Officer We are not exactly trained for that sort of operation. I think we had better leave it to you. In the meantime, if you like, we could overawe the crowd? Are they armed?

Police Officer Somebody is.

Exit.

Army Officer (*to his men*) Load your rifles. Assume a grim demeanour. MacTavish, I'm talking to you. Wipe that nervous grin off your face, boy. My God, this is not funny!

The SOLDIERS *start marching, and the* CROWD *gathers around them, hampering them and mocking. The* ARMY OFFICER *sings*:

And so we marched to Bachelor's Walk
The crowd around began to talk
Began to talk, began to sing
Until we came to the river's brim.

The SOLDIERS *have marched right to the edge of the stage and can go no further. One by one they turn to face the* CROWD.

If we marched any more we'd be into the tide
There was no room on either side
The crowd around began to roar
At the soldiers who could march no more.
If you're jammed up tight against the wall
And you have no choice but fight or fall
And a loaded gun is in your hand –
How long in patience will you stand?

One of the SOLDIERS *fires his rifle. A* CIVILIAN *falls. There is sudden dead silence. Then a roar of anger. More shots from the other* SOLDIERS. *The* CROWD *screams and scrambles for safety. The* SOLDIERS *make their escape. The* SUBSIDIARY DEMONS *mix in the confusion, swirling all round the stage.*

At the opposite side from PRINCIP, *the* ARCHDUKE – *a gloriously-uniformed dummy – is hauled up on the end of a line and hangs facing across at* PRINCIP.

Princip Death to the Archduke!

PRINCIP *rushes across the stage and shoots the* ARCHDUKE – *the dummy falls. The whole of this episode is very rapid: and the deaths must appear almost simultaneous. There is a great noise of percussion. The* WAR DEMON *takes the centre of the stage – in the midst of a frozen tableau of death. He screams.*

Connolly (*still at his table, out of the action*)

> Three were killed and thirty hurt
> And the rest ran away through the Dublin dirt.
> The soldiers who had done this deed
> Were those who at their country's need
> Refused to march on their kith and kin.
> But now at last they are men again.
> They have shot and they have killed
> And the promise of their uniform has been fulfilled.

War Demon (*indicates* PRINCIP)

> He has shot and he has killed
> And the promise of his Brotherhood has been fulfilled.
> August nineteen hundred and fourteen
> The greatest war the world has ever seen.

All round the auditorium, NATIONAL VOLUNTEERS *appear, running with bundles of rifles, and handing them on excitedly to others.* BOYS *and* GIRLS *of the Fianna (if convenient) marshalled by the* COUNTESS MARKIEVICZ, *race up and down collecting the weapons.*

Volunteers (*severally*) These are for Cork – Limerick here – Galway – take this lot to Waterford – Wexford – Sligo – Mullingar – the Connemara men will want these – all these for the Dublin Battalions – I said *all* of them for Dublin – you're not to let them fellers from Athlone get their hands on them – *etc., etc.* . . .

Countess Markievicz Two hundred and fifty – three hundred, with that lot there – no, I can't let you have a dozen, they are to be looked after in a *safe* place, do you hear me – silly boy, they are not playthings! Belfast – what about Belfast – where's Nora Connolly – Nora! All these are for the Citizen Army, and these –

NORA CONNOLLY *comes up to her, as a Fianna-girl.*

Can you and your sister take the train to Belfast and give these to your father – I don't believe anyone will be bothered about two girls – but if they ask any questions remember your training – you'll have learnt enough to baffle them. Lose no time . . .

NORA *takes the bundle of guns, wrapped up in a blanket or tent-cover, and runs in and out to reach* CONNOLLY – *she hands him the guns.*

Connolly At innumerable socialist conferences, notably Stuttgart in nineteen hundred and seven and Basel in nineteen twelve, resolutions were passed proclaiming that no interests of the people can serve to justify war waged for the sake of profits, the ambitions of dynasties, the power of the ruling class. I am confident that the international socialist movement will unite throughout Europe to prevent inconceivable holocaust . . .

Exit. The stage rapidly empties.   **END OF ACT 1**

ACT 2: 'World War to Civil War'

SCENE 1

A landscape devastated by war – broken trees and buildings, wrecked vehicles, dead men and horses, etc. (Backcloth 4).

Liberty Hall in the midst of the Dublin dockland, the river on one side, the Custom House on the other (Backcloth 9).

Enter CONNOLLY. *He takes his place at his table (with a label over it reading 'ITWU Belfast'). He works at his writing. As he speaks, the* WAR DEMON *paces slowly around the stage.*

Connolly The movement towards war on the continent of Europe makes it impossible this week to write for my newspaper upon any other question. I have no doubt that to most of my readers Ireland has ere now ceased to be, in colloquial phraseology, the most important place on the map: and that your thoughts must be turning gravely to a consideration of the position of European socialism in the face of this crisis – the whole working-class movement stands committed to war upon war – and stands so committed at the very height of its strength and influence...

> Example, Germany: the civilisation of philosophy and ordered
> thought
> Whence Engels and Karl Marx between them both have brought
> Throughout the whole wide world the truth we now pursue,
> The paradise we look for, the dawn we greet, the due
> Deliverance by means of science for every living human creature –
> Inconceivable the German workers can repudiate their own class-
> nature...

Enter GERMAN SOCIAL DEMOCRATS. *During the ensuing episodes the* WAR DEMON *and* SUBSIDIARY DEMONS *hang up, busily and silently, recruiting posters and mobilisation orders at the back and sides of the stage.*

1st German Social Democrat The German Social Democratic Party immediately undertakes active propaganda against the imminent threat of war.

2nd German Social Democrat I propose we send a deputation to the French Socialist Party in Paris, assuring them of our firm intention to stand by the resolutions of the Second International.

Enter 1ST EMPLOYER (*as a German*).

Connolly Example, France: from the first great revolution to the Paris
Commune
For liberty, fraternity, each red bonnet flies over the moon.

Inconceivable they should not now recognise the enormous
urgency: it is now their *turn*!

Enter FRENCH SOCIALISTS.

1st Employer (*to* GERMANS) The threat of war against the fatherland comes not
from France but from the east – Russia: the breeding-pit of reactionary
autocracy and despotism!

German Social Democrats We stand firm by the Second International!

Ignoring 1ST EMPLOYER, *they greet the* FRENCH *with mutual effusiveness.*

1st French Socialist Liberty equality fraternity – we expose the blatant false-
hoods of the capitalist warmongers!

Enter 2ND EMPLOYER (*as a Frenchman*).

Connolly Example, Britain: the chief trade unions have already declared a
general strike:
Inconceivable these men can follow the road that their rulers would
take...

Enter BRITISH TRADE-UNION LEADERS.

2nd Employer (*to* FRENCH) German militarism has consistently plotted to continue the shameful conquest of French territory of half a century ago – we
must once again defend the integrity of our soil and recapture the lands
lost to the Prussians in eighteen seventy.

French Socialists We stand firm by the Second International and the revolution of ninety eight and the revolution of eighty one!

The BRITISH *greet both the* FRENCH *and the* GERMANS.

1st British TU Leader It's nothing but a load of East European nonsense: if
Austria and Serbia want to have a conflagration, there is absolutely no
reason why any of us should be dragged in: we've far better things to
attend to. Let's get on with it.

The three groups all cheer.

Enter 3RD EMPLOYER (*as an Englishman*).

Connolly So far it will be observed
They will hold to it good and hard:
How long before expedient argument
Robs all of them of their intent?
The year nineteen hundred, I remember it too well
How Millerand and his confederates were ready to sell
Every principle in the book for one small place and token
Of acceptance by the capitalists ... Are we always so easily broken?
God help us, I hope not: but in Dublin they throttled our throat...

2nd Employer (*to the* BRITISH) The root cause of the whole thing is the fundamental jealousy of German business interests towards the prosperity of the British Empire. The Kaiser of course is not interested in Serbia – he looks towards Suez, and beyond Suez towards India.

British TU Leaders We will not be diverted from our struggle for the living wage!

The groups of socialists stand rigid, propping each other up – the FRENCH *lean on the* GERMANS *and the* BRITISH *lean on the* FRENCH, *while the* EM-PLOYERS *run round them with insinuating slogans:*

1st Employer Russia – autocracy – despotism – Russia –
2nd Employer Germany – militarism – eighteen seventy – Alsace-Lorraine –
3rd Employer Germany – the British Empire – the prosperity of India – Africa – Canada – Australia ... *etc.*

The WAR DEMON *beats his drum.* DIPLOMATS *and uniformed* OFFICERS *scurry in and out across the stage, whispering, muttering – rhythmical exclamations from the* SUBSIDIARY DEMONS.

Connolly How long can they hold firm while the whole of Europe can now hear
The rumble of the troop trains and the clicking down every wire
Of the telegraph to call together the reservists from far and near –
The movement of men and the awakening of old alliance,
Sleeping treaties new-invoked, ultimata, defiance –

From Austria to Serbia, from Russia back to Austria, from Germany to Russia, from France suddenly called upon by Russia to Germany, from Germany to Belgium, from Britain suddenly called upon by Belgium to Germany ... my God: we are at war.

SCENE 2

The WAR DEMON *suddenly breaks off with a final clash of his drum. Dead silence and everyone freezes. The propped-up huddle of socialists remains in a precarious position, just balanced, and teetering.*

War Demon
At war according to the proper protocol:
The declarations pass from hand to hand and so into the file:
Ambassadors pack their baggage, close their doors, depart.
The last act of the old diplomacy: the last chance of a second
thought.

The DIPLOMATS *slip away. The* OFFICERS *remain, and are joined, on the one side by the* KAISER, *on the other by* ASQUITH.

1st German Social Democrat (*after a pause*) Nevertheless, we do accept that a defensive war against Russia and therefore against her allies is essential for the preservation of the socialist movement in Germany.

Kaiser The subhuman hordes of Tartary now sweep across Europe. Are you prepared to vote war-credits to my Government?

2nd German Social Democrat We reserve to ourselves the objective political right to overthrow the German Empire by proletarian revolution once Czarism has been defeated. In the context of that perspective we are prepared to vote war-credits.

German General (*to* KAISER, *confidentially*) It is now possible, All-highest, to move our troops into Belgium for the attack upon France.

Exeunt KAISER *and his* STAFF, *with German* SOCIAL DEMOCRATS *stooped obsequiously before them. As a result, the French* SOCIALISTS *collapse.*

1st French Socialist Objectively we must accept that the German Socialist Party has become an active accomplice in the imperialist schemes of the German General Staff.

2nd French Socialist For the preservation of the French Revolutionary Republic it is incumbent upon proletarians to take up arms for the defence of France.

The FRENCH SOCIALISTS *hurry out, leaving the* BRITISH TU LEADERS *to collapse in their turn.*

1st British TU Leader If the neutrality of Belgium has been violated with the treacherous support of the German labour movement, we realise our own best interests might well have to give way to an issue of principle.

Asquith The principle of international agreements arrived at by a sovereign government which includes representatives of the Parliamentary Labour Party.

2nd British TU Leader Right. And in that context: where does the government stand upon employment, wage-rates, and conditions of work in a state of hostilities?

Asquith In return for the voluntary repudiation of industrial disruption, we are happy to guarantee that the coal-mines, railways, docks and all other industries of national importance, will come virtually under state ownership – with trade union representatives given seats alongside the employers and alongside government officials upon every board of control. And a guaranteed minimum wage. And a guaranteed cabinet portfolio for certain members of the Labour Party. I call upon Mr Lloyd George to amplify my benevolent pledge.

Enter LLOYD GEORGE.

Lloyd George I would describe this benevolent pledge as a charter for labour! The most radical measure ever taken by a British government, opening up a great new chapter in the history of labour in its relations with the state. And dependent upon no coercion, but the voluntary agreement to hold all wage disputes over for the duration of hostilities.

Asquith Which will not be very long.

Aside to LLOYD GEORGE.

To be on the safe side, we will reserve compulsory powers.

Lloyd George (*aside*) In point of fact *draconian* powers – to be on the safe side.

To TU LEADERS:

Well?

1st TU Leader Well . . .! My word, Mr Asquith – with one stroke of your pen you have turned the whole country half-socialist!

2nd TU Leader Why, we never expected this – no, not in our wildest dreams . . .

Exeunt TU LEADERS, *with* LLOYD GEORGE, *leaving* ASQUITH *with* GENERAL WILSON *and an* ADMIRAL. *The latter begin to dance to a new rhythm played by the* WAR DEMON, *short sharp stamping steps at first, on either side of* ASQUITH.

Connolly No not in my wildest dreams – ! These feet these feet
Are left alone to beat
Our faces into pulp and blood and broken bits of bone . . .
What will this do to Ireland? No that's not true –
The question now, is what will Ireland do?
Can they in Westminster so soon forget
Last week in Dublin three good men were shot –
No, they remember, and they take their time:
Into their murderous scheme
They fit
Each little bit:
And shape, they hope
A world that will hold no more hope . . .

SCENE 3

ASQUITH *clumsily begins to dance as well.*

War Demon (*sings*)
Now at last your chance –
All your burdens now are lifted
These foolish feet have drifted
Into one great glorious dance – !

Enter BONAR LAW, *dancing to the same steps, but vigorously.*

Bonar Law
It is the dance of war!
Where in chaos and confusion
Every Liberal illusion
Will never be heard of more!

War Demon (*sings*)
>> Blood blood blood...

Asquith (*sings*)
>> I am now a national leader
>> The Conservative is my brother
>> And unity is the mood!
>
> Mr Bonar Law, sir, your hand.

The dance stops.

Bonar Law (*shaking hands*) So long as the experience of the General Staff is permitted to prevail, the Conservative Party will accede to all decisions taken by the cabinet in connection with the prosecution of the war.

WILSON *whispers in his ear.*

But I warn you – if things get difficult, we shall press for a coalition.

Exeunt WILSON *and* ADMIRAL.

And I warn you, we are not satisfied with trade-union leaders upon industrial boards of control –

Asquith They will be brought into line by compulsory powers. No problem.

Bonar Law There are other local difficulties –

Enter MIDDLE-CLASS SUFFRAGETTE.

Suffragette Votes for Women! If you don't give the women the vote, we shall boycott the war.

Asquith You don't *want* to boycott the war?

Suffragette On the contrary: we are eager to play our full part in it alongside our gallant men.

Asquith If that's what you want the vote for, madam, you can most certainly have it! All ladies at present in prison will be instantly let out, and I give my solemn promise that female suffrage will be brought in before the next general election – provided I have *your* promise that you will not force a general election before the war has been won...?

This last question to BONAR LAW, *as* ASQUITH *turns away from* SUFFRAGETTE.

Thank you very much, madam – we're getting along famously: next problem, if you please?

Suffragette (*on her way out*) England at long last has proved true to her destiny! I shall rip up an old bolster: and every young man not in uniform shall receive one white feather...!

Exit.

Bonar Law Next problem.
Asquith Next problem.

Connolly (*as they pause, and look away from each other*)
>The next problem will be *my* problem: I well understand
>They can find no solution but black treachery on every hand.

Bonar Law
>I will repeat once more and never again, the Irish Home Rule Act
>Will never be accepted as a fact
>By Ulster: and if the heart of Ulster now should fail
>There is no chance this nation can prevail
>Against the furious discipline of German power.

Enter CARSON.

Carson Sir Edward Carson, speaking for
>Each loyal Ulster Volunteer,
>Desires at once to make it clear
>That to a man we'll fight the German war –
>Provided that Home Rule at once is dropped!

Asquith The Bill is passed: it cannot be revoked.
>Postponed, perhaps: but would not that provoke –

Re-enter WILSON.

Wilson Reinforcement of rebel sentiment in the catholic two-thirds of Ireland? Oh yes. What the deuce are those provinces good for but to supply us with soldiers? If the nationalists in Dublin are allowed to believe that very shortly they may determine their own destiny, why on earth should they risk their lives for us? Home Rule should be abandoned altogether, Prime Minister: the Conservatives agree with me.

Exit WILSON. *Re-enter* ADMIRAL.

Admiral Naval bases on the south-west coast of Ireland are essential to the survival of Britain. Any suggestion that one day that coast will no longer be *our* coast will seriously endanger the security of the bases. Home Rule should be abandoned altogether, Prime Minister: the Conservatives agree with me.

Exit ADMIRAL. *Enter* MRS ASQUITH.

Mrs Asquith
>The only means you can be sure of Irish bodies and Irish land
>Is to have John Redmond deliver them over of his own free will and
>   generous hand.
>Today is the day for all men to make war:
>Keep out of this, my dear, stand over by the door –
>Your faithful wife will do the best she may
>To make not war but peace, and that in her own sweet way . . .

She nods and winks at BONAR LAW, *who takes the hint and slips out.*

Call him.

Asquith Redmond, my dear fellow – the lady is waiting!

> ASQUITH *admits* REDMOND *after the style of a brothel janitor.* MRS ASQUITH *disposes herself seductively.*

Redmond

Madam, the kingdom's parliament has passed the Home Rule Act:
I beseech you use all your efforts to make sure that it takes effect!

Mrs Asquith

And I beseech you that you will not neglect
The magnanimous character of the people of this realm.
Consider the huge gratitude that would at once overwhelm
Every problem that lies between us, should you today declare
That the gallant aspirations of each National Volunteer
Would be totally devoted to the liberty of us all
In the teeth of the German threat! Sir, respond to my call –
Offer your troops without condition to my husband, to the King,
To myself even – Mr Redmond you would bring
Such reward from this nation for your heroic sacrifice
That not one man in the whole of England would withhold from
you your price...!

Redmond (*suffused by her ardour*)

You mean after the war, Home Rule, confirmed –
But what about partition...?

Mrs Asquith

Assuredly that condition
Would no longer be of account:
Mr Redmond, this is a peoples' war:
The wellbeing of all people must alone be paramount.

Redmond We the Irish are men of principle: I want a statement of principle that we are involved in a foreign war on account of –

Asquith (*involuntarily interrupts*) Belgium!

Mrs Asquith (*gestures her husband to silence*) *Catholic* Belgium...

Redmond Now that would be the principle of the right of self-determination for small neutral nations – it wouldn't be altogether out of place to apply it locally ... Mrs Asquith, whatever possessed the man that he never got you do to his business for him before – sure the lion would lie down with the lamb for one dimple of the roses in your beautiful cheeks –

Mrs Asquith (*sharply*) Home Rule after the war, Redmond: goodbye – go and make your speech!

> *He gets up guiltily from her bosom and advances nervously downstage – stops to think a second, clears his throat – addresses the* AUDIENCE.

Redmond My speech ... I must make my speech ...

We offer to the government they may take their troops out of Ireland,

> and that, if it is allowed us, in comradeship with our brethren in the north...

Mrs Asquith (*collusive to* ASQUITH, *on their way out*) Tell that to Carson!

Redmond

> ... We, the volunteers, will defend the coasts of our own country, against all enemies of the British Empire!

> Now, how do you think the Irish newspapers are going to take that?

SCENE 4

Connolly *The Irish Worker* – the one newspaper for which I am prepared to
>   speak –
>   Will take it as all capitalist hysteria should be took.
>   Within one month all Europe lost its wits
>   Within four years half Europe was destroyed:
>   I intend to stay alive and I intend to keep my head.
>   My socialist pen is in my hand
>   My rebel rifle underneath my bed.
>   I let the pen speak first:
>   It said –
> 'Ruling by fooling is a great British art, with great Irish fools to practise it on! The signal for war should have been the signal for rebellion: and the National Volunteers should have been the first to respond to it!' Instead of which they –

Enter a number of VOLUNTEERS, *who divide into two groups, noisily. The larger group stands by* REDMOND: *the smaller is clustered on the opposite side with* MACNEILL.

MacNeil They split! For Redmond and his proposal to devote the Volunteers to the defence of the British Empire – one hundred and eighty-eight thousand have offered themselves. Myself, Eoin MacNeill, opposing this decision, received support from no more than twelve thousand.

Enter WILSON *and goes up to* REDMOND.

Wilson (*prompts* REDMOND) The situation is now grave.

Redmond The situation is now so grave, that I do not think it right to confine the services of the Volunteers to home-defence only!

His VOLUNTEERS *cheer.*

D'you hear, sir, they give three cheers.

He hands WILSON *a green banner which one of his* VOLUNTEERS *has brought him.*

This banner, sir, is yours, to set forward at their head in the forefront of the hardest battle. Sir, my own son takes his rifle and prepares to march.

Wilson Lord Kitchener is most sensible of your very gallant offer – but this damned flag won't do, you know – put it away – it's a rebel flag – shan't have it.

He tosses the flag back to REDMOND.

Redmond But the Ulster Volunteers have been permitted their own flag . . .

Wilson These people of yours are not sound and never have been. We'll split the battalions up, put them under British officers, have them marched at once to commence their basic training – from the very beginning, mind! Bogmen . . . don't know left foot from right . . . March!

A SUBSIDIARY DEMON *in a soldier's helmet marches the* MEN *off with a great deal of screaming and yelling.*

Subsidiary Demons
> The war, the war, now forward to the war
> And reap the reward of glory and gore . . . !

REDMOND *goes off with them.* MACNEILL *and his* VOLUNTEERS *remain behind, in a despondent huddle at one side.*

SCENE 5

Connolly (*with reference to* MACNEILL *and companions*)
> Some few small voices so, which may be raised
> Against this lunacy . . . in Ireland raised . . . alone . . . ?
> I look across the world in my despair and find –

War Demon
> Some few small voices petulantly raised
> Against what history alone has done:
> The men of destiny of this great world
> Can shut and muffle them one by one . . .

Enter LIEBKNECHT, KEIR HARDIE, ROSA LUXEMBURG, MACLEAN, JAURÈS, *and* LENIN. ASQUITH *enters on one side and the* KAISER *on the other.*

Liebknecht In Germany, Karl Liebknecht, socialist deputy and undaunted opponent of militarism, has accused the Social Democrats of being seduced by political fraud to vote funds for the Kaiser's war.

War Demon That voice for a start –

Kaiser Conscript him for war service.

SUBSIDIARY DEMON *in a soldier's helmet, leads* LIEBKNECHT *away.*

Keir Hardie In Britain, Keir Hardie, pioneer member of the Parliamentary Labour Party, denounces the alliance with reactionary Czarist Russia.

War Demon That voice. Muffle it. Quick . . . !

Asquith You have already been told our ally is plucky little Belgium!

Keir Hardie There's no doubt it does depend upon which way it is looked at . . .

> SUBSIDIARY DEMON *gives him a pair of spectacles and a war poster. Peering through the glasses at the poster,* KEIR HARDIE *goes out.*

Rosa Luxemburg In Germany, Rosa Luxemburg, socialist agitator and delegate to the Second International, continues to publish her clandestine newspaper – read *Die Internationale* – buy *Die Internationale* – the only paper in Germany to oppose the imperialist war!

War Demon Muffle that voice!

Kaiser Put her in prison!

> SUBSIDIARY DEMON *in a police helmet arrests her and takes her out.*

MacLean John MacLean, Glasgow labour leader, agitates all down the Clyde for political strike in opposition to the war.

War Demon You need more than a Liberal argument to successfully muffle him. What about your draconian powers?

Asquith If he goes on any longer, we shall serve him with an order to deport him from Clydeside to an ineffective rural residence – I don't want to have to do it yet – but –

MacLean I take occasion to express my complete solidarity with James Connolly and the Irish cause. Man, they sold ye down the river in the lockout last winter – but all Clydeside stood with you – with you and Big Jim Larkin!

Asquith Censor his utterances in the national press!

> SUBSIDIARY DEMON *in a bowler hat snatches away the script for* MACLEAN'*s statement and runs off the stage, pursued in vain by* MACLEAN.

Jaurès In France, Jean Jaurès, leader of the French Socialist Party, reminds the labour movement of the international undertakings they had all put their names to – to resist by militant action all capitalist armed conflict –

War Demon This voice cannot be muffled – he is a *leader* of those socialists – it must be stopped and stopped now – *Messieurs les assassins, à Jaurès, s'il vous plaît!*

> SUBSIDIARY DEMON, *in a wide-brimmed hat and cloak, shoots Jaurès.*

Lenin The revolutionist V. I. Lenin
In Switzerland so far undisturbed
Puts forward his views on the war
To be translated and smuggled abroad:

It is almost universally admitted that this war is an imperialist war. Imperialism is the highest stage in the development of capitalism reached only in the twentieth century; capitalism now finds the old nation-states too cramped for it. Almost the entire globe has been divided up among the syndicates and trusts until we find that six great powers have grabbed twenty-five million square kilometres of land and enslaved five hundred and twenty-three million people in their colonies. Competitive conflict between these powers therefore . . .

Kaiser That voice among all voices –

Asquith Must be muffled and buried at once – he's a Russian ? We don't forget nineteen hundred and five . . .

Kaiser This war is a war between sovereign monarchies and constitutional republics : we cannot admit the possibility of anything else !

War Demon Don't worry, his voice is already well-muffled –

Asquith No it's not –

Kaiser I hear him muttering –

War Demon He's in Switzerland –

Kaiser and Asquith Ah . . .

> *The* KAISER *and* ASQUITH *go out, severally.* LENIN, *muttering over his notes, also leaves, in a different direction.*

Connolly He is in Switzerland and is not heard –
> I cock my ear to catch one further word –
> And there is –

War Demon
> Nothing. Silence. They have left you all alone
> In your far distant Irish corner where there is nothing that can be done . . .

> *The* SUBSIDIARY DEMONS *carry off* JAURÈS' *body.*

Connolly (*as the corpse is taken past him*) All hail to at least one continental comrade who showed mankind that men still know how to die for the holiest of all causes, the sanctity of the human soul, the practical brotherhood of the human race.

> *With a triumphant clanging and screaming, the* WAR DEMON *also goes out.*

SCENE 6

> CONNOLLY *sits writing at his table. He speaks furiously across towards* MACNEILL.

Connolly Nothing that can be done . . . ?
> There is everything that can be done
> And by no other men than these –
> The only organised group in Europe
> Who deliberately refuse
> The war the war, to go into the war –
> Sirs, do you dare commit
> Yourselves at once upon this wind that blows
> The whole world inside-out – ?

MacNeill Mr Connolly, I am a scholar and a patriot and – I hope – a man of some precision of thought: I must ask you in what direction you believe this wind to be travelling?

Connolly International war is disaster for the international working class, bringing death upon the battlefield, starvation in the home, slavery in the places of work. I foresee six months, nine months of unprecedented carnage, followed by a patched-up peace, followed by year after year of unemployment and misery in a devastated continent. Unless out of it, Professor MacNeill, we can drag hold of revolution. Oh revolution of some sort will inevitably arrive: but it won't work without we are ready for it, without we have already banded together the force and the intention to control it for its full potential. Under Larkin and myself the Irish Citizen Army – we have no more than one-twentieth the strength of your Volunteers, but we are representative of the whole of organised labour. Do you not see that together with you we could – –

MacNeill We are a constitutional, national-minded, responsible body, Mr Connolly, devoted only to the integrity and freedom of our beloved country. If I take you aright, sir, you are expecting us to foster some sort of repetition of last year's industrial violence?

Connolly It will not need to be *fostered*. I said it is inevitable. But the working people of Ireland will be on the receiving end of it unless we can –

MacNeill Unless you can strike first and do hurt to the Irish people, yes? The very function of these Volunteers is to *prevent* such an outrage. We want nothing to do with your divisive ideology, sir.

CONNOLLY *abruptly returns to his work with an explosive exclamation.* MACNEILL *is about to leave, when he is detained by a Volunteer* (PEARSE).

Pearse (*confidentially*) Mr MacNeill, if you do not look for revolution, just why do we remain here, in arms?

MacNeill I conceive, Mr Pearse, that when the British imperial war is ended, our undiluted power will be required to remind Westminster of their promise about Home Rule and our own aspirations towards an entire republic.

Another Volunteer (MACDERMOTT) But nothing until then?

MacNeill I do not at present anticipate the necessity. In the meantime we must accustom ourselves to vilification, not only from the socialists of Belfast, but also from those far closer to us, who only a few weeks ago seemed our blood-brothers to all eternity . . .

Enter a group of EMPLOYERS (*Irish*) *and a* PRIEST, *carrying placards with recruiting slogans – some of which they also post up round the stage. They assail the* VOLUNTEERS.

1st Employer The nuns of Louvain have been raped in their convent –

3rd Employer The priests of Louvain were tied to the clappers of the church bells and hammered to death for refusing to ring a peal to welcome in the German Army!

Priest How can you as catholic Irishmen remain indifferent to the horrors
    that are now wreaked upon catholic Belgium!
2nd Employer Illustrated history of the German atrocities – publishing rights
    to the Dublin edition now available at competitive prices!
Priest Does it have the *Imprimatur*?
2nd Employer (*dances and yells*)
        Imprimatur-stabat-mater
        In-excelsis-paracelsus
        The war, the war, now forward to the war
        And reap the reward of glory and gore – !

Exeunt PRIEST *and* EMPLOYERS *cavorting and whooping, as* RECRUITS *for the
war come rapidly across the stage all shouting the chorus, 'The war, the
war'*, etc.

Connolly The war, the war – I've heard it all before –
        Against South Africa against the Boer –
        MacNeill will shout as I did then
        But we know now that he will do no more –
MacNeill and Volunteers (*vainly, against the rush*) Don't join the British
    Army, don't join the British Army, don't join the British Army –
Connolly DON'T JOIN THE BRITISH ARMY!!

The stage empties. PEARSE *and* MACDERMOTT *remain behind, discreetly in a
corner.* CONNOLLY *is standing at his table, roaring helplessly.*

SCENE 7

Connolly (*sits down again*)
        Write my pamphlets
        Write my leaflets
        Write my newspaper
        Write my book –
        In Belfast like a helpless gudgeon
        Entangled squirming upon the hook –

PEARSE *and* MACDERMOTT *are joined by* CLARKE (*in character as a tobac-
conist*): *a conspiracy scene which* CONNOLLY *is not aware of.*

Clarke We keep well away from that lad Connolly, except in a general sense
    he might be useful for propaganda – sure there's no harm in joining voices
    with him in opposition to recruitment. Even MacNeill would discover no
    problem about that: and Arthur Griffith with Sinn Fein has his own pub-
    licists in the same cause. But for *our* purposes: England's difficulty must
    be Ireland's opportunity. So let's examine the possibilities . . .
MacDermott A re-creation of what ought to have happened in seventeen
    ninety-eight? Bring the Germans in to help us with a nationwide insur-

rection. The Brits would have a battlefront to the east of them as well as
to the west. They'd be bound to make peace, and at the peace conference
the German government sure would guarantee the independence of the
Irish Republic.

Pearse Or a similar re-creation of what ought to have happened in eighteen
sixty-seven? Get the Irish-American exiles to set a nationwide insurrection under way from across the Atlantic. The American government
to be forced to support us, in that case.

Clarke Either way we are dependent upon overwhelming outside help. And in
both instances by means of America. Casement is in America at the
moment, Plunkett is in Germany, but our contacts with Germany can be
made only through neutral New York. Both of them must lose no time –
themselves and the Irish-Americans must impress whoever they meet
with our serious professionalism. Ninety-eight and sixty-seven were
destroyed by informers. It mustn't happen this time. Hold hands on it . . .
We talk to nobody, however much we believe they are sympathetic to our
intention. We hold no public meetings, publish no Jacobin pamphlets,
salute no revolutionists in any foreign country.

Pearse We can of course declare we are opposed to the war?

Clarke If Connolly, or Griffith, or MacNeill should desire to say so, we say it
too. But afterwards, not before. The Brotherhood must not appear to be
leading towards anything. And in any case we can say it with all the more
security because we know that in fact we do not oppose the war – we
intend to take part in it . . . So that's our secret: keep it.

Exeunt CLARKE, PEARSE, MACDERMOTT.

As they cross the stage CONNOLLY *finishes his writing, gets up, sees* CLARKE
*and moves down to greet him, but like men meeting in the fog they miss each
other . . .*

SCENE 8

Connolly Marooned in Belfast I cannot expect
This Brotherhood to treat me with respect:
Am I a fool because I still suspect
They each of them know well in their dark mind
Exactly what it is that they intend . . . ?
They have their own men in the North – a friend
Of mine has put the word out – crafty and quiet . . .
What is the answer? God, I already know it . . .

Enter NORTHERN IRB MAN, *furtively, approaches* CONNOLLY *sideways.*

Northern IRB Mr Connolly, your desire to get in touch with the Republican
underground has been put forward to the proper quarters – but nobody in

this city at the present time has anything to say about anything in that line of business...

Connolly Is that a fact?

Northern IRB Man Your own Belfast socialists have refused to support you in denouncing the war: and why wouldn't they? They're shit-scared. The protestant trade unionists have the whip-hand and they make it sting.

Enter a SHIPYARD WORKER. *He addresses the* AUDIENCE *directly, taking no notice of the other two men.*

Shipyard Worker To put a battleship in the water and make sure she neither sinks nor yet fails to sink the enemy takes a degree of skill, ye damned Fenians, that not one of youse in Dublin or up the Falls Road has the remotest conception of. Don't youse talk to me of international solidarity for the rights of the working class – our right is to see we get properly paid for our services to the United Kingdom: and we're well able, I'm informing youse, to look after it for ourselves! Pride and craft in the work, pride and craft in the trade union, and pride and craft in our own boys who wear the uniform in our own ships. Pride and craft – that means loyalty. And loyalty in Belfast means no damned Teague dare open his mouth!

Exit SHIPYARD WORKER.

Northern IRB Man The point about being underground is that that's where we are and that's where we must stay. Oh, I heard you were putting out a class of a manifesto against recruitment for the Army. D'you suppose the IRB here would ever be so stupid as do anything so overt as that?

Exit NORTHERN IRB MAN.

SCENE 9

CONNOLLY *snatches the 'Belfast' label off his desk and tosses it away.*

Connolly No question now, in Dublin town alone
       I can find out what the hell goes on –
       The *war* goes on, month after month –
       The Citizen Army sits as still as any stone –
       Dublin and no other place
       I must force forward my red swollen face!

Exit, all his papers in his arms.

Enter COUNTESS MARKIEVICZ, O'CASEY, *and* CITIZEN ARMY *council-members for a meeting.*

Countess (*to audience*)

> I have tried so hard and done my best
> To keep all contacts wide and open –
> But with Larkin sick and Connolly away
> Are they all asleep and cannot be woken?

(*To Citizen Army.*) I put it to you – are you all of you asleep here or what are you? This war might be over and a treaty made with the Germans in a matter of weeks – from the Citizen Army not one move to even let the world know we exist! Mr Secretary O'Casey –

O'Casey May I refer you, Madame Markievicz, to Jenerski's *Thesis on the origin, development and consolidation of the evolutionary idea of the proletariat* –

Enter LARKIN.

Larkin Which nobody here but yourself will have read. There's a practical formal question to be put before this meeting: how far are we going to continue our attempts to associate ourselves with the Independent Volunteers under Eoin MacNeill? You gave notice, did you not, Sean, of a resolution bearing on this. So let's have it for God's sake.

O'Casey I put it before you, to take it or reject. It concerns Madame Markievicz – through her membership of the women's section of the Independent Volunteers – the *Cumann na nBan* – she's attached to the Volunteers and on intimate terms with many of their leaders. Now the Volunteers in their efforts and aims are inimical to the interests of labour. It can therefore not be expected that Madame can retain the confidence of this council: and I move that she be now asked to sever her connections with either the Volunteers or the Citizen Army.

Larkin Would you keep personalities out of it! Sure we all have the utmost confidence in Madame Markievicz as an individual and – –

O'Casey I want you people to tell yourselves, if there was a revolution over the water for a *British* socialist republic, how much support would they get from MacNeill? And by extension from Her Ladyship here? I want me resolution put forward to the vote!

Larkin You can wait till I've put another one. Vote of confidence in Madame Markievicz and her integrity in all the work she's done for the furtherance of this body.

O'Casey (*comes forward and addresses audience*) As organising secretary my function is to record the vote. The vote of confidence is carried by seven votes to six.

To the meeting.

Very well, I withdraw me motion. I had hopes I could speak freely in Liberty Hall of all places without having me own damned integrity defamed! Well, it seems I was mistook. So I'm better off outa here. I'm going. I resign.

Exit O'CASEY.

The meeting breaks up in some dismay.

CONNOLLY, *all his papers under his arm, marches in and takes his place again at the table, placing a label reading 'ITWU Dublin', firmly in view.* LARKIN *and the* COUNTESS *remain to confront him. The* COUNCIL MEMBERS *straggle back when they become aware of his arrival.*

SCENE 10

Connolly There's a time and a place to strike yourselves rigid on a pose of no compromise, and this isn't it! From one end of Europe to the other, labour and the socialists are compromising with the *war*: and anyone who refuses to do that is on *my* side, nowhere else. Whoever is not willing to go along with this policy should resign like Sean O'Casey! Well?

Citizen Army Men No no – we go along with you – we're all behind you – it's all right, Jim, it's all right – *etcetera* ...

Connolly So from now on a continued and intense preoccupation with our military training and proficiency as the defence force of the working class! Okay?

To one of the CITIZEN ARMY OFFICERS:

Michael, I want a plan worked out, and you can give it me over the weekend, as to how with the available men we could surround and capture Dublin Castle. Make it good.

Citizen Army Officer Right away then.

Connolly (*whispers to him*) And another matter. Redmond's Volunteers have a whole shed full of good rifles at the north end of Amiens Street Station. Get hold of as many railwaymen as you have in your company, and see what you can do about a crafty infiltration of the yard after dark ... No end of good practice for you – get along with you – do it ...!

CITIZEN ARMY OFFICER *nods acknowledgement and leaves with the* MEMBERS.

Larkin Now about Sean O'Casey – you know that that lad was always contrary – a minority out of a minority out of a minority I always called him – an unskilled socialist labourer with literary leanings and a protestant into the bargain ... But what *I* want to know is this: is it true you've been signing political statements on the same paper as Arthur Griffith? Arthur Griffith supported Murphy and the employers in the lockout – have we forgotten? And he now ––

Connolly Is involved in a campaign for Irish neutrality which neither affirms socialism nor denies it. But in the present state of affairs it can only be described as a revolutionary posture. Very well: so I go along with it. Because I am a socialist and I therefore must affirm that in this one particular Arthur Griffith is correct! In token of which – Winifred! Do you have that new banner prepared – I want it up across the frontage of Liberty Hall – now!

WINIFRED CARNEY *and* O'BRIEN *come in with a long banner and hang it up across the stage, where it remains till the end of the play.* CONNOLLY *reads out the slogan on it:*

'We serve neither King nor Kaiser but Ireland!'
Supposing it did prove possible to pull Ireland out of the war – and it turned out in the upshot that our movement had played no part in it?

Exeunt WINIFRED *and* O'BRIEN *when the banner is hung.*

Countess (*in support of Connolly*) Supposing it did prove possible to proclaim a republic, and it turned out in the upshot that our movement had played no part in it?

Larkin On his present form Arthur Griffith would have played no part either.

Countess And is not that exactly what we are calculating upon?

Larkin (*in disgust*) Sure a slogan is one thing – but republicanism, secret societies . . . boy-scout passwords in the night . . .

Connolly Jim, there is more than that, five hundred times more than that – !
Will ye not listen to what goes on!

SCENE 11

Enter ASQUITH *at a distance.* GRABITALL *and* EMPLOYERS *greet him and bring him on to the stage.*

Asquith   Month after month the war goes on,
              And every day one thousand men
              In Flanders fields are dead and blasted
              Their bodies flung into red rags of ruin –
              I see no way, my generals see
              No way to break the ironclad cage of war –
              We must have men and more again
              And men to fight and die and more and more – !
I particularly appeal to the citizens of Ireland, to the masters and employers of that patriotic community –

Grabitall and Employers (*in chorus*)
              The war the war now forward to the war
              And reap the reward of glory and gore –

Connolly Come on now, Citizen Army, are we going to let him get away with it – ?

Countess Come on now, Independent Volunteers, come on now, altogether – !

ASQUITH *is assisted to a rostrum by* GRABITALL. CITIZEN ARMY MEN *and*

VOLUNTEERS *assemble, with rifles.* ASQUITH *notices* CONNOLLY'*s new banner and recoils.*

Asquith My friends, this war is a moral war, a crusade for the principle of the right of small nations to their self-determination –

He is interrupted by a chorus of 'Don't join the British Army' repeated each time he tries to speak. He gets no further in his speech and is compelled to stand down. The CITIZEN ARMY *and* VOLUNTEERS *cheer triumphantly and exeunt. He turns in disgust to* GRABITALL.

Mr Murphy, is this usual?

Grabitall Not at all, sir, most *un*usual, a totally isolated expression of – of –

Asquith Of an attitude that can only be solved by some degree of coercion, I think. I leave it to you. In the meantime –

On the banks of Clyde and in South Wales
There is strike and trouble and strike again –
I am going to require to coerce them there:
I shall soon have not one single gun –
The war, the war, now forward to the war
We must have men and more and more and more . . . !

Exit ASQUITH.

Grabitall Declarations of redundancy of one-third of the unskilled labour employed by the Dublin employers –

1st Employer Let them be told if they join the army their wives will be compensated with the government allowance –

2nd Employer Sure they'll never have had so much cash in the house in the whole of their lives –

3rd Employer Sure one small demonstration and a ruction in the street is like nothing in comparison with the hard economic facts!

Grabitall (*leads the* EMPLOYERS *again in chorus*)

The war, the war, now forward to the war
Coercion coercion for glory and gore!

Again a hastening of RECRUITS *across the stage all shouting out the chorus. Exeunt* GRABITALL *and* EMPLOYERS.

SCENE 12

Connolly What have we left to counteract
The economic bloody fact?
The Transport Union must support
All strike or stoppage of any sort –

General meeting in Liberty Hall – Miss Carney, let's have a look at the books – William, I want an opinion on the overall viability of each individual branch – Jim, can we have your views of the –

WINIFRED CARNEY, O'BRIEN, DELIA LARKIN *and* ITWU OFFICIALS *assemble at his call.*

Larkin Insanity beyond measure to attempt now to start
Strike upon strike with no money in the bank –
Oh yourself and William O'Brien were always the buggers to look
For every penny in every column of every ledger and every book –
How comes it then that it falls to me
To be the only one to see
The Irish Transport Union is almost finished, man, flat broke!
Our only hope, I told you – America. I must go to America to see what I can raise for us there – sure national neutrality for the United States is the main platform of the socialist movement there at present – Debs, Haywood, the lot of 'em have nothing else between their teeth – it wouldn't be too hard to incorporate Ireland into the argument – well? In the meantime, the Red Army, the Citizen Army of the working class – we must keep it in being ... Wire New York to get me home again the day MacNeill and Arthur Griffith inaugurate the government of the Irish Greengrocers' Republic ...

Exit LARKIN.

Countess O'Casey gone, now Larkin gone, Sheehy Skeffington three parts underground:
How many tiles, nails, rafters must fly before the rooftree comes down with the wind ... ?

Connolly The greatest leader of labour who in Ireland was ever known
Like a dog must he be driven out before the struggle can even begin ... ?

O'Brien Before eulogy, before epitaph, don't you think we should find out Exactly what Big Jim Larkin has left behind for us on our plate ... ?

Winifred Carney
The answer to that one's easy – page upon page upon column of bad debt.

1st ITWU Official I have demands from the casual workers at the docks for industrial action upon forced redundancies –

2nd ITWU Official I have demands to back a strike from the labourers in the railway yards –

Enter CITIZEN ARMY OFFICER *and whispers to* CONNOLLY.

Connolly Just a minute – Madame Markievicz, would you attend to this, please.

The COUNTESS *takes the* CITIZEN ARMY OFFICER *aside.*

Countess We were just hearing about the railway yards, – did you get hold of the guns?

CITIZEN ARMY OFFICER *nods and grins, confidentially.*

Countess Bring them into the basement and for heaven's sake don't disturb the meeting...

The CITIZEN ARMY OFFICER *slips out. During the rest of the scene he and one or two others of the Citizen Army are seen passing across the back of the stage behind the meeting carrying bundles of rifles and ammunition boxes. The* COUNTESS *makes a thumbs-up sign to* CONNOLLY *and resumes her place. The meeting continues.*

3rd ITWU Official I have a whole list here of wage demands from the boatmen, from the coal-porters, from the carters at the brewery.

Delia The Women Workers' Branch of the union demands action on the dismissal of women in factories to replace them with child labour –

1st ITWU Official Is that a fact? I have complaints here that there's a number of employers bringing in a crowd of women to replace *men* –

2nd ITWU Official So that the men can be shifted off into the recruiting offices for the bloody war! So what d'you think of that, Miss Delia Larkin, you and your women workers –

Delia Easy enough to be blackguarding me now my brother's been driven to America! And driven by what? By what else but this fool republicanism, militarism, private armies with nobody in them but six so-called officers and a handful of ragamuffins. Don't think I haven't noticed who's been slipping in and out of the basement – do you mean to tell me that such cowboys-and-Indians is better expressive of the needs of the working class than honest-to-goodness industrial struggle? I haven't forgotten how –

Connolly Delia, I will tell you one thing you *have* forgotten! And let no-one here make the mistake of ever forgetting it again. As soon as this war broke out, the Irish Trade Union Congress passed a formal resolution declaring the conflict to be solely for the aggrandisement of the capitalist cartels: and demanding all suitable measures of resistance on the part of the workers.

Delia And is that supposed to mean collaboration with the Republican Brotherhood? Must the Citizen Army pool its resources with the National Volunteers? Resources raised exclusively from the subscriptions of trade unionists for the defence and protection of trade unions in the course of legitimate disputes!

Connolly I believe and I have stated that republican struggle is the most immediate available form of resistance in this country. Who agrees with me? Madame...? William...?

Delia (*as* COUNTESS *and* O'BRIEN *signify agreement*) I'd like to enquire then who *doesn't* agree? And I'd like to ask also by what process of democracy this decision has been arrived at? Well?... Has he torn out the tongue of every one of you on this executive?

She gets no response: stands waiting a moment: silence: she walks out.

Connolly Winifred, will you please see that a committee is formed to consider replacement leadership for the women workers. Right. So we have no money. Every strike or go-slow that can be supported, will be supported. And wherever we can make use of bluff to compel employers to negotiate, then bluff will be resorted to. But that's all. We are in a cul-de-sac. Will you think, please, how to get out of it? Thank you.

The meeting breaks up, irritably. CONNOLLY *and the* COUNTESS *remain.*

Constance: my whole assessment of the industrial situation has been founded upon a fundamental mistake.

    A year and a half this war goes on and on

    They lay men off and force them to the front:

    Yet for those whose jobs are safe the wages rise

    And rise again beyond all precedent –

Countess Six months of war, did we not say,

    And then catastrophe of mass-starvation –?

Connolly With every strike we call, the state concedes

    New terms for new negotiation . . .

    I've no experience to solve

    The whole insoluble contradiction!

Goddammit, the Irish workers have the one sole incentive, to eternally carry on like a flock of blind eagles, flying higher and higher into the thick of the storm-cloud: supporting the war, supporting recruitment, supporting the endless insupportable casualty lists –

Countess Which already are stretched out from that blood-bucket in Flanders as though a huge poisonous dragon was smearing its foul tail over the map of the world!

Connolly Constance, we must look and at once for a fresh priority . . .

SCENE 13

Enter ASQUITH *at a distance. The* WAR DEMON *rears up alongside him.*

Asquith Industrial trouble held at bay

    With new concessions every day –

War Demon

    Indefinitely –?

Asquith Not at all. There is a reason behind this mess –

War Demon

    The reason is the subversive press–

Asquith I know: it aggravates it: yes.

    I did reserve, you recollect,

    Draconian powers–

War Demon

    So put them to effect!

Asquith Do you think I must – ?
      I am a Liberal – after all –

War Demon
      If you do not, the war is lost
      So beat your head against the wall
      And wipe your tears and sign the order – now!

Asquith But how?
      My dear sir, where to start – ?
      Glasgow, South Wales – or perhaps some other part – ?

Enter GRABITALL *at the far side from* ASQUITH.

Grabitall (*calls across to him*)
      Prime Minister – Ireland! And I will list
      The papers I require suppressed:
    Firstly *Sinn Fein* – controlled by Arthur Griffith and vehemently inimical
    to the recruitment of soldiers.

Asquith The newspaper *Sinn Fein* is accordingly prohibited.

Grabitall Secondly, *Irish Freedom* – an organ for extreme Republicans, Pearse,
    MacDermott and so forth – surreptitiously giving support to the notion
    of a secret Brotherhood and reminding its readers of the Fenian rebellion
    and the terrorism of the last century.

Asquith Historical reminiscences are particularly dangerous. The newspaper
    Irish Freedom is accordingly prohibited.

Grabitall There are several subsidiary sheets of equivalent tendency – Dublin
    Castle will give you the names. But third, and perhaps most perilous
    because of the place whence it issues – Liberty Hall, the home of Larkin,
    the home of syndicalism, the home of red revolution and destruction of
    all that is held most dear to the soul of the Catholic Gael – the third paper,
    Prime Minister, is James Connolly's *Irish Worker* – the one rag respon-
    sible for every strike, every picket, every union agitation from the Dingle
    Peninsula to the top of Loch Foyle. Prime Minister, this James Connolly
    is –

Asquith Is an inconsiderable little nuisance: but you're right: he should be
    stopped. *The Irish Worker* is prohibited. If he endeavours to print it, I
    will put him in prison.

Exit ASQUITH. *The* WAR DEMON *withdraws.*

Grabitall Sure, if you can catch him, you dithering fool –
      Don't you know your police won't *touch* Liberty Hall –
      Don't you know the employers in this city for years
      Are banged and blown-at by the transport union till they bleed at
        both ears –
      Don't you know – oh you will learn it late or soon
      What you do should have been done in nineteen hundred thirteen … !

Exit GRABITALL.

SCENE 14

Countess John Maclean in Scotland will organise the printing of our news-
paper over there.
Connolly John Maclean in Scotland is himself in some fear
That he himself will be suppressed.
Constance, we must do our best
To get the paper out ourselves – in secret, with another name.
Constance, don't you see, all the rules of the game
Are from this day completely changed?
Constance, we have been *observed*.
Our overt labour movement at last has found
For the first time ever it must go underground.
Countess No less than if we were the secret Brotherhood itself.
Connolly All normal process now is put upon the shelf.
Our posture is that of Paris in the days of the Commune.
Our posture is that of Russia in nineteen hundred and five.
In order to remain alive
We must be ready to deceive
Our very friends, must plot and plan
And tell the truth of it to none
We cannot absolutely trust.
In Moscow and in Paris the peoples' battles were both lost.
Countess We must discover why, and how, we must make sure
We do not likewise waste away our power.

Enter LILLIE. *She comes in at the back and sits down with her mending in
the middle.* CONNOLLY *and the* COUNTESS *walk away from each other and
stand at either side, where they talk quietly to the* AUDIENCE, *as though
unaware of each other. A very formal hieratic scene.*

Connolly Specifically about Moscow. The regular army remained loyal to the
Czar. The peasants outside the city remained loyal to the Czar.
Countess There was no insurrection in other major cities of the Russian
Empire. The attention of the Czar's army was therefore not seriously
diverted.
Lillie I couldn't stand it in Belfast. You'd have thought in the catholic areas
there'd be less of it than among protestants, but even up the Falls they get
the messages every day. Mrs McManus at number twenty-three had the
telegram only yesterday – her son Declan was gone. Old Mr Farrell at
the corner beside the hospital lost his two boys in the one week. Gallipoli,
he said, they were killed in the first landing.
Connolly The regular soldiers were forced to attack the revolutionary partisans all the way down built-up streets where there were hundreds of
people just living in the houses. They were obstructed at every block by
barricades and overturned vehicles.

Countess In Paris the barricades were the first things they organised when the insurrection began. They kept the government troops out until the artillery was moved onto the hills outside of the town.

Connolly Eighteen thousand of the Russian regulars were held up by barricades for one week and two days.

Countess The Communards could have lasted longer if the city had not already been besieged by the Prussians, right through the previous year.

Connolly If they'd had only eight hundred rifles the Czarist artillery could have been dealt with. Fifteen hundred insurgents had nothing but pistols and petrol bombs.

Lillie And now that I've come for a few days to Dublin it's exactly the same as Belfast. I spoke to Riordan who used to live in Sullivan's Buildings when my husband was involved in the rent resistance fifteen years ago. His boy Sean is dead in France, Willy John had been taken prisoner: his wife's young cousin had lost both legs.

Connolly John Maclean could pull his people out in a general strike along the Clyde.

Countess Nearly three hundred men available in the Citizen Army and at last they have all got rifles.

Lillie Nearly a quarter of a million from Ireland alone have already joined the forces. My husband has joined nothing. Has not needed to. He was a part of this war before it even began. He was a part of it the day he took off the old Queen's red coat and chose his battle for himself. And yet in the worst of the slaughter it appears he has *no* part. Will they murder all these people and let him find not one chance towards acting to prevent it? Have all of those who could help him gone away from him, all of them...?

Connolly Nearly twelve thousand available as they always have been available in the Independent Volunteers. Are they never going to declare themselves and tell MacNeill just who they are?

Exit LILLIE. CONNOLLY *and the* COUNTESS *stand silent for a moment. Then enter* CLARKE, *walks across to* CONNOLLY, *misses him, then turns round him and catches him.*

Clarke Mr Connolly, the old Fenian, O'Donovan Rossa, whose body has been brought back from America for burial: the independent units of the National Volunteers and related organisations have a funeral ceremony planned, of considerable importance, we believe, to the public political sentiment in this country. I am deputed to invite you, as a trade unionist and also as the head of the Citizen Army, to take part in the deliberations of the organising committee...?

Connolly And why not, Mr Clarke? I'll be very glad to oblige.

Clarke We thought you'd want to.

Connolly Tell me though – who will give the graveside oration? Professor MacNeill?

Clarke I've no doubt he'll be there. Padraic Pearse will be the principle republican speaker, Mr Connolly. We're most grateful for your co-operation.

Exit CLARKE. CONNOLLY *and the* COUNTESS *break out of the formality.*

Connolly Oh when are these fellows going to stop blethering about dead Fenians and give us a few live ones for a change?

Countess It says in the constitution of the Republican Brotherhood that before war against England can be inaugurated, the decision of the majority of the Irish people must first be obtained.

Connolly It must? And so what? Would they hold an election?

Countess If they can't hold an election, public opinion must be tested somehow.

Connolly I'll believe it when I see it. Dammit, I'll buttonhole Padraic Pearse, put it squarely to him – what are you playing at?

>Hole-and-corner hugger-mugger
>Secret societies, the wink-and-the-nod –
>Declare yourselves declare yourselves
>Declare yourselves in the Name of God . . . !

SCENE 15

A guard of CITIZEN ARMY MEN *enters.*

Connolly Soldiers of the Citizen Army, at the salute to honour this funeral!

The coffin of O'DONOVAN ROSSA *is brought in with an escort of* VOLUNTEERS. PEARSE, CLARKE, MACNEILL *and* SHEEHY SKEFFINGTON *are among the mourners. The funeral is observed at a distance by* ASQUITH *and* GRABITALL. CONNOLLY *steps forward.*

Connolly We honour the memory of O'Donovan Rossa, who fought for his cause in Ireland, was imprisoned in England, and died in exile in America. Karl Marx spoke loudly for him against his tormentors in the gaol –

Sheehy Skeffington (*aside to audience*) On his release he repudiated the red ravings of Karl Marx . . . Not respectable, you see, for an Irish patriot to be associated with such alien notions . . .

Connolly We are here by our right of our faith in the separate destiny of our country and our faith in the ability of Irish workers to achieve that destiny.

Pearse (*steps forward to address the gathering*) They think they have foreseen everything, think they have provided for everything – but, the fools, the fools, the fools, they have left us our Fenian dead – and while Ireland holds these graves, Ireland unfree can never be at peace.

MACNEILL *expresses some alarm at these sentiments.* CONNOLLY *goes across to shake hands with* PEARSE, *but misses. The cortège moves on and out.*

Grabitall I watch, I listen, I report:
>Prime Minister, you must act!

Asquith Another example of the kind of attention
They are always trying to attract.
Leave them alone –
They'll all go home …

Exeunt ASQUITH *and* GRABITALL, *severally. The funeral party has left the stage, except for* CONNOLLY *and for two* IRB MEN *who have detached themselves from it. One of them waylays* CONNOLLY.

1st IRB Man Mr Connolly, Mr Pearse would like a word with you – now.
CONNOLLY *sees that he is holding a pistol.*
Connolly Now look, laddie, you know me. You do not play games the like o'that with *me*. Besides, I don't believe you. Padraic Pearse? The special branch!
2nd IRB Man (*behind* CONNOLLY *with another pistol*) You'll find out when we get there. Come.

They blindfold CONNOLLY *and lead him out.*

SCENE 16

Enter PEARSE, CLARKE, PLUNKETT, MACDERMOTT, *and other* IRB LEADERS.
CONNOLLY, *blindfolded, is brought into them. His eyes are uncovered.*

Connolly Just what the deuce is going on? I am perfectly capable of coming to your house by tramcar or by bicycle or on my own two feet at any time without –
Pearse This is not my house. It belongs to a highly respectable business-man who is in no way under surveillance and has conveniently gone to Limerick to secure a contract in building materials. May I offer you a glass of whiskey?
Connolly I don't drink, Mr Pearse.
Pearse I wasn't asking you to *drink*, but to confirm our good fellowship. Mr Connolly, I do apologise. But you are altogether too direct for us: and we cannot afford to make it known that we are direct with you. I think you know everyone – Sean MacDermott, Joseph Plunkett, Eamon Ceannt, Tom MacDonagh, Tom Clarke. Sean?
MacDermott We want to ask you, Mr Connolly, is it true that the Citizen Army combined with the trade unions is about to spring on to us –
Connolly I can assure you, Mr MacDermott, nothing will be *sprung*.
MacDermott – a unilateral insurrection?
Connolly Unilateral's a quare word. We're talking of the inevitable historical process involving the mass action of the greater part of the working class –
MacDermott Yes: but how soon?
Connolly The only way you can tell is the time ripe for revolution is to let fly your revolution and find out if it succeeds. Scientific analysis is a high-

falutin fine phrase, but it only goes so far . . . My assessment is within six weeks.

MacDermott Too soon.

Connolly I tell you there's no such thing as to pre-ordain the exact date.

Pearse But that's exactly what we've done.

CONNOLLY *gasps*.

Pearse Easter Sunday. Which falls this year upon the twenty-third of April. Three full months from now. I don't know about scientific, Mr Connolly: but militarily precise.

MacDermott One hundred percent military, Mr Connolly. We're in a war, so it has to be. The plan we have made does not and cannot depend upon the popular will.

Clarke Though we do take the results of the O'Donovan Rossa funeral to indicate that the popular will is broadly in favour of what it is that we intend. I have reports from our friends in all parts of the country agreeing that the publicity over the burial was startling –

Connolly Not quite good enough, Mr Clarke. It's a fact that you gentlemen, or your predecessors in the Brotherhood, have devised such schemes before, many times in point of fact; and they've never come off. With your permission – which I shouldn't need – I will continue my own course.

Pearse Please don't. Not just yet. It really would be quite impossible if you were to jump the gun on us like this. We chose the date of Easter because Easter is the earliest we can possibly get all our work together. All our work includes you. And the trade unions. And the Citizen Army. We *must* have it co-ordinated. Mr Connolly – please?

Connolly You'll have to tell me more about what your work includes.

Pearse We'll tell you all of it.

Connolly Military . . . ? How many men?

MacDermott Ten thousand.

Connolly You must be joking.

MacDermott By no means. In arms and fully organised. We pull all the Volunteers out of the hands of MacNeill.

Connolly When?

MacDermott Easter Sunday. Not before. It'll take us that long to have it fixed – without any chance of an error, you understand.

CLARKE *and* PLUNKETT *unroll a large chart* (*Military dispositions for the Rising*) *which falls to cover the backcloth of Liberty Hall, etc. It is divided into two separate maps – one of the whole of Ireland, and the other a large-scale street plan of Dublin. Military dispositions are marked with coloured symbols, and illustrate the ensuing dialogue.*

The weekend of the Easter festival there will be general manoeuvres called for the entire corps across the country. MacNeill has agreed to it – indeed the good man is of opinion it is all his own idea. Local commandants will make certain that the manoeuvres are embarked on with live rounds in the magazine. The Cork Brigade is to move into positions on the north and north-west of the county – here – making contact with the outposts of the Kerry Brigade – here. The Kerry Brigade to the north is to link with Limerick. Limerick, Clare and Galway hold the line of the Shannon along here – to Athlone. We thereby cut off the south-west of the country. We shall need to do that because the Germans require a beach-head.

Connolly Germans? Real Germans . . . with spiked helmets and the goose-step? How many?

Plunkett At least five thousand – maybe ten. Roger Casement has also enlisted his Irish Brigade among our people in the prison camps over there. There's been a difficulty of communication with him – but –

Clarke We are assured via New York that it really *will* be a brigade. A large consignment of first-class weapons and ammunition will be supplied by Berlin.

MacDermott We have a policy throughout Waterford, Wexford, Wicklow, to attack, seize, and hold all towns and strong places. The British garrisons are minimal, their security is a joke. In Dublin, we take the city. We have five thousand men here – that's half of the whole force.

Plunkett We will occupy and fortify the Castle, the Post Office, the Four Courts, various factories, hospitals, warehouses and so on. We will isolate and reduce the military posts in different quarters of the town.

Pearse We had hoped that the Citizen Army would be of great value here – the industrial areas, docks, railway yards, factories – clearly we need men who know their way around. In fact, I'd go so far as to say, Mr Connolly, that without the Citizen Army and its background and experience, a successful battle in Dublin would hardly be possible. So what do you think?

Connolly I'll tell you what I *don't* think, I don't think any longer that I am 'too direct' for you people! Sir, you have amazed me . . . I can't possibly give an answer, just like this, sat here . . . I'd be glad if you'd let me think about it. Twenty-four hours should be enough to consider the implications.

Pearse You'll not object if we ask you not to go home? Security . . .

Connolly You understand my decision will be on political potential as well as on the military . . . I'm not afraid: but I'm not seduced. My profession tends to make me both sceptical and critical. I'm no cynic.

Pearse We'll leave you to it. You'd like some sandwiches . . . ?

They all go out and leave him alone with a small tray of food.

SCENE 17

Connolly There's ham and there's butter and there's bread upon the plate

And cups of tea for a night and a day for the man that has to wait
Till his mind and his heart and his stomach and his brain
Have overtaken these great tidings that have overtaken him.
These tidings, these tidings distort me back and side
My mouth is grinning behind my ear, my nostrils run with blood.
My bones beneath my flesh beneath my skin turn round and round
Two flat feet like boats on the water pitching up and down –
These tidings these tidings I never even dreamed –
The horn of war is roaring like a boulder in the stream
The severed head upon the roof of the house-place of the king
Cries 'awake awake you Irishmen you lie in bed too long...!'

Behind him lines of SOLDIERS *cross and re-cross the stage, with banners and bayonets – dark, unidentifiable, marching to a repetitive low drumbeat.*

Sprinkled all over the land, the blood of the dead head
For sixty years will pour down rain and even then will not be dried...
Too much noise, said the king:
But he rolls out of his bed...

A question how truly we need to disturb him? I who have fastened my cloak around me with hoops of twigs, and must hold my hacked joints from coming asunder with a stuffing of dry wisps, and who have endured the whole long winter unsupported, unassisted: at the breaking-open of spring and the unfreezing of the rivers, do I require to give over the integrity of my battle into the swirl of the wheels of the chariots of opportunity? To be rescued...? Maybe. To be made captive...? Who can say? To take help: or to give hostages...?

Suppose I should refuse
The self-delusive fervour of this man Pearse,
This poet possessed,
This fledgeling schoolteacher quite lost
Between the broken eggshell of his safe and bourgeois past
And the new huge flapping flight he means to launch tomorrow –
If I were to take care now and so carefully tell him – No:
What would there then be left for the Irish working class to do?

From among the marching SOLDIERS *a number of* SHAPES *materialise – these have the voices of various characters out of earlier episodes of* CONNOLLY'S *life: but they should not look exactly like the characters remembered. A kind of distorted imitation of the faces, perhaps, with the bodies and costumes not fully seen.*

1st Shape (*British trade-union leader*) At the same time in all war industries a guaranteed minimum wage: at the same time members of the Labour Party accorded office in the War Cabinet: at the same time a voluntary agreement to hold all wage disputes over for the duration of hostilities: in point of fact draconian powers – to be on the safe side. For Godsake

you stupid Irish, don't you think we don't know what we are doing in
our own areas...?

Connolly And this time round not even one shipload of Liverpool food –

Do I dare once more to offer them to bring them once more down to
hell

Choke their throats once again with the dust of betrayal...?

What else if we go on and on all on our own –

Support from whom? Perhaps from John MacLean.

But Larkin's gone: and Sean O'Casey's gone

And Sheehy Skeffington has turned his back

And Delia Larkin chose to break

Away from all of us and – what, go with her brother?

O'Brien and his committee men are buried now in fuss and bother

Debit-credit, ledgers, cashbooks, in the dust of Liberty Hall –

If I say *no* to Padraic Pearse: what help from these at all...?

And yet if I say *yes*: I must embrace

What prohibitions on my socialist course?

A large white egg-shaped screen has become visible behind him. More
SHAPES *creep forward.*

2nd Shape (O'CASEY)

The Volunteer Association is in its methods and aims inimical to the
interests of labour.

3rd Shape (1ST EMPLOYER)

A highly respectable business-man in no way under surveillance,
conveniently gone to Limerick...

4th Shape (3RD EMPLOYER)

Will you mention my name and the name of my firm, my God if a
Dublin merchant cannot at a time like this leave his latch key for
the glory of the people of Ireland...

With a high scream the head of a great red BIRD *breaks through the egg – a
claw comes out to widen the aperture, and part of one wing is visible.*

Bird Prohibition number one:

No tactical collaboration

With an element of the bourgeoisie

From an inferior situation

Unless you can foresee

Strategical advantage

Upon the turning of the next full page.

Connolly The book is closed and glued

With soot of cordite

And with blood

If the pages will not open

They must be torn out at the root.

> The working class is not alone . . .
> The grave-heaps in Flanders at Mons, Ypres, Bethune,
> Loos, Albert, Armentières, cover severed heads and splintered bone
> From man upon boy upon man who have no name
> Nor class nor even unity of their own body –
> We must take things as they come . . .

5th Shape (DE LEON)

> First the master, then the disciples, then the completely informed
> and corrected nucleus of activists and agitators – and finally, the
> masses . . .

Bird Prohibition number two:

> There is nothing you can do
> To advance the revolution
> Without a party to determine
> The scientific meaning
> Of your intended contribution.

Connolly There is no scale can weigh and measure

> The imperative desire
> Of a people for their liberty:
> If they want it, they will take it, they will take it today.
> Leave the party in the meadow to be counting the grasshoppers:
> If they have not their sharp sickles
> They will cut not one blade of hay.

5th Shape (DE LEON)

> If James Connolly is not an undercover Jesuit, I ask you very care-
> fully to consider what else he may be . . .

6th Shape (BISHOP)

> Lillie Reynolds, you understand there can be no nuptial before the
> altar of the church: you understand there can be no common grave
> for both yourself and your husband. Your children belong to *us* in
> a land full of heresy . . .

Bird Prohibition number three:

> Do not permit factitious deity
> Invented in man's brain to oversee
> The work that brain of man alone should order:
> Keep God enclosed in His own proper border –
> Let Him out and you will find
> The crooked devil on His holy shoulder
> Controls both you and Him and every project of your human mind.

Connolly God may have made mankind

> Mankind may have made God.
> Whichever way how dare I stride
> Upon the secret pathways of another man's soul –
> If people call on God, they call
> On man for help: I must accept it, or reject it all.

7th Shape (WALKER)

We would ask you, Brother Connolly, to confine yourself to the class of workers you were sent to represent. Ulster will fight and Ulster will be right!

Bird Prohibition number four:

Your proletarian power
If it dare to ignore
The opposition of a third
Of the workforce of the nation
Will survive on no foundation
But collaboration
With the Catholic bosses
Who oppress the Catholic masses:
Wolfe Tone made no such error.

Connolly Wolfe Tone had not with horror

Observed the workers of the North
March forth
To France with sword and gun,
To strike all hope of revolution down.
I piped to them, they did not dance.
It is too late: they now must take their chance.

8th Shape (LARKIN)

We serve neither King nor Kaiser . . . sure a slogan is one thing . . .

Bird Prohibition number five:

How can your revolution live
Dependent on an eagled emperor
To give to you the needful power
To fight the people's independent war?
Wolfe Tone made no such error:
He brought from France the naked rights of man
To set them up alone
Against the strength and terror
Of the crown.

Connolly Who can predict what would Wolfe Tone have thought

Had he had access to the swollen heart
Of General, Consul, Emperor Bonaparte . . . ?

Bird Prohibition number six:

Secret signs and traps and tricks
Produce no revolution but a private plot.
You tell the people: 'For you, we have done *this*.'
They answer you: 'So what? We wanted *that*.'
Wolfe Tone and the United Irishmen
Ten years in public laid their statements down.

Connolly And yet they left the people with no plan

When they were caught and throttled one by one.

I *have* a plan and I have written it
Book after book with my right hand.
They may not understand
This year or next –
May sink the volume of my text
In the deepest midden they can find –
I know, in the end, they cannot keep it hidden:
It is not mine alone,
Thousands have shared this work –
By thousands upon thousands upon thousands
In the end it will be made known …
And add to it too that I have lately heard
Of what has taken place at Zimmerwald,
In Switzerland, where the new wild geese
From all of Europe found one narrow resting place
To fold their wings, set down their feet
And for a few short days could meet
Upon a patch of neutral ground:
They offered to the world the muffled sound
Of international socialism cut to shreds
By national war – yet still held firm upon one perilous thread …

A group of DELEGATES, *wrapped up against the cold, are seen grouped in a distant corner. They include* LENIN.

Lenin Turn the imperialist war into civil war! Proclaim a new International! Stand up for your own cause, for the sacred name of socialism, for the emancipation of small nations as well as of the enslaved classes, by means of irreconcilable class struggle …!

Connolly What they so helplessly have said
In Ireland I will make our very deed.

Bird Prohibition number seven:
Do not deceive yourself that you are given
By Jesuitical justification all the cause
You need to make upon your own your private wars!
Private perhaps, so slyly personal the real deep guilt and grudge
That drives James Connolly to this sharp knife-edge …

9th Shape (LILLIE)
In order to provide for six children in a small dark flat
Lillie Connolly must take in washing, mending clothes, and that's
that.

Connolly See the slave of a slave taking orders from her boss
So that *his* boss may be toppled with the minimum of loss …
Very well: I am a man who will hazard his whole life
And those of his friends, because he knows his wife
Has got from him alive such little good.

Very well, perhaps I do shed blood
Perhaps I do make war
For no-one else but her–
What's wrong with that : she is a legion, I can't count
How many of her there are, and what they want
I do not know how to explain –
But I do know that to do nothing
Will do nothing to relieve their pain.
Away away, you undistinguished bird –

The BIRD *cries out and waves its head.*

Your feathers are all borrowed
And your beak is made of mud . . .

The BIRD *withdraws.*

Mr Pearse – shall we have a word . . . !

Exeunt.

END OF ACT 2

ACT 3: 'The Rising'

SCENE 1

A landscape devastated by war – broken trees and buildings, wrecked vehicles, dead men and horses, etc. (Backcloth 4).

Military Dispositions for the Rising (Backcloth 11).

Enter CONNOLLY *and* PEARSE.

Pearse You have made up your mind – you will come in with us in the Rising?

Connolly If you want us, you must meet our terms. We, as the Citizen Army, created for our own purposes and independent of the National Volunteers, must continue to retain our independence, our chain of command, our own commandant –

Pearse You.

Connolly I become in effect the second-in-command of the entire operation.

Pearse Are you willing to be inducted into the Irish Republican Brotherhood?

Connolly I am not. We are public people, in the labour movement, we are accustomed to declare ourselves. I must know that no-one under me in your chain of command is in fact my concealed superior.

Pearse But you see, we take an oath –

Connolly For security. Yes. It is prudent: because you answer democratically to no-one.

Pearse Except our conscience.

Connolly For which you require God to stand guarantor. I understand all that, yes. But *I* have to answer to one hundred thousand trade unionists, Mr Pearse: don't you suppose that ought to be enough?

Pearse Leaders of labour are as corruptible as the rest of us.

Connolly If so, they are no longer the *leaders* of labour.

Pearse The very materialist basis of the business they conduct –

Connolly To be sure there's no idealism: we just rescue human beings from being turned into animals.

Pearse My remark was unworthy. I apologise.

Connolly But, as you say, we are fallible. It's a question which you think the greater deterrent – God: or God's voice . . . ?

Pearse *Vox dei vox populi* . . . ?

Connolly God's voice within *my* conscience is the voice of the people, yes. I had hoped you would be prepared to put trust in it. No oath.

Pearse Your point is made: and taken. We'll consider you a full member of the military council. In any case you are already privy to nearly everything we have planned.

Connolly Except this. In what name do we raise our flag on Easter Sunday?

Pearse What else but the name of the Republic of Ireland? To be defined in a proclamation.

Connolly May I ask you your collective views upon the issue of private property?

Pearse I fancy I know yours...?

Connolly We want and we must have economic conscription in Ireland. Socialism. Common ownership of the resources of the land. Under one, common, direction; that Ireland may live and bear upon her fruitful bosom the greatest number of the freest people she has ever known.

Pearse This could cause difficulties.

Connolly Aye... Now, your turn.

Pearse I base my views upon James Fintan Lalor.

Connolly Very good. So do I. But interpreted how?

Pearse Four propositions. One: the end and purpose of freedom is human happiness. Two: the end and purpose of national freedom is individual freedom. Therefore individual happiness. Three: national freedom implies national sovereignty. Four: national sovereignty implies control of all the moral and material resources of the nation. Not really so very different from what you said.

Connolly Yes it is. Your word 'nation' includes all, excludes none. 'We can support ourselves,' said Wolfe Tone, 'by the aid of that numerous and respectable class of the community, the men of no property.' 'Merchants,' said Wolfe Tone, 'make bad revolutionaries.' Company directors, says James Connolly, turn government into mass murder, religion into a confidence trick, and nationality into an increased margin of profit upon their books. Don't you see, if you once permit their way of life its very existence, it will continue to amass power, and there will be nothing for anyone else except the servitude of that power?

Pearse Class conflict within a nation is more destructive than anything else.

Connolly Class conflict is inevitable, until the nation itself agrees to put it out of the law by making outlaws of all exploiters. There's no compromise.

Pearse Would you accept a declaration of the right of the people of Ireland to the ownership of Ireland?

Connolly To let William Martin Murphy remain the despot of all his enterprise?

Pearse It would also let you in the fullness of time bring in your legislation to strip the coat off Murphy's back.

Connolly Provided I can find the votes...? Dammit, Mr Pearse: I haven't even got them in your military council. I must make do with limitations... What do we propose to say about the protestant north?

Pearse A specific guarantee of political and religious liberty.

Connolly I wonder will they believe it?

An inordinately lengthy pause. They look at one another.

Pearse (*without much conviction*) Fortunately the greater part of Carson's army is in France.

Connolly Fortunate? The casualties of those regiments have been enormous beyond nightmare. Do you know that in one day the scarlet bicycles of the telegraph boys came to every street off Sandy Row and nearly every house in every street with the news of someone's death?

Pearse I intended to mean *fortunately* from a purely military point of view. We must take a cold account of the opposition to our venture.

Connolly The military point of view is the worst in the whole world.

Pearse Oh surely, surely not. Why, Mr Connolly, the last six months have been the most glorious in the history of Europe. It is good for the world that such things should be done. The old heart of the earth needed to be warmed with the red wine of the battlefield...

CLARKE, MACDERMOTT, PLUNKETT, *etc.*, *with other* IRB MEN, *have slipped in and are listening behind.*

IRB Man (*in a whisper*) Padraic has won him over. He has compelled him to the struggle by the grace of divine poetry...

Pearse Such august homage was never before offered to God as this, the homage of millions of lives given daily for love of country.

Connolly You mean the Germans?

Pearse The English, if it comes to that, the French, Russians, everyone... But not us. Ireland will not find Christ's peace until she has taken Christ's sword. What peace she has known in these latter days has been the Devil's peace, peace with sin, peace with dishonour – for that matter, Mr Connolly, *war* with dishonour, because our soldiers in Flanders fight not for their own but for the alien who oppresses them...

Connolly Yes... well... At all events, we can put a stop to that.

Pearse We shall win through, Mr Connolly; and those of us who survive shall come unto great joy. I think we shall come unto great joy even if we do not survive.

I have turned my face
To this road before me
To the dead that I see
And the death I shall die.

The VOLUNTEERS *all break into a stirring song in Irish, 'oro se do bheatha bhaile', and the meeting breaks up.* CONNOLLY *is left alone.*

Connolly I myself am *not* determined upon death. The plans of these people have a basis of practicality: my concern, to substantiate it.

SCENE 2

A NEWSBOY *crosses the stage calling 'Irish Independent':* CONNOLLY *buys a paper. Enter* O'BRIEN *and the* COUNTESS.

O'Brien In the Name of God, where have you been?

Connolly Considering, among other things, the continuation of the current dock strike.

Countess Jim, this is no time to talk about the dock strike –

Connolly It's every time to talk about it. Listen: William Martin Murphy has published an appeal from a unionist general – don't interrupt, William, you must hear this.

> 'I exhort all deputy-lieutenants, magistrates, and employers of labour within this city to lose not a moment in making clear to their employees that not only will no hindrance be placed by them in the way of young men desiring to join the army, but that special privileges will be given to those who show themselves worthy of support by patriotically responding to the country's call in its hour of da-da-da . . .'

O'Brien Sure we've heard all that before – they've been saying that since August 'fourteen.

Connolly In August 'fourteen there was no strike at the docks. What Murphy has done now is to put the clock back one more year – August nineteen thirteen, what happened then?

Countess He imposed the great lockout.

Connolly So he did: and so he *does*. Will ye look: in his leading article he makes use of the general's letter in relation to the dock strike to back up his own appeal to the Federation of the Dublin Employers to lock out every single member of the Transport Workers' Union! I knew it would come: I've been waiting for it, here it is: after eighteen months of war they have finally found a way to use the jingoes of the war hysteria to destroy the labour movement.

O'Brien D'ye suggest then the dock strike was a strategical error . . .? Like playing into their hands with it like a crowd of damned eedjits?

Connolly By no means: the reverse! We are *given* into our *own* hands an industrial crisis of the first potential magnitude!

O'Brien God knows what the dock dispute alone is costing the union – Jim, we can never afford another general strike!

Connolly We may not have to. In fact we may need no more than the general agreement through all parts of the working class that we *ought* to be affording one . . .

> We need fury against Murphy
> We need fury against the state
> We need a rage of recollection
> Of how when we were locked out
> Through a whole winter William Murphy
> Could get through his gate
> Not one cart-load of cargo – once again we can breed
> In all of our people the old hope and the pride
> Of that victory for which they starved
> And which they damn well nearly had . . .!

Countess Jim, will you please put your first intention
Into the middle of the scene –
Here. You have been missing for three days
We think we know where you have been.
Jim, I cannot believe either Pearse or Tom Clarke
Kept you all that length of time talking over your plans for a
strike...

Connolly No they didn't. You understand I cannot tell you now
Exactly what was said, by whom, or how
It will be put into effect. But if I do explain
That very shortly every working man
Within the union will have his chance to gain
A full, a very full revenge for what was done
To him and his in nineteen hundred and thirteen,
I fancy you will catch at least the corner of what I mean...?
This news from the employers has got to be made the keystone of trade-union policy over the next few weeks; William, I want every convenor, every shop-steward alerted to the immediate probability of a particular drastic action on the industrial front. Tell them not to worry about the details of finance. The funds will be found, in some most unexpected places...

O'Brien Are we waiting for some sort of signal or what? There's a class of a prophetical vagueness about this which I must say I don't appreciate...

Connolly William, when the time comes to declare to the movement just where we all are,
They will know that it has come, and their purpose will be quite clear.

Exit O'BRIEN.

Countess To me already clear as the new moon
So suddenly exalting her bright horn
Above the water of a mountain lake
White and alive at once where all was cold and black.
You look at me as though you have been drinking wine –
Red wine for blood...?
Did Pearse project on you his mad sweet mood
Of naked, flower-crowned sacrifice hung by the wrist
Upon the pillar-stone before the people for the thrust
Of spear or arrow in his bleeding side?
Do you at last believe with him
That for this people now a given god
Must give himself to death for them
To mark their scarlet smears on lintel and doorpost –
And so march out at last
Their own deferred passover

> To the promised land . . . ? James, you have set the date!
> James, is it Easter . . . ?

Connolly And how did you discover?

Countess For a man like Padraic Pearse what other possible feast?

Connolly No. Too much poetry. It didn't go at all like that.

> Anything later would be too late
> Anything sooner too soon.
> Constance, *my* mind at least –
> And I think also his – turned powerfully upon
> These rumours that already talks have been begun
> Between the British and the Germans about peace –
> Negotiated truce – an armistice . . .

On the Western Front they have reached deadlock, bound down in the mud and wire. Gallipoli, which might have broken the war decisively open, proved a complete failure. If hostilities were to be negotiated now to a temporary end, inevitable they should resume in a matter of a few months or a year or two at most. But, during the respite, all resistance in Ireland to renewal of the war could be crushed by the entire British Army, conscription could be forced onto us, national independence would not only in that case be indefinitely deferred but forgotten for ever!

Countess But a negotiated peace, immediately *after* an Irish revolt, would tip the scale against Britain in their haggling with Berlin; an Irish Provisional Revolutionary Government – however tenuous – however impotent – by the very fact that it existed –

Connolly Would have to be recognised, because the Germans would have supported it, and the Germans would insist! America would be called in as a so-called neutral arbitrator – neutral in favour of the Irish and no-one else: and as part of the terms of truce Britain would be compelled to give up any further claim to the lordship of this island. For the whole of the past year we have been agitating for Irish neutrality – and Britain has refused to even consider it. But don't you see – the whole thing's changed! If only a fraction, a significant fraction of the people of Ireland, can be seen, under arms, to be presenting so much as the illusion that Ireland is from now on the *ally* of Germany – then our neutrality will be *begged-for* by the British at any price!

Countess And our price is the Republic! And from the day we get that it will no longer be possible for Britain to renew the war against Germany – their naval bases will be lost – their training and supply and recruitment of troops will be withered away – God knows what proportion of their own working class will suddenly become suspect –

Connolly As you see, all this talk from Padraic Pearse about blood-sacrifice is in fact quite irrelevant. By joining for our own cause in the war, at this time, with the uninvolved proletariat at last, thank God, aroused by the bloody-mindedness of William Murphy, we can conclude the entire conflict: and unhindered we can set forward for the socialist revolution...!

Exeunt, exalted and exultant.

SCENE 3

Enter KAISER *and* GERMAN GENERAL.

Kaiser   Question of negotiated truce
From America supervised
Our own terms could be imposed
Don't you think it could be of use?

German General All-highest, there is no doubt that our own terms would be much more advantageously imposed once we have broken through the French fortifications at Verdun. You are recommended by your general staff not to rebuff the American intermediaries: but commit your government to nothing. Be discreet, and procrastinate.

Exeunt.

Enter ASQUITH *and* WILSON.

Asquith   The Americans suggest
That the Germans are so hard-pressed
They may very well think it best
To cut their losses, as it were,
And call a halt to this endless war...?

Wilson Prime Minister, there is a plan in the War Office operations room for an attack at the River Somme of such unprecedented magnitude that the entire present picture of stalemate will be reversed. Any attempt to make terms with the Hun, before that attack can be logistically supported, will be seen by the army as a betrayal of all the casualties they have suffered up to this time. We must keep faith with our dead men, Prime Minister. The Conservatives agree with me ... whom, remember, you were induced to bring into your war cabinet because the Liberals on their own were losing the war. It is therefore for the Conservatives politically exigeant to hold out for complete victory...

Prime Minister, I do beg you, as it were, to wait and see...

Exit WILSON.

Asquith

That bloody man, of all men, has to use those words to *me*...?

Exit.

SCENE 4

Enter CONNOLLY *and the* COUNTESS.

Connolly The line is drawn upon the ground

The arched feet poised to take the running leap

The whole world changed into a quite new size and shape –

And I myself must now put on

A change of shape at every turn.

In the office above, the advocate of the dockworkers' wage:

In the basement below, with yourself and a young priest,

Co-director, with Kitchener, with Hindenburg, of the crisis of our age.

Where's my daughter, where is Nora; Liam Mellows, are you there?

Enter NORA *with* MELLOWS *disguised as a priest.*

I do hope you were unobserved as you slipped down round the turn of the stair . . .

Countess Liam! Since when were the officers of my Fianna inducted in holy orders?

Mellows Time to take them off, Madame Markievicz, I think.

Connolly (*as* MELLOWS *removes his collar, etc.*) He goes to Galway on the afternoon train. On behalf of the Volunteers. But there's a few points of view from the Citizen Army that need to be made in the West, and there's no better man to make them. It's for you and nobody else, Liam, to take control of things in Galway: if the revolt is successful the men from the rural areas will have a preponderance in the new counsels of the Provisional Government. I want Galway at least to be solid for revolution – there'll be gombeen opportunists and every breed and class of land-grabber trying to climb upon your back – keep 'em out!

Countess Will you tell me how he ever got out of Scotland, this young man? Weren't you served with a deportation order under the Defence of the Realm Act – and isn't he liable to instant arrest if they discover him back in Ireland?

Connolly Nora got him out, via Glasgow, via Belfast, hence the clerical get-up.

NORA *is helping* MELLOWS *to dress up in a new outfit.*

Mellows Hence a prosperous young cattle-dealer making a good thing out of War Office meat contracts – would I pass muster, do you suppose in the fair of Oughterard?

Connolly Good. Very good.

Mellows Mr Connolly, there is one thing – in the western counties, the small farmers: all this talk in your manifestoes of the confiscation of the land – won't it confuse them, don't you think . . . ?

Connolly The only successful sustained revolutionary struggle this country has had was the Land League War of the eighteen eighties. Not a small farmer in County Galway but has his memory of his father's memory of that! You remind them of its principles.

Mellows Let him who lifts his spade to till

Take title deed to all the soil

Let him who would grab another man's land

Have his fat beasts driven to the stony strand . . .

Countess Let you tell them it in Irish and after that you can tell them anything . . . !

Connolly Good luck.

Exit MELLOWS.

Now Nora, when you passed through Glasgow

Did you have words with John MacLean?

Nora I did, but I couldn't tell him

What it was you were doing –

He wouldn't let me – too well-watched –

He said, any loose talk, the whole business is botched.

Countess I hope he knows what he's about.

There was a hundredweight of gelignite

Came to my house last night

From a messenger of MacLean: I got it into a safe place

But straightway came in the police . . .

Their information, thank God, was confused:

But they had it from Scotland and I am inclined to think

Our contacts there should not be used

At least until we are over the brink.

Connolly I don't believe they'll need to be

If all goes now as I foresee.

When the Glasgow men hear what we've done

They'll all know very well it's time

To kick their ball into the game.

In the meanwhile into this basement, every cartridge, every gun,

Every document that gives a hint we are no longer on our own –

Today we lock the door between the office and the stair.

Nora – unfasten the bag –

Members of the CITIZEN ARMY *begin to come in carrying boxes and parcels, etc., some of them clearly containing weapons, and stowing them away at the side.* NORA *has a bag from which she takes out a green flag.*

Countess That's prudent – yet this flag –

Connolly For the roof – for the open air!

A flag states an attitude

But a document betrays a plot.

I have never been ashamed of any attitude yet.

He gives the flag to a CA MAN *who takes it to hang it up over the stage.*
O'BRIEN *enters.*

O'Brien (*calls from the other side of the stage*)
>There's a suggestion of some doubt here about the size of the dockers'
>claim...

Connolly William, it's still the same.
>No concessions. If the bosses remain firm
>We step up our own terms.

TU OFFICIALS *have come in with* O'BRIEN.

O'Brien Jim, the committee says –
1st TU Official
>That flag must come down.
O'Brien Jim, the committee says –
2nd TU Official
>All these quare goings-on...
O'Brien Jim, the committee says –
1st Union Official
>We want to know who are these men?
>We want to know why Liberty Hall
>Should all of a sudden become so full
>Of non-affiliated this and that
>In and out o'the bloody basement like some class of a dangerous rat –
O'Brien They mean, Jim, constitutional
>As a matter of proper principle
>We've got to keep our proper business
>Very clearly in the clear...

A cry – 'Police!!' Immediately the CA MEN *and various* VOLUNTEERS *who
are helping them begin to rush all the dunnage out of sight. A* POLICE
OFFICER *comes strolling past the* TU OFFICIALS, *oblivious to all the* PEOPLE
milling about, and starts looking through a burst parcel of newsprint.

Connolly You have a warrant?
Police Officer Defence of the Realm Regulations, not required, you know that.
It's been reported you may have here some copies of illegal newspapers –
in particular *The Gaelic Athlete*: a publication presenting matters of
football and such in a manner subversive of public order in wartime...
Countess (*points a pistol*) If you don't drop those papers, Inspector, I shall
drop you.
Connolly Inspector, this building is called Liberty Hall – the working class of
Dublin require a warrant to disturb their liberty – if you don't know *that*,
you should go back to your superiors and find out where they draw the
line. I think they will inform you that a general strike in wartime is *not*
adequately balanced by the prevention of subversive football... Well?

Police Officer (*retreats*) Mr Connolly, I suggest you should be very very careful...

He goes out.

Connolly From henceforth Liberty Hall is under armed guard day and night. I will sleep in my own office.

The TU OFFICIALS *look alarmed.*

Yes, I know, I see your faces. Your problem is not improved.

He blows a whistle and CA MEN *in uniform with rifles come in and stand guard.*

If we can't share the use of the building, my brothers, there are some of us will have to go. Now then, who do you think will be able to turn out whom? I warn you, if we split, I stay with the Citizen Army.

O'Brien (*to* TU OFFICIALS) You'd be satisfied if the Chief promised it was only a temporary measure?

Connolly Oh, it's that all right, temporary. Be assured of that – yes. When we leave, we don't come back. From the day that we do leave, you'll have no more cause to worry. Agreed?

O'Brien Agreed?

Dubious nods from TU OFFICIALS.

Agreed.

Exeunt O'BRIEN *and* TU OFFICIALS.

Enter SHEEHY SKEFFINGTON.

Sheehy Skeffington
Larkin from New York
Says leave alone this dangerous work.

Connolly Over three thousand miles, Skeffy,
His voice can not be heard...

Sheehy Skeffington
Over three thousand miles his head reels with what *he* has heard.
Tell me, does that lad there with his gun
Now speak for Marx and Engels and Wolfe Tone
And Lalor, *and* yourself? If so, his voice is very short.
No different from a bullet shot
From any other firearm in the world.
You wrote a history of the Irish people once:
It is as though you reached the present tense
In your last chapter and then drew a line
Across the page and wrote –
'All the above no longer makes good sense:
If you have read it, then forget it.'
I'm sorry, James, you count me out.

This crank, this small arm, has become disconnected from the shaft of
the piston. You should look out for a new spare part . . . one that fits.

Exeunt.

SCENE 5

Enter KAISER *and* GERMAN GENERAL.

Kaiser   General, you cannot really mean
            In the midst of your great attack upon Verdun
            To let the Socialist Irish have ten thousand men?
General Oh we never did approve it:
            Roger Casement misconstrued it.
            Roger Casement is a fool.
            Indeed it would do no harm
            If the Irish were to rebel:
            And so for Casement, we send him home,
            A consignment of guns as well:
            They are old, they are clogged with dirt,
            Not accurate: they could divert
            A British regiment or two away from France . . .
            Ten thousand German soldiers, though,
            As you say, would be not good sense.

Exeunt.

Enter LLOYD GEORGE *and an* ADMIRAL.

Lloyd George
            Admiral, you cannot really mean
            That all this time your intelligence men have known
            The secret of the German naval code?
            From their espionage transmissions from America you have heard
            Of an armed insurrection in Ireland? It's absurd.
            If true, why has not the Prime Minister been told?
Admiral (*to audience*)
            Sir Roger Casement under water
            Like a voracious barracuda
            Swims toward Kerry. We could and should
            Pass on this news to Dublin, but we won't.
            For if we do, the government will shunt
            So many troops to Ireland the whole thing will be called off.
            No, they must first rise and then be beaten down!
            And then, my friends, they'll never dare again.
            There is no other way our Atlantic bases may be secured.

To LLOYD GEORGE:

Mr Lloyd George, would the Prime Minister be really reassured
If we told him what we knew? Were he taken by surprise
And thus apparently confounded, would not a man more wise
And more far-sighted in his views,
Thereby obtain the chance to rise –
I will not say *displace* the present leader of the state –
But we do feel it is not yet too late
To put the affairs of Britain into the hand
Of one who has the confidence both of the land-
Commanders and the rulers of the fleet . . .
Mr Lloyd George, we all know well how very well you can be
   discreet.

Exit LLOYD GEORGE, *slyly.*

By God, I would not trust him a foot nor an inch
But he's better than Asquith when put to the pinch!

Exit.

SCENE 6

Enter a BRITISH GENERAL *and* GRABITALL.

General MacNeill has ordered some sort of march
For Easter Sunday. I don't know where.
Grabitall Perhaps to church? Leave it alone.
MacNeill would never dare . . .

Exeunt.

Enter a VOLUNTEER.

Volunteer
I am a conscientious Volunteer.
My secret orders I have had.
On Easter Sunday Dublin runs with blood.
I hope not mine . . . But I must go
Prepare myself, first at confession, then with the firm
Who have insured my life. I want to know
If they will pay upon my policy, were I to fall
Fighting for Ireland as a proclaimed rebel?
A British bullet here or a German one in France
Equally would kill . . . Why should my wife
Not benefit, to whichever side I give my life?
It is all too complicated: yet I must try
To sort out my affairs the most straight and scrupulous way . . .
I have hardly time to think:
I work, d'you see, in a bank.

Enter COUNTESS.

Countess I want to draw all my money, please, out of my account.

Volunteer (*as cashier*) I'm sorry, Madame Markievicz, but I'm afraid you have none in.

Countess It doesn't matter – not to worry. After the Easter holiday I can assure you things will be different . . .

Aside:

If this bally revolution doesn't take place soon, I don't know how I'm going to live . . .

Exeunt.

Enter a DOCKER.

Docker I am a docker at the port.
We're out on strike
We won't go back.
The Transport Union gives support
In all our struggle for a living wage.
Their strike-pay, though, is very small indeed.
I think I am a damnfool to engage
On Easter Sunday in Jim Connolly's deed of blood.
As it is my wife and six young kids
Have barely a bite of food.
And yet if we refuse to march
We leave Jim Connolly in the lurch.
And I believe if we leave him
It is ourselves are left to sink or swim.
Sure there's no future for this country
But that which the short squat Jim
Day in day out in rain or snow
Has told us is the only way to go.
'Tis him or Murphy, and by God
Rather than Martin Murphy I'll lie dead beneath the sod . . .

Exit.

Enter CONNOLLY *with a bicycle, meeting* DE VALERA *with a bicycle.*

Connolly Traversing the town by foot and upon my bike
Looking over the strong points we are shortly to attack
I confer with a long schoolmaster whose business is the same.
He tells me his name.

De Valera De Valera.

Connolly He tells me he regrets he has never read any of my books.

De Valera But I must take occasion to study them when all this is over.

Young Plunkett now impresses me as having given very fruitful thought to the art of fighting among city streets.

Connolly Moscow nineteen-o-five: that's what we fix our minds on. The entire working class came out in support of five hundred. Barricades on every street, tramcars turned over, telegraph-poles cut down and lashed across with rope between the houses. Your job is to guard the flank of Michael Mallin and the Countess up there in Stephen's Green, and to hold this road here against any troops brought up from Dun Laoghaire.

A POLICEMAN *passes.*

Make normal conversation . . . !

De Valera Do you commonly attend the late Mass at Haddington Road?

Connolly Eh? Oh, yes, certainly, that is when I – I don't go elsewhere . . .

De Valera I forgot you were a protestant. I should have chosen a better – –

Connolly Keep your eye on that canal bridge.

Exit DE VALERA.

> Though courage and will must wait to be proven
> The plans themselves are all made: they are good: I daresay heaven
> Is not without some accident to drop upon us yet . . .

Exit.

SCENE 7

Enter LLOYD GEORGE *and* ASQUITH.

Lloyd George

> John Maclean in Glasgow's gone too far.
> He and his friends imperil the whole war –
> Munition works and shipyards blighted by strike all down the Clyde,
> Prime Minister –

Asquith I have heard you. I agree. Here is what I decide.

> By virtue of my draconian powers all left-wing agitators in the Glasgow area are at last to be deported –

Lloyd George (*aside*)

> At last. I do believe it is too late.
> Too late at least for Mr Asquith's fate
> To be postponed. The Tories all and Bonar Law agree
> The seat he sits on is the chair for *me* –

To ASQUITH:

> Your Cabinet will be pleased indeed
> That to this violent Red you have put paid.

Exeunt.

MACLEAN, *under arrest, is brought across by a* POLICEMAN.

MacLean

> Aye let the bosses' war run on to its bitter end –
> They will know in the future years which one was the workers'
> friend!

Enter CONNOLLY.

Connolly We know already who has been the friend
> Of the Irish worker: now they've got him.
> Sure we must do what we do without him:
> But this must mean, if our backs go to the wall
> There's no hope of help from Scotland
> For the boys in Liberty Hall . . .

Exit.

Enter MACNEILL *in charge of* PEARSE.

MacNeill Mr Pearse . . .! Mr Pearse . . .! I am informed I have been deceived!
You intend on Easter Sunday to – to engage in physical force, sir! I
demand an explanation!

Pearse (*gives him a paper*) Mr MacNeill, would you read this, and then tell me
what you think of it.

MacNeill It appears to be an official order emanating from Dublin Castle and
arranging for the arrest of every nationalist in the country –!

Pearse Including yourself and including the Archbishop. Under the circumstances, sir, do you suppose that we have any choice but to fight?

MacNeill Mr Pearse, this news is devastating . . . I had been so confident all
this time that the passive existence of the Volunteers would of itself be
sufficient reminder to the British that their pledge of Home Rule at the
end of the war – and so on . . . Mr Pearse, we must make a plan!

Exit MACNEILL. *Enter* MACDERMOTT.

MacDermott

> Did you show him the Castle letter?

Pearse Oh I did and he's all of a jitter.
> Who wrote it? Did you?

MacDermott

> Did you ever hear me tell you a thing that was not true?

Enter 1ST VOLUNTEER MESSENGER, *followed by* CONNOLLY.

1st Messenger

> Casement is caught!

Enter 2ND MESSENGER.

2nd Messenger

> The German ship that brought
> The guns is caught: and scuttled!

MacDermott

> The whole of our plans are baffled.

Pearse Not at all. We carry on.

1st Messenger

> Casement, you know, was landed here *alone*.

Connolly You really believed the Germans were not going to let us down?

> An Emperor who'll help another empire pass
> Into the common hands of subjects is as rare
> As bulls who eat roast beef instead of grass.

Enter 3RD MESSENGER.

3rd Messenger

> The men we sent to Kerry to prepare
> Our radio link with Germany and the world
> Have in their motor car by night been hurled
> Into the sea!

Pearse It seems that we

> Have gaps in our line of battle that will have to be made up.

Connolly Don't talk about it. Spread the map.

Enter MACNEILL, *at the far side*, *as* PEARSE, MACDERMOTT *and* CONNOLLY
crouch over a map.

MacNeill

> How can how can a serious-minded Gael
> Like Padraic Pearse become so double faced!
> This document is forged!
> A second time they have deceived MacNeill!
> I must make haste ...

Enter GRABITALL. MACNEILL *scurries round the stage and up to him, gives
him a paper.*

Grabitall In my newspaper the *Independent* this statement forthwith is
placed:

'Owing to the very critical situation, all orders given to the Irish Volunteers for Easter Sunday are hereby rescinded: and no parades, marches, or
other movement of Volunteers will be commenced on that day.'

> I am very glad to see
> Professor MacNeill agrees with me
> And is determined to prevent
> All provocation and discontent.

Exeunt GRABITALL *and* MACNEILL.

SCENE 8

MACDERMOTT, PEARSE and CONNOLLY have heard GRABITALL'S announcement in horror.

MacDermott Betrayed again betrayed again betrayed again . . . !

Pearse Mr Connolly, I assure you – I knew nothing of this.

Connolly Mr Pearse, we do not purchase Murphy's papers in Liberty Hall. Of what you did not know, we are still unaware. And moreover, we have our orders.

He walks away from them, calling:

Constance – Winifred – mobilisation three-thirty!

Enter the COUNTESS, WINIFRED CARNEY *and* O'BRIEN.

William, if you have not gathered what is happening this afternoon, I do not propose to tell you. But if all goes off as it should, you will find yourself nominated as a member of a provisional government, to look after the general civilian affairs until the fighting is concluded. You agree?

O'Brien Tell me – is Arthur Griffith going to be in this provisional government?

Connolly Not possible, just yet, William, to make sure it will be a *Labour* Government. But at least it will be Republican.

Exit O'BRIEN.

Countess There's a whole rack of rifles there have not been cleaned for a week. Disgraceful! You have ten minutes . . .

CITIZEN ARMY MEN have come in and are bustling about, bringing out the weapons and accoutring themselves. PEARSE *comes over to* CONNOLLY.

Pearse Mr Connolly – we can't do it – not today! Do have some sense. You must cancel your orders . . . !

Connolly No! This is the last time in this history and in the work of my life
    The bourgeoisie will make a haystack out of every single hope!
    The troops of labour march out to revolt:
    You come or you stay behind
    You make up your own mind.
    Today the working class will fight
    Without ten thousand faint-heart friends to punctuate
    Our statement with their *if* and *and* and *but*.
    Soldiers, are you ready?

Pearse You must give us time to cancel the cancellation of our orders, Mr Connolly!

Connolly But you can't do it.

Pearse By tomorrow –

Connolly It won't work, Mr Pearse. You have lost your Volunteers.

Pearse Mr Connolly, I believe that you *want* to have them lost! You desire to be betrayed by the idealists, by the mystics. I won't let you. You are with *us*: and we, such as we are, are with *you*, Mr Connolly . . . !

Connolly The one last prohibition that I thought need not be broken

> All of a sudden I have agreed to the wiping of it out. The complete token
>
> Of the fallible betrayed humanity
>
> Of careful international theoretical James Connolly –

He grips PEARSE *by both hands.*

> – and yet who could do other
>
> Than call a man like this his brother?

Postponement for one day . . . is it practical: that's all?

Pearse Just.

Connolly Then it's agreed.

The COUNTESS *comes in with* CONNOLLY'*s uniform coat and hat and gun-belt: she helps him to put them on with a deliberate formality.*

I'll hold my men tonight bivouacked here in Liberty Hall. With as many Volunteers as you can bring to keep us company. The rest to assemble at – twelve o'clock noon . . . ? Constance, you go direct with your command and be ready to take hold of St Stephen's Green. Good luck.

He shakes hands with the COUNTESS *and she goes off.*

Pearse In the meantime, the proclamation. We have the agreed text already drafted.

Connolly You'll find the printing-press over there. There are three paid-up members of the Dublin Typographical Society ready to set the type.

He calls the CITIZEN ARMY MEN *and* WOMEN *to him confidentially.*

Citizen Army – come here a moment. Whatever happens tomorrow, hold on to your rifles. Those with whom we are fighting may stop before our goal is reached: remember *we* are out for economic as well as political liberty.

Winifred Carney For both sexes . . . ? The women want to know why we are not being given guns.

Connolly We haven't got enough. Don't you know the whole thing is going off at half-cock? Who shoots a gun best, shoots. There are pistols as well, you know. I want *you* to use a typewriter. And in no back room. At my elbow. D'ye know anyone else who can do it as deftly?

> So, after all the excitement and the urgency and the heat
>
> We discover after all we have nothing to do but wait.

They all sit down with their weapons and equipment, patiently waiting. PEARSE, *with some* VOLUNTEERS, *are attending to the proclamation in the rear.*

SCENE 9

Enter at a distance, NORA *and* LILLIE.

Nora   In Belfast, on Holy Thursday, the twenty-sixth anniversary
Of her marriage in Scotland, to the Irish revolutionary:
Lillie Connolly has been told, by her daughter, what is afoot.

Lillie   Lillie Connolly has known, twenty-six years, that it would come.
He doesn't think I'll stay in Belfast, washing blankets, in this small
    home?
I would stand with him and his guns in Liberty Hall, if I could.
But someone must survive and tell his children what he did.
Nonetheless I will be in Dublin. Before I go there I will burn
Every paper in this house that incriminates a single one.
Light the fire: and the flames will rise.
Flames everywhere before the eyes
Of Ireland – dark smoke over the low roof.

She and NORA *burn letters and other documents.*

Nora   Countess Markievicz says you stay in her house in Dublin.

Lillie   Ah the beautiful Countess . . . Yes I will: and is not that proof
That James Connolly and myself are one flesh in death and life.

She sings:

> Can I say that I had rather
> Have married for your father
> A draper's clerk, a minister,
> Or a sober quiet schoolmaster,
> Who would come home and live at home
> With his regular weekly pay?
> While the wild women of Dublin
> Would be left alone to play?

> James Connolly is my man
> I had rather let him roam
> With the wildest in the world
> Be they women or be they men
> Than lie beside me night by night
> With broken heart and frozen brain –
> For the life of his wife he must go to sleep again?
> For the life of his wife all our liberty fell to ruin

Now that all is secure here, towards Dublin we take the train . . .

NORA *and* LILLIE *go out.* NORA *re-enters on the main stage.*

Nora   And myself, on Easter Sunday, stand in Liberty Hall, appalled.

You all sit here, you do nothing, I thought the whole thing had
  already begun –

In the North there is such confusion, they think everything's been
  cancelled –

They can't decide whether to go home or to march out and take the
  field,

At least, I told them, Dublin, you would know here what is to be
  done...!

Connolly Indeed it is a confusion, it's a comical Irish muddle: but it's no
worse. Now look, Nora, you'll not want to do this: but you must go back
to Belfast.

Pearse (*comes over with the proclamation*) We need you to take the proclamation
to the North. In your mind: not your hand. Too dangerous. You could
be caught with it.

Connolly Memorise it. And then make haste to the station. Don't miss the
evening train. There isn't going to be another one.

Nora (*reads*) 'Poblacht na hEireann: the Provisional Government of the Irish
Republic to the people of Ireland. Irishmen and Irishwomen, in the name
of God and of the dead generations from which she receives her old
tradition of nationhood, Ireland – through us – summons her children
to her flag and strikes for her freedom...'

She goes out.

SCENE 10

The CITIZEN ARMY *and* VOLUNTEERS *get up and form up in two squads with
their respective flags.* CONNOLLY *and* PEARSE *step forward and address the*
AUDIENCE.

Connolly Monday morning. There is a race-meeting at Fairyhouse. Bank
holiday and an indolent city. Bank holiday and a few men, some in
uniform, some in their own clothes, one or two in rags and tatters, look
around at one another and wonder – is this all? Have you any reports in
from the rural counties?

Pearse From the rural counties I have heard nothing.

  Indeed before I died I never did.

  But outside Dublin there were some who rose.

  Thomas Ashe in County Meath played games

  In and out the small towns with the police.

  Killed eight, lost two: captured one hundred guns.

  Paul Gilligan in Wexford made attacks

  Upon the railway-line and blocked the tracks.

Connolly In County Galway Liam Mellows fought

  At Clarenbridge and Oranmore and Gort:

  Caused panic in Galway, frenzy in Tuam,

Held his men together unbeaten,
In the end he got them home . . .

Pearse Out of the five thousand who were predicted in the plan to invest
Dublin – just over one tenth: maybe six hundred, maybe seven . . .

Connolly Absentees from the Citizen Army, I am glad to say, negligible.

O'BRIEN *has entered.*

William, it's time we were off. We're going out to be slaughtered.

O'Brien Is there no chance of success?

Connolly None whatever. Go straight home and stay there. There is nothing
you can do now, but you may be of great service later on. Commandant
Pearse: sir, the parade is yours.

PEARSE *draws his sword and turns to give orders to the* TROOPS.

Pearse Army of the Irish Republic: attention! By the right, right turn! To the
Post Office, quick march!

*They march around the stage, etc. Business now follows the description in
the next two speeches.*

O'Brien I went back in to Liberty Hall
And took my bicycle and began to wheel
It through the crowded door and so on to the road.
In O'Connell Street the flag went up: a bewildered crowd
Watched men with bayonets suddenly turn and run
Into a public building –

The VOLUNTEERS *and* CITIZEN ARMY MEN *thrust a* BRITISH SUBALTERN *out.*

British Subaltern
I had gone in
To buy a stamp. They threw me out. I am quite sure
Behaviour of this sort is not allowed.
Someone is reading something. I can't quite hear . . .

PEARSE *is reading the Proclamation.*

A mob of men with rifles give a cheer –
My commanding officer has gone away
To the racecourse this Bank Holiday.
I don't know what to do. I think I ought
To find my way to him and to report . . .

He carefully edges himself out of the CROWDS, *and goes.*

The stage now represents the Post Office, and the VOLUNTEERS *and* CITIZEN
ARMY *set to work with vigour tearing down as much of the structure as is
practicable and erecting barricades, etc.* CONNOLLY *tries to clear a corner
for himself.*

Connolly Would you mind: this is an office! I want all these fellows out of here
and let Miss Carney and myself set up a headquarters. If you've nothing
to do, then find something to do – break the windows, block the openings,
secure for yourselves loopholes. You, you, and you – barricades in the
adjacent streets!

*There is furious activity for a few moments, until they have all settled their
military arrangements: then calm.*

Well . . .! Isn't this glorious! We're in: and they've not stopped us.
Pearse What happens next?

At a distance, re-enter BRITISH SUBALTERN *to a group of* RACE-GOERS,
including a GENERAL (*throughout this short episode the* AUDIENCE *see only
the back of the* GENERAL). *They are cheering on the horses.*

British Subaltern

When I got to the racecourse all of a sweat

I found my officer had placed a bet

On a horse I could have told him had never a chance –

He could barely spare me a passing glance.

General (*behind his binoculars*) No no no you three-legged mule, he's coming up
outside you, keep *out*, dammit, *out* – or he'll pass you at the corner!
Aaargh . . . I knew it! Damn fool let him pass him on the very point of the
turn! What is it, boy, what d'you want?

British Subaltern

Excuse me, sir, I have to say

There's a sort of revolt in Dublin today.

General Don't be a fool, if they tried that

They'd all be in gaol in five minutes flat.

Go away, get lost!

British Subaltern

I did what I was told.

In the end though, they caught hold

Of what it was was going on.

Down in the town

The bullets began to fly

And one by one

Men saw their fellows die.

*The race-going party has left its position. The stage representing the Post
Office is now under siege. Cracks and volleys of small arms fire. Some of the
men on the stage are wounded.*

A group of WOMEN *from the slums appear in the auditorium in front of the
stage, screaming abuse at those on it.*

Women The dirty bloody bowsies are taking away our men's lives, why don't you get out and fight the Germans like men, why don't you fight the Huns like my Paddy – Jimmy Fogarty, ye bloody lowser, what about separation allowance – what about our soldiers' pay . . . !

Connolly The Government Separation Allowance for the families of men at the front is the only regular income some of these women have ever had. There's nothing we can do about their abuse except take no notice – and keep them as far as possible out of the line of the shooting . . .

Enter at one side JAMES STEPHENS.

James Stephens James Stephens, Curator at the National Museum, novelist, poet . . . On this day the rumours began, and I think it will be many a day before the rumours cease. I met one man who spat rumour as though his mouth were a machine-gun or a linotype machine.

Persons slip up and down the AUDIENCE, *whispering rumours earnestly and rapidly to those within earshot.*

Rumours German submarines have landed machine-guns and rifles and
ammunition at thirty different places within twenty miles of
Dublin . . .
The barracks at Cork has been captured by the Volunteers . . .
Thousands of Irish-Americans with horse foot and guns have been
landed at Bantry Bay . . .
The whole of Cork, town and county, has been captured by the
Volunteers . . .
etcetera . . .

Enter at a distance ASQUITH *and* WILSON.

Asquith Report at once upon the Irish news!
Rumours are all I hear.
I was informed – by whom? – that nothing near
As bad as this was to be feared
From who is it – Sinn Fein?
Wilson I think it's worse. I think Berlin
With loads of German gold
Has got the whole thing going.
Not possible the nationalists with all their booing,
Jeering, hooting in the streets could ever hold
Themselves together long enough like men
To get assembled such a foolproof plan –
Our chaps were at the races! Filthy trick
So typical to stab them in the back.

Enter ADMIRAL: *to* ASQUITH.

Admiral Prime Minister, the German High Seas Fleet has made attack
Upon the English East Coast ports!

> Diversionary scheme to draw support
> Away from Ireland where I have no doubt
> A full-scale landing will be carried out!

Wilson The only way to put this rising down
> Is treat it like a total new campaign
> As great as Flanders or the Hellespont:
> Dublin from now must be a first-class front
> For every weapon we can muster – whole regiments must be sent
> – Lord Kitchener and the Tories all agree –
> Surround the town, destroy it by land and sea.

Exit ASQUITH, WILSON *and* ADMIRAL.

Connolly They've tried with cavalry, God help them, we beat them off . . . they've tried with infantry and we're beating them off.

Pearse D'you suppose they'll bring artillery?

Connolly In my analysis of Moscow in nineteen-o-five I made the point that a regular bombardment of the city could only have been possible if the whole loyalist population had withdrawn outside the insurgent lines, which couldn't happen there and it can't happen here – our positions are too dispersed. There's also the crucial question of the damage to capitalist property. Do you really believe Murphy and his political friends will allow them to shell O'Connell Street?

Re-enter ASQUITH *and* 1ST TU LEADER.

1st TU Leader
> Prime Minister, is it true that Jim Connolly's gone stark mad
> Taken hold of these raving Fenians and put himself at their head?
> Oh always such a silly bugger, but I never even dreamed
> He would ha'let things come to this. Oh, sir, I am ashamed
> Of the very name of socialism – please don't let
> This make any difference to my place in your cabinet –
> I beg you to believe that British labour still holds staunch:
> And we back our boys in uniform to the very last trench!

Asquith We don't want to make too much of this Irish affair –
> Connie Markievicz, I understand, quite driven to despair
> By her bankrupt bank-account, threw her petticoat over her hair
> And exhibits herself like a harpy with a gun in each fist –
> My wife knew her once, said she should have been kissed
> A little more often: oh we'll soon sort it out –
> Our General in Dublin will take a very firm line.
> In the meanwhile, Mr Henderson, I'd like you to maintain
> More sugar for civilian rations, running short, please take note.

Exeunt ASQUITH *and* 1ST TU LEADER.

James Stephens Looting began. The department stores in O'Connell Street were among the first buildings to be invaded – the crowd knew that they were unprotected because of the very danger of their position – between the bullets the people ran, making up in one wild spree for all the years they had gone without.

LOOTERS *run backwards and forwards among the* AUDIENCE, *their arms full of goods, screaming improvised encouragement to one another. They dodge bullets – there is continuous small-arms fire – now added to by the rattle of machine-guns: and intermittent crashings of broken glass.*

Connolly (*watches the looting*) If that doesn't stop, we're going to have to shoot them.

A Citizen Army Man D'you want me to do it now?

Connolly (*as a new burst of firing comes at them*) No ... Leave it a while ...

The REBELS *beat off an attack, while the* LOOTERS *all run out of the way. Then the looting begins again.* SHEEHY SKEFFINGTON, *with an umbrella, appears in the middle of the* AUDIENCE.

Sheehy Skeffington If the looting doesn't stop, these foolish people are going to be shot! There must be someone here will join with me to form an unarmed citizens' police to try to check this dangerous rapine. Volunteers?

Captain BOWEN-COLTHURST, *his uniform awry, a Bible in one hand, lurches through the* AUDIENCE. *He wears the mask of a* SUBSIDIARY DEMON.

Bowen-Colthurst

My name is Captain Bowen-Colthurst and I know
The Pope of Rome is Lucifer, Beelzebub, the foretold Antichrist –
He raises up upon our Protestant Empire this great waste
Of blood and shame – this repugnant flow
Of hidden Celtic excrement upon the dead white face
Of Dublin. I hold God's Book, and here I find the text
To tell me what it is I must do next ...

He sees SHEEHY SKEFFINGTON.

You – I know you. I have heard you speak in public.

Sheehy Skeffington Socialism? Votes for Women ...?

Bowen-Colthurst (*beckons for the* SUBALTERN, *who comes running*) Oh Lord God, if it should please thee to take away the life of this man, forgive him for Our Lord Jesus Christ's sake! Kneel, Titivullus: Apollyon, say your prayers!

The SUBALTERN, *dubiously, obeys his gesture and forces* SHEEHY SKEFFINGTON *to his knees.* BOWEN-COLTHURST *reads from his Bible:*

'But those Mine enemies that would not that I should reign over them, bring them hither and slay them before Me!'

He draws his pistol and shoots SHEEHY SKEFFINGTON *dead. He then goes out with the* SUBALTERN. *The episode has not been seen by the characters on the stage.*

James Stephens The rumour of the death of Sheehy Skeffington is persistent in the city. The most absurdly courageous man I have ever met with or heard of...

Connolly Winifred: take care of this. If I don't survive, all my papers, books, poems, the lot – they must go to Sheehy Skeffington. There is no better man to watch over my inheritance.

A CITIZEN ARMY MAN *approaches* CONNOLLY.

CA Man Commandant, there's a question. Like, the Bank Holiday being now over – some of the lads is after wondering, would it be all right to go back to work? I mean, ye wouldn't really want us to be docked a day's pay – would ye, Commandant?

Connolly The flag we hoisted up? What does it mean to you?

CA Man Sure the freedom of Ireland. But the question of a day's pay –

Connolly Your employer?

CA Man Dirty Murphy.

Connolly And ye would give him *again* the benefit of *yourself*? When the gun in your hand and the flag above your head has told him that you are free? You know we have another flag. I think it's time we put it up where it can really make its point. Take the Plough and the Stars, make a dash across the street: and hang it on Murphy's hotel.

CA Man I will so, sir: at the double!

He takes the flag and runs out into the auditorium, dodging bullets. He fixes the flag to some convenient place on the wall opposite the stage, and then scrambles back.

Connolly (*as the* CA MAN *goes*) And then no more nonsense about wanting to go back to work!

Enter GRABITALL *and the* BRITISH GENERAL, *at a distance. It is now seen that the* GENERAL *wears the mask of the* WAR DEMON, *and some of his accoutrements.*

Grabitall General, General, please, I beg you to spare
　　　　　Just one moment of your time! Oh General, my dear sir –
　　　　　You must understand
　　　　　The most part of the Dublin people are as loyal as any in the land –
　　　　　The Federation of Employers is exceedingly concerned
　　　　　Lest property of great value should inadvertently be burned
　　　　　– General, don't you see, what a terrible disaster
　　　　　If Connolly, the damned ruffian, or that crazy schoolmaster –
　　　　　What the devil is the feller's name, Padraic Pearse, were to cause

> The operations of the military to in any way infringe the laws
> Governing breaking-and-entering, or trespass, or the like of that . . .

General Mr Murphy: all rebels caught in arms in time of war will be shot.

Grabitall Very good, sir, very good, sure the safety of the nation
Comes first, they must be shot: can't it be done with moderation –
I mean, as it were, in the *street* – ?

General Mr Murphy, they are not in the street: they are inside!
If need be every wall in Dublin will be opened as wide
As the mouth of the Liffey – I alone have the power to decide.
Go on, get lost.

Exit GRABITALL.

Where are you, boy? Come here!

The SUBALTERN *comes up to him.*

Any news from the fleet?

Subaltern
Yes sir. HMS *Helga* is in position in the tidal pool:
She is ready to open fire.

General Tell the Captain first of all
To blow the roof off Liberty Hall.
Tell the Captain after that
The GPO must be laid flat.
Tell the Captain not to trouble
If anywhere else gets turned to rubble.
I have orders, sir, to lay the iron hand
Of ruthless chastisement upon this land.
We told the Irish England had expected
A certain duty from them: they defected
And they must bear the consequence alone.
The face of what they call the Famine Queen
Today they shall find carved from a rock of stone.

Exeunt GENERAL *and* SUBALTERN.

After a pause, deliberate heavy shelling is heard – not salvoes: one rever-berating explosion at a time. CONNOLLY, PEARSE *and their people stand transfixed at the sound. This shelling continues through the ensuing dialogue.*

Enter LLOYD GEORGE.

Lloyd George
Each shell that falls on Dublin now will make
An opportunity for *me* to take –
When all is done and brought through to the end
A quick and clever man will have to send

> Commissioners, diplomatists, and such,
> To fix some sort of settlement and patch
> The whole thing up again
> With eager sympathy for grief and pain . . .
> I do believe that I
> Of all Westminster best will qualify:
> Good. Not only will I win the war
> But Ireland too I'll solve for evermore.

Exit LLOYD GEORGE.

The shelling suddenly becomes louder – the men on the stage are thrown about by the blasts. CONNOLLY *looks out into the* AUDIENCE.

Connolly There's a barricade over there that badly needs checking – no, no you stay here – I'll take a look at it myself.

He jumps down from the stage, and is suddenly thrown over by a shellburst. Some of his MEN *come after him and drag him back to the others. His leg is wounded.* WINIFRED *attends to it.*

KARL LIEBKNECHT *enters at one side with a handful of leaflets.*

Liebknecht

> Karl Liebknecht in Berlin
> Hearing the Irish news
> Decides he has been too feeble
> In propagating his socialist views:
> Goes out into the street and takes his stand,
> His pamphlets in his hand –
> I cry the name of *Spartacus*:
> I make indeed a grotesque fuss –
> NO WAR NO WAR NO WAR!

A GERMAN SOLDIER *strikes him down.*

> They knock me to the floor.
> Of course I knew I was premature:
> But how could Connolly be so sure
> That he would endure
> For as long as he did ? Five days ? Six ?
> Asquith's soldiers could not lose.
> But *Mein Gott* such a pile of bricks
> Broken glass, broken men, broken stone
> That once had been proud Dublin town . . .

He is dragged out under arrest.

James Stephens Saturday. A red glare tells of fire. The rumour now grows that the Post Office is evacuated.

Pearse Too many civilians have been killed. It would be wrong to prolong it.

James Stephens The rumour also grows that terms of surrender are presently being discussed.

Connolly (*seated in a chair, unable to put his foot to the ground*)

> I dream a dream that I have dreamed before
> I am in prison by the fire and in the fire
> There is no way I can get out of here
> Except to let the flames run over all
> Burning the floor the window and the wall
> And I am free and all the bread is burned to ash . . .

Pearse The Provisional Government has agreed to an unconditional surrender.

Connolly I agree to these conditions. For the men under my command.

James Stephens None of these men were magnetic in the sense that Mr Larkin is magnetic. But if Larkin was the magnetic centre of the Irish labour movement, Connolly was its brains.

The BRITISH GENERAL *walks on to the stage. The men there all stand to attention.* PEARSE *hands over his sword. The* GENERAL *looks at it in surprise. He turns to the* SUBALTERN *who is just behind him. The gunfire has stopped. Everything is lit by flames.*

General Formality with a soldier's sword:
> Good Lord . . . !

Mocking laughter and jeering from all sides during this speech.

> D'you suppose the feller has the intention
> Of invoking to me the Geneva Convention?
> Because, if so, in double-quick time
> I think he'd better think again.
> I'd have you know, you bloody little men,
> To rebel against your King is a matter of *crime*.
> I have the honour to proclaim
> A Martial Law upon this wretched town.
> Trial before a drum-head court
> Will serve you now both sweet and short.
> Read out the names and I will call
> The sentences for one and all.

Subaltern Patrick Pearse. Thomas MacDonagh. Thomas Clarke.

General Death.

A volley of shots. All the REBELS *shudder, but stay where they are, at attention, in a rigid tableau.*

Subaltern Joseph Plunkett. Edward Daly. Michael O'Hanrahan. William Pearse.

General Death.

Another volley. Same business. A whooping cheering exhilarated group of BRITISH SOLDIERS *run in. They are loaded with all sorts of looted gear – from Liberty Hall – posters, flags, bits of furniture,* CITIZEN ARMY *uniforms, a sewing-machine ...*

Soldiers (*generally – some of the remarks directed to* SUBALTERN, *who is temporarily distracted from the list of names*) Excuse me, sir – some of us was into that dump they call Liberty Hall – nothing left of it really – seems that the navy blokes didn't know it wasn't garrisoned – we found all sorts of stuff there – abandoned – books, printing-presses, loads o'that daft get-up like they use for the Irish dances – hey, look mate, I got a fuckin' harp – Christ you're a fuckin' angel – look here, sir, there's loads o' these –

– referring to sewing-machine.

Notice on the door says 'Women Workers' Clothing Co-operative' – do you know what they was doing there – making use of their damn trade-union hall for stitching up the rebel uniforms – how come we was told it was all Jerry gear they was wearing – this jacket's like regular British – all right, sir, if I take this sewing-machine home with me? Like, my sister she makes underclothes for the troops at the front – Christ but we didn't half shake these fuckin' paddies up – right? There's fifty blubbering judies in front of the Custom House this minute – wanted to know could I tell 'em the list of the prisoners ...?

Subaltern And did you tell 'em?
A Soldier Well, I couldn't, could I? No. I don't know the names of the fucking prisoners – not at all *my* department.

Exeunt SOLDIERS.

General Carry on, boy, what are you waiting for?
Subaltern John MacBride.
General Death.

Another volley. Same business.

Enter at a distance, ASQUITH, GRABITALL, 1ST TU LEADER.

1st TU Leader
       Prime Minister, the Labour Party would prefer
       These deluded fellows treated as prisoners-of-war.
Grabitall The Forces of the Crown, you fool,
       Inevitably must take control.
       Indeed, sir, for the safety of the state
       We all of us appreciate –
Asquith That for me to interfere with what my generals decide
       Would be a most imprudent act indeed.
       Leave it alone.
Subaltern Edmund Kent. Michael Mallin.

General Death.

Another volley. Same business.

1st TU Leader

> I can't go against the operation of the law
>
> But, sir – there is a protest – George Bernard Shaw –

Asquith No. I do not hear. The cabinet had decided –

1st TU Leader

> Also *The Manchester Guardian* says this cruelty is misguided:
>
> Prime Minister, it is a *Liberal* newspaper I quote!

Asquith Mr Henderson, are you in my cabinet: or not?

> If Labour desires to govern, then Labour must keep quiet.

Grabitall I am very glad to say, sir, with the exception of but one,

> The Home Rulers in parliament approve of everything you've done.

Asquith There you are then: protests only from cranks: the lunatic fringe

> With a concept of politics as outdated as Stonehenge.

1st TU Leader

> True indeed, throughout the world
>
> The socialist movement is appalled
>
> The way James Connolly has sold out
>
> His principles and joined the rout
>
> Of nationalistic nonsense. I don't doubt
>
> That Labour's patriotic place in England's history will augment
>
> Great future gains from this most sad event.

Subaltern Thomas Kent.

General Death.

Another volley. Same business.

LENIN *enters at a separate corner.*

Lenin In the spring of nineteen sixteen

> In the very midst of the First World War
>
> The revolutionist V. I. Lenin
>
> In Switzerland had this to declare:

The misfortune of the Irish is that they rose prematurely, when the European revolt of the proletariat had not yet matured. Capitalism is not so harmoniously built that the various springs of rebellion can immediately merge into one, of their own accord, without reverses, and defeats.

Subaltern John Heuston. Cornelius Colbert. John MacDermott.

Asquith No – wait a moment: General! Don't forget

> This is a Liberal government that you serve – I would regret
>
> To have too many dead upon our record – perhaps we should stop soon?

General Prime Minister, would you wait, please, till my duty has been done...

> Just read those names again.

Connolly Out in the street the people throng and rush
   And cry aloud 'Bread, bread, where is our food –
   This child destroys our life,' they cry.
  It would not have been done had there been any other way.
 They'll never understand why I am here. They all forget I am an Irish-man...

Asquith General, I would now, if I may
   Take advantage of this delay –

Grabitall The man with the wounded leg is still alive:
   Let the worst of the ringleaders be dealt with as they deserve.

General I said read those names again!

Subaltern John Heuston. Cornelius Colbert. John MacDermott. James Con-nolly.

General Death.

Subaltern The last one, sir, is unable to stand.

General Then shoot him sitting. Fasten him to his chair.

 Another volley. Same business.

Connolly For nearly thirty years I tried
   To clear the world of those who now have had me tied
   Into my chair and shot at till I died.
   They always claimed that they were here to stay.
   They did not ask us if they may.
   And altogether they asked so very few
   That when the fire and sword and fury flew
   At them in Russia, China, Cuba, Africa, Vietnam
   And indeed once more in Ireland, my own home,
   They could not credit what it was they'd done,
   Or what it was in Dublin we'd begun
   At Easter nineteen hundred and sixteen –
   We were the first to roll away the stone
   From the leprous wall of the whitened tomb
   We were the first to show the dark deep hole within
   Could be thrown open to the living sun.
   We were the first to feel their loaded gun
   That would prevent us doing it any more –
   Or so they hoped. We were the first. We shall not be the last.
   This was not history. It has not passed.

         END OF PLAY